BINDING PASSIONS

TALES OF MAGIC, MARRIAGE, AND POWER AT THE END OF THE RENAISSANCE

Guido Ruggiero

New York   Oxford
OXFORD UNIVERSITY PRESS
1993

Oxford University Press

Oxford   New York   Toronto
Delhi   Bombay   Calcutta   Madras   Karachi
Kuala Lumpur   Singapore   Hong Kong   Tokyo
Nairobi   Dar es Salaam   Cape Town
Melbourne   Auckland   Madrid

and associated companies in
Berlin   Ibadan

Copyright © 1993 by Oxford University Press, Inc.

Published by Oxford University Press, Inc.,
200 Madison Avenue, New York, New York 10016

Library of Congress Cataloging-in-Publication Data
Ruggiero, Guido, 1944–
Binding passions : tales of magic, marriage, and power at the end
of the Renaissance / Guido Ruggiero.
p. cm. Includes bibliographical references and index.
ISBN 0–19–507930–2—ISBN 0–19–508320–2 (pbk.)
1. Sex customs—Italy—Venice—History.
2. Sexual ethics—Italy—Venice—History.
3. Marriage—Italy—Venice—History.
4. Renaissance—Italy—Venice.   I. Title.
HQ18.I8R83 1993
306'.0945'31—dc20   92–24005

1 3 5 7 9 8 6 4 2

Printed in the United States of America
on acid-free paper

For all those who have shown the way
and especially
Natalie Z. Davis and Gaetano Cozzi

Slowly as the ages passed living among signs had led to seeing as signs the infinity of things that in the beginning were merely there without marking anything but their own existence. Now they had become transformed into the signs of themselves and added to the series of signs intentionally made by those who wanted to create a sign. . . .

ITALO CALVINO, Le Cosmicomiche, p. 50.

ACKNOWLEDGMENTS

Writing a book, much like making a long journey, is an adventure in which, if one is fortunate, one may encounter interesting and fine people who help show the way. Great writers like Dante may have completed their literary peregrinations with only one or two guides, but happily, much less accomplished writers on much more humble journeys often need more guidance than even a Virgil or a Beatrice could provide. That is certainly the case in the journey that produced this book; I have enjoyed an embarrassment of riches when it comes to help along the way.

Perhaps most important have been the people who have made research in Venice and the Veneto so rich and rewarding. The staff of the Venetian Archivio di Stato has been particularly helpful in good times and difficult ones, especially Michela Dal Borgo, Sandra Sambo, and the hard-working *Uscieri* there. The staff of the Archivio della Curia Vescovile of Feltre was also most accommodating and welcoming, as were those of the many other libraries and institutes where I have worked in Italy over the years. Special thanks are in order for the many friends in Treviso who made my time there enjoyable, rewarding, and at times even possible, especially Laura and Delma Giannetti.

Colleagues, students, and friends in Europe and the United States also contributed a great deal to this journey. Again, a list can only begin to suggest those who have helped, but especially significant have been Bob and Mary Jo Nye, Jim and Joanne Farr, Phil and Gillian Tabor, Jonathan and Beth Glixon, Edward Muir and Linda Carroll, Judy Brown, Gene Brucker, Gigi Corazzol, Gaetano Cozzi, Natalie Z. Davis, Bob Davis, Joanne Ferraro, Mary Gibson, Felix Gilbert, Ronna Goffen, Paul Grendler, Michael Knapton, Patricia Labalme, Mary Lindemann, Richard Mackenney, John Martin, Lauro Martines, Lori Nussdorfer, Paolo Preto, Brian Pullan, Dennis Romano, Margaret Rosenthal, Kenneth Setton, and Anne Jacobson Schutte. Chapters of this book were presented in early form at a conference on Love, Sexuality, and Marriage at the National Humanities Center in 1987; at a symposium on Sex, Love, and Marriage as part of the Appleby Memorial Lecture series at San Diego State University in 1987; at the Third International Association for the History of Crime and Criminal Justice conference sponsored by the Maison des Sciences de l'Homme in Paris in 1988; and as public lectures at a number of universities in the United States, Italy, and England. At each stop on this grand tour, people offered suggestions and asked questions that have contributed to this book, especially Elena Fasano Guarini, Sarah Hanley, David Halperin, Daniela Lombardi, Robert Muchembled, Gherardo Ortalli, Lawrence Stone, James Turner, and Stephen Wilson.

While working on this book, I have received much appreciated support from my colleagues at Syracuse University in Florence, the University of Tennessee, the University of Cincinnati, and the University of Connecticut—particularly the last, where virtually every member of the department has at one time or another aided significantly in this project. The staffs at all four institutions have been unusually helpful, providing a consistently warm and supportive environment even in the worst times of economic hardship. My students have also done much to enrich this project and this journey, especially Michelle Laughran, Lee Penyak, Susanne De Lucca, and Meg and Mary Gallucci. Much of the writing was done in the idyllic setting of the Institute for Advanced Study at Princeton and Harvard's Villa I Tatti. There too, fine colleagues and excellent staffs made the supposed labor of this book a special pleasure and privilege. I Tatti is set in the hills above Florence where Boccaccio's band of young people retired from the troubling world of 1348 to tell their tales of the *Decameron*, and there were many days there in 1990–91, surrounded by minds always young and lively (not just of the fellows but also of the staff), when I felt that they were really writing the tales of this book. Much the same could be said of Princeton, the Institute, its fellows, and its staff. Crucial for research time in Italy and writing at the Institute and I Tatti were a series of much appreciated grants provided by the John Simon Guggenheim Foundation, the National Endowment for the Humanities, and the Research Councils of the University of Connecticut and the University of Cincinnati.

Finally, I owe a very special debt of gratitude to those who have read this manuscript with such thoughtful care and who have provided a host of useful suggestions for improving it. Jim Farr, John Martin, Lauro Martines, Edward Muir, and Kristin Ruggiero have each read it all, and some have read it in more than one draft. The book and the journey were much improved by their suggestions, help, and friendship. Kris Ruggiero especially has made this journey possible and special. Thanks to all these fine people and the many others not named here, this book is a better one, and the journey involved in writing it has been a rich and rewarding one.

CONTENTS

BINDING PASSIONS

INTRODUCTION

Carne Vale and **Carnival**

For Bakhtin, in his beautiful study of Rabelais, the carnival is always a primary source of liberation, destruction and renewal, but the scope it is allowed changes in different periods. Before the existence of classes and the state, the comic realm was equal to the serious; with slave and feudal societies, including that of the sixteenth century, the carnival became a second life, a second reality for the people, separated from power and the state but still public and perennial; in bourgeois society (and alas, one feels, in Bakhtin's socialist society as well) it is reduced to home and the holiday.[1]

It was carnival—to be exact, Giovedi Grasso of 1571 in Venice. It was the season of festivities, when the passions and the flesh were unbound and ruled for a moment openly and when the people came out into the streets to play at turning their world upside down. Perhaps 1571 was not a good year for turning the world upside down in Venice, for the world was in many ways too topsy-turvy already for the city that longed to live up to its own label as the Most Serene Republic, *La Serenissima*. Most important, Venice was locked in yet another costly and destructive war with the Turks that was going badly on all fronts, straining its economic and social order at home and its already tenuous ties with its Christian allies. The great naval victory of Lepanto that would calm for a moment fears and to some extent reestablish the city's reputation as a great power was only months away but largely unanticipated. If anything, Venice's days as a major power must have seemed dangerously numbered. Yet even war and a looming bleak future did not stop carnival; in a way, looming misfortune made its unbinding of the passions and celebration of the flesh even more attractive.

On that Giovedi Grasso two young men, both in their early twenties, costumed as priests, were lustily singing their way through the streets of Venice not far from Saint Mark's Square. Saluting others in masks and making obscene gestures with a broom, singing ribald parodies of the litany of the Mass, they wound their way from the Church of San Moise toward San Luca, a nearby square close to the heart of the city, in search of a party, a good time, or something more. One of the men was a recently married, promising young lawyer who served in the Ducal Palace, named Zaccharia Lombardini. He had been eating dinner with his wife when a young neighbor, Giacomo Zorzi, had dropped in to ask him if he wanted to go to a party. Zorzi, a noble from a good family and also recently married, was not someone Zaccharia could turn down.

In Venice nobles, even a youth like Zorzi just beginning to grow a reddish blond beard, were the contacts that ensured success, and even their whims were to be cultivated. The nobility, a herediatry ruling class defined by the fact that they sat automatically on the Major Council, the theoretical font of all authority in the Venetian state, had by the late sixteenth century become a much more aristocratic and less mercantile group than when they had first legally declared themselves noble in the early fourteenth century. Some, of course, were still involved directly in commerce, but a large percentage at least of the rich nobility had diversified their wealth, investing in trade, land in the city's empire on the mainland (the *terraferma*), banking and government bonds, and even cloth and other artisanal forms of production.

Significantly, by the late sixteenth century, the qualification "at least the rich" was necessary for the nobility, because the group had become much more diversified in terms of their wealth. In fact, a sizable number were actually relatively poor and made their living by holding minor posts in government (virtually a form of charity), indulging in petty graft, or even selling their votes. At the other extreme, however, the truly rich had become ever more aristocratic, with ideals that would have fit comfortably with most of those espoused by the sixteenth-century codifier of aristocratic ways, Baldesar Castiglione, in his *The Book of the Courtier*. In theory, immediately below this nobility fell another hereditary legal class, the *cittadini*, in turn divided into subgroups defined legally. Certain offices in government were reserved for them, as well as a fairly large number of economic privileges. But this group was less exclusive than the nobility, in large measure because the demanding rules for gaining this status were often bypassed if one had powerful noble friends. Moreover, to take advantage of the potential privileges such rank offered, one usually needed the support of nobles who sat on the councils of government that actually consigned those privileges in the form of minor posts or opportunities to participate in the city's trade. As a result, the *cittadini* that mattered to a great extent had become the clients of the nobility—men like young Zaccharia, a lawyer working for the government, anxious to please his noble neighbor Giacomo Zorzi. Thus when he was invited to go out with Zorzi, Zaccharia left his wife to finish her dinner alone and went out to enjoy with him the last night of carnival.

In the streets the two young men were surrounded by the masses of Venice, a city of about 170,000 inhabitants at the moment—a moment, however, that was to be short-lived, as the plague would return with renewed furor in 1575–77, carrying off at least a quarter of the population. The vast majority of these people were lumped together as a group below the nobles and the *cittadini* that was less well defined legally and less clearly thought about by political thinkers at the time. Even today it is only recently that historians have begun to look more closely at the divisions in the *popolo* (the people), as this mass was often loosely styled following late medieval tradition. But the Venetian *popolo* may be broken down broadly into subgroups of artisans, servants, sailors, day laborers (the honorable poor), and marginal people (often considered as outside the *popolo*). In addition, Zaccharia's and Zorzi's costumes for carnival remind us that there was another social hierarchy in the city—a clerical one. Ideally more spiritual than mundane, in many ways this hierarchy mirrored the secular one, with clerics from noble families on top and a range of progressively poorer and less significant priests, monks, and nuns reaching down even to the relatively marginal with, for example, ex-prostitute nuns at the convent of the Convertite. Finally, of course, as a trading city still, Venice had a large foreign population as well, including Arabs, Germans, and the perennial outsiders, even when they had been long-term residents of the Ghetto, Jews.

In those streets, surrounded by those people all intent on enjoying the most important evening of carnival, Zorzi revealed to his friend that the party he had been contemplating would be with a certain Letitia Parisola, wife of Antonio Banchini, called the "Little Bird,"[2] who until recently had been his mistress. Here we find ourselves in a different social world that does not show up well in the more traditional social breakdown of the city outlined above. Letitia was apparently a prostitute of some status; her husband may well have been her pimp, especially given the phallic charm of his nickname in Italian. The term "Little Bird" may lack the poetic charm of Caterina da Valbona's captured nightingale (in Boccaccio's famous tale from the *Decameron*), but it may well have made a similar humorous play on the Italian association of birds (*uccelli*) and phalluses (also referred to as *uccelli*). The world of Letitia and Little Bird also had its hierarchy. In fact, it seems to have had its customs, values, rules, and, in a way, its culture as well, all of which we know little about. Thus, following our young revelers, although we know a great deal about their world in theory, we are following them into relatively unknown territory. And suggestively, that is true even if Letitia lived also at the heart of the city in San Luca, hardly a five minutes' walk away. So the two revelers wound their way to their anticipated small pleasures, and we may follow them into the relative unknown of their evening and through their carnival into the relatively unfamiliar world where *carne vale*, literally where the "flesh mattered," and not merely for a season.

When the two youths arrived, they began to sing Letitia a serenade under her window. Hearing their song, she came out onto the balcony and greeted Zorzi warmly, calling out, "Good evening, Zorzi, do you want to come to the celebration with me?" He replied, "Sure."[3] The evening seemed to be shaping up nicely. And pretty much as one might expect for a Giovedi Grasso toward the end of the Italian Renaissance— young men of good family in costume, taking advantage of the freedom of the season and the power of their families and position to enjoy the illicit pleasures of a young woman apparently anxious to be enjoyed by the rich and powerful.

But as typical as the scene may have been, it did not work out as anticipated. After a moment inside, Letitia returned to say that she would not go with them, offering the rather lame excuse that she had decided to go to bed instead. Presumably that seemed as unlikely on Giovedi Grasso in 1571 to Zorzi and Zaccaria as it does today, for after wishing her "good night" they moved off to the nearby square with the idea of looking for some dancing there, but apparently also in order to keep an eye out to see what Letitia actually had decided to do for the evening. Not long thereafter their suspicions were rewarded. Letitia came out of her house with four young men, also in carnival costume. They went off through the streets, followed at first discreetly by the rejected suitors to a mask shop, where Letitia had her companions buy her a new mask. Meanwhile Zorzi and Zaccaria began to cut up outside, singing loudly again and insulting passers-by with obscene remarks and gestures.

Letitia and her group left the shop and headed on to Saint Mark's Square, the ceremonial center of the city, where traditionally on Giovedi Grasso a large public festival was held with a fireworks display provided at government expense. The square in many ways represented the city to itself. Throughout the sixteenth century, this central urban space had been redesigned to express the grandeur and importance of the Most Serene Republic to its inhabitants and its vistors. By 1571 it looked much as it does today, rather like a large open outdoor room surrounded by the office buildings of government and capped by the twin pillars of rule—the Church of San Marco, the burial place of the patron apostle Saint Mark, who had both predicted and guaranteed Venice's greatness; and the Doge's Palace, where the chief executive officer of the city, a noble elected for life, lived and worked as the symbolic head of state. Lying side by side in their splendor and magnificence they proclaimed many things, but perhaps most important the greatness and longevity of the city republic—a lesson most important as the republic's maritime empire and commercial wealth, already considerably weakened, seemed gravely in danger from the Turks.

Unlike today, however, the square was open on its western edge, that is, on the way that our would-be partyers came to join its festive crowds. Entering the square, Letitia and her friends hoped the two young men following them would be distracted by those crowds and other activities of carnival. Instead the two men followed them doggedly as they walked up through the square, between the colonnaded buildings of state, turning right to walk along the Doge's Palace, and came out before the *bacino*, the open body of water that lies before the palace. In fact, they stopped right in fromt of the Columns of Justice, where the state, with often elaborately symbolic ritual, carried out capital punishment in the name of Justice, God, and the Doge. There gondolas tied up and then, as now, could be hired.

Letitia and her friends decided to give their followers the slip by hiring one and literally leaving them in their wake. But none was available. Thus, with the evening threatening to get nasty, especially as their followers had somehow picked up four armed soldiers crossing the square, they decided to return home. Barely had they left the crowds of Saint Mark's, however, when the two men and their soldiers attacked with weapons drawn, crying, "Kill! kill!" Letitia's admirers, perhaps regretting their good fortune at having won her company away from two such violent young men, did, if not the gentlemanly thing, at least the wise one. Being unarmed, they fled. Letitia and her servant (who had come along for the festivities) were quickly overpowered and bustled along with knives at their throats by the two men and their *bravi*. At first the men threatened to kill both, but as tempers cooled and they tried to decide what to do with their prey, they were talked into returning them home. A wise decision, for men from powerful families like Zaccharia Lombardini and especially Giacomo Zorzi could get away with many things in late Renaissance Venice, but murder committed in public was normally not one of them. Thus Letitia and her servant, both scared and roughed up, had their carnival brought to an unhappy end by the harsh realities of unbound passion and power, both masculine and social.

But carnival was just about over for Zaccharia and Zorzi as well, for within a few days they found that their unbridled passions had put their own lives, at least for a moment, in the hands and at the mercies of more powerful men. First, in a move that they may well have expected, they were called before the Avogadori di Comun, roughly speaking the state attorneys. It seems that some of Letitia's young masked friends, although not nobles, were men with connections in government. In fact, the father of one was a minor official; thus, he brought a complaint to the Avogadori about the assault.[4] This was the normal procedure for dealing with such matters when they were not handled by summary justice involving small fines levied right in the streets by the police patrols that guarded the peace. For more serious crimes or ones that escaped the patrollers, the Avogadori were the normal magistry turned to. They or their minions investigated allegations, prepared the case, and if prosecution was in order presented it to the correct judicial body or council for a decision.

This whole process, however, could be and often was short-circuited by the supreme secret police of Venice, the Council of Ten. Originally an ad hoc body designed to limit the danger of conspiracy, it had during the Renaissance become virtually a shadow government, especially when matters of state broadly defined were involved, thanks in large measure to its virtually unlimited powers, secretive and efficient operating procedures, and powerful membership.[5] At times, the Ten was not above dealing with a carnival assault like this one, for important people were involved on both sides and a decision by the Ten put everyone on notice that the most important men of the city had heard the matter and decided. It appears, however, that the case as a carnival assault was fairly quickly dropped; thus we know little beyond the fact that all involved were called in to testify before the Avogadori.

Shortly thereafter, however, Zaccharia and Zorzi were called in by the Holy Office of Venice to explain what they had been doing that Giovedi Grasso. This body was a local reflection of a more general drive to reform Catholic society and the Church in the late sixteenth century. In 1542, Pope Paul III had rejuvenated the Inquisition of the Church, establishing the Congregation of the Holy Office of the Roman Inquisition to counter the perceived threat of the Protestant Reformation and heresy. In most of the Catholic world, this institution rapidly became an important arbiter of orthodoxy, a tenacious opponent of the new creeds facing Catholicism, and a significant bureaucracy for extending more effectively the Church's power. It may also have been in many ways central to the formation of the modern mind and body, with its often highly visible and intrusive investigations of people's beliefs, values, and even ways of perceiving.

Be that as it may, not all of Catholic Europe rallied behind this institution without reservation. Venice, long noted for its independence vis-à-vis the hegemonic pretensions of the Catholic Church, opted for a compromise position designed to contain heresy and discipline an avowedly Catholic city without compromising the prerogatives of its own secular government—a Holy Office of its own. In 1547 the Doge and the Collegio (the top executive committee of the city) appointed three secular officials known as the Tre Savii sopra l'Eresia to serve with the Papal Nuncio, the Patriarch of Venice, and a clerically appointed Inquisitor to investigate, try, and correct heresy in the city. This became the Holy Office of Venice, its local Inquisition advised by but theoretically not controlled by Rome.[6]

From the start, this institution was ideally a form of cooperation between the secular government of Venice and the reforming hierarchy of the Church. And although in theory it might have been expected that its ecclesiastics would provide the drive for eliminating heresy and its secular Savii the sage council on political realities, things were considerably more complex. As both the Patriarch and the Inquisitor usually had close ties to Venice and its noble ruling class and often saw that group as crucial for their success, they could be quite politically sensitive. In turn, the Savii were frequently very concerned about the Christian moral society that they perceived Venice as being; thus they could be hard-liners when it came to orthodoxy. The upshot was a complex institution that did not behave in accordance with many of the received stereotypes about the Inquisition. Most notably, procedures were relatively strict and correct, torture was used sparingly, and penalties tended to be restrained and ameliorative even in the context of Italy, where recent scholarship has shown that, on the whole, the Inquisition proceeded with comparative restraint in the late sixteenth century.[7]

It was this body, then, that called in our two young carnival revelers, apparently much to their surprise. That surprise was probably due in part to the fact that the Holy Office had in its early years largely concentrated on heresy in the sense of confessional issues—Lutherans, Anabaptists, and other reformers more difficult to classify, who were seen as immediate threats to Venice and its territories as a Catholic society (as the special city of the Apostle Saint Mark).[8] But as those formally more dangerous threats had been brought under control or, perhaps more accurately, had been limited at a level where they did not seem to be as threatening, the Holy Office became more and more concerned with a range of practices that seemed to undercut or dishonor the faith.

Thus the 1570s saw a gradual shift in the focus of the Holy Office. Heresy remained important, but progressively heresy shared the council's attention with witchcraft, magic, superstition, and misuse of the holy. And as the Holy Offices both of Venice and of the broader Inquisition of the Church spread their nets more widely to discipline Catholic society, they became a significant element in reformulating not just the Church and Christianity, but also the world view of the West. That, of course, is a large claim that goes well beyond the scope of this book and certainly light years beyond our young revelers' crimes of Giovedi Grasso. Yet Zaccharia and Zorzi symbolize nicely one aspect of that change. In a way, as others have noted, in the second half of the sixteenth century carnival seemed to be ending and Lent beginning, not just for our revelers but for society as a whole. Suggestively, however, the way it ended for Zaccharia and Zorzi in 1571 brings us, as well as them, face to face with a central institutional factor in and reflection of that change.

Zaccharia and Zorzi found themselves before the Holy Office because it was claimed that they had dishonored the Church with their carnival pranks. In deciding to investigate the two young men, the Holy Office had concluded, "Putting behind them the fear of the Divine Lord and the justice of the world, dressed with the surplices of priests, they went about screaming the litany with most evil and dishonest words dishonoring the saints of heaven and doing other things against the honor of God and Religion."[9] Their assault on Letitia and her friends was of little concern; that was a matter for other courts. It was their disrespect, their dishonoring of God, the saints, and the Church, that required action. Honor and respect should have bound their carnival passions within a narrower field of play; at least that was one idea the Holy Office was attempting to propagate by bringing these important young men to trial.

And to give the Holy Office its due, the reports on their activities revealed a disrespectful attitude toward the things of the Church that seemed to go well beyond playfulness. One priest reported hearing the youths passing in the street "singing a type of litany, which went more or less, 'Who will be that devoted soul who will give herself to me to be screwed one time? Who will be that soul of God who will give herself to me to be screwed for the love of God?'"[10] While Zaccharia refused to admit singing these verses, and also tried to dissociate himself from Zorzi and the revels of that night, he did admit that the latter, as he went through the streets dressed like a priest, "had a broom in his hands and when we encountered other people dressed in masks he said making [an obscene] gesture with the broom, 'Lord sprinkle me [*Asperges me Domine*].'"[11]

Certainly such behavior was disrespectful to God and the Church, but carnival had traditionally been a time of license when one could say the normally unsayable and turn the world on its head for a moment in play. As Edward Muir in his masterful study of ritual and festival in Venice pointed out, "All the carnival images . . . [of Venice] turned everyday society on its head. Most masqueraders identified themselves ritually or dramatically with their social opposites" *popolani* dressed themselves as officials, nobles as peasants, men as women, harlots as men; likewise destruction led to birth and sex to death; the old became young and the decrepit potent."[12] But as Muir and others have noted, carnival implied more in the Renaissance. It was the special time when the illicit became licit, when masked passions won out over public restraint, when the flesh won out over traditional morality and honor, when the customary ties that were perceived as binding society were dissolved in the passions of the body—when literally *carne vale* (flesh mattered), and broke through the multiple bonds that restrained it and was celebrated.

Interestingly, although *carne vale* does not seem to have been the etymological root of the Italian word *carnevale* (carnival),[13] it does express to a large extent what carnival was about. There was a subtext to carnival, however, that was increasingly articulated across the Renaissance and the early modern period. In the theories of the Church and its theology, the state and its ideology, and the family (at least elite families) and its values of honor and reputation, *carne vale* was ideally to be for only a season, carnival. A question that is seldom asked is why. Why could the flesh rule for only a season? Why were its passions and pleasures perceived as so dangerous that in normal times they had to be bound? The question is seldom asked because at one level the answer has seemed so obvious. Across the span of the Western tradition from Aristotle to Machiavelli and on to Freud and Foucault, the flesh and its passions have remained a tremendous threat, perceived perhaps in quite different ways, but with disturbing consistency as dangerously uncontrollable forces that threaten to destroy, both at the level of the individual and of society.

Society, the groups within it, and the people who constitute it have been perceived as ordered by many things: by reason, morality, honor, family, government, religion—the list could be extended and would need to be modified for different societies and cultures—but with amazing consistency, those ordering principles have been threatened by passion, especially the passions of the body. Nonetheless, at the same time, virtually all these principles of order have also attempted to bind passion to their service; thus reason, morality, honor, family, state, and God usually have had "correct" forms of passions associated with them, and incorrect passions have been seen as in opposition. And again with impressive consistency, the negative side of these equations has been associated with the passions of the body, although again in historically different ways at different moments and in different contexts. The point is simply that there is a history to be told of the binding of passions and the desire to do so; a history intimately intertwined both with the broad issues of order, stability, and power and with the more everyday issues of how people live together in families, neighborhoods, and larger solidarities.

The dangers of unbound passions at the end of the Renaissance, of course, were not illusory, as the violent attack on Letitia and her maid by Giacomo Zorzi and Zaccharia Lombardini indicates in a small but suggestive moment. The latter were not important figures in the great course of history, not even in the smaller course of Venetian history, but in their highhanded violence and in their passion at being rejected and perhaps dishonored, Zorzi and Zaccharia bring us face to face with a concrete

moment that, when multiplied countless times in different social, cultural, and temporal contexts, has seemed over and over again to test the
fabric of society. And binding their passions and the passions of people in
general was a particularly acute concern of the Renaissance and the
early modern period. Thus, at least at the level of ideals, passions and the
flesh were with increasing insistence to be allowed to rule only for a
specific time each year, and that meant crucially that their potential for
misrule would be contained during "normal" times.

Yet the passions have refused to be bound, the flesh to be fully
civilized, and that has meant, much as Mikhail Bakhtin suggested and
Natalie Davis echoed in the quote that began this introduction, that there
has come to exist a parallel world that to some extent mirrored, and in
mirroring reversed, the normal order of the everyday world: "the carnival became a second life, a second reality for the people, separated from
power and the state but still public and perennial." That second life was
largely lived in a world (or worlds) that was seen as illicit, that grew
apace in some ways with the increasing desire to separate out *carne vale*
as a limited time of the year and of life itself. There, however, the passions, especially passions of the flesh, rather than destroying all social
organization, as the theories of the licit world would have it, seemed to
become themselves one of the organizing principles of a counter society
and order with a history and at times a culture and values of its own.

Originally, continuing in the line of an earlier study of fourteenth-
and fifteenth-century Venice (*The Boundaries of Eros: Sex Crime and
Sexuality in Renaissance Venice*), I set out to explore in this book that
parallel world at the end of the sixteenth century, when it seemed that it
should have been more visible and perhaps more unified and coherent
as a result of the reforming attacks of Church, state, and civic morality
across the century: visible, because those attacks created an extensive
bureaucratic record and a lively literature supporting and questioning
them; unified and coherent, because those attacks to some extent isolated the illicit world and turned it in upon itself. In a series of tales or
microstudies designed to open up the complexity of some of the issues
involved and confront them at the level of daily life, then, I planned to
examine the functioning and significance of the major features of that
world at the end of the Renaissance: prostitution, concubinage, love
magic, renegade clerics, as well as a double standard that winked at male
promiscuity, a social hierarchy that largely overlooked the victimization
of lower-class women, and a vision of sex as fitting within a passive-
active dialectic that easily slid into violence.

The theoretical issues involved in such a study particularly interested
me, for the world of the illicit seemed to contradict one of the most
enduring underlying presuppositions of social order: that *carne vale*
could not rule, that for society to exist the passions had to be bound.
Research revealed, however, that that apparently clear-cut theoretical

opposition was less evident in the concrete historical setting of the late Renaissance than I had assumed. Rather than Sadean solipsists of *Philosophy in the Bedroom* or neo-libertines competing for pleasure and power in a society of moral victims and amoral victimizers, I found an illicit world where often passions were bound in a number of ways that clearly drew on the forms of licit society and culture, and at times even in the name of the pleasures of the body and passion itself.

Thus, recalling a metaphor from *Boundaries of Eros*, rather like Alice I found that in trying to tell the tales of this book, I had stepped through the looking glass, expecting (as perhaps she did not) that the world of my tales would be reversed, just as it seemed to be in the ideology of carnival and in the mirror. But what I found was a world that was eerily familiar: not so much reversed as shifted in such a way that known things were not quite known, accustomed signs marked slightly different meanings, familiar people were not as expected, nothing was quite the same. Yet curiously, the resulting disorientation, like that of the readers of Alice's adventures, was not one that made understanding impossible; rather, many of the shifts made eminently good and often rather poetic sense. It was not, then, the world of the most radical deconstructionists or the one feared by their opponents—a world where any meaning would do. It was instead a place where other meanings less often thought were given play or perhaps their due.

There abbesses ruled houses of prostitution rather than convents. The host of the Eucharistic ceremony bound the love not of God but of everyday men and women. Courtesans, the nobles of their profession and of the illicit world, married nobles to become domesticated in the regular social hierarchy and live as wives. Hammers hammered phalluses and hearts, and in the process both broke apart and bound together people in love. Women seemed to be priests and in their spititual endeavors empowered the male hierarchy of the Church. And priests were masters of evil arts, selling their powers to those seeking illicit goals for handsome profits. As a result, again rather like Alice's adventures beyond the looking glass, the tales that make up this book can be read merely as tales of the illicit because they come from that world or its fringes, but they have become more. They have become a series of stories about the binding of passions at the end of the Renaissance. Stories that provide a rather different perspective on what was perceived as making that society cohesive, and on the sometimes unexpected people who were perceived as wielding the power to bind it together or tear it apart. Still, I hope that I have been able to tell good and historical stories, so that they can be read simply as tales.

The strongest theme that comes out of looking through the late Renaissance looking glass that separated theoretically the licit world is how significant binding passions were for forming individuals and society on both sides of that divide. The perception that such binding was necessary was not only reflected in life, culture, and society, it played in many complex and revealing ways a central role in each. Marriage, perhaps the most significant binding for society, was much different from its modern namesake. In the broadest sense, it was not a love match between two individuals; it was an alliance binding two families together. Contemporary rhetoric, both legal and moral, often stressed that a married couple were sharing the "yoke" of wedlock, and although that rhetoric had a long tradition, it described a significant ideal. Binding husband and wife together like two oxen, the marriage yoke was one that was worn in order for the couple to work together, to till effectively the fields of life. If emotional ties were to strengthen the bonds of wedlock, they were ideally to be ties of affection that grew after a time of working together under that yoke. A reason why such affection might grow up and could be legitimately hoped for in arranged marriages was that normally the future couple was selected in terms of contemporary perceptions of what would make a good pairing. This evidently changed as one moved across the social and economic spectra, but relative economic and social parity was an ideal even if at times social advancement or economic goals might undercut it. Simply stated, marriage was a significant form of social and economic placement for all involved, and the easiest and surest placement was one where both partners and their families belonged. It was also normally a highly public moment of measurement of status; thus too much mobility in marriage could not be allowed. Ideally, the passions that worked to bind people in marriage were duty to family and the desire to correctly place and to be correctly placed in society (often expressed in terms of honor), plus, if all went well, a certain affection between the spouses.

But marriage was merely the first binding of passions that licit society generally agreed was central to its existence. In a way, even the humorous and/or misogynistic attacks on marriage so popular in the Renaissance were a reflection on that; attacking marriage and women, they nonetheless assumed that marriage was a bind difficult to avoid. Beyond marriage and in a way created by it was the family, usually construed as the crucial building block of larger solidarities and society itself. It was tied together with bonds of "natural" affection and obligation reinforced with codes of familial honor and reputation. And from the family quasi-familial groupings swung out, organizing much of Renaissance social life: the *famiglia*, the larger household unit that included servants, boarders, and even clients; the "friendship family" that ranged from legally recognized godparents (*comare* and *compare*) to special friends who were given similar titles or even referred to as brother or sister; and more formal brotherhoods such as guilds, confraternities, and at times even business and contractual relationships. Beyond and to a degree constructed upon these familylike solidarities were larger and more problematic ones such as the community, which ranged from neighborhood and village to emerging concepts of state. Usually the ties that bound one to these larger solidarities were viewed as stemming from the family. In turn, family placed and to a great degree bound one to even more important social systems such as the social hierarchy and class; and one's placement in those systems bound one and one's passions in a host of ways both small and great but often unrecognized.

Culture, of course, was intimately interrelated to this system of binding, providing in a way its ideology and, perhaps more important, revealing the deep ties between such binding solidarities and the very order of things. At the highest level, while the passions of the social world required correct binding ideally for civilization to endure, in the natural order of things the world itself was literally full of passions and bindings, for the cosmos itself was alive. From God to the humblest pebble, there was a continuum of passions just as there was a great chain of being. One has only to remember that a pebble, when dropped, fell because of a natural *attraction* to the earth or because earth things *desired* and *sought out* their natural place at the center of the universe. The world was alive, and passions correctly ordered were what made it what it was. As a result, at the highest level, nature provided a model for the human binding of passions, for in nature order existed not merely because God in his creation had placed things in a hierarchy, but crucially because he had bound the passions of things to fit his grand design. Guaranteed by God, this order of nature was rendered problematic, however, by the Devil and his minions both at the level of theology and at the level of the everyday. If evil was for Saint Augustine the willful breaking of the ties of grace that bound the elect of God naturally, for most people it was a more problematic force based on unbound or incorrectly bound passions often associated with the ultimate exemplar of unbound passions, the Devil.

But attempting such distinctions even in a very loose and general way brings us up against another central issue that stands behind the themes that to some extent tie together the tales of this book. It is evident that not all people in a society participate in culture in the same way, and often it appears that rather than one culture in a given society, we are encountering various shades of culture or even several distinct cultures. At the least, it seems necessary (especially for complex premodern societies) to deal with real disjunctions in a general shared culture often turning around strong divides between urban and rural, between classes or social levels, between the genders, and between the literate and the illiterate. At times these disjunctions may be merely areas of poor fit in a shared culture—in a way, shadings of it. At times they may describe major ruptures that reflect very different ways of encountering the world and very different worlds to be encountered.

To a great extent, while at the end of the Renaissance elites and the rest of society shared a passion for binding passions, the structure and methods of the bindings that were seen as crucial shift rather dramatically when one moves from a learned perspective to a more popular one. But closer study of popular culture and its many shadings reveals that both the learned and the elite at times participated in and learned from the popular world that surrounded them, especially when it came to the passions and the flesh. Thus even as the intellectual, ecclesiastical, and secular elites of the period were working at many levels to limit *carne vale* to carnival and make even carnival itself more decorous and controlled, members of those elites like Zaccharia and Zorzi, attracted to the pleasures of the flesh, were pulling in the other direction. This disjunction between elite values and practice within a general culture meant that in reality, through the Renaissance and well into the early modern period, passions, and especially the passions of the flesh, refused to be limited to carnival or bound by the Church, the state, or the family for that matter. In large measure, that is because a great range of elite values and the learned culture that stood behind them often had only limited impact on everyday life.

Actually, when it comes to the flesh, elite values and culture seem to have had often rather limited impact on the elites as well. Perhaps this is revealed most forcefully in the increasing time and effort governments and the Church spent in trying to regulate sex and carnality. In fact, in many ways one might posit a demarcation between the premodern world and the modern that turned on the transition between a time when, notwithstanding elite values and learned culture, *carne vale* ruled and a time when the flesh and its passions were bound by a "modern discipline"—bound by marriage and family, bound by Church and state, bound by work discipline and the work day, bound by elite and learned values finally shared by a broad segment of society, and, most difficult to chart but perhaps most significant, bound by the internal control of the individual conscience long theorized by the Church and theologians. That transition is difficult to trace and chart for many reasons, but clearly one of the most significant is the simple fact that the primary factors in that transition moved on different timetables driven by often quite different concerns.

But a crucial moment in that transition was the second half of the sixteenth century; a crucial place was late Renaissance Italy, both in the great urban centers like Venice and in the countryside as well. And the bringing of Zaccharia Lombardini and Giacomo Zorzi before the Holy Office of Venice was one small sign that the rules were changing: the binding of passions had begun to shift away from popular culture and toward the learned, and with that the formation of the modern mind and body was well underway. Their carnival was over and their approach to *carne vale* was threatened. When the long transition was completed, mind, body, sex, and their value to society and individuals had become decidedly different.

One area where that shift was most important for the binding of

passions was magic and witchcraft. In the late Renaissance and presumably earlier as well, both played a significant role in the binding of
passions; in fact, another theme of this book is that their binding powers
were much more central than has been recognized. A significant factor
in this tendency to underrate their importance has been the triumph of
science, which undercut the power of both. Yet behind and before the
scientific revolution there stood a despiritualization of the world picture
that helped make science possible and at the same time made witches
and magic less likely. And rather paradoxically the Inquisition, in close
alignment with a more general rethinking of the role of the priest and
religion in the world, played a major part in that transition. The reduc-
tion of the cosmos accessible to everyday people to the material three-
dimensional world that is the basis of Newtonian physics was prepared
for by the sixteenth-century drive to limit access to the spiritual realm to
ecclesiastics. In this drive the Inquisition played an important role, pro-
pagandizing for and enforcing a withdrawal of the spiritual at the level of
both high and popular culture. More particularly, as medicine and science lost their spiritual dimensions; as healers, magicians, and witches
lost their claim to manipulate the spiritual forces of the world, the
ground was prepared for a mechanization of the world picture. The
documents that stand behind many of the tales in this book were created
in part by the desire of the leaders of the sixteenth-century Church to
withdraw spiritual power, to take that power back into the Church and
out of the hands of lay people, especially women. In turn, that means
that the magic and witchcraft dealt with here are rather different from
the traditional vision of both.

Witchcraft in these tales has little to do with the Sabbat, riding
brooms, or sucking the blood of babies. In fact, in this it merely follows
the Venetian Holy Office in the second half of the sixteenth century. That
institution, apparently following a more general Italian trend,[14] seemed
to be relatively uninterested in such phenomena and seldom pressed
witnesses in that direction. It was much more concerned with and aggressive about the misuse of the sacred and the spiritual powers of the
Church: at the lowest level when such powers were used by nonec-
clesiastics, at a higher level when they were used for illicit ends, and
finally at the highest level when they were reversed or denied in such a
way as to call on the aid of the Devil or evil spirits. For the Venetian Holy
Office, those were the real dangers of witchcraft. Magic both high and
low presented a similar threat in their eyes. And in a way, that common
concern meant that in the records of the Holy Office one tended to slide
into the other. *Magia* (magic) tended to slide into *stregeria* (witchcraft) or
fattucheria (evil magic) or *herberia* (herbal magic).

My sense is that this was not the case solely for the Holy Office, but a
more general phenomenon. The world was perceived as a complex field
of intersecting powers (perhaps ultimately arranged in a hierarchy if one

was keeping track), and those seeking power had to understand merely where to hook into the system to have it. But clearly, magicians and witches went too far, in the eyes of the Church, when they stepped into the spiritual world to use the Christian powers of that world for their ends or rejected the spiritual powers of goodness and light for those of evil and darkness. Centrally, they were frequently seen as doing so and appear to actually have done so to bind passions and gain power.[15]

One question remains: how can we know such a complex and significant transition? Perhaps the best answer is that ultimately we cannot: at the theoretical level, because the changes involved were so wide-ranging, there is a virtual infinity of interconnected factors impossible to unravel; and at the human level, because such changes were often lost in the also nearly infinite contingencies of everyday life that masked them. But having said the obvious—that historical knowledge is difficult to have—I would like to try an approach that goes back to the very beginnings of telling history and at the same time responds to contemporary reconsiderations of its potential. Simply I would like to tell tales, stories told in a way like those told by the first storytellers. Elaborate, rich stories that, for all their potential untruths, overstatements, and misunderstandings, and all their latent multiple levels of meaning, nonetheless provide underlying proximate truths about how life was led and how the passions were bound in the late sixteenth century. Like those of the early storytellers, my tales have been limited, first, of course, by the limits of my understanding, then by the reality that I share with today's culture, and finally by the nature of the storyteller that I am, a late-twentieth-century historian trying to tell stories that do justice to the richness of the texts that stand behind them.

Reading these tales, it will be clear that my view of how they would best be told has been greatly influenced by the work of the Italian scholars who have developed and defended microhistory. Especially important have been the widely read books of Carlo Ginzburg, *The Cheese and the Worms* and *The Night Battles*,[16] along with the less well known work (at least in the English-speaking scholarly world) of Edoardo Grendi and the circle of scholars associated with the journal he edits, *Quaderni Storici*. That journal has to a great extent led the debate on this innovative approach to history in Italy.[17] Needless to say, the methodological ground for this book was also well prepared by a number of histories of great importance written outside of Italy. Readers will note the influence of the historical storytelling of Natalie Z. Davis, Gene Brucker, David Sabean, and Robert Darton. Finally, John Demos's sensitively expressed desire to do justice to the rich complexity of the people (especially women) who in a very real way he had met and learned to respect in writing *Entertaining Satan* has also been a guiding principle.

If this book has stories that have the potential to move in such circles, it is largely because of the exceptional women and men of the sixteenth century whom my researches have brought me into contact with. Their lives, struggles, and values have been preserved with remarkable vividness in the complex records of the Holy Office of Venice, as well as in the extensive archives of that city and its mainland empire. Those records are layered with a wide range of perspectives and values that each in its way speaks from the past and often speaks eloquently through the filters of scribes, bureaucratic structures, time, and culture that separate us from them. And, of course, as Natalie Z. Davis has so carefully demonstrated in her book *Fiction in the Archives,* many of those voices were themselves telling artfully constructed tales of their own. But rather than retelling their tales, I have attempted to use the techniques of microhistory to craft their truths, half-truths, and evident lies into stories that reveal the underlying complexities of late-sixteenth-century culture and values, shared (and at times not shared) from which their tales sprang and drew meaning. Moreover, approaching the archives as a storyteller as well as a historian has helped me to better appreciate what a rich pool of insights on the human mental world past, present, and possible lies buried there overlooked, to our aesthetic and intellectual loss.

I must admit, however, that attempting this mix of storytelling and microhistory also helped me to better understand the dangers of both and to appreciate that storytelling has some rather different ways of showing proximate truths. Ways the discipline of history might well reject, even if they are often to be found unrecognized in the most traditional of histories. First, the aesthetics of a tale has a tendency to empower one way of telling a story over another and thus may privilege one potential truth over another. For Renaissance intellectuals that would not have been a problem; to a great extent in the Platonic tradition, truth was beauty and beauty was truth. That is no longer self-evident in a world where often the most beautiful everyday images we see are television commercials and where the poetics of the political half-truth has been raised to an exquisite art form.

But, as with television commercials, if we recognize that the aesthetics of a tale has this potential, a writer can try to use that reality of storytelling to highlight what analysis has marked out as worthy of note and a critical reader can read with an eye for those aesthetic keys that should give pleasurable food for thought and perhaps disagreement. Unfortunately, I can make little claim to be such a skillful writer; thus I will place my hopes on skillful readers and my ability to resist the most attractive explanation in order to hold out for the one that gives the richness of the documentation and the complexity of late Renaissance life its due as much as possible.

Equally important, telling a story does not limit one to merely the narration or description of events; stories, I would assert, seldom merely list in temporal or visual terms, especially modern and postmodern ones.

In storytelling there is analysis that builds proximate truths first, of course, in ways familiar to historians; the storyteller stops the tale to provide description and context, to explain, to consider the various possibilities, even to tell what is actually happening. But in addition, the storyteller today can shift perspectives and times, layer events, repeat a theme and slowly expand it, until its deeper meanings become clearer and its significance more evident. Rather unwittingly as I wrote out these tales, I came to see the potential this has for the historical storyteller, and I hope I have taken advantage of its potential in my revisions. Once again, it is an analytical technique that has an aesthetic dimension that I hope will make the reading of these tales more pleasurable.

It also has a potentially negative dimension. Most significantly, it may well be easier to win support for such analysis, because even a careful reader may have trouble seeing that an argument is slowly building as one moves from tale to tale until what was once a tenuous hypothesis has become through repetition an apparent given. While I am aware of the danger of this, the material of these stories is unusual enough and my treatment of it, I believe, hypothetical enough that I am relatively certain that the doubt level of readers will remain high even as I hope that they enjoy the tales told and come to understand rather than merely believe.

The first tale of the book is the story of Andriana Savorgnan, a Venetian courtesan, who married Marco Dandolo, a Venetian noble from one of the most important families of the city. It is no surprise that his family was not particularly happy with the binding passions that they saw involved in this match. In fact they attempted to have it annuled by the Patriarch of Venice, and at the same time they attempted to have Andriana punished by the Holy Office for her purported use of love magic to literally bind Marco's love and force him to marry her. In their claims and in the development of the case against Andriana before the Holy Office many of the themes of this book are introduced, beginning with the formally illicit but fairly open world of sex that involved courtesans and the elites of the Renaissance. The story from this base moves on to consider the binding nature of marriage, family, social relationships between the classes, illicit sex, and love magic. But the central theme remains the life of prostitutes, the controls formal and informal that disciplined their lives, their powers, their problems, and their own social order.

The second tale continues with the theme of the ties of matrimony, focusing on the problems that developed when Elena Cumano found that her noble lover, Gianbattista Faceno, would not honor his promise of marriage to her. Along with marriage, this story returns to the issues of family, social hierarchy, and love magic, but this time from the perspective of Feltre, a smaller provincial center at the edge of Venetian territory just over the front range of the Alps, and involves a young woman of much more legitimate status, the daughter of a lawyer. The angle of analysis also changes; thus the issue of marriage is looked at with special attention to the binding power of reputation, honor, and words in late Renaissance society. In addition Elena's tale begins to open out the question of the relationship between love magic and accusations of witchraft, and to consider what it really meant to be labeled a witch and perhaps to be one as well.

The third tale continues with the issue of love magic and witchcraft, looking at the complex love stories that turned on the unlikely-sounding teaming of Paolina di Rossi, another Venetian courtesan, and Don Felice di Bibona, a cleric of dubious reputation. Marriage, status, and honor, although they remain significant in the unfolding of the tale, take a back seat, as does the tale itself at times, to the spinning out of a number of related stories that open the complex, rich, often virtually poetic world of love magic dominated largely by women and women's networks, first in its spiritual dimension, then in its bodily, spatial, and verbal dimensions. By the time this tale is finished, *carne vale,* love, flesh, and the binding of passions shoud have taken on new late Renaissance meanings.

The fourth story again leaves Venice for the countryside, this time moving to the edge of the area that Carlo Ginzburg made famous with his studies of the cosmology of the miller Mennochio and the theology of his night-battling Benandanti—the Friuli. The story, however, continues with the theme of love magic as it was practiced by Apollonia Madizza and her compatriots in the little town of Latisana, attempting to put it in a local context. Love magic in Latisana was integrated into a range of largely spiritual practices that turned on the ties that bound society together and healed its wounds, illnesses, and discords. These "arts" made Appolonia and her fellow practitioners much more than the witches they were accused of being by the authorities; in many ways it made them the true priests of Latisana. To a degree, Apollonia's tale might even be seen as a form of apologetics for witchcraft and a popular religion that has been lost. That, however, was not my intention. Given the general mindset that sees the witch as destructive and antisocial, it seemed that allowing the defense of Appolonia a stronger voice in her story was warranted. And in the end there does seem to be a good case for the women priests of Latisana and, by implication, for women priests elsewhere in the premodern period. At the least, Apollonia's story provides a useful cautionary tale about a number of stereotypes that have developed about witches, magic, the power of women, and the binding of passions to create society.

Finally, the last tale of the book involves the priest and friar Aurelio di Siena. In a way, Aurelio ties together or marries the tales that go before literally for better and for worse. Over his more than seventy years of life he was consistently a renegade cleric, moving in and out of the world of sex and power where the flesh ruled. He may have kept a house of prostitution and he almost certainly kept several mistresses, including the illegitimate daughter of the famous Venetian diarist Marin Sanuto. Yet more certainly, he sold at high prices the binding magic of love and health, as well as prophecies on the probable success of marriages, elections, and gambling. And he sold these things to everyday people as well as the rich and famous, becoming involved even with the love life of the noted love poet and cardinal Pietro Bembo. At least three times he fled from monastic orders, only to return to join new ones and move ahead with his ecclesiastical career. Four times he was investigated by the Holy Office and once sentenced to ten years in prison followed by perpetual banishment. Nonetheless, in his seventies he was still a major player in the illicit world of Venice, binding the passions of the rich and famous as well as the humble and was, once again, a relatively well-to-do man.

Fra Aurelio was perhaps one of the most outrageous examples of the many clerics who were still living beyond the discipline of the Church in the second half of the sixteenth century; thus, his story reveals their world with some exaggeration perhaps, but it is an exaggeration that reveals and highlights how that world could work and how far the disciplining drives of the period still had to go to bind the passions and the flesh, to tie and limit *carne vale* to carnival. From another perspective, he provides a masculine outlook on a world that was in many ways dominated by women and women's networks, and in doing so I believe reveals more clearly the contours of their dominance. Also, his story and his gender provide the opportunity to look more closely at a question that runs through the book even if it cannot be answered here: the relationship between levels of culture and gender at the end of the Renaissance. Fra Aurelio moved easily between the aristocracy and the elites of his age, whether of Venice or of the Church, at the same time that he moved easily among midwives, prostitutes, and marginal women; he moved easily as well between the popular magic associated with women that was so important to his profits and the high magic, assumed to be male, that allowed him to ask for and receive high fees; and he moved regularly within the power dynamics of Church, status, money, and sex, regularly turning all to his profit.

After Fra Aurelio's tale, the reader should have plenty of meat with which to ponder what *carne vale* actually meant in the late sixteenth century and how the passions were bound and ideally to be bound. Before beginning to tell their tales, however, Zaccharia and Zorzi deserve their due. For we have begun with their tale. And although Zaccharia and Zorzi are far from the most attractive of the people to be encountered in this book, they seem to have escaped the binding passions of the Holy Office in a manner fairly typical of the relatively rich and powerful. Zaccharia before the Holy Office, as already noted, tried to shift as much of the blame as possible to his friend, taking the correct social line that nobles decided and others followed. Zorzi, in turn, simply denied everything. Suggestively, after early testimonies that were quite detailed and damaging against the young men, as the investigation wore on people became more and more vague and forgetful. One or two did admit that they had been warned by unspecified people about testifying before they had been called in, but they assured the Holy Office that they were nonetheless prepared to tell all that they could remember about the events of Giovedi Grasso. Then, when questioned, they remembered little.

Slowly the case melted away and was allowed to drop. The powers of Zaccharia and Zorzi, the more traditional focus of history, had apparently won out. Family, status, wealth, and the ability to wield influence both political and personal had undercut the attempt of the Holy Office to punish what they had decided needed correction in 1571. Had Zaccharia and Zorzi's moment before the Holy Ofiice, then, in the end been enough to make them aware that *carne vale* was ending? Probably not. That was to be a long transition and crucially, like all great transitions, to be effective it had to be much more broadly cased, the sum of thousands of similar moments across society. Moreover Zaccharia and Zorzi's escape from their would-be repressors underlines another aspect of successful broad transitions: they seldom undercut openly the traditional centers of power. Change of such a major type usually comes at society from one or several oblique angles, often seemingly unrelated and perceived as traditional rather than radical.

Thus while we will be looking at binding passions from the perspective of magic, marriage, amd power, we will be constantly reminded that that complex of issues, although most important for the way life was lived, cannot be studied in a vacuum. The binding of passion and flesh intersected with the binding powers (and passions) of society, politics, and family in a rich dynamic that is central to the understanding of each. That appears to have been very much the case at the end of the Renaissance both in Zaccharia and Zorzi's failed prosecution and in the tales that follow.

1

Love Bound: Andriana Savorgnan, Common Whore, Courtesan, and Noble Wife

A Question of Honesty

"I believe you should make your daughter Pippa a whore," Antonia concluded after listening to Nanna contrast the dishonesties of her life as a nun and a wife with the successes of her life as a whore. So Pietro Aretino, the famous sixteenth-century writer and polemicist, had his women narrators conclude their discussion of the best life for a woman in his sixteenth-century satire the *Sei giornate*. Antonia summed up their reasoning: "the nun is a traitor to her sacred vows, the wife an assassin of holy matrimony; but the whore attacks neither the convent nor the husband. In fact . . . her shop sells that which she has to sell. . . . So be open-handed with Pippa and make her a whore from the start. . . . For in the end, as you yourself have said, the vices of the whore are virtues."[1]

Aretino's logic and perverse wit only slightly mask the revolutionary import of his message, for it is in reality nothing less than a sustained attack on the social morality and civic society that others were so aggressively defending in the early sixteenth century.[2] And crucially, the prostitute and the illicit world that surrounded her were key figures in Aretino's attack. As the title implies, Aretino's dialogues span six days; during the first three, Nanna, a Roman prostitute herself, and her friend Antonia considered the real options that women faced in the Renaissance, deciding that prostitution offered the only honest life. The last three days were dedicated to instructing young Pippa how to be the best prostitute possible.

The argument of the dialogues develops out of Nanna's autobiography because she had experienced each of the three options—life as a nun, as a wife, and as a whore. As a young girl just reaching sexual maturity, she had entered a convent. This was the Renaissance norm for many who became nuns. She had assumed that she was joining a world of religious commitment and fervor by taking vows that bound the passions she had already felt for a man in the outside world to God. But she was quickly disabused, discovering that the fervors of her sisters were quite other than religious. With a voyeuristic brush, Aretino's Nanna painted a lurid picture of the dishonesty, predominantly sexual, that she found in her convent. Behind the salaciousness of her tale, however, lay a truth that many in the Renaissance understood. The convent was not simply a spiritual retreat for women committed to a religious life; it was a form of social and sexual bondage that socially placed young women. For many, especially upper-class women, the convent was a life pressed upon them by their families to salvage family honor when a dowry could not be raised or a suitable marriage could not be arranged. As a result, when the discipline of the convent broke down, when its carefully bound passions were released, some convents were, not surprisingly, virtually as scandalous as Nanna claimed. But more significantly for many nuns, their vocation was not a true one.[3] Quite simply, their "shop," in Aretino's terms, was not producing the true spirituality claimed; thus, in his perverse way, Aretino could argue on the basis of Nanna's history that nuns were dishonest, and his attack could be heard by his Renaissance readers.

Nanna fled the convent to seek the honest life of a wife and another form of correctly bound passions in wedlock. But she found little that was honest there either. Without a father to arrange a match for her, she was forced to fall back on her mother, who "began to let it be known that she wanted to arrange a marriage for me, giving out now one story now another about me leaving the convent. . . . An old man, who only lived because he was still eating, having heard about this decided to have me for his wife or die. And as he was well-to-do my mother . . . concluded the marriage."[4] Clearly this arranged match, typical especially of the upper classes, had little chance from the start. The lively and independent Nanna found herself virtually sold into slavery labeled marriage with an old man "who only lived because he was still eating." Quickly Nanna learned all the dishonesties of life as an honest married woman, beginning with learning from her mother how to recover her virginity lost in the convent. Neighborhood women and friends continued her education, showing her how to escape her prison through adultery.

Finally, in a description that may have caused the voyeuristic laughter to stick in the throats of many a male reader comfortable with the Renaissance double standard that winked at male infidelity but frowned upon that of women, Nanna explained the end of her married life. Quite literally, she escaped wedlock by fulfilling her husband's initial desires. In the beginning he had wanted "to have me for his wife or die." Caught in bed with a lover and attacked by her irate husband, she coolly concluded, "I buried a little knife that I had in his chest and his pulse beat no longer."[5] Thus the wife became "the assassin of holy matrimony," as Antonia was to conclude.

Once again Aretino exaggerated the case against Renaissance marriage for effect, but his point had real bite. Arranged marriages, marriages contracted for larger family objectives, marriages formulated for economic motives, especially in the context of a double standard of sexual behavior, could be dishonest and little better than a form of servitude for women. As the correct place for licit sexuality, marriage had little chance of success and, as a result, many marriages were dishonest and a tissue of lies. Thus Aretino and his characters, Nanna, Antonia, and Pippa, could say to their readers that there was only one honest life for women in the Renaissance—that of the prostitute—and they could be heard. In the *Sei giornate* Aretino had turned the Renaissance world of marriage on its head and, consciously or merely moved by the inherent illogic of the structures of the dominant discourse, he did so by attacking the very ideological base of the central institutions that placed, disciplined, and correctly bound the dangerous passions of women in society: the honesty of marriage and the convent. The very honesty of the morality of society had been called into question—a revolutionary challenge indeed. But without seeing Aretino as a revolutionary, his perverse commentary on social morality brings us face to face with a crucial perspective on prostitution in sixteenth-century society: its potentially subversive nature in a society that saw itself based upon marriage and family.

The Marriage of Andriana Savorgnan

But rather than pursue the subversive nature of prostitution in the sixteenth century in a general theoretical way or from the perspective of literature, I would like to suggest some of the complexities of the issues involved by imitating Aretino and telling a tale not so perverse and cynical as his, but hopefully more based upon events and less upon literary imagination. Significantly, it is a tale of crime, discipline, and the binding of passions; for although prostitution was legal in the Renaissance, prostitutes were increasingly disciplined by society across the sixteenth century in ways and for reasons often surprising and telling. The case is that of Andriana Savorgnan's encounter with the Holy Office of Venice.

Early in 1581 the Venetian noble Marco Dandolo married the daughter of Laura Savorgnan, Andriana. The event, as retold by Laura, seems prosaic enough: "The week before the feast day of San Francesco, Signor Marco called me into the room where he was with my daughter Andriana and he said to me 'Grandmother please consent that your daughter become my wife.'"[6] One can well imagine the pleasure that this woman of humble origins from the Friuli felt when she heard that proposal from a scion of one of the oldest and most important noble families of Venice.

"And I," she continued, "made the sign of the cross saying, 'if that is pleasing to you sir, it is to me as well.'" That was Sunday. The next day, Marco returned to work out the details of the alliance and marry Andriana. "And thus Signor Marco on that very Monday took the hand of my daughter in my house in Santa Maria Formosa."[7] Present at the wedding as witnesses were Monsignor Alessandro Contarini, the ring bearer named Simon, Laura's parish priest, and, of course, the proud mother, Laura Savorgnan. After the marriage the young couple (he was twenty-two, she about twenty-three) moved into the palace of Monsignor Contarini in San Filippo a few hundred yards away on one of the back ways through to the central square of Venice, San Marco.[8] This was ideal; it promised that mother and daughter would remain close, and in a way it symbolized their new, more central place in the world of Renaissance Venice.

But to the disciplining eye of the late sixteenth century, Laura's description of her daughter's marriage already suggested problems. First, it was simply too quick. Although Laura claimed to have sought permission from the correct authorities, there had not been time to post bans, as the new marriage regulations of the Council of Trent required. Before Trent the Church had required solely the consent of the couple involved to constitute a marriage. Such a straightforward requirement had created, however, a host of problems. Most significantly, an exchange of consent was virtually impossible to discipline and control by Church, family, or government. As a result, when the fathers of the sixteenth-century Church met at Trent at midcentury to define the parameters of their faith, they were anxious to impose a tighter discipline on marriage. Among other things, they required the posting of bans before a marriage and a priest to officiate the ceremony. Thus, after Trent, a Sunday proposal and a Monday marriage were no longer possible.[9]

There were, however, other forms of discipline to enforce norms that had a wider social consensus than those of the Church. Honor was especially important in binding the passions that might lead to an unwise match. In this case, the quickness and privacy of the marriage would have been deemed as hardly honorable given the noble status of Marco Dandolo. At his social level, marriages were affairs of pomp and ceremony to be savored by family and supporters and evaluated by peers. If he had considered his honor and that of his family, he should have resisted the match for numerous reasons, but its speed and privacy should have been telling signs of its dishonorable character. Both honor and the rules of the Church, then, could discipline marriage: a marriage partner had to be selected not with dangerous passions such as love, but with great care, for a family's reputation and honor were made public at such moments as at virtually no other. Marriage was a crucial rite of passage for the Renaissance family.

In terms of family, Laura's account of the marriage of her daughter to Marco Dandolo leaves another question. Where was Marco's family, the famous and powerful Dandolo clan? We can excuse the absence of Marco's parents; he was an orphan. But his brother, Francesco, had missed the ceremony, as had his deceased mother's brother, Marco Michael, also a noble of major family. Both men were intimately involved in the tutelage of the young Marco. Much of the haste and the absence of relatives might be explained by the fact that Marco was marrying down the social scale. Such marriages were not unheard of, especially when the bride brought with her a large dowry and significant family connections. The Savorgnan family was, in fact, an important provincial clan, presumably an interesting match for an orphaned younger son of a major family. But the Dandolo family's absence suggests what Laura ruefully admitted as she proceeded with her tale of the wedding. Her dead husband had not actually been a Savorgnan. Rather, he had been a retainer of theirs who had taken their name and died fighting by their side against the Turks.[10] Others were not so generous. An old friend agreed that Laura's husband had died fighting the Turks on a galley captained by a Savorgnan, but as a rower, not as a retainer. In fact, she clarified that he had been sentenced to the galley as a common thief.[11] Hardly a family tradition worthy of the Dandolos; their absence underlined the faultiness of the marriage between Andriana and Marco. Without the Church, without law, without criminality per se, we are in an area where the powerful disciplining forces of honor and public reputation made such marriages, if not impossible, at least unlikely.

By itself this might be enough to explain the haste and relative privacy of the ceremony, but there was another and more important problem. Aloisio Soranzo, a long-time noble acquaintance of Andriana, put the issue bluntly: "I have known for many years the woman called La Savorgnan [Andriana]. I have been in her home and I heard that she was married to the Magnificent Messer Marco Dandolo, gentleman of Venice. This seemed very strange both to me and to the entire city—that a young man so honored, esteemed, and noble would be joined in marriage to a woman of such low birth, infamous morals, and a public whore. All the city judges that that woman led him to do it with potions and witchcraft."[12] Marco Dandolo had not simply married down the social scale; his passions had run amuck, perhaps aided by witchcraft, and he had married a "public whore." Even young Soranzo, who admitted having enjoyed Andriana's favors over a long period of time, claimed to be deeply troubled by the match. Significantly, Andriana had been quite the darling of a circle that included prominent nobles and clerics of the city. Yet with her marriage to Marco Dandolo, she went rapidly from being the darling of that group to being labeled "a woman of . . . low birth, infamous morals and a public whore."

The deacon of the Church of Santa Maria Formosa, who apparently was not an entirely innocent observer of Andriana's sexual activities either, suggested quite a different noble perception of her before her marriage: "The Magnificent Messer Fillipo da Canal told me three or four times that Andriana could not be the wife of anyone but him at least in the eyes of God, because they had given their hands in marriage to each other and had sworn [their marriage] before a crucifix that was over the door. . . . He told me this several times over the course of this last year."[13] Again following Trent, this was not a legal marriage. Fillipo's styling it a marriage "at least in the eyes of God" seems to have been an equivocation still used fairly frequently in the late sixteenth century to qualify the new regulations of the Church. It appears that marriage "in the eyes of God" was often adequate for initiating sexual intercourse, with the result that a new range of problems arose in regard to premarital sexuality, quickly followed by new attempts at disciplining such activity by ecclesiastical and civic authorities. But leaving aside for now those problems,[14] it is clear that Andriana was quite capable of securing marriage commitments from nobles no matter how much custom and social values militated against such matches.

In fact, there had been another, earlier attempt to secure a noble marriage for Andriana with the Count Scipione Avrogado. An old acquaintance of Andriana and her mother reported that they had obtained from a Greek witch a special potion that had been mixed with the food of the count's wife. "It was done so that the wife of the said Count Scipione would shrivel up and die. Then Count Scipione was to have taken Andriana for his wife as at the time he was so in love with her that he could not live without her. Not very long after the wife of Count Scipione died, but I don't know if she died because of that."[15] By then, however, Andriana was working on a better match, Marco Dandolo. Nonetheless Count Scipione and Fillipo da Canal, bound by their passions, continued to pursue her.

The Power of Andriana Savorgnan

Clearly, the power of this prostitute from a humble background in her early twenties was impressive, and although her trade was legal, it equally clearly required discipline. One key to that discipline was conceptualizing her power as not so much sexual as magical. The Dandolo clan used just this rationale as the basis of their two-pronged attack on Andriana. On the one hand, they argued before the Patriarch of Venice that the marriage of the young couple was not valid because Marco had been bound by Andriana's love magic and thus had not consented to the matrimony of his own free will. They also argued that the forms of Trent had not been observed, but the magical binding of Marco's love and thus his lack of free will was the focus of their case. In addition, they brought proceedings against Andriana and her mother before the Holy Office of Venice, accusing both women of using witchcraft to win and hold the love of Marco and other nobles. Such claims were not limited to the Dandolos; by the late sixteenth century, they had become regular and helped to swell significantly the number of accusations brought before the Holy Office in Venice and Inquisition tribunals elsewhere.

One central concern about prostitution in the sixteenth century turned on the power prostitutes had over the passions of men. In theory, the client, by buying or "renting the prostitute's body," as authorities often phrased it, should have been in control. Commercializing sex, in a way much like marriage, disciplined it; in one case, the control was provided by a husband reinforced by family and Church; in the other, the control was provided by money reinforced by the regulations of commercial transactions. In both cases in theory, passions were to be correctly bound and contained, leaving men on top. But in practice, as Andriana's noble lovers make perfectly clear, it was not unusual for passions to confuse the issue. Her lovers were rich, powerful men who nonetheless had become powerless before her wiles; they were described by sympathetic observers as "not being able to find any peace or rest without her," "mad about her," or even "not being able to live without her." Such language has become so familiar today that one misses much of its weight in the sixteenth century. Certainly in the literature of the period, one finds plenty of similar rhetoric, and as we shall see in Chapter 3, this language of accusation echoes the standard language of accusation used against love magic. Rather than stale conceits, however, we are dealing here with claims that Andriana truly and willingly damaged her male victim lovers by binding their love. Certainly at the end of the sixteenth century, the Holy Office was aware of the import of such language and pressed a number of witnesses to detail her magic and its impact, especially on Dandolo. Most admitted that Dandolo had lost his ability to act independently and was completely at the mercy of Andriana. This was not modern romance; it was sixteenth-century binding magic. As one witness sympathetic to Dandolo's plight related, "I believe that this marriage was put together more with witchcraft than with other things, I do. In fact, I noted that he did not even know how to give his opinion or how to move from her side."[16]

Although it is possible that the accusation of witchcraft against Andriana was totally false, totally fabricated to undermine her marriage with Marco, the weight and detail of the evidence suggest that there was some witchcraft or, more specifically, love magic involved. Andriana and her women friends were accused of a wide range of activities that seemed to have been quite common and an important part of the renaissance prostitute's tricks of the trade (as we shall see in Chapter 3). Most of these aimed at binding the love of clients or evaluating that love. For the latter Andriana relied heavily on the casting of beans, the relationship between beans after they were thrown, and between them and other objects thrown with them signifying the relationship of people to each other.[17] To bind clients, she apparently had a rich lore that she had learned from her mother and several other women, including the famous healer and magician la Draga, who will be discussed in Chapter 4. But without anticipating too much, one example of the magic she was accused of may suffice to provide a sense of this important part of the Renaissance prostitute's world and a sense of the reality behind the accusations against her.

Franceschina, wife of Vicenzo Savoner, known as China, admitted that she had helped Andriana with magic designed to bind the love of the noble Nicolo Corner. She and Andriana had collected olive branches given out in church and brought them to Andriana's kitchen, where they burned the tips. Then they tied each one and dipped it in holy water, and Andriana said the following words: "As I bind this wood with this string, so too may be bound the phallus of Nicolo Corner so that he may not be able to go to any woman other than me." The women then went down to a ground-floor room, where Andriana planted the branches in the ground and said: "As this wood both will not grow again or branch out again, so too Nicoleto Corner may not be able to have relations with other women than me."[18] Although this specific magic using olive branches was unusual, its form was typical, as we will see, in its binding, its use of the holy, and even in the rhetorical forms used. Interestingly, however, in this case there is fairly good evidence that the magic did not work, for there exists a will of Nicolo Corner's wife, Laura, written, as was often the case, as she neared the term of her pregnancy a little more than a year after this magic was attempted.[19] Thus Andriana's magic seems to have failed.

Or maybe not, for if we suspend disbelief, the timing of events allows a different interpretation. Following China's testimony in late October 1581, the Holy Office, not willing to rely on her word alone, sent their officers with her to Andriana's house. There they found the olive branches bound and planted as China had testified. And with the logic of inquisitors they dug them up as evidence, thus presumably breaking the spell. A little more than a month later, in January 1582, Laura and Nicolo were married, and a year later Laura was pregnant, about to give birth. The timing, therefore, allows a thoroughly nonmodern retelling: Nicolo had actually been bound and was incapable of marrying until the

Holy Office discovered and undid the binding magic of Andriana. Fortunately, however, that does not have to be accepted to understand the central point: love magic was an important weapon of prostitutes and also of those who wished to accuse them of illicitly binding the passions of men.

Accommodating the theory of disciplined commercial sex with such realities was essential for Renaissance society. Passions that broke down the theoretical economic control of the client over the prostitute, when conceptualized in terms of magic or witchcraft, shifted the focus of the problem from the male client to the female prostitute. Thus neither prostitution as an institution nor powerful men as individuals were responsible for the mad and disruptive passions engendered at times in such relationships. Rather, evil women using binding magic were—just as Marco Dandolo's family had claimed. Crucially, that meant that such passions could be handled in traditional ways by disciplining those who used such love magic, that is, prostitutes. Men like Marco Dandolo could remain victims even when they insisted that they were willing ones; and in more normal moments, they could perceive themselves in control even as they worried that they were not.

Perhaps such ambivalence is not pleasing to our desire to order that past; but then, desire and order fit only imperfectly together whether we are speaking of sex or of history. And here we are at the heart of a complex web of perceptions and values that give the lie to the simplistic vision of prostitution as an economic transaction. In a way also we find ourselves here with Andriana and Marco at the nightmare edge of what such relationships could entail, at least from the perspective of Renaissance elites and their conceptions of order: the prostitute daughter of a peasant thief had by the wiles of her craft captured a place in the central institution of aristocratic society, the marriage bed of Marco Dandolo, scion of the Venetian nobility.

Even language itself was marshaled against this. Accounts of Andriana's snaring of Dandolo stressed the fact that she was a common whore or public prostitute, in other words, a prostitute of the most base reputation. That unanimity in labeling Andriana, however, does not square well with the details of the case, nor obviously was it supported by the testimony of her family and remaining friends. As one might expect, Laura Savorgnan presented a different picture of her daughter. The Holy Office asked her, "Could you clear up for us whether your daughter has been a courtesan or a public prostitute here in Venice?" Laura answered, "She has been a courtesan given her clients." Accepting her logic, they asked, "Could you tell us those gentlemen who have had contact with your daughter and slept with her?" Her reply was impressive: "They were Santo Contarini, Piso Pisani, Fillipo da Canal, the Count Scipio Avrogado, Paolo Robazzo—but it would take a much larger brain than mine to be able to remember them all. . . . And then there was the Celsi called Lorenzo and Messer Nicolo Corner son of Messer Zorzi and Marco Dandolo who has had relations with her for two years."[20]

Laura's give-and-take with the Holy Office reveals a shared standard; notwithstanding the claims to the contrary, Andriana's clients revealed that there was little that was common in her prostitution. Any doubt that remains is put to rest by a letter in the Medici Archives in Florence written to the Duke by one of his men in Venice. In the midst of reporting the important events of the city the Duke's correspondent noted, "Andriana Savorgnan, *famous courtesan*, having fled her home to avoid arrest, Saturday was arraigned before the Holy Office for having used witchcraft and evil arts to lead the Magnificent Marco Dandolo to marry her."[21] Andriana was not a common whore but a "famous courtesan," the type of high-class, refined prostitute for which Venice had already become well known. And as a courtesan, she was famous enough to have her binding of the passions of Marco Dandolo brought to the attention of the Duke of Florence.

Social Distinctions and Prostitution

As such, Andriana was at the top of a social hierarchy of prostitution, a hierarchy that, much like the regular social hierarchy, had significant disciplining functions. Just as knowing one's place in the social order controlled behavior in myriad ways—Castiglione's Perfect Courtier comes immediately to mind—so too did the social order of prostitution form and control the behavior both of the prostitute and of her clientele. The criteria that measured such distinctions and reinforced such hierarchies are difficult to sort out, however, largely because the records of the period provide so many different perspectives on prostitution, ranging from moral condemnation and outrage to joyous male-centered celebration.

Most governments still required the registration of prostitutes both for tax and disciplining purposes, and occasionally evaluated them as they were registered. In Florence in 1560, for example, the office of the Onestà, which was responsible for regulating prostitutes, compiled one of their periodic censuses of prostitutes, which has survived. It divided the women registered into the categories of "rich, middling but comfortable, poor who would be able to pay their tax, and truly poor." Respectively, they reported numbers of sixty-eight, ninety-seven, sixty, and fifteen for each category.[22] Evidently the numbers themselves must be treated with suspicion, as they were generated largely by a desire to tax, and as such were deformed in ways difficult to evaluate by a counter-desire to avoid being taxed. Taxation also clearly has colored the categories themselves, with their focus on the ability to pay taxes and wealth. But wealth was a significant measure of status in the Renaissance and perhaps an even more significant one for women like prostitutes, who had theoretically sacrificed their honor to their profession.

Literature is also full of interesting hints of such distinctions, largely overlooked because we have only just begun to consider the meaning of such hierarchies and their disciplining potential. Niccolò Machiavelli's misogynistic description of the very Machiavellian disjuncture between appearance and reality at the bottom of the hierarchy is fairly well known. Writing to Luigi Guicciardini, he reported an unseemly encounter with a common prostitute in a dark room. Afterward wishing to see his "merchandise," he lit a lamp and almost "dropped dead." There follows a long, destructive description of the poor old woman he discovered. Meaning to be clever, Machiavelli's humor was designed to work at several levels: it played on the gap between appearance and reality; it suggested the demeaning absurdity of his own passions; and it detailed the simple ugliness of the woman. We can be spared his description, which no longer reads as humor, but his concluding remarks are particularly telling about social placement and behavior: "as soon as she began to speak there came from her mouth such a stinking breath that the portals of my two most shocked senses, my eyes and nose, were overwhelmed by that plague. Then the shock settled into my stomach, but not being able to swallow it, there began a great heaving, and heaving, suddenly, I threw up all over her. And so having paid her with the exact coin that she deserved, I left."[23] Even allowing for Machiavelli's exaggeration for effect, such literary visions of the common prostitute reveal clearly their low status and suggest why Andriana's attackers were so anxious to label her a common whore.

From Machiavelli's common Tuscan whore to the noted sixteenth-century *novelliere*, Matteo Bandello's depiction of the aristocratic Roman courtesan Imperia, celebrated by poets and noted "friends" like Agostino Chigi, is a short jump in time and space but a very long one indeed in terms of status and behavior. Even Imperia's lodgings evoked her virtually imperial position in Roman society. "Her house was furnished in a manner that was all carefully planned so that whatever foreigner entered seeing the furnishings and the discipline of the servants would believe that here there lived a princess. Among other things there was a hall, a main room and a bedroom all so richly decorated that there seemed nothing else but velvets and brocades and on the floors the most beautiful carpets. . . . In the bedroom where she retired when she was visited by some great personage there were draperies that covered the walls . . . layered with gold and much beautiful and delightful work."[24]

The "humorous" conclusion of Bandello's tale is an almost perfect reversal of Machiavelli's letter. Imperia's brilliant chambers were visited by the Spanish ambassador, who was attracted by reports of her grace and beauty. He was not disappointed. "Upon seeing the woman as she was so very beautiful, he marvelled greatly at her and the rich furnishings that surrounded her. After the ambassador had been with her for some time, feeling the desire to spit, he turned to a servant and spit in his face. For this he apologized by saying to the servant, 'I hope that you do not mind, but in this place your face is the most base thing.'"[25] Imperia, being a woman of refined sensibilities, thanked the ambassador for his compliment but suggested that in the future he should spit on the carpet, which, elegant as it was, was placed on the floor for just that purpose. The cruelty in both stories worked as humor, in large measure because of a strong sense of hierarchy in society and in prostitution. Vomit and spit did not so much demean as measure the immense social gap that yawned between the common prostitute and the courtesan.

In the highly stratified society of sixteenth-century Italy, that there would be several levels of prostitution covering the social spectrum from Machiavelli's old prostitute to Andriana Savorgnan and Bandello's Imperia comes as no surprise. Already by the early sixteenth century it is possible to distinguish five or six levels of prostitution in the major cities of Italy. At the humblest level fell the numerous women who drifted in and out of the trade as necessity or chance moved them. They operated from the streets or from taverns and inns, drawing their trade mainly from the lower social levels. As they attempted to avoid taxes and registration, their activities were formally illegal. But the irregularity of their practice and their limited earnings made such part-time women both difficult and unrewarding to attempt to bring under the law. They exist in the records primarily when they began to congregate enough in one area of the city to create disorder or change the nature of an inn or tavern enough to create complaints. Much more visible, in the records at least, were the registered prostitutes who worked in large houses sometimes publicly run, sometimes run by prominent families. It appears that their clients were most frequently local artisans and foreigners. Suggestively, many of these houses were organized much like a convent with an "abbess" responsible for the discipline of the "sisters" and a form of cloisterization that severely limited a sister's time outside the brothel. It seems almost as if, consciously or unconsciously, the binding and disciplining functions of the convent and the house of prostitution were being equated.

A third group of prostitutes comprised registered women who worked independently, usually managed by a procurer or procuress. Reputation, appearance, manners, and cost were central in determining the social level of their clients. But the ability to support a procurer and pay the taxes that came with registration while living independently suggests a higher level of patronage. Unregistered women who worked for a procurer may well have comprised two groups: less appealing women who avoided registration because their earnings were small, and more expensive prostitutes whose trade benefited from the greater freedom of movement and the higher status offered by avoiding registration.

Also, by avoiding registration, the latter group could attempt to evade the increasingly strict sumptuary legislation that theoretically was designed to keep prostitutes from dressing like upper-class women. If such legislation had worked, it might have helped to restrict the hierarchical differentiation of prostitutes, as dress was a major public measure of status. Not registering was just one ploy among many for avoiding laws that were generally avoided by the more powerful in the profession. Often these latter unregistered women were much like Andriana early in her career, that is, professionals who maintained their independence in the hope of finding noble supporters who would allow them to enter the much more lucrative ranks of the courtesan.

In the Venetian comedy *La Bulesca,* first performed in the early years of the century, the young prostitute Marcolina explained to her sister Zuana (and to her aristocratic listeners who attended the performance) some of the advantages of practicing outside a bordello. "If I had remained in the house of Marietta [a bordello run by the latter] I would never have had more than a little money and I would have always been under her power. . . . It is good also to be one's own master, to live in one's own house rather than to have to screw this one and that in the bordello. If you earn a dress, it is yours, while there [in the bordello] you must pay a third of your earnings for expenses and constantly sweat under this one and that. . . . Now everything is mine. I do not give up a quarter or even a third of my earnings." Later in the comedy, Zuana underlined the significance of this change by noting in a soliloquy how far her sister had risen in life after leaving the bordello. She labeled Marcolina "a refined whore" and was especially pleased that in her independence she had escaped the clutches of the low-life ruffians Bio and Bulle, whose swaggering, threats, and insults make up the heart of the play. Rather, she could now take the lovers she wished and operate at a higher social level. Perhaps, in fact, at just the level of the young male aristocrats who heard and apparently commissioned the play, for it appears that the play was first performed in 1514 before one of the famous Venetian Compagnie di Calze, youth groups of the best families dedicated to the display of status and power at the level of public festivals and private events.[26]

Beyond Marcolina at the top of the hierarchy of prostitution, courtesans usually went unregistered and lived on their own, with as much style and grace as possible in the manner of Imperia. If such a woman had a manager, by the sixteenth century it was usually another woman and often her mother (either actual or adopted), as was probably the case with Andriana. But what gave the courtesan the power to transcend her more humble compatriots was one or a series of upper-class male sustainers who provided the wealth and the protection to allow her to move securely beyond the restrictions, both legal and social, placed on regular prostitutes. In this context, the list of Andriana's gentlemen re-counted by her mother to the Holy Office demonstrated to all that her daughter was a courtesan. But crucially, when Andriana stepped beyond that protected status, broke the unwritten regulations of a code of honor that accepted sex with prostitutes but not marriage, her detractors, in-cluding many of her ex-supporters, declared with even their language that that protection was null and void. She was no longer an honest courtesan, but rather a "common whore." In a way, that label de-meaned Andriana in a manner very similar to Machiavelli's vomit. And, of course, in that demeaning, in that loss of status, there was a strategy of control as surely as there was in the attempt to prosecute her for witchcraft before the Holy Office. Here we are well into a complex web of forms of discipline that controlled prostitution without labeling it illegal per se and often without having to call on more formal disciplin-ing structures.

Andriana, however, was not a woman to be so easily labeled and dismissed. For if she had not legally married Marco Dandolo, she had come close enough to warrant the launching of a major counteroffensive by his family and their supporters. And more important, she appears to have built some ties to very important friends in her career as a courte-san, friends who were reluctant to come forward and testify in her behalf but who worked behind the scenes to help her. One telling indication of this was the fact that when, shortly before her marriage, she had been held in jail for a short period (perhaps after being condemned by the Magistrato alle Pompe in April 1581), she had been allowed to have private quarters there and to keep at least one servant to take care of her needs. The servant was also necessary because she entertained regularly while in prison, receiving visits from admirers and even wining and dining her jailor. Apparently her quarters included more than one room and a private kitchen as well, for her servant reported that he had been kept waiting in the kitchen with some noble admirers while Andriana and some of her women friends retired and locked themselves in an inner room for about a half hour. The servant supposed that this secre-tive absence was for magical purposes: "While this Andriana was in jail . . . there came to visit her an old woman dressed in a black cape and hood plus a pair of gloves. At the bidding of Andriana and her sis-ter Ippolita the women entered into that room and they locked them-selves in. . . . And thus they stayed locked in for a half hour. Mean-while I stayed in the kitchen talking with many nobles who came to talk with the said Andriana."[27] One may justifiably imagine that while courtesans, with their powerful protectors, might occasionally win such conditions in jail, their more common sisters encountered much less comfortable situations there: social distinctions colored even life in jail.

The Origins of the Renaissance Courtesan:
Social Imperatives, Social Arbiter

The Renaissance origin of the courtesan is an issue that has engendered
debate. Some have suggested that the courtesan was just another aspect
of the Renaissance of classical culture—a modern form of the Greek
haeterae. Others have argued that the courtesan developed in Rome in
the fifteenth century around the courts of increasingly princely popes
and cardinals. An aristocratic and courtly environment with limited access to aristocratic and courtly women, so this thesis runs, engendered a
higher caliber of prostitute—a woman who was not only young and
beautiful, but who could grace with wit and charm a dinner or an
evening otherwise dominated by male clerics. From such newly perceived necessities in an environment of unusual wealth, power, and
culture, the courtesan flourished as an elite form of prostitute quickly
copied by an increasingly aristocratic upper class throughout Italy.[28]

Unfortunately, there is little information to prove or disprove such
conjectures. What seems clear is that the style caught on quickly because
it satisfied new social imperatives. In the increasingly aristocratic world
of the Renaissance, upper-class males found in the courtesan, as they
found in expanding interests in display and manners, yet another area of
life where they could fashion themselves as a Renaissance elite. As virtù
left the marketplace and the halls of government, it came to inhabit the
court, the dining hall, and the bedroom—new aristocratic spaces where
the courtesan was groomed to move with uplifting grace and ease. In
fact, with time the courtesan became not simply an accessory but also
an arbiter of status. Imperia's elegant bedroom and the Spanish ambassador's highly cultivated sense of manners, as crystallized in Bandello's story, merely reflect one facet of that brilliance. Only the best men
were admitted to her chambers to admire her princely style, and with a
chuckle the Renaissance reader found that there was nothing more common to be found there than the face of a servant. The ideal was that
unlike the common whore, who was available to all, the universal victim at the bottom of the hierarchy of prostitution, the "honest courtesan" was an exacting mistress, a woman not unlike the court lady of
Castiglione in her disciplining function, who judged honestly her suitors,
accepting only the best. With honest courtesans, men were measured by
connoisseurs in the art of love, and the truly deserving—those with
aristocratic manners, grace, and wealth—would be made manifest to all.

Another story from Bandello provides a fictional portrayal of how
this arrangement supposedly worked in Venice, as well as some interesting details about how courtesans practiced their trade, all wrapped up
in a morality tale that stressed the danger of the courtesan for young
nobles. Bandello introduced this *novella* by explaining that he had been
told it in the context of an ongoing discussion about the diverse stu-

pidities that young men committed when they became the victims of love—a rubric under which Bandello and most of his readers probably would have included Marco Dandolo as well. "In Venice," he related, "there is also another thing: an infinite number of whores, who as in other cities are called with honest language courtesans. One notes there, however, a custom which has not yet been heard of elsewhere; namely that there are courtesans who will normally have five or six Venetian gentlemen for their lovers. Each of these men has a night of the week when he goes to dine and to enjoy her. The day belongs to her, free to be invested in the service of whoever comes. . . . If it should happen that some outsider arrives with a fat purse and asks to spend the night with her, she may accept him. But first she must tell the man to whom the night belongs that if he wishes to grind his grain he must do so during the day. . . . And thus organized these lovers pay a certain amount monthly and it is formally included in their agreement that the women may receive and lodge for the night outsiders."[29]

A young noble from Milan became the victim of this system. Visiting a Venetian courtesan and falling in love with her, he decided to purchase her favors, as Bandello implies he would have been able to do without a problem in more normal places like Lombardy. Instead he found that he could buy no more than her conversation, and that he was consistently passed over for others more favored. As Bandello played on the traditional conceit of the prostitute's greed and duplicity, he drew out the point that this treatment only increased the young man's passion: "She . . . seeing him richly dressed and looking like a man ready to spend realized that he was a pigeon ready for plucking; thus, she began to play him making eyes at him and giving him quite sweet looks. All of which drove the young fool mad. Finally one day as he was giving her his alms, pricking up his courage and being close to her he asked for a kiss. She immediately reprimanded him saying that he was too presumptuous and that he did not merit one. At the same time, however, she lovingly kissed another who was there. Then to increase his passion for her she said to another, 'Let's go in the bedroom and grind two sacks of grain.' That they did."[30]

Bandello's unnamed Venetian courtesan in her free time literally kept court. Men gathered around her, paying their "alms," as he ironically labeled them, in order to try to win her favor and favors. The chosen few could grind a sack or two of grain; the others waited until they merited such honors. Certainly there is satire, misogyny, and overstatement for effect in the tale, but it is the courtesan's freedom to chose and her role as judge that make the story work. It might be that this was merely a fictional contrast with the correct way that things were done in Lombardy, but Andriana's case suggests that this was not mere fiction, and certainly even the tale works better if the courtesans of big cities like Venice had this reputation. Bandello took the tale a step further, however, pointing out that the normal rules of jealousy seemed to be curiously reversed in such situations, an unlikely detail if the practice was merely fantasy. Rather than being upset by the courtesan whose favors they shared, men seemed to feel a stronger passion for her. And that was true whether they were Venetian nobles sharing their kept woman with outsiders or Bandello's young noble from Milan seeing the object of his desire giving the kiss refused him to another.[31]

The story's tragic conclusion allows Bandello, true to his dark vision, to bring unbound passion's folly to its dark flower. Having failed for three months to win the love he had paid for with both money and courtship, after yet another refusal, he dramatically drank down a draught of poison before his courtesan love. But one last irony remained: "She thinking it a joke, laughed. And he went home to bed where that night he died without anyone knowing it." In a way this was the ultimate futile gesture in a society so attuned to the public construction of self; it was literally the deconstruction of a noble at the hands of a courtesan. Bandello's victim had been denied, in front of other honorable men, every public favor that status and wealth required, and in the end he had been denied by his poison and by his perverse passion even the satisfaction of a last heroic deed, dying publicly before his tormentress. Instead, with the public last laugh of a powerful woman ringing in his ears, he retreated to die unremarked in his own bed—truly the period's highest condemnation of mad love's effect on young men.

Still, discounting the details required by the symmetry of the tale and what was perhaps the stereotypical emphasis on the avariciousness and commercial greediness of Venetians compounded with similar stereotypes for prostitutes, the courtesan of this tale shines through as an independent woman who judged men. Turning to other realities, however, it is evident that the economics of the everyday world of practice beyond literature implied that men with enough money could be relatively sure of their judges. Even if one was rejected by Imperia, with a certain level of wealth, there were other courtesans like Andriana Savorgnan, at least in her earlier career, to reinforce an aristrocrat's status. Still at the level of the courtesan there was considerable overlap of status and sex in relationships, which means once again that we are faced with more than a simple economic transaction. Status, place, and honor had to be factored into the relationship as much as or even more than pleasure, and even the power of money could become ambiguous in the context of a Renaissance courtesan.

Things, however, could become yet more complicated, requiring qualifications of our qualifications, as the curious case that the young Venetian noble Luigi Dolfin became involved in in Florence in 1563 suggests. It appears that when a Venetian noble was abroad, at times even money and status were no match for a powerful courtesan. Dolfin had had a run-in with the Florentine courtesan Giulia Napolitana and complained to the perhaps most important criminal magistracy of that city, the Otto di Guardia: "It occurs my Lords that as men living without wives sometimes have resort to women and prostitutes, it happened to me a few days ago that . . . I agreed with Giulia Napolitana that she come to sleep with me at my house and I left her four gold *Scudi*. . . . It seems, however, that either on her own or pressed by others this woman decided to scorn me and thus she made a fool of me before an infinite number of her friends and favorites."[32]

Guilia was no common prostitute. She did not appear in the 1560 list of Florentine prostitutes compiled by the office of the Onestà discussed earlier, not even among the category of the rich, but this is probably merely an indication of her status, power, and support. Courtesans, as noted earlier, were usually able to avoid such demeaning requirements as registration, and that, of course, meant that they also avoided taxation. But even if she was not registered there, she was well known at the Onestà, as Dolfin ruefully complained. It seems that he had attempted first to bring his complaint to the Onestà: "Thinking that there [at the Onestà] there would be given me the correct and good justice, it turned out instead that I saw clearly the unmeasured and open favors given to her by some in that office." Not only had Giulia bantered with the judge like an old friend, he lamented, the latter had even had the gall to reassure her that he would not listen to Dolfin's complaints.

More troubling yet to the Venetian was the fact that the judge had allowed her to enter the court "accompanied by about 150 young men making a great din all to my dishonor." Dolfin had not been able to take advantage of the power that money and status theoretically provided him over a courtesan, and he had compounded his loss by making that public in court, where by being mocked by the young friends of Giulia, he had lost his honor as well.[33] Literature also delighted in such reversals of honor and status worked by clever women or prostitutes on powerful but often not too clever males. Aretino's Nanna, for example, provided a long list of tricks the courtesan could play on such men. But once again, literature probably made more of the range of these opportunities than real life actually offered.[34] Dolfin's case reveals that in life such things could happen, but Andriana's suggests that even for very powerful women with powerful friends, things could unravel quickly when one stepped beyond the accepted boundaries of behavior.

Andriana's case raises one other major issue: where did these brilliant, mannered, and attractive women come from? How did they learn the skills that enabled them to move in such demanding circles, not merely as participants but also as arbiters? How did they escape the discipline of social place to become educated and relatively cultured women? A corollary of these questions is also worth considering: did acquiring such manners and culture serve to discipline them in the same way it did their aristocratic clients? Literature again provides some tantalizing suggestions. Aretino, for example, while coloring his narrative with considerable irony in the *Sei giornate,* presents an account of the training and indoctrination of a future Roman courtesan, Pippa, by her mother, Nanna. Nanna, as we have seen, having decided that the only honest life for Pippa was as a prostitute, decided to make her the best prostitute possible, that is, a courtesan. For Nanna that meant superficial culture and refinement to match that of her clients and a bag of tricks to milk the most profit out of the trade.

Reselling virginity, refurnishing expensive lodgings, and cadging expensive gifts all figured large in Nanna's schemes. But in part they figured so large because Aretino delighted in using Nanna's mercenary desires to satirize the supposedly aristocratic and powerful men who were, in fact, the victims of his "honest" heroines. And honest they were in Aretino's eyes because they sold exactly what they claimed to sell, sex *and* illusion: the illusion of men being elite, refined lovers; the illusion of men being discriminating in their choice of mistresses; the illusion of men being mannered and intellectual. In sum, they sold to the upper classes the very illusion the upper classes had created of themselves. Such illusions always sell dear. And they were more expensive yet in a society where they often masked more mercenary and unseemly realities; that was the heart of Aretino's perverse satire.

Still, behind that satire, one sees the illusion of learning and refinement being orchestrated in Pippa by her mother. The first-generation prostitute, Nanna, had learned the basic tricks of her trade; Pippa, the next generation, could be developed to go beyond with at least the veneer of refinement and culture. Andriana Savorgnan's life history reveals a certain level of accuracy in Aretino: "It is true that I know everything about this Andriana because she was born in Udine in my house," Catarina, wife of Joseph, told the Holy Office, "she would now be about 23 or 24 years old. Her mother called Laura lives with her in her house. . . . This Laura being left in poverty [after her husband went to serve on the galleys] came to stay in Venice with certain gentlemen as a servant."[35] Others were not so discreet and labeled Laura a concubine or prostitute. Andriana soon found herself a victim of her mother's service; Catarina explained, "according to what Laura and Andriana told me when Andriana was ten or eleven she had her virginity taken while her mother worked as a servant. After that Andriana was continuously a public prostitute here in Venice, in Padua, and all over."[36]

Laura Savorgnan told a similar tale of her early years, even if, for obvious reasons, she couched her account in a more positive light. She stressed that her years of service in Venice had been in noble households, with her young daughter Andriana at her side. After allowing her to establish this positive picture, the Holy Office asked pointedly, "What work did this child Andriana do after she reached the age of ten?" Laura replied, "From about ten on, I had her learn to read and write and make lace in the Neapolitan manner."[37] Although this was not the anticipated response, it reveals that Laura had higher aspirations for her daughter. Reading and writing were not the skills required to be a servant, the wife of an artisan, or even a simple prostitute. They did, however, begin to prepare Andriana to be something more, the educated and refined courtesan capable of attracting aristocratic male lovers. And significantly, growing up by the side of her mother in the homes of Venetian gentlemen, she also had the opportunity to observe and assimilate their manners and style.

Those illusive questions—How were Renaissance courtesans made? Where did they come from?—begin to gain focus and form from Andriana's life. The Holy Office, however, was less interested in those aspects of her biography than in her career as a prostitute: "Could you clarify," they asked, "what your daughter's life was like in terms of her reputation and honesty." Here we are back to evaluative and disciplining language that was understood by all, and Laura did not hesitate to provide the response expected by her examiners: "My daughter was about thirteen when her virginity was taken by a Frenchman. From that moment she regularly had gentlemen that slept with her."[38] Under further questioning, as noted earlier, she labeled her daughter a courtesan and provided a list of her noble admirers. Andriana emerges from such testimony as a young woman not unlike Aretino's Pippa. Benefitting from her mother's experience and a training that prepared her for the highest level of the profession, at a young age she moved ahead rapidly, becoming by her early twenties a famous courtesan. One advantage she had over Pippa was her direct exposure to aristocratic lifestyles as the daughter of a woman who lived in that environment. Manners, refinement, and the ability to read and write all came together in Andriana, allowing her to move beyond the common to claim the status of courtesan.

Others followed a similar path, as the sixteenth-century records make clear. Giacomina di Seravallo was a woman in her early thirties and apparently at the end of her career when she came to the attention of the Holy Office, charged with using love magic to bind her clients. Significantly, one form of that magic involved *carte di voler bene*—written prayer spells used to touch and bind the love of patrons—that she had been accused of writing out herself. Under direct questioning, however, she denied this, admitting only that "I have certainly kept books to read, histories and other things because I enjoy reading."[39] While admiring her evident good taste, it must be conceded that Giacomina apparently never gained the status of courtesan. Perhaps her greatest success was in having been recruited for a private *casino* kept by young nobles in the Ca Loredan. Exactly what went on there is unclear, but her onetime lover, a tailor named Marco, discussed in his testimony her recruitment and service there: "I do not know where this Giacomina would be if not perhaps in the Ca Loredan. That is a *casino* in Calle della Testa which is kept by a few gentlemen including a Loredan. . . . Messer Ottavian Pisani came to my house with two gentlemen from the *casino*. They spoke with Giacomina and agreed that she should go and serve there. Afterwards she came back to my house two times and told me that once she had had to stay on her feet until the ninth hour and another time until the eleventh and she was not sure she could continue."[40]

Was Giacomina's service as a prostitute in a private bordello, or was it as a servant in a private social club maintained by nobles of important families like the Loredan and Pisani? Unfortunately, the Holy Office, with its usual tact in regard to the great families of the city, did not inquire further about this *casino* or about why Messer Ottaviano Pisani, along with two other gentlemen, was out recruiting for such a place, especially women like Giacomina, whose apparent familiarity with love magic and checkered past seemed to have made her not well suited for merely pouring wine or cleaning. Giacomina, however, was not a success at their *casino* and left after only a few months to sell her favors in Padua. There also things did not go well, and when she fell ill she wrote to Marco, asking him to come and get her. Against many of the stereotypes of a deserted male lover, Marco went immediately to Padua to rescue Giacomina, and it seems that the couple eventually married and settled down in Venice.[41]

Cassandra Lizzari was a younger prostitute, also the daughter of a prostitute, who had mastered written culture as well, and seems, from her confidence and assurance before the Holy Office, to have felt that she was operating from a position of strength, perhaps because she had noble supporters. Asked about her literacy she replied with evident pride, "I know how to read and write and I say the office of the Madonna. I've read Petrarch, the Furioso, the Lives of the Saints and I have composed many sonnets just to pass the time and to work on my writing." The Holy Office actually showed interest in her poetical abilities, asking her to write two or three sonnets for them. Unfortunately, there appears in the transcript in a strong, clear hand, presumably hers, only "I Cassandra do not recall the sonnets that I wrote to pass the time,"[42] Returning to their original concern, they showed her a sheaf of papers one by one, all of which were forms of *carte di voler bene*, which they feared she had used to bind the love of her clients. At first she tried to deny this, claiming that she had merely copied them for an old woman who had asked her to do so as a favor. The Holy Office dutifully followed her down this aside, trying to get the name of the old woman or a physical description and receiving only the most vague responses. Cassandra did specify that the copying of the first *carta* had been quite difficult because it "was old, so much so that it was difficult to make out."[43] If this was not entirely a fantasy concocted to lead the Holy Office astray, we may have here a glimpse of a written tradition being passed on by women, one that had endured long enough to have created paleographical problems for this young scribe.

But in the continuing give-and-take on the central issue of the *carte di voler bene,* Cassandra revealed a confidence and strength that are unusual and impressive. Asked point blank if she thought such *carte* were good things, she replied, "I believed that they were good things. If I had believed they were bad I would not have written them." That, obviously, was the wrong answer, as the Holy Office made clear with their next rather discursive question: "Does it seem to you a good thing to wish to bind the soul of certain men to love a woman and to make it so that one cannot eat, drink, sleep, or do other things?" High Christian culture had come head to head with a literate young lower-class woman who sensed her own power. And once more, Cassandra gave her answer, not the one that the Holy Office had virtually demanded: "It seemed to me a good thing then and it seems so even now," she replied unperturbed.[44]

Cassandra was a self-confident woman in a relatively strong position with her mastery of reading, writing, and the magical powers that, most agreed (including apparently her ecclesiastical interrogators), could bind a man in love. Whether she was in fact a courtesan or, as seems more likely, on her way to becoming one, we find ourselves at a noteworthy nexus in a network largely composed of women who utilized the world of love and passion to implement significant strategies of power. Those strategies were not always effective; in fact, most of the cases discussed in this book involve moments when those strategies had broken down, were becoming ineffective, or were encountering other strategies or structures of power that were momentarily more effective, such as those of the family or the Holy Office. Yet the courtesan who could write, like many other women who were literate and had mastered the word, was much more than an object.

Power over words implied in many ways power in the world and over men, and this was especially the case in the binding magic of love. As a result, at times even the most famous and literate courtesans were not immune to suspicions about the powers that their ability to read and write had given them. Veronica Franco, the queen of the Venetian courtesan poets in the second half of the sixteenth century, provides an excellent example of the problems such suspicions of literacy could entail. The high point of her career may well have come in 1574 when the future king of France Henry III slipped away from the elaborate public festivals designed by the Venetians to win his favor to enjoy the favors of Veronica. What we might think of as an escape from the public to the private world of illicit pleasure became for both Henry and Veronica a public event. Each gained in reputation and stature from the encounter. And, in fact, Veronica attempted to immortalize it with poems and letters that painted the meeting between the future king of France and the Queen of Courtesans as important for both Venice and France, as well as for the individuals involved.[45] Significantly, this vision was taken seriously, seriously enough even to be attacked.

Veronica, although clearly unusual, was, like most courtesans, much more than a beautiful woman. At the time of Henry's visit she was respected for her poetry; noted for her artistic sensibilities; and famous for her wit, intellect, and conversation. In addition, she numbered among her admirers and supporters some of the most powerful and influential men of Venice. More publicly, she also entertained some of the most renowned artists and intellectuals of her day. In sum, she was a major figure, and tellingly, much of the reputation that made her one was based upon her literary skills and her ability to create a public persona for herself using her mastery of words.

But even she was not exempt from the suspicion of using love magic and magic in general to her advantage. Just a few years after Henry's visit, in fact, she found herself brought before the Holy Office by her son's disgruntled tutor, Rodolfo Vannitelli. His deposition of 1580 accused Veronica of attempting to identify the person who had stolen some goods from her home using a magical technique based on calling a White Angel (Angelo Bianco) to reveal the culprit in a vase of water. It appears that Vannitelli was concerned that Veronica would accuse him of this theft, and thus he wanted to take the offensive by accusing her of witchcraft, perhaps forcing her to back down. Whatever his motive, he did not hesitate to fill out his accusation with other innuendos about illicit magic often associated with prostitutes that might catch the eye of the Holy Office. "Your most holy reverences ought to punish and have punished the said Veronica Franco and the others who helped with the said incantations and invocations of demons in accordance with the sacred and divine laws concerning such deeds so that she becomes an example for everyone else. For if this mistress of evil magic, this public and common whore is not punished, many others will follow her example against the Holy and Catholic faith."[46] Much as in the case of Andriana Savorgnan, Veronica was labeled a "public and common whore" by her accuser. If naming could create power over another, in both cases it is evident that men were not merely trying to cut these powerful women down to size using such words; they were literally trying to name them back into the place that traditional values had created for women.

But Veronica, like Andriana, was not so easily *re-placed*. And she was no common prostitute either; if anything, even Rodolfo's accusation revealed that, obliquely providing a glimpse of some of the additional attributes of the courtesan: "Moreover she holds private sessions of forbidden games especially cards. . . . She never goes to church as you can have attested by the whole neighborhood and by the parish priest. . . . In the two and a half months that I lived in her house, she never went to Mass. Rather she concentrated on her games and other dishonest and illicit business with various men and her lovers. But in truth she has much too much help in this city and is the favorite of too many. . . . Still I pray and call upon you that notwithstanding her supporters you punish her as she deserves and quickly, very quickly so that she does not further infect this city."[47]

Again Rodolfo's language sought to place Veronica, first by giving her attributes perceived to be common to courtesans: gambling, avoiding church and Mass, and engaging in illicit activities; then more aggressively by playing upon the powerful supporters that empowered her; and finally by returning to one of the commonplaces of antiprostitution rhetoric of the late Renaissance—the prostitute as an infection that threatened the city. Veronica the common whore infecting the city; Veronica the courtesan, with her powerful friends, moving beyond the law of the city; Veronica the evil woman, corrupting the men of the city—the illogic and self-contradictions of the vision that Rodolfo was drawing upon should not mask its power. Veronica was a major figure and a powerful woman in a society that had little way of dealing socially, politically, economically, or imaginatively with such women. As a result, it was all too easy to reverse her brilliance and turn it against her.

Rereading his testimony, Rodolfo added further details about the evils of Veronica that the scribe diligently squeezed into the margins of the transcript. He reported that Veronica had eaten meat on holy days several times, and in what must have been a particularly tasty mixing of sins, he noted that once she had even eaten meat on a holy day while playing cards with two young men at the same time! Again, however, he came back to love magic and the power that it gave her to bind the passions of men, claiming that she "carried out several other incantations of demons in order to make certain Germans fall in love with her."[48] Veronica, when faced with these accusations, needless to say, denied most of them. She did, however, admit to having tried calling on the Angelo Bianco to attempt to find her lost goods, even admitting that as a young girl she had participated in such magic. The Angelo Bianco was supposed to reveal the location of lost goods or the identity of the thief who had stolen them, usually to a virgin, and Veronica as a child had served as the virgin in such a ceremony. In fact, she even explained to the Holy Office that the magic had worked when she was a child. She had seen that the lost belt sought had been stolen by her father from her mother, and he had later admitted this to her. Nonetheless she expressed contrition at having attempted such magic as an adult and asked for forgiveness. The rest of Rodolfo's accusations she rejected, especially all claims of love magic. When asked specifically about calling upon demons to bind the love of Germans, she replied nicely, "My Lords no! As

God and the Madonna are my witnesses, I am the most timid woman in the world when it comes to demons and the dead."[49]

Perhaps. But, of course, Veronica was no mere victim of Rodolfo's accusations; she was a clever woman who was as capable of using labels and stereotypes to further her case as he. If the subtext of her accusation was that she was an unusually powerful woman, an illicitly powerful one, what better response than to take up the rhetoric of the stereotypical weak and frightened woman? It may be reading too much into her words, but "I am the most timid woman in the world" was one of the best answers possible for what appears to have been the real fears about Veronica and courtesans in general. If anything, such fears were fueled even more by Andriana Savorgnan's marriage to Marco Dandolo. Moving from graceful, mannered, cultured arbiter of status to wife was not criminal—it was simply not done. And things that are not done, when they happen all the same, reveal how complex the forces of social discipline can in fact be in a society.

Binding Prostitution

Although prostitution remained legal across the sixteenth century, its perception changed in major ways. Courtesans like Andriana, at least when she was still seen as honest, could be famous, literate, and arbiters of social status, but lesser prostitutes had become to a great extent a disease that infected licit society, worthy only of Machiavelli's vomit. Reflective of this newer, sterner vision, a host of initiatives were undertaken that went beyond the medieval goal of containing and disciplining prostitution by limiting it to certain well-policed areas. While continuing and reinforcing such traditional measures, Venice, like many other cities, created a much more articulated institutional structure that attacked prostitution on several levels. The attack focused, however, on three areas: keeping the trade as decorous and unobtrusive as possible; restricting the profits and the infrastructure of procurers and procuresses who recruited and controlled many prostitutes; and attempting to limit the number of women who entered the trade and remained in it.

Keeping the trade as decorous and unobtrusive as possible was in part the natural outgrowth of the failure to keep prostitution limited to one area of the city. In Venice this area had been the Castelletto, an isolated zone near the commercial center of the city, the Rialto. There early on, led by the Council of Ten, the city fathers had attempted to contain prostitution and control it. Special policing patrols were created and the trade was essentially licensed out to several noble families, most notable among them being the colorful Malipiero clan. If that containment ever worked, by the early sixteenth century it had been long ignored. Prostitutes were plying their trade all over the city when in 1502 a general restatement of the laws concerning prostitution required them to return to the Castelleto, and the state licensed brothels there. A herald was instructed to go to the main areas where prostitutes were practicing to announce that they must return within four days or face a penalty of six months in jail, twenty-five lashes, and a fine of 100 lire. The announcement was to be read: "In San Luca in the street of the house of the Corner family, in San Luca at the bridge of the Fuseri, in San Anzelo in front of the house of the Malipiero family, in San Samuele that is in Santa Margarita and San Rocco, in San Moisè in the street of the house of the Barozzi family heading towards the Ternita in the Frezzaria, in San Salvador, before the houses of the Nani family, in San Lio, in Santa Maria Formosa on the Ruga Giuffa, in Santa Maria Formosa on the Calle Longa, in San Antonio at the arch, in San Giovanni Bragola [today Bandiera e Moro], in Santa Trinita [today Ternita], in Santa Maria Mater Domini along the street, in San Stin in the square, in San Cassiano, in San Simeone Grande over the bridge of stone, in San Silvestro in the street of the Tagliapietra, in San Aponal in the square, in San Polo in the street of the Cavalli, in San Pantalon in the street of the Castelforte, in San Leonardo, at the bridge Dalazedo (that is of vinegar), at the Bari in the street of the house of the Zusto family [probably campo Riello today], in San Basso at the wooden bridge of the Angel, in Santa Margarita of the Tagliapietra at the house of the Barbaro family, at San Sebastiano in the middle of the Calle del Forno, in San Sebastiano in the group of houses just over the bridge, in San Barnaba in the Calle Longa, and in San Stai in the Calle del Forno."[50]

Clearly this list demonstrates that prostitution was no longer confined to the Rialto area, if it ever had been. Thirty-one locations, many of them in close proximity to the homes of major noble families, apparently had enough prostitution to warrant the herald's announcement. Equally evident from a perusal of the laws passed subsequently and the criminal records that make reference to prostitutes' activities is the fact that this attempt to confine prostitution to one district was as much a failure as earlier attempts.[51] Instead the Council of Ten and its policing bodies, as well as other councils concerned with prostitution, concentrated on attempting to keep the trade away from the main public spaces and from churches and convents. They also attempted to limit the movements of prostitutes, keeping them out of churches as much as possible and away from the public eye.[52]

Moreover they regularly passed sumptuary legislation designed to both identify in public and limit the display of prostitutes. In the early sixteenth century in a moment of crisis (1514) a new council, the Provveditori alle Pompe, was created to deal with concerns about excessive display in general. It systematized and extended earlier legislation, and one of the focuses of its activity quickly became the dress and public display of prostitutes. In this area its goal was relatively clear: to keep prostitutes in their place by controlling their public appearance. Again we are in the realm of Renaissance self-fashioning: the perceived danger was that class and gender barriers could be threatened and honorable upper-class women confused with dishonorable prostitutes if dress codes were not defended. The enforcement, or rather selective enforcement, of these regulations may have helped to create, however, a slightly different situation. When Andriana Savorgnan was the darling of a coterie of important Venetian nobles, she, like other highly visible courtesans, had the support to ignore the sumptuary legislation of the Provveditori alle Pompe. Lesser prostitutes, however, were not so protected; thus sumptuary legislation may have actually strengthened and helped to reify social distinctions among prostitutes, much as they did for society in general.

Another institution created just before the sixteenth century also became heavily involved in binding prostitutes in their place, the Provveditori alla Sanità. Created in 1485 with broad authority to deal with issues relating to public health, they found that authority suddenly extended in the 1490s by the rapid spread of syphilis. Even before that, however, as prostitution had become associated with the dissemination of disease in general and especially the plague, the Sanità had been empowered to control the movement of prostitutes. At one level, this association may even account for the use of disease metaphors to describe the the evils of prostitution well before the spread of syphilis. But it is clear that with the spread of the disease and its immediate association with prostitution, the metaphors became both more powerful and ubiquitous. And the Provveditori alla Sanità became major players in the growing complex of Venetian institutions designed to contain and discipline prostitution.

The Provveditori alla Sanità and the Provveditori alle Pompe were joined in the late 1530s by another council, the Esecutori contra la Bestemmia, which quickly gained wide responsibility for prostitution as well. The Esecutori, as their name implies, were in theory to be primarily concerned with *bestemmie* (that is, curses), a particularly troubling subset of crimes of speech in the eyes of the authorities. Speech had long been regulated in Venice, as had crimes that in any way seemed to threaten the honor of God.[53] Previously, speech crimes had been the responsibility of the Council of Ten, which dealt with a broad spectrum of language perceived as dangerous, running the gamut from insults to conspiracy. In 1537, however, as part of a reforming drive to make the Ten more effective, it delegated its authority over *bestemmie* to a subcouncil the Esecutori. Quickly unseemly and disrespectful behavior of any kind was drawn under their control and that meant that they became leaders in the disciplining of prostitution.

These three new councils formally remained concerned with containing prostitution, much as earlier governmental bodies such as the Ten and the Signori di Notte had done. But, in fact, they subtly shifted the ground of that containment, or to be more accurate, they revealed the desire of government to shift that ground. Spatial isolation remained important, and decorum had always been one goal of that isolation—the indecent and illicit had to be kept away from the eyes of the decent and licit as much as possible—but now decorum became central. The late Renaissance city, much like the courtier, seemed to be much more concerned with constructing a public image of itself as decent and licit, an image that had little place for the earlier medieval and early Renaissance celebration of the pleasures of the flesh and prostitution that are found even in the laudatory literature that cities promoted about themselves. The mannered, decorous body in the aristocratic, honorable city with passions correctly bound was replacing the boisterous, bustling city of artisans and merchants. Both ideals had stressed a moral city, but in the former, body and the illicit had their place and were even celebrated; in the latter, they were to be masked and made in a way invisible. For those bodies that rejected these new goals, there was the Pompe to enforce the dress codes of the aristocratic hierarchy of society; there was the Sanità to restrict movement that threatened that order at the level of health and much more broadly as well; and there was the Bestemmia to make sure that words and increasingly deeds lived up to the decorous ideals of the well-mannered city—the Serene Republic of Venice.

Of course, these institutions were merely institutions, and like most, their records reveal the futility of their efforts to implement the policies just outlined. The body and the body politic remained frequently indecorous and passionate, the illicit and indecent often showed through and, at times, were celebrated. The discipline of institutions was simply not enough. In the late Renaissance, in large measure it was doomed to fail as far as prostitution was concerned because it could not deal effectively with the large number of women involved. But perhaps more important, it could not work because it made virtually no attempt to deal with the men who created the market for prostitution. Still, as a sign of the changing perceptions that were helping to prepare the ground for a society of ever more disciplined bodies, cities, and aristocracies, these institutions and the binding they envisioned were most significant. Even today institutional discipline seldom carries the true weight of creating an ordered society. Crucially, however, it does publicly mark and demonstrate the boundaries between acceptable and unacceptable passions and behavior—boundaries that in the Renaissance were built upon concepts of honor, family, Christian and often local civic values, and social expectations. Such a diverse and potentially fluid base for boundaries can at times (moments of stress or transition perhaps) be guided or strengthened by institutions. At other times it may merely ignore them.

It appears, then, that the Provveditori alle Pompe, the Sanità, and the Esecutori contro la Bestemmia were not so much causes of change as signs of change. And in that context, it is significant that the sixteenth century saw the proliferation of similar institutions in many Italian cities. One area where these institutions may have been somewhat more effective was in trying to break the power of procurers and procuresses over prostitutes. From the last decades of the fifteenth century, tough laws had been passed to limit the exploitation of prostitutes by procurers through forms of debt slavery and the recruitment of poor girls into the profession with promises of marriage or economic reward. Both types of legislation had important antecedents, but the pace and strictness of legislation increased across the century. Periodically, procurers and procuresses were even banned with dramatic results. Once again, however, such provisions do not appear to have limited prostitution per se; rather, they seem to have encouraged an increase in the number of women operating on their own or within the potentially more supportive context of women's networks. The aggressive and powerful *ruffiano* and *bertoni* (the former a pimp, the later a pimp with at least the implication of being a lover as well) remained important stock figures in literature but may have become less so in practice. Systematic research, however, will be necessary to test this tentative hypothesis. Yet clearly there was a concerted effort at the level of law and institutions (not limited to Venice) to destroy rather than contain procurers and procuresses.

Perhaps most interesting of all in this attack on prostitution was a series of sixteenth-century public initiatives to reclaim prostitutes and keep young women from becoming trapped in the trade. Venice provides a good example, although once again, the city appears to have been less an innovator than an eclectic follower of others. Early in the century the Incurabili was founded as a hospital for those suffering from syphilis where numerous prostitutes were interned. They were treated for their illness, of course, but as the Incurabili was mainly concerned with quarantine in the medieval tradition of leper hospitals, the institution's main goal in interning prostitutes was to limit the infection of society in the medical sense. As a result, it became to a large extent a holding house for infected prostitutes, especially older ones, and local satirical literature would label it early on the "courtesan's purgatory."[54]

The Convertite, founded about 1530, offered in addition to quarantine a newer path to the decorous, moral city—the conversion of repentant prostitutes to an "honest" life.[55] Originally prostitutes were helped there to prepare to reenter society as wives or nuns by living an austere, disciplined life, learning domestic skills, participating in cottage industry, and receiving a heavy dose of Christian morality. Slowly the monastic discipline of the institution won out, and after 1551 the Convertite became officially a convent where women made the impressive leap from being prostitutes to nuns. The leap was not always successful, it should be noted, as in 1561 a major scandal broke out at the Convertite. It seems that some of the nuns were still selling their favors from within the much more secure walls of their convent, while their father confessor served as their pimp.

Interestingly, this scandal so caught the public imagination that it provided one of Laura Savorgnan's first memories of Venice. When testifying about her life before the Holy Office, she dated her arrival in Venice in terms of the public execution of the priest involved, Pietro Leon da Valcamonica: "In that year when they burned the priest of the Convertite, I came to this land and Andriana my daughter was born."[56] In addition to serving as pimp for his charges, it was claimed that he had had sexual relations with at least twenty of the ex-prostitutes living in the Convertite. This extreme breach of faith probably was the reason for his extreme penalty and the public example that was made of him; most priests were treated much more leniently for their sexual exploits even with nuns, as we shall see.[57] His public confession and a sermon that he preached against his sins before his execution were made into major events; the newly arrived Laura, probably already embarked on a life of concubinage and perhaps part-time prostitution, appears to have been one of those impressed.[58]

Shortly after the Convertite became a convent, a new home was founded in Venice in 1560 designed to keep young women from being lured or sold into prostitution. This had long been a goal of government designed to limit the moral damage of legal prostitution. As early as the fourteenth century, men and women were being prosecuted for luring young women into the profession, and in the sixteenth century both the prestigious Council of Ten and the Provveditori alla Sanità regularly issued legislation designed to limit such activity. One piece of legislation, passed in 1542, provides a good picture of the mix of moral and practical values that legitimated such initiatives: "There is no doubt that there is nothing more gracious in the sight of God than the elimination of the first cause of the abuses committed. For we see clearly every day that there are diabolical persons who at the instigation of the Devil are continually watching to seduce and lead astray poor orphans and girls who are forced to beg for their living in the city, or even poor servant girls who are on their way to lodge with our nobles and citizens, by offering to clothe them and be their mistresses, with many blandishments. Once they have fallen into the hands of these bawds (*ruffiane*), they hire them chemises, headdresses, stockings, shoes, dresses, cloaks and capes, and by means of this the bawds keep them at their mercy and live off the earnings of their girls, who can never free themselves and are constrained of necessity to commit wicked sins and become accustomed to these meretricious vices. This is a most potent reason for the infinite number of such disreputable prostitutes now in the city and increasing daily."[59]

The response was the Zitelle (literally, the House of Old Maids), which sought to attack prostitution at its source, the recruitment of young unmarried women. That it was not intended merely as an orphanage was made clear by its entrance requirements. To qualify, girls had to be at least nine years old, beautiful and healthy, and threatened with being forced into prostitution.[60] Yet another tack was taken by the Casa del Soccorso, founded about 1577. It was designed to allow unhappy wives to escape untenable family situations without having to live on their own. The implication, made clear in the founding charter of the Soccorso, was that such women were highly likely candidates for prostitution; women who were sexually active and living outside of marriage, it was assumed, had few other options.[61] At the Soccorso, women could theoretically stay as long as they wished in a communal environment largely run and controlled by other women. The potential subversiveness of the institution to family and patriarchal imperatives was not unrecognized and was undercut by its aggressively pursued goal of reconciling wives with husbands or, failing that, helping wives to prepare to accept a new discipline, that of the convent.

This whole range of initiatives, implemented in slightly varying forms in many Italian Renaissance cities in the sixteenth century, with its interesting blend of morality and charity, was quite clearly aimed at limiting prostitution, protecting the moral fabric of society, and placing women in the accepted disciplining institutions of society for women—family or convent. Yet the efficacy of this initiative and these institutions was undercut by their inability to deal with the scale of the problem: they offered charity (and discipline) to a few, hundreds at best, while thousands plied the profession.[62] Moreover, they attacked merely one side of the problem, and the more symptomatic side at that, while with a stubborn patriarchal myopia, they overlooked the fact that male clients created a lucrative market for prostitution that would not disappear simply by luring or pressing a few women to abandon the profession.

Yet even if only small numbers of women at best were "saved" from prostitution, the force of such initiatives should not be underestimated. Each new institution was in its way a public restatement of the civic and moral ideals of the Renaissance city, and as such, each continued and expanded what disease metaphors had begun—to portray prostitution in a new and more negative light. Prostitution was no longer a necessary minor evil or a slightly sinful pleasure. It was a trap for women that was difficult to escape, as the Convertite symbolized and publicized; it preyed on the economic problems of the young and defenseless, as the Zitelle demonstrated; it broke apart marriages, allowing wives to escape their husbands, as the Casa del Soccorso warned. And perhaps worst of all, it infected civic society with a moral disease that threatened to be incurable, as the Incurabili concluded. Thus, the symbolism of these institutions and the civic initiatives that created and sustained them in the sixteenth century catechized for a moral, civic society and mobilized public and private support in ways not to be underestimated. And significantly, all this happened while prostitution remained legal.

Perhaps most significantly for the prostitute and those who frequented prostitutes, such symbolic action allowed the vision of a decorous moral city to triumph without dismantling the world of illicit sexuality that turned around prostitution. Society was moral, as these multiplying institutions insisted, even if within society sin persevered. Yet the nice illogic of such a vision only begins to scratch the surface of the deeper issues that maintaining the legality of prostitution in the sixteenth century faced. Already at the beginning of the century, Pietro Aretino, with his perverse wit, had cut to the heart of the matter. Nanna and Antonia had concluded that the primary contemporary forms of binding women's passions and sexuality, with their focus on arranged marriages at an early age or internment in convents, were not just unhappy, but ultimately dishonest and immoral. The counterworld of the prostitute and illicit sex were, in turn, the only honest ones because they sold exactly what the Renaissance needed—not just sex, but status and illusion in a rich mix that stretched from the great courtesans on top to the humble part-time prostitute at the bottom of society.

And in the end, disciplined but legal prostitution continued because even with its new, more negative reputation, Renaissance society, or at least its male rulers, managed to maintain the concept of prostitution as a controlled, disciplined form of sexuality that bound and placed women. Andriana Savorgnan's attempt to move beyond that discipline reveals well some of the levels of controlling response available to neutralize the dangers of even the sexually powerful courtesan. But as we have seen already, in matters sexual nothing is ever unambiguous, and there is one last uncertainty in Andriana Savorgnan's case. The records of the Holy Office do not report what action, if any, was taken against her or even the fate of her marriage.

Still, the archives do contain tantalizing hints. The marriage records of the Avogadori di Comun that registered legitimate noble marriages—that is, where both partners were from noble families and thus their children would be nobles as well—provide some negative evidence. Marco is not listed there as ever marrying. Of course, his marriage with Andriana would not have been registered, but apparently he did not go on to do the "correct" thing and marry a noble woman. More important, as the case progressed, it came out that although the couple had been ordered to separate by the Patriarch of Venice, they had not. Instead they had fled to Padua, where they lived together in secret, supported by friends.[63]

Moreover, when Andriana had been ordered to come before the Holy Office to testify, she had not done so. Thus learning where the couple was hiding, the Holy Office sent their minions to arrest her. But that mission ended in failure. The young lovers, as befitted their binding passions, were caught in bed together; nonetheless, Marco managed somehow to help Andriana escape. He, however, was forced to return to Venice, where he testified before the Holy Office late in October, defending his marriage, denying that he had ever felt the effects of any magic, and insisting that he had always loved Andriana.[64] At virtually the same moment, a letter arrived from Cardinal Savello in Rome, which informed his interrogators that at his petition, Rome had decided to look into the case. Clearly, Marco was not prepared to let his marriage fold under the pressure of his family or of the Holy Office.

It seems highly likely, given the fact that Marco had gotten the attention of Rome, that he had begun to rally support for the marriage. Nonetheless, the Venetian Holy Office continued examining witnesses, and it appears that Marco even offered to arrange a meeting between Andriana and officials of that body to hear her defense outside of Venice.[65] There is no record, however, that such a meeting ever occurred, and in the early days of 1582 it is clear that the Holy Office's investigation was losing steam. The last witness was heard on March 10, and the case was dropped.

Had Marco and Andriana won? Had their passions, however bound, triumphed against the imperatives of honor, family, and caste? One last questionable clue suggests that they had. In the useful but often inaccurate genealogies of Venetian noble families attributed to the sixteenth-century noble Marco Barbaro, one finds an entry for Marco Dandolo. There he is reported to have married "Andriana Savorgnana Courtesan" and to have gone on to serve as Provveditore in Legnano and as Podestà of Bergamo.[66] Did Andriana escape the discipline of Renaissance prostitution, then, to marry into the powerful Dandolo clan and become a noble wife? Did Marco escape the discipline of noble values and family honor to marry his love? Perhaps so. But perhaps in the end it would be best if we retained some doubt on the matter, for the cases of the Holy Office are so complex and speak with so many different voices that doubt normally seems in order. And, nicely, with such doubt, each of us is free to give Andriana's tale the ending that we feel would be best; thus, for once, not unlike Andriana, escaping the binding discipline of this discipline of history.

2

"More Dear to Me Than Life Itself": Marriage, Honor, and a Woman's Reputation in the Renaissance

A Troubling Mass in Feltre

In early May 1588, three priests were celebrating Mass in the Cathedral Church of the small Alpine town of Feltre when, just before the *Lavabo*, the subdeacon, Andrea da Canal, noticed hidden near the altar "a small figure of a child." Quietly he nudged the deacon, Geronimo Lusa, whispering to him, "Look there, it's a small child."[1] Geronimo motioned to him that they should finish the service, and the Mass continued as it had presumably done since the Council of Trent in the sleepy little town of the northern Veneto, lying just over the front range of the Alps on one of the pass roads connecting Venice and northeastern Italy with Austria and southern Germany.

After the Mass, Andrea and his fellow priests took a closer look at the figure and found it a very troubling little package indeed. They discovered wrapped in a white veil not the figure of a child, as Andrea had assumed, but rather a detailed wax figure of a nude man with "many needles stuck all over it, especially the eyes, temple, heart, and phallus. Then the statue was wrapped in three places, with a piece of fabric around the eyes, a second around the stomach, and a third black sash around the genitals full of bent needles."[2] All three clerics were troubled. What the figure meant, what it was doing hidden near the altar of San Prosdecimo, who had put it there, and what should be done all were unclear. On the last point—what should be done—they were of two minds: destroy it as a work of the Devil and forget it or turn it over to the Bishop of Feltre for investigation.

Perhaps as little as a generation earlier, the matter would have been allowed to drop, but by the late sixteenth century the reformed Church was not only busily working to bring the large urban centers of Italy under its more aggressive discipline, as we have seen in the case of Andriana Savorgnan, it was reaching out to the smaller centers as well. Not that Feltre was that small. The chief Venetian official there at the time, the Podestà, Vicenzo Capello, reported upon the return from his posting: "The site of this city [is] hilly and blocked in by mountains although it has some level land lying over towards Belluno. The territory extends in length 25 miles and in breadth seven and has in all about 22,000 souls [in the town itself there were only about 8700]. . . . But what is most important is that it has several difficult and mountainous passes that mark the border with the territories of the Duke of Austria . . . which make the place most significant."[3] As it was a border area with Austria, the peace and stability of this little town were more important to Venice than its size or wealth might seem to warrant. Even apparently minor disruptions of the status quo could be viewed as threatening. Thus this small wax figure, caught between the Church's drive to discipline Catholic society and Venice's desire to maintain the stability of its border territories, was saved to create a little ruffle in the quiet flow of provincial life, a ruffle that slowly circled outward to involve the hierarchy of the Church, the courts of Venice, and ultimately us as well.[4]

Quickly, however, gossip and rumors spread through Feltre, and the local bishop began an investigation to determine who was responsible. Both the rumors and the investigation focused on a rather unlikely group of women. Foremost among them were Elena Cumano, the eighteen-year-old older daughter of an important local lawyer; her mother and their household women; and finally, Lucretia Marescaldo, a woman in her early fifties reputed to be a witch. After the investigation had gone on for a couple of weeks in Feltre, a denunciation sent to the Venetian Holy Office by a powerful local family, the Faceno clan, outlined one case that was being built on these rumors—theirs: "In the city of Feltre there is a woman named Giulia Cumano, wife of Messer Zuan Cumano doctor of law, who has several children, among them a daughter of about eighteen. This mother decided to have Gian Battista Faceno, a young citizen of Feltre of about twnety-two, take as his wife her daughter. Not able to secure her ends legitimately, she turned to evil ways and witchcraft. With the aid and instruction of other women knowledgeable in these arts she had specially made at a workshop . . . a figure of white wax about one foot high in the form of a naked man. . . . Then with the help of these women, witches and evildoers, she inserted many needles in all the parts of the said statue."[5]

The recourse to magic and a group of women knowledgeable in witchcraft by the wife of a prominent lawyer to secure a match for her daughter with the son of a major local noble family does not square well with received notions about how marriages were arranged in Renaissance Italy, even if it echoes in many ways the accusations made against Andriana Savorgnan and anticipates similar accusations that we will discuss later. Marriage, especially upper-class marriage, was normally a carefully negotiated joining of families contracted by their leaders primarily for dynastic, economic, and political motives. And, as we have seen, at midcentury, the Council of Trent attempted to clarify doctrine in this area. The earlier position, which held that only the consent of the couple involved was required, had created myriad problems. Most significantly for family marriage strategies, it allowed young couples to subvert privately the most careful plans of families and clans with clandestine marriages.[6] Trent attempted to clarify marriage in part so that consent would remain central, but also so that broader dynastic interests would be respected. The new requirements of published bans and clerical participation ideally made marriages more public and gave families more opportunity to intervene before consent could be given against their wishes. But legal niceties and family interference aside, our needle-pierced doll and the recourse to magic it reveals open a perspective on a different range of problems that grew up around marriage and sex, at least in part, in response to the reforms of Trent and, in addition, to a continuing range of problems with premarital sex that Trent did not address.

Society, however, had not ignored these problems. Crucial was the disciplining power of a complex web of concepts that turned on honor and reputation and their association with female sexuality. Broadly sketched, while male honor was variously determined given the intricacies of public and private behavioral expectations for men, for women public and, to a degree, private expectations were more limited. As a result, female honor focused more narrowly on sexual concerns—chastity and fidelity in marriage and virginity before it or at least before a promise of marriage.[7] Sexual honor, however, was not limited to women. With a nice irony in this patriarchal society, men found that their honor was intimately intertwined with that of the women they claimed to control; thus, the chastity and fidelity of wives, the virginity of daughters, and even the sexual conduct of female dependents reflected on the honor of men and, in turn, on the family as a whole. Strikingly, a female's sexual honor was not solely or even perhaps primarily her own; it was bound up in a much more convoluted calculus of honor that involved her family and the males who dominated it.

Yet even in this patriarchal society, the sexual component of a woman's honor did not come close to exhausting the standards that measured her life. Beyond honor, but closely related to it, stood more nebulous concepts of public reputation (*fama*) that for women went well beyond the sexual. *Fama* was constantly evaluated in late Renaissance life by means of public evaluation and gossip. Significantly, women played a central role in this in theory, as gossip was widely recognized as a woman's prerogative.[8] Certainly men participated in gossip evaluation also, and ultimately it may have been their evaluation that mattered; but gossip, even women's gossip in a patriarchal society, should not be underrated. For what was often labeled idle words, in an environment so finely attuned to reputation, actually was a potent form of power. Power, because the world of gossip evaluation had the ability to create crucial realities: honor, reputation, and, of course, at times even husbands, wives, and witches.

The Marriage and Reputation of Elena Cumano

Which brings us back to the plight of Elena Cumano. For her much more than marriage was involved. At age eighteen in 1588, she found herself seduced, abandoned, and pregnant and her life relentlessly laid out before the courts of Feltre, the Church, Venice, and the public of her community in ways that allowed the complex web of honor, reputation, and gossip in which she was entangled to be evaluated by all. At the very moment that she and her mother were being accused of using witchcraft to win a husband, her father was suing the family of her erstwhile husband to force them to accept her as his wife. Testifying before the Podestà of Feltre, Vicenzo Capello, Elena laid out her vision of her situation, a vision that, self-servingly or not, excused her behavior and sought to save her reputation. She claimed that Gian Battista Faceno was already her husband and, in fact, had been so long enough to make her legitimately pregnant before deserting her. "I wish to say concerning my husband signor Gian Battista Faceno that having promised to make me his wife, he insisted even before he knew me [sexually] that I ought to say in confession to my confessor at Easter a year ago that he was my husband."[9]

Apparently here we have a traditional secret exchange of consent that Elena suggested Gian Battista was anxious to formalize to a degree even before sexual intercourse began by having it reported to a priest. While not quite up to the standards of Trent for marriage, consent and a priest's involvement came close, and it may have been hoped that this would win a certain sympathy for Elena's plight. It was at least a promise of marriage, which for many was adequate for initiating honorable sexual contact between future spouses. Of course, before Trent, if Elena could have proven her assertions, she would have had her husband and her honor and the case would have been closed. By 1587, when this promise was given, things were more problematic, and Elena went on to try to demonstrate more effectively that Gian Battista had married her.

["He continued always to pledge that I was his wife and that he did not intend to have any other woman but me. . . . I said that I wished two witnesses to the marriage. He asked me if I wanted a greater witness than our Lord God. Thus we called upon him for our witness with very great oaths."[19]

Duped by Gian Battista, Elena nonetheless presented a case that went a long way to reestablish her honor and reputation even if it did not meet the legal requirements for marriage. She portrayed herself as accepting an apparently honorable man's word, with God as her witness. Soon Gian Battista began visiting her at home under the pretext of being a suitor and a friend of the family. Unfortunately for her, however, he did not visit merely to talk, and shortly she found herself pregnant. Elena reported the strains this put on their relationship in a manner that again added to her reputation and continued undermining that of Gian Battista. "Thus I became pregnant. He began to say, then, that he wanted me to have an abortion, but I did not want that at all. He said to me that he had spoken with the physician Rizzardo, but that he did not want to give him any medicine [for an abortion] and that he had gone to Venice for advice. . . . But I said that I did not want to lose my body and my soul. He replied that he had had other women abort and that they had not died."[11] A good Christian operating in good faith found that her presumed husband was neither; clearly, honor and reputation fell on her side in her telling of the tale.

It is interesting to note that Gian Battista turned to a male doctor for advice on abortion. Apparently men used male networks for such things, just as they used male networks to hire wet nurses for "their" children—almost as if the aspects of the female body and reproduction that concerned men and their honor directly had to be controlled by other males. This is not to suggest, however, that women's networks did not also deal with abortion. Rather, it appears that women turned to other women more in the context of acting against the wishes of the males who were responsible for them, whether that meant husbands, fathers, or brothers. It also seems that among women the lack of a period was often construed as an illness, rather than as a sign of pregnancy—an illness that could be treated. And, of course, the cure for such an illness was to invoke menstruation.]

A woman <u>healer named Elena</u> reported one such remedy to the Holy Office in 1571: "To cure a woman whose period [*fior*] has not come, I take some sage and I grind it very fine for three mornings and I give some of the paste of it to her for three mornings and she will be freed."[12] It appears that in concentrated enough form, sage is a poison that can induce abortion; as such, it is a remedy with a long tradition.[13] But suggestively, by treating a late period as an illness rather than as a pregnancy, women healers conceptualized the problem and women's bodies in a radically different and less threatening way than male networks. Only more systematic research will confirm if this apparent distinction was a consistent one; but if so, it would be a significant break between a male culture and vision of birth and a female one.

During their discussion about abortion, Elena reported yet another admission by Gian Battista. "He said that there was no question that I was his wife, but that he had suggested an abortion because at that time he had other business to do before making the marriage public."[14] Elena, deeply troubled, continued to follow the reputable path. She visited her confessor to ask his counsel. He suggested another meeting between the couple; thus Elena claimed to have summoned Gian Battista to one more secret meeting in her bed. But the events of that encounter, which occurred on December 7, 1598, even in her testimony engender suspicion. Undressed together in bed, she reported, "he said that he wanted to keep the promise that he had made me." Apparently a moment of warm reconciliation that fulfilled her confessor's optimistic hopes and hers as well, the scene rapidly degenerated. "At that moment Gian Battista was discovered . . . by chance by my father, two of my brothers and two of my uncles . . . they were lamenting the situation when he said to them that I had been his wife for four months. . . . Then my father called two witnesses and said 'In confirmation of this contract made give her here this ring in pledge.' This he did putting on my finger this ring."[15] At this point in the transcript the scribe inserted in Latin that Elena displayed to those present "a gold ring on her ring finger adorned with a pearl."[16] Again with her ring and its display, Elena was building her reputation in a public forum before the Podestà of Feltre.

She continued undermining the honesty and, in turn, the honor of Gian Battista, "My father also wished to call a priest, but Gian Battista said, 'Sir, don't bother because tomorrow I will return with my brothers to do what is necessary . . .' and he added, 'Do not believe that I have been forced to do this, because I have wanted to do this for months.'"[17] After numerous apologies again reflecting on his dishonorable treatment of the Cumano family, he left, taking with him the accoutrements that presumably many a young rake took to a tryst—a stiletto, pistol, and a rope ladder used to gain entrance to Elena's room. Gian Battista, however, did not keep his word, or at least the words Elena put in his mouth. That night was the last time Elena was to see him.

As soon as he escaped from her bedroom and the hands of her father, brothers, and relatives, in fact, he began trying to escape from his problematic marriage, claiming that it had been forced on him. That night he waylaid one of the witnesses and tried to convince him, mainly with threats, that he had been forced to agree to the ceremony. The next day his family took up the case, also trying to press witnesses to portray the events of that evening as a trap and Gian Battista as a victim rather than as a happy husband relieved at last to have his marriage finalized and public, as the Cumano telling of the tale would have had it. Thus, for

a time, a war of words and tales raged in Feltre until finally, after a
month of public claims and counterclaims, the city's bishop, Giacomo
Revelli, ruled that the marriage was not valid because the forms of Trent
had not been followed. In addition, he ordered that Elena must stop
claiming that she was Gian Battista's wife and defaming him. Theoretically the war of words was over.[18]

What for an evening had appeared to have been a triumph for the
Cumano family—Gian Battista's "willing" confession of marriage before
witnesses and the exchange of a ring—thus collapsed before the new
requirements of the Church. As Zuan Cumano, Elena's father and a
lawyer, must have been uncomfortably aware, he and his family lacked
the canon law prerequisites to have a binding marriage. Nonetheless, as
a lawyer, he was well aware that the Venetian government had become
increasingly concerned about young men taking advantage of women
by consenting to marriage; convincing them that that alone constituted a
marriage; then robbing them of their honor and occasionally of their
dowries as well; and finally, deserting them with the unwitting support
of the Church, which declared such presumed marriages null because
they had not followed the new forms of Trent, just as Bishop Revelli had
done. Already in 1577, Venetian authorities had begun to pass legislation to limit such practices, legislation that Zuan cited in his case against
Gian Battista.[19] Clearly, he hoped to win support for his and his family's
plight from those concerned authorities.

In a formal complaint written to the Podestà of Feltre, Zuan Cumano
summed up the situation after that night nicely from a male perspective:
"Thus I expected that shortly there would be done what should have
been done before the Church [*in faciem Ecclesia*] but that wicked and
most evil man thinking to increase his honor and reputation with his
new addition of this evil wickedness began to refuse, making the claim
that he violated my daughter without any promise of marriage and to
have fooled and made a joke of me [*burlato*]."[20] After admitting bitterly
Gian Battista's treachery, Cumano's testimony swung to a more evaluative mood that says much about a masculine vision of the double standard of honor and reputation involved in premarital sex for women and
men. "He burned to make himself renowned for his great and evil be-
trayal, holding for himself as a signal trophy the prostitution of the
honesty of my house and the awful violence to his given and obligated
pledge [of marriage]. He hoped also to make himself glorious for having
scaled the walls [of my home] with a rope ladder and at the same time
for having violated the security of my house and the honor of all my
family preserved forever intact by my ancestors. And surpassing all iniq-
uities . . . he has gone to the reverend vicar of our most reverend
Bishop and secured a formal admonition against my daughter that she
must desist from claiming this marriage."[21]

Cumano's perspective is instructive. Clearly he was laying out his problems in terms designed to play on the concerns of Venetian authorities about such matters; yet his words struck deeper chords by playing on references to his family's honor and reputation in terms of the marital and sexual problems of his daughter. From Cumano's perspective as the male head of his family, a predatory Gian Battista had created serious difficulties for his daughter's honor, his own honor, and that of his family. Significantly, even the issue of the unwed pregnancy tended to be evaluated in terms of family honor. Equally suggestive was the strong appeal Cumano made to a double standard of honor. He assumed that the very same events that had dishonored his house, as Gian Battista presented them to the public, would bring honor and glory to the young man. For Cumano even the violation of the walls of his house had been given a heroic twist that added to the culprit's honor. It should be noted, however, that this double standard was not perfectly symmetrical here. All agreed that Gian Battista, to gain fame and reputation at the expense of the honor of a woman and her family, had to claim that he had violated both her house and her body "without a promise of marriage" or at least a serious promise of marriage. The breaking of one's word seriously given undercut even a rake's *fama*, changing him from the fantasy of many a Renaissance male to the feared predator of family honor that haunted the worst nightmares of those same men.

Yet when Zuan Cumano claimed that Gian Battista had "fooled and made a joke out of me," he may have been trying to deal with this also at the level of honor evaluation. If the promise had been merely a joke, as was often claimed, no one was supposed to take it seriously. A joke did not bind a man as his word, and thus his honor was not involved. The problem for men or their families in making such a claim was that it was difficult to prove that they had been merely joking. One proof, however, was particularly effective. If the social distance between the man and the woman was great, courts and the community were often predisposed to accept the claim that the man was not serious in his attentions. Moreover the woman and her family—especially her family, with their greater experience of social realities—were expected to be aware of the fact that the word of a man in such circumstances, no matter how serious it might sound, was not serious.[22] For Gian Battista and Elena, in theory and perhaps in her father's rhetoric as well, such a social gap existed. Although Gian Battista, as the youngest son of the Faceno clan, probably did not have outstanding financial prospects, and although Zuan Cumano was an important lawyer in Feltre, the former was a member of the hereditary local nobility that sat on the Major Council of the town and the latter was merely a member of the *cittadino* class that formed an intermediate group between the nobility and the *popolani*.

In this context, labeling Gian Battista's broken promise a joke might seem a tactical error. But suggestively, at the very moment that this case was being argued, the tranquility of Feltre, so valued by its Venetian

rulers, was being disturbed by growing tensions between the local nobility and the *cittadini*. It seems that the *cittadini*, upset by the nobility's
high-handed ways, had organized to protest formally the latter's privileges and asocial behavior, and Venice feared that perhaps they were
prepared to do more. Thus it may have been that Zuan Cumano chose to
characterize Gian Battista's broken promise as a cruel joke to place it
squarely in the context of the ongoing unacceptable behavior of the
nobility, attempting to put pressure on the Venetian authorities to act in
his favor to demonstrate that things were not out of hand. If so, he had
chosen a dangerous forum, for the Podestà, Vincenzo Capello, to whom
he directed his complaints, seems to have sided with the nobility in
general and the Faceno family in particular in this case. Elena demonstrated the Cumano family's awareness of this when she testified in
Venice before the Holy Office in July. Taking advantage of a question
about whether she had told the truth in her earlier testimony before the
Podestà, she replied: "My lord no, I did not tell the truth to him. I told
him that I did not know anything because while his lordship questioned
me the brothers of my husband were there at the door. His lordship got
up . . . and went to speak with them four or six times, even though his
lordship had promised me that when he examined me he did not want
to have my adversaries present."[23]

It appears that from the first, the Cumano family and their supporters had been concerned about the Podestà. Thus when he ordered the
bishop of the city to turn over the investigation to him and the secular
authorities of Feltre at the instigation of the Faceno family (on May 19)
and the bishop concurred, the Cumano family apparently saw that the
case was slipping even further beyond their control. And that may have
been why Zuan Cumano decided to go on the offensive before the Podestà at just that moment, bringing his own complaint before him and
loading it with the rich rhetoric of honor and reputation. A rhetoric that
before him and his local noble advisers might have appealed to common
values and fears, but at the same time publicly put the nobility on notice
that, all claims to the contrary, this was not merely a youthful prank. It
was a serious matter threatening the *cittadini*'s honor. Moreover, at a
moment when the *cittadini*'s murmuring about the nobility's high-
handed ways was already threatening to come to a boil, it was a matter
that required serious attention. On this score, it is significant to note that
the Argento family, named frequently as leaders of the *cittadini* faction at
this time, were closely related to the Cumano family. In fact, Galeazzo
Argento was the son of a sister of Zuan Cumano who had married into
that family. He had actually been at the bedside of Elena and Gian
Battista as a witness of their ill-fated "wedding" and would testify before
the Podestà as one of Cumano's star witnesses. And tellingly, he was to
be identified several times for Venetian authorities as one of the more
potentially violent leaders of the *cittadini* faction.[24]

Perhaps Cumano hoped that by going on the offensive, drawing out the honor dimension of the conflict, and demonstrating that potentially dangerous tensions were being exacerbated by it, pressure might be brought to bear on the nobility and the Podestà to back down on the issue of the wax statue and perhaps even support the marriage of the young couple as a way to defuse the situation. Certainly, as noted earlier, he knew that the Venetian authorities were concerned about men taking advantage of the new rules for marriage, and he was probably aware that they were also concerned about the growing split between the *cittadini* and the nobility in Feltre. Thus, even if the Podestà and nobility did not respond to his case, he may have hoped that the Venetian authorities would. And in the end they did, at his petition. One final bit of evidence based on the timing of Vincenzo Capello's resignation from his post as Podestà reinforces the interpretation that this case had taken on broader social and political dimensions. After being quietly reprimanded for his handling of the investigation by Venetian authorities in 1589, Capello stepped down before his term was up, ostensibly to accept another post. His replacement, Francesco Sagredo, wrote to his superiors in Venice that when he arrived he found the city hopelessly divided between the *cittadini* and the nobility, and was forced to spend most of his term cleaning up the mess he had inherited and pacifying the enraged *cittadini*, whose unrest was perceived as most dangerous for Venetian interests.[25]

In the light of this complex calculus of reputation and honor, the Cumano family's stress on Gian Battista's frequent admissions of marriage and intention to marry take on additional meaning as well. As noted earlier, while that marriage could not be established before the Podestà of Feltre, his court provided an ideal public forum to try the honor and reputation of Gian Battista Faceno. And while no formal verdict could be given on that, a less heroic view of the rake's progress could be publicly presented—one that stressed that with false promises he had led astray an innocent Christian girl and a trusting father who had had faith in the binding honor of his word and pledge. The Cumano family may have even hoped that whatever the outcome of the case, making public this vision of events (whether they were true or not) might have forced the Faceno family to reconsider their own honor and reputation and decide on marriage.

This, of course, was the perspective of the Cumano family, a perspective that, given a modern sensitivity to the evident plight of Elena, deceived, abandoned, and pregnant, may miss the way the Faceno could read the same tale. A healthy corrective is provided by the literature of the period. For while Shakespeare might at times show sympathy for his star-crossed lovers, other perspectives on star-crossed love, especially when it involved class, were well represented. Bandello, in novella 31 of part II of his *Novelle*, tells the tale of a Milanese nobleman who fell in love with the daughter of a substantial commoner, much as young Gian Battista seems to have done with Elena. He, however, did do the correct and honorable thing. After courting his love from a suitable distance, he approached the girl's father for her hand. Bandello reports that the father, in turn, did the honorable thing, going to the young man's mother (his father was dead) to warn her of the unwise love across class lines. Together the parents plotted to send the young man away and marry his love to someone of her own station while he was gone; they plotted, that is, to respect the normal imperatives of family and social order that the unbound passions of love had blinded their children to.

The successful outcome of the tale for Bandello, and presumably for his readers as well, was underscored by the clever metaphoric ending he provided. When the young man returned, learning of her marriage, he rushed to see her. But he was surprised to find her less beautiful than he remembered and blind in one eye as well. Once more, however, the young noble behaved correctly, congratulating his ex-love on her marriage and expressing his condolences for the accident that he assumed must have caused her to lose the sight of one eye while he was away. She replied warmly, "And I say from my heart to you that I am happy that you have recovered the sight of both your eyes." Her remark, and his moral, Bandello explained as follows: "She had been blind in that one eye ever since she was a small child. . . . Thus love often blinds incautious lovers." And thus, from the patriarchal perspective of the late sixteenth century, Gian Battista's timely withdrawal to the wars of Flanders may have prevented blind love from doing harm. In such a reading, Zuan Cumano becomes the person who acted dishonorably, and the Faceno family, Gian Battista, and his own daughter were the victims.[26]

Be that as it may, it is Zuan Cumano's complaint that we have on the broken pledge. And that complaint is also eloquently evocative in its metaphors of sexual victimization and honor that figure so prominently in the description of Gian Battista's deeds. Again, it was not so much Elena's victimization that was central, but rather a form of familial reputation expressed in sexual terms. Gian Battista had "violated" [*violata*] the walls of Zuan's home by physically scaling them. "Violated" was used in just this sense to describe in criminal records the taking of a woman's virginity. In the process, Faceno destroyed the honor of Zuan's family, "always conserved intact" [*conservato sempre intacto*] by his ancestors. Again, "intact" was the usual way of referring to honorable unmarried women still virgins [*vergine intacto*], and "conserving" that virginity intact was a central goal of the family. In sum, Cumano was describing literally the sexual desecration of his family's honor, and it is not at all surprising that he concluded that Gian Battista had gloried in the "prostitution of the honor of my house."[27] Cumano was not only clever in this use of metaphor, he was following a normal pattern of language found in many such cases. Regularly there was a metaphorical wedding of the sexual and the honorable that saw a woman's body and honor being bound up with the tradition/body of a family and its honor.[28]

That symmetry of vision could hardly be better exemplified than in the opening lines of Zuan Cumano's written complaint: "Giovan Battista Faceno . . . a youth most arrogant and audacious, destroyer and prostitutor of the honesty of families had the desire under a false and wicked promise of matrimony to *violate* the security of my house in order to wickedly betray and deflower Elena my daughter . . . carrying off [*levando*] her virginity and carrying off [*levando*] eternally the honor of myself and my entire family which has always been *more dear to me than life itself.*"[29] Again Zuan's house is portrayed as violated in conjunction with his daughter's "deflowering." The parallel is reinforced by the repetition of "carrying off," which is explicitly used to describe the loss of Elena's virginity and the loss of his and his family's honor. As a result, as Zuan makes absolutely clear, he finds himself facing in the loss of his daughter's virginity a loss of personal and familiar honor more dear to him than life itself.

Such rhetoric may have been overblown, but it suggests a central perspective on why such tight control of a daughter's sexuality was deemed necessary, especially by upper-class fathers. Not only was a daughter's honor and, in turn, her marriageability crucially colored by perceptions of her sexual purity; in much more complex and subtle ways, a family and the men responsible for it found the honor of all of them turning on the intactness of a daughter's virginity. As has been well documented, upper-class daughters were expensive to marry and difficult to place well in the Renaissance; in addition, when not bound by marriage and unplaced, their passions were very dangerous for the honor of father and family as long as they remained so.

One might well ask if daughters and women in general saw their situation as equally perilous. Did young women see that they had honor to lose, and did they evaluate it from the perspective of their virginity before marriage and their chastity thereafter? Could it be that that intactness that meant honor in a male world was less significant for women; that women did not evaluate themselves by the codes evolved for them by men, and that Elena and many other young women like her were less concerned about their virginity than their fathers and brothers? Perhaps. But the answer to that question is a complex one that requires more extensive research. Nonetheless Elena's case and its broader context provide some suggestive insights on the matter. First, Elena's sacrifice of that which her father held more dear than life itself needs to be more carefully considered. It might well be argued that, in fact, Elena only put her honor at risk in sexual intercourse in return for Gian Battista's putting his own honor at risk by giving her his word even before God "with very great oaths."[30]

Throughout her testimony before both the civil and ecclesiastical authorities, Elena was most concerned to demonstrate that she had given herself only after a promise of marriage reinforced by oaths to God and discussions with her confessor. Without mentioning her honor, as noted earlier, such testimony reinforced her honor by demonstrating that she had given her virginity with the assumption that she was acting correctly as a wife in the eyes of her Church and community. Suggestively, however, Elena seemed to imply that her vision of her reputation and honor went beyond the sexual. For example, when referring to a conversation that she had heard about between Gian Battista and several local notables, she reported a telling detail. One of those notables, responding to Gian Battista's proclamation that he was leaving for the wars in Flanders, objected, according to Elena: "it is not well to run off to Flanders when you have taken for a wife that woman *who is well-born, intending by this me.*"[31] Elena implied, using the words of another, that she was honorable on more than one level in the eyes of the community. First, of course, she reinforced her primary line of attack by revealing that members of the community perceived her as Gian Battista's wife. But in addition, she was an honorable woman because she was well born into that family whose tradition her father was anxious to defend. And finally, of course, that honor would be secured by a marriage tie to another prominent family of Feltre, Gian Battista's, and perhaps even increased, as his family was a noble one. In fact, this goal may come closer to explaining the risk she took in exchanging her honor with his: if the risk had succeeded, she would have secured for herself and her family the correct place in society for a well-born woman— marriage into another important family.

Magic, Marriage, and Reputation

Honor, status, and family power, however, were not enough to secure Elena's marriage. For that matter, neither was the entrapment of Gian Battista, apparently engineered by her father, or even the public pressure reported from the community. But Elena, disappointed, still did not see herself as without hope, which brings us back to the wax figure found hidden near the altar in the Cathedral Church and eventually to a larger circle of the residents of Feltre and their perceptions of reputation and honor. When her case was brought before the Holy Office of Venice, Elena provided an explanation for the statue: "sleeping with my husband [Gian Battista] one night, he said to me that many times he had heard that men made women come to them with a statue. They bound the statue and needles were stuck in it to give the hammer [*martello*] to those women whom they wished to have come. . . . The next day my husband left after he had been found in my house and I did not see him again."[32]

Elena had begun to set the stage for the dangerous admissions that were to come. Her husband, before he deserted her, had described a magical way men used to bind women to themselves. But again, nicely, she demonstrated to the Holy Office that she had at first avoided such questionable tactics, adopting instead the correct Christian approach— prayers, Masses, and a good life to win the support of God, Mary, and the Church: "I was pregnant by him so I hoped to make him return with prayers and I sent a woman . . . to light eleven candles, have a Mass said and ask for the grace to see the road to be reunited [with my husband]. I also had a Mass said to the Holy Spirit and sent alms to the Monastery of the Angels and Santa Chiara. Moreover I had us inscribed in the school of the rosary so that I could say the rosary for us both. I also had a prayer said at the chapel at the door of San Lorenzo where there is a Christ, a Madonna, and a Santa Lucianna that have done many miracles in order to ask the grace that things be made right and my husband return."[33]

Thus, following the correct Christian path with candles, masses, prayers, alms, and even the new fashion of the rosary, Elena demonstrated her faith in the power of the Church. And for a moment it seemed that the path of the good Christian would work. Just before Easter, Gian Battista's brothers were reported to be talking in public about how Gian Battista had confessed, been forgiven, and, having taken advantage of a special general indulgence offered by the Pope, was planning to return to Feltre. Elena saw this as a sign that her prayers had been answered. She explained to the court that it had seemed clear to her that if he had confessed and been forgiven, he must have certainly been convinced by his confessor to honor his promise of marriage. Once again with an apparent artlessness in her testimony, Elena had suggested that the Church's power should have been adequate to bring her husband back and properly bind their passions. If candles, Masses, prayers, and alms were not adequate, surely the Church's control over confession and the central mystery of the faith that it provided access to—the Eucharistic Ceremony—should have carried the day and secured her husband's return.

Gian Battista did return, but not to Elena. Rather, he slipped in and out of town on his way to the wars in Flanders. The Church had failed her. But there was another range of binding powers available to Elena, powers that often were not so distant from Christianity as it was commonly practiced as the Church might have hoped.[34] "Having learned this [that Gian Battista had fled to Flanders], I resolved to try to make him return using the statue that I had heard him speak of himself." Thus she began to reveal the love magic used to try to force her husband's return. "I gave four *soldi* . . . to Lucia my maid, so that she would buy a statue of wax."[35] From the beginning, however, the plan did not go smoothly. The first statues delivered were rejected. And when an adequate statue was brought, Elena reported that there was an extra two-*soldi* charge, which wisely she did not explain to the Holy Office. It seems that she had sent her servant to buy the wax statue from a local craftsman, Pietro Grevo, who specialized in wax figures as *ex voto* and funerary ornaments. Normally, these were dressed and hung in the churches of the city as a memorial, a request for divine aid, or an expression of gratitude for aid received. As such they lacked an element essential to the magic at hand; thus the first statues sent had been unacceptable because they lacked "a virile member and testicles." As a proud craftsman, Pietro, when called to testify, even explained how he modified his regular molds for making the statues, using beans to achieve the desired additional physical details, and noted that when he delivered his revised work, Elena's servant had informed him that "the statue was pleasing to her mistress."[36]

Elena admitted to the Holy Office that the evening the correct statue was delivered, "after dinner while the rest of the house rested, I wrapped my white veil that I wear on my head at night around the statue in order to tie it up and stuck a needle into it so that it would stay bound. Then I stuck eight or ten needles in diverse places as seemed fitting to me all over the statue. But as I was doing this the leg broke off, so I used a bit of taffeta to put the pieces back together and tie them back in place. Then I gave it to my maid and told her to carry it to the cathedral and leave it at the head of the altar behind the altar cloth . . . because this would make my husband return either tomorrow or shortly. But he never did return."[37]

Although Elena's story put the blame for her actions squarely on her own shoulders, exculpating her mother and the other women accused of complicity, it also placed her actions in the best possible light. Having failed to win back her husband as a good Christian with the aid of the Church, she had in a way tried the next best avenue open to her as a good woman: as a good wife, she had tried to win her husband back following the advice of that very husband! Gian Battista had explained to her the magic of the wax statue, which apparently worked as a *martello*, or hammer, to force a person to return. The *martello* was a widely used form of magic, as we shall see, often adopted to punish enemies— to hammer them or, as in this case, to force them to act to avoid the pain and suffering that the hammer created for its victim.[38] Usually the hammer was activated by prayerlike language that used Christian imagery to call on God or his heavenly supporters to punish/hammer the victim until they fulfilled the hammerer's desires. Elena, however, did not admit to using such language; rather, she turned to the Church to trigger her hammer in a more formal way. Her hammer was to have been activated by the Masses said over the statue, and it was in that context that the statue had been discovered near the altar in the Cathedral Church of Feltre.

Her interrogators in the Holy Office were particularly troubled by her use of the Church in conjunction with the hammering magical wax figure. They noted that seeking the aid of the Church "for good things is licit and laudable, but evil with illicit means." Then they asked, "Could you clear up whether or not you understood that you were doing evil?" Elena admitted, "At the time I believed that I had done a good thing, but later when I confessed during the Jubilee to an Observant Friar he told me that I had sinned . . . thus at first I believed it was not a sin, but after the friar explained I believed it was."[39] Once again Elena was putting her case in the best possible light, but her examiners were suspicious about her account of the magic and how she had come to know about it. In part they were suspicious because another woman reputed to be a witch had been implicated in the case by the investigation in Feltre, but in part they were troubled by Elena's claim that her husband had provided the idea for the magic used. Statistically speaking, that claim was unlikely; in this period, most of the people tried for the use of love magic were women and, more important, the cases themselves, as we shall see, suggest an underlying assumption common at several levels in society: that women were the masters of such magic. In turn, those few men prosecuted were usually priests, not husbands.[40] This is not to argue that men did not practice such magic, but merely to point out that Elena's examiners were predisposed to be suspicious about her claim that a man had taught her the rather complex magical program that she had followed. In fact, they were quite concerned to discover the women's networks that they assumed lay behind the wax figure.

Witchcraft, Reputation, and the Power of Words

Significantly it was a woman's reputation that forced the direction of the original inquiry by the Bishop of Feltre. Lucretia, a woman of about fifty and married to a builder known as Giorgio Marescalio, immediately became the focus of the investigation there, in large part because she had the public *fama* of being a witch capable of such magic and also of being particularly adept at securing marriages between unwilling partners. A large group of neighbors and local ecclesiastics testified to her evil *fama* in disturbing detail, claiming not only that she knew and used binding love magic, but also that she destroyed children, hammered her enemies, and knew what people said about her in secret. A neighbor, Bartolomeo Bressano, gave a typical account of her activities. He claimed that Lucretia had put a spell on [*fatturato*] one of his children. Moreover he reported that "while visiting my house Lucretia's daughter told my wife that once she had given birth to a badly deformed child which no one dared to touch except her mother. She [Lucretia] killed the child and said that it had a blessed cowl which her husband wore thereafter. It had the power to protect one from enemies."[41]

Such destruction of deformed children was apparently common, often done by the midwife who oversaw the birth. But Lucretia's interference seemed to imply several things to her neighbors and to the ecclesiastics who heard the case as well. First, monstrous births threatened the regular order of life in a community. They suggested that things were radically out of joint in the family involved and also in the larger community; hence, their frequent association with other portents and God's judgment.[42] The reported reluctance to touch the child seemed to reflect a deeper fear of its significance as well. In turn, Lucretia's lack of fear suggested that she was familiar with the powers that stood behind such things. With a familiarity and a coolness that impressed, she killed the child and, in addition, demonstrated enough understanding to draw out the magical implications of the baby's cowl to benefit her husband.[43] Bartolomeo continued: "And moreover I heard from Zuan Battista Galletto that if it had not been for this Lucretia, messer Piero Sandi would never have married his wife and also that Francesco Ochies one time was ready to strike her because she had made a male child of his die. He brought a case against her, but because he was poor, he could not prove what was being said publicly. Concerning her evil *fama* one may question all our neighborhood in which there are Vicenzo Busiga, Antonio Gallot, Michael Forner, messer Zan Vettor Capra the barber, Francesco the apothecary and many women whose names I do not know."[44]

Clearly, we have in Lucretia another woman whose reputation was evaluated by her neighbors on broader criteria than her sexual behavior or chastity. As Bartolomeo had promised, those neighbors called before the court confirmed that they viewed her as an evil woman and a witch. The widow Giacoma Patugalla provided an account of a damning incident of a type often associated with witches. Lucretia had visited her house one day about five years earlier and, seeing her young son, had placed her hand on his head, saying, "Oh, what a pretty child." Shortly thereafter the child became sick, and Giacoma began to suspect Lucretia of being a witch and of having made her child sick. Witches were, of course, well known for destroying children; the frequent wasting diseases of childhood were regularly assumed to be the result of their spells. Giacoma tried an experiment, however, to test her hypothesis; she was no credulous victim of superstition. She had learned that there was a way to determine if a witch had cast a spell over a child: "I had been taught that one had to beat the clothing of the child and that the person who had given the sickness/evil [*male*] to him would come. Thus I tried it and the day following the said donna Lucretia came to my house and told me that my child would no longer have the sickness/evil. Nonetheless the child died and I had the impression that the child died because of her."[45]

While Giacoma's account is clear and virtually stereotypical, right down to her experiment to determine if Lucretia was a witch, one thing in her account is less clear: why did Lucretia want to destroy her child? In some regions, witches were reputed to destroy children by sucking their blood and causing them to waste away simply for the malicious pleasure of destruction or as a mark of their full commitment to evil. Lucretia's neighbors, although ready to accuse her of heinous crimes aplenty, were silent on her reasons for killing children. But a hint to their perception of her motives, and perhaps to their deeper fears of her as well, is provided by the testimony of another neighbor named Giacoma, Giacoma dal Cumo. She reported that Paolina, the daughter of Lucretia, had asked her to do a favor for her and keep it a secret from her mother, apparently because her mother would have disapproved. Somehow, however, Lucretia found out.[46] As a result, Lucretia came right to her and, after giving her a punch or two, "she put a hand on me . . . which made a tremor and fear come over me and I shook so much that I did not know what I was doing." Giacoma was so frightened that she confessed the secret favor, and Lucretia then "made the sign of the cross over me and said, 'Go and be blessed. Go in the name of God.' Immediately that fear went away and I went home without feeling any more pain."[47] Here Lucretia was punishing a neighbor for acting against her interests and implicitly against her wishes. In other words, her spells gave her a power over her neighbors, a power that could punish them for acting against her or even her desires. It may well be that neighborhood babies were seen as having been destroyed in much the same context. Rather than mere evil, their destruction was evil to an end.

Perhaps the best example of Lucretia's use of her punishing powers is also the most apparently banal. Orsola, wife of Vettor Buziga, had gotten into an argument with Lucretia while washing clothes almost a decade earlier, perhaps about who was first. The discussion passed from words to deeds, and water was splashed by each woman on the other. After Lucretia left, however, Orsola was suddenly paralyzed and unable to move for two days. A number of people still remembered this incident years later, perhaps because it epitomized the power and danger of Lucretia's reputed use of punishing witchcraft.[48] It may be that Orsola's splashing and public argument with Lucretia should be read as well as a public affront to the latter's honor. In that light, Orsola's punishment could be seen as a form of vendetta, as well as a demonstration of Lucretia's power. And neighbors remembered the incident, if that interpretation is correct, because even a minimal dishonoring of Lucretia carried with it a threat of vendetta in the form of witchcraft. It may be that given the brief accounts of Lucretia's magic, most of it could be explained in simple terms of power, but it is worth considering in this late Renaissance society so rife with concepts of honor and vendetta that the power of witches could serve as a significant tool in the vendetta side of the honor dialectic. The person who dishonored a witch could expect the treatment that Orsola received or perhaps something worse, like the death of a child. If this were true, then the honor of witches had to be treated with unusual care by those who associated with them either voluntarily or involuntarily as neighbors—and one can see another possible reason why Lucretia's neighbors were so troubled by her.

Less evident, however, is the positive side of this ability to pursue vendetta with witchcraft. In the Renaissance, ideally, the honor dynamic, with its threat of vendetta, was supposed to limit the level of violence in society. One did not cross the honor of another, one did not do violence to another, because that would require vendetta, that is, violence and dishonor in return. Thus, ideally, violence was avoided without formal institutions or additional violence within a community or group simply by maintaining a balance of honor. Violent passions were literally bound by the threat of vendetta. But, of course, that simply required the threat of vendetta to back it up. If one did not have the power to pursue vendetta, the support of threatened violence fell away, one's honor became problematic, and violent passions became easier to indulge, especially for the powerful.

Enter the witch. The witch's power allowed virtually everyone an option of vendetta, and as such, it could be, if used well, a positive force in society. The good witch in a way could serve as the underpinning and defense of the honor of the more humble, protecting them from violence by offering them a proven and visible form of vendetta. Thus when someone seemed to fall victim to witchcraft, people asked who had been wronged by the victim or his or her family and suspected the wronged person of being the source of their problems. But in theory, those moments should have been rare; more often, neighbors treated each other well for a host of reasons, one of which may well have been a fear of their neighbor's power to pursue vendetta using witchcraft. If this hypothesis is valid, every neighborhood needed a witch, at least a good one. Whether it is true or not, as we shall see, it appears that they had one. Certainly this is leaping far beyond Lucretia's problems with her neighbors, but it is a speculation worth considering and suggests another reason why people turned on her so violently. Her vendettas had gotten out of hand; they no longer seemed to serve the community. Instead they had come to focus on her petty quarrels, such as the splashed water at the wash.

The investigation of Elena Pedra, accused of witchcraft by her neighbors in 1589, reveals this honor dynamic well, again in the context of a negative case where vendetta had gotten out of hand. It seems that there had been a long-term disagreement between Elena and a certain Faustina, widow of Giovanni Dominici Nordio. As the conflict developed, one of Elena's children, Antonio, became ill and was confined to bed. Nothing would cure him, and as the illness dragged on, one day, according to Faustina, Elena approached one of her daughters to tell her that the child's illness was a direct result of the vendetta that she had launched against them. Faustina even claimed to remember Elena's words to her daughter: "You thought to do your worst [to me] and I did my worst, because two or three times I went to call vendetta by asking God to put a demon on him [the child]."[49] The magic involved seemed to be largely based on hammering prayers to God and on a tablecloth over which a number of Masses had been said, much as over Elena Cumano's wax statue. Elena Pedra claimed that as the tablecloth slowly wore out, so too would the child. That promised a long illness, and at the time the matter was brought to attention of the Inquisition, it had lasted for three years.

Elena Pedra, perhaps moved by the denunciation of her deeds to the Holy Office, tried to end her magical vendetta tellingly, using the customary forms of the vendetta. Faustina reported: "This Elena the other day sent to me to ask to make peace. And she promised me to liberate him [her bewitched son] by praying to God that he cure him. The day of the Madonna of the Candles this Elena came to my house to ask forgiveness of my son and to drink with him in his bed."[50] Here witchcraft, if not actually taking the form of vendetta, was at least being packaged in that form for the Holy Office. For whether Elena had actually bewitched Faustina's child is much less significant than the fact that apparently everyone involved in this case—including the Holy Office, which heard it as a matter of witchcraft—could operate under the assumption that witchcraft had this dimension. Of course, the Holy Office (and therefore we as well) tended to see such issues only when vendetta got out of hand. But even on that score, Elena's case is revealing. If the two women had made peace earlier, for example when Elena had explained that the child's illness was her doing—and presumably many families, seeing a child threatened, might have done so—the matter would have been settled and the community would have returned to normal, with another small demonstration that honor and vendetta worked even at the level of the neighborhood and the relatively humble.

To return to Lucretia, neighbors feared her as a witch, but her reputation had spread more widely and even local clerics were convinced that she was one. Perhaps the most revealing testimony came from the cleric Zuan Victor, who reported spying on Lucretia in the cathedral shortly after the discovery of the wax statue. In a long testimony he described her movements around the church, movements that an innocent eye could easily have read as those of a devout woman involved in her private devotion. But lurking in the choir, the cleric watched with a suspicion that layered her every movement and glance with dangerous implications. Reading his testimony, one sees how a woman with the reputation of being a witch, whether she was one or not, underwent a scrutiny that made it almost certain that she would become one in the public eye at least.

"I put myself to walking there in the church," he reported, "and while I strolled through the chapel of San Zuane, there entered four or five women whose names I do not remember. Also there entered Lucretia wife of messer Georgio, the builder, who is reputed to be a witch and who has been given the nickname Circe. . . . Lucretia kneeled on the first step of the steps that go into the choir from the side that overlooks the altar of San Prosdecimo [near which the wax figure had been found] . . . seeing her there I moved back very slowly behind the altar painting of San Rocco in order to clearly see the woman and not be seen. After all the other women left, remaining alone in the church. . . . This Lucretia began to make the sign of the Cross. . . . Then she began to kiss the floor and for this reason I knelt down [in order not to be seen]. But at that moment some people arrived . . . and donna Lucretia stopped right where she was. After those women had left for a time, this woman returned to making the sign of the cross and kissing the floor. She repeated these things four times because when she began to make the sign and kiss the floor people came in. Finally after the fourth time, I believe that was after about three quarters of an hour . . . there arrived messer Vettor Guslin and a peasant. And this time Lucretia got up from where she had been and it appeared to me that she was trying to look over towards the principal altar of San Prosdecimo. She went towards the part of the church that is towards the Church of San Lorenzo near which again lies the altar of San Prosdecimo. When she arrived at the font for Holy Water she turned giving a quick glance [*un occhiata*] as they say around the Church and then slowly left walking over to San Lorenzo."[51]

Lurking in that silent church with the cleric Zuan Victor, one gets a sense not only of how his suspicions magnified the significance of Lucretia's every action, but how the Church was for at least some women in the late Renaissance a special and familiar space. Witch or merely good Christian, Lucretia had her own sense of the Church and used it for her own programs with a familiarity that comes through even Victor's suspicions. In many ways the churches of the late Renaissance were a special place for women. First, of course, women operated there in an environment where in theory they were the equals of men. Both were ultimately involved in the same battle for salvation. But beyond that much circumscribed and overlooked point, in many ways it appears that church space had been appropriated quite aggressively by some women. It was one of the few public spaces where women could move freely with a certain lack of suspicion. Perhaps this is one reason why public officials had been worried for a long time about the potential for illicit sexual contacts in church.[52]

Clearly, church space had an important social dimension for women, and it may have been more significant than for men, who had a wider range of social spaces to frequent. In some ways, we might even conjecture that the church played a role for women similar to the role that the bar and later the coffee house would play for men. More significantly for understanding Lucretia and her reputation, however, there is much evidence in the cases heard by the Inquisition in Italy that certain women, struck by the deeper meanings that they perceived as underlying the special space and objects of their churches, had attempted to use those powers for their own programs of magic and witchcraft. The same was true for domestic space and objects, as we shall see. Altars, the Mass, holy oil, holy water, the Host, blessed candles, and the very geography of specific churches, as well as domestic doorsills, hearths, stairways, beds, hearth chains, pans, beans, salt—together they make an unlikely list, but all shared the status of familiar yet special places and things where women moved and that women used. And certain women discovered in and around these places and things a world of deeper meanings that created a special culture and a range of deeper powers that they drew upon at times most effectively to bind people and their passions.[53] Victor's suspicions and his testimony were probably designed to play on fears of just that, fears that were shared more broadly. When we read of Lucretia's movements about the church from that perspective, they become rich with meaning and threat.

Lucretia's interruption of her prayers when others entered the church, her repetition of certain prayerlike actions, and her glances thus confirmed her guilt. In the end, however, Zuan Victor admitted that there were earlier reasons for his suspicions, "This reputation [*fama*] is further confirmed because I remember that when my father . . . was troubled by a diabolical spirit, he was exorcised in the Church of All Saints. Before the main altar the Spirit [that had possessed him] said that he wished to reveal the queen of all the witches of the city and said that she was this same Lucretia. Another time in Padua when my father was being exorcised . . . the same spirit said that he remained in his body because of spells, magical signs, and bindings as he had said other times. Forced with the greatest exorcisms to tell who had done these magical deeds he remained firm in naming Lucretia."[54] This had led to a careful examination of Victor's father's home to determine if there was some sort of hammering magic that could be discovered there. The search bore fruit, for in his father's bed were discovered "two pieces of wood like cypress, and in addition some pieces of stone, some twine, a plum pit with a feather stuck in it so well that it seemed natural, and a few little curls of feather as well as other things which I do not remember, all of which were burned. . . . Because I remembered all these things when I was in the Cathedral Church I watched that woman more carefully."[55]

Exactly. Lucretia found herself in a precarious position because, witch or not, her public reputation had made her a watched woman—a woman caught in the measuring gaze of her community—virtually a witch waiting for an incident major enough to bring her to ecclesiastical justice. One could argue that for her as for Castiglione's Perfect Courtier, her *fama* was becoming her reality, although in this case with less positive results. And the very afternoon of the discovery of the wax statue, true to her reputation, she was the first woman called in to be examined by the bishop about her role in the matter.

Unlike Elena Cumano, who could attempt to draw on her family's status and connections and her father's legal knowledge in the courts of Feltre and even Venice to regain her honor and reputation, Lucretia had to rely largely on more personal methods. As gossip was undermining her reputation she went about speaking to her neighbors, trying to defuse that gossip. Also, her husband and at least one daughter were reported to have done the same and to have talked as well to local church leaders, trying to show that she was really a "good woman" [*donna del bene*]. It appears, however, that earlier, even she had had recourse to litigation in the local courts of Feltre, forcing her most vociferous accusers to refrain from their attacks on her reputation.[56]

But with the discovery of the wax statue and the rapid focusing of public accusations on her, it seems that Lucretia moved her campaign up a notch and began to try to control the development of public opinion and the case the Church was building against her in some interesting ways. It is clearly dangerous to try to read too much into the not disinterested accounts of her activities. But curiously, an investigation that seemed destined to lead so smoothly from Lucretia's *fama* as a witch involved with marriage and love to her conviction as same had a tendency to keep jumping off the track. In my first readings of the testimony, I found these derailings interesting because they provided suggestive details about private life that seemed irrelevant to the case and thus appeared less likely to be skewed by the necessity of arguing it. The priest Andrea da Canal confessed, for example, that he had gone to Lucretia for magical help to overcome his love for a young woman; help he admitted that she denied, suggesting that instead he would be better off as a priest praying to the Virgin Mary for such aid.[57] This testimony did little to support the case against Lucretia, but it did provide a fascinating picture of the spiritual dilemmas of a young priest facing the conflict between the renewed moral drive of the late-sixteenth-century Church and his own sexual desires.

Yet as I worked over the body of testimony collected against Lucretia, the suspicion began to grow that these derailments were not quite the innocent asides that I had at first assumed. In fact, when looked at more closely, they seemed to have a pattern all their own, and the thrust of that pattern was that Lucretia was a Christian woman who had been badly misunderstood by her neighbors. Of course, this could have been

simply because Lucretia was just that, not a witch, and over the course of
a careful investigation this truth came out. Upon review, this is apparently what the ecclesiastical authorities of Feltre and Venice concluded;
at least they concluded that the evidence was not sufficient to sustain a
formal charge against her.[58] But another and considerably more interesting reading of the testimony is possible, one that would see Lucretia as
in a way a real witch or master of folk magic who used the skills she had
developed as a manipulator of reality to derail the case against her.
Especially important in this vision of Lucretia was her clever use of
words to create conflicting visions of who, in fact, the people were who
were interested in magic and witchcraft in Feltre.

One of the first clues that conjured such suspicions was Lucretia's
anxiety to go to confession after the wax figure was found in church.
That very day she confessed not once but twice, and both times under
rather suspicious circumstances. Pietro Trento, her regular confessor,
talked with her in the early afternoon, and although she asked that their
conversation be considered a confession, curiously she did not insist on
it or protest when the priest did not follow regular forms. Pietro pointed
out, "I did not absolve her . . . nor did I give her any penance . . .
actually in the act I did not have the intention of confessing her or of
administering the sacrament of penance."[59] To his credit, however, Pietro still informed his superiors that he intended to keep the "quasi-
confession" secret.

The deacon and chancellor of the Cathedral Church, Antonio Argento, was not so scrupulous. He reported that later in the day Lucretia
and her husband had visited him at his home, asking to speak with him
in secret. His report of the conversation is revealing: "She repeated what
she had said . . . *implying almost* that she wished to speak under the
seal of confession. I replied 'say what you wish,' as I realized that confessions are not made in the presence of another and there was present her
husband." With his "implying almost," Antonio left room for his
hearers to assume that what he had heard was not actually a confession.
As an almost confession, the legalistic quibble of the presence of Lucretia's husband took on additional weight, and eventually, after some
soul searching and encouragement from his ecclesiastical superiors con-
ducting the investigation, he decided to disclose what she had said. She
began, he revealed, by apologizing about complaining about others in
confession because she understood that confession was not the place to
complain about the sins of others; in other words, theological niceties
aside, she was treating her revelations as a confession and therefore was
providing in secret the truth of what had happened.[60] This she claimed
she was doing because others were committing "cunning and evil
deeds" that were being attributed to her; thus her desire to confess and
to get his advice. The heart of her confession focused on the priest
Andrea da Canal. Argento reported that she had spoken about meeting

Andrea on the way home from church that morning: "'He said to me,' 'Donna Lucretia, did you know that there was found today a statue wrapped up with needles in it behind the altar . . . of San Prosdecimo and that you have been accused of the deed?'. . . . This donna Lucretia speaking with me [Argento] said that she knew nothing about it and that she was a good woman but that he [Andrea] must have put it there and wished to put the blame on others."[61]

Out of the secrecy of what Lucretia appeared to have assumed was a confession emerges proof that she really was a good woman and evidence that someone else seemingly above suspicion, the priest Andrea da Canal, was responsible. Yet by the time this testimony was given, Andrea was no longer above suspicion, as Lucretia had with apparent innocence in her own earlier testimony reported that Andrea had been for quite a while interested in using magic and witchcraft to solve his love problems and secure his ecclesiastical advancement. In fact, Andrea, pressed by authorities in Feltre with threats of excommunication and loss of benefices, confirmed her testimony, at least in part. "After last Easter," he admitted, "I went to find Donna Lucretia at home . . . and I said to her that I felt very tormented in my heart because of the love of a woman and that I would hold her dear if she would give me some remedy if she knew of any." But Andrea had to concede that rather than giving him a magical solution to his problems, she told him to "confide your problems in the Virgin for she will help you." Andrea, however, reported that he had then shifted his request after concluding that "this love of a woman would eventually pass." Instead he asked for her help in gaining the grace [gratia] of his superiors so that he could secure new benefices and move ahead with his career. Again Lucretia counseled prayer rather than magic and vaguely promised that she would pray for him as well. He confessed that he returned to her eight days later to press his pleas and was again counseled to entrust his cares to the Virgin.[62] In addition, Lucretia had confided to him that she was praying for him to the Virgin and beating her breast as well.

We find ourselves before a curious juxtaposition here: the young priest Andrea came to the reputed witch Lucretia for binding love magic; instead he was instructed by her to have faith in prayer and the Virgin, that is, in what was theoretically at least his own power and tradition. But it seems significant that Lucretia waited until the wax figure was found to relate in the secrecy of confession Andrea's much earlier quest for magical power. And then she reported that interest, as she herself admitted, to point out that Andrea was to blame for the wax figure, not her. Yet could it have been that she rushed in to confess about Andrea's magical interests to shift the investigation away from herself, a relatively unimportant old woman after all, and to Andrea, a cleric of some stature in the community and perhaps from the Venetian noble da Canal family?

I am suggesting that perhaps Lucretia was building her own case against Andrea: a case that developed out of her testimony, her two "secret" confessions to two confessors in one day, both intriguingly flawed in ways that might have allowed those confessors to reveal her secrets, and finally, the conversations that she, her daughter, and her husband had carried on with neighbors and ecclesiastical authorities. With these things, Lucretia appears to have been intentionally creating a web of words with the power to bind her potential adversaries and shift the blame to others. In this she was, if this interpretation is accurate, acting much like a true witch, using the power of words and relationships to shape and coerce the future to her ends.

This is not to suggest that the web of words that Lucretia had constructed was entirely false. Rather, as a wise and powerful master of words, she appears to have selected a strategy that allowed her to use troubling truths—the kinds of secret truths the "witch"/powerful woman must have often known about her community to be successful—to construct a reality that had verisimilitude because it was largely true. For this, shifting the blame to Andrea da Canal was ideal, because it appears that much of what she claimed about his search for power over love through magic was true. It was also ideal because, given the fact that he had gone to Lucretia for help on these matters, he was one of the people who had to be most careful about testifying against her. Thus she could subtly shift the focus of the investigation by leaving a trail of words that would eventually ensnare him at the same time that he, in his testimony, was trying to exonerate her.

Early in May 1588, Andrea was called to testify in Feltre about his knowledge of the statue. He began by recounting the discovery of it during the Mass. After the furor died down, on his way home he had encountered Lucretia by chance: "As I was headed home near the walls . . . Lucretia caught up with me because I had stopped to pull up a garter on my socks. I asked her where she had been. To which she replied that she was coming from Our Lady of San Lorenzo, where she had heard the Mass . . . I asked her if she knew anything about the statue which had been found under the altar of San Prosdecimo and she with great surprise said that she did not have any knowledge of it crying 'Oh me, oh me, but what can this mean?'"[63]

An apparently innocent encounter with Lucretia gave Andrea the opportunity to introduce evidence that revealed her surprise and lack of knowledge about the statue. While virtually everyone else was relating their suspicions about her, the priest seemed to be building a case for her innocence. But, of course, the authorities were already suspicious about Andrea's relationship with Lucretia; thus, ignoring his implications, they pressed him about that relationship. Asked about any recent contacts between them, he replied, "Since Easter, if I remember correctly I talked with this Lucretia two or three times because she lives in my neighborhood. But I do not remember precisely what was discussed." Again his examiners focused on his vagueness; they called upon him to try to remember exactly what had been said. Andrea, however, attempted to give as little information as possible, sticking with creating a sense of everyday conversations between a priest and neighborhood women: "I do not remember that we talked about much of anything but the things that one says in conversation such as 'How are you donna Lucretia?' and she responded, 'Troubled for the poverty of my poor widowed daughter,' and similar words." Still not to be put off, they asked him what he had heard about her reputation. Clearly, they assumed that they were putting him in a bind, for they were well aware of her reputation as a witch and they knew already that he had come to her for aid. But again Andrea resisted, claiming, "I hold this Lucretia to be a good woman [*donna da ben*]. . . . I do not know that the said Lucretia has the reputation [*fama*] of being a witch nor have I heard others say this."[64] Again the ubiquitous reference to *fama*, but here Andrea was trying to make it work to Lucretia's benefit and perhaps his own as well.

The authorities were unimpressed with Andrea's waffling, and after some aggressive questioning that forced him to admit that he had known Lucretia for many years, they sent him off with the threat that if he did not become more forthcoming, he risked excommunication and the loss of his benefices. A day later, Andrea was back before his examiners in a much more contrite and open mood. Perhaps the threats had loosened his tongue or perhaps the realization that he could not count on Lucretia to cover his questionable testimony about his contacts with her had done so. Whatever the reason, this second testimony revealed one priest's faith in the magic of a woman and, incidentally, as noted earlier, the troubles a young priest could still face with love in the late sixteenth century. Trent may have changed the rules, but it had not yet succeeded in changing the players. As we have seen, in his second testimony Andrea confirmed that he had gone to Lucretia first with a request for aid in overcoming the love he felt for an unnamed woman. But rather than magic, he had gotten the advice that he should pray to the Virgin for help with his problems. Even after admitting that he had asked for her help with love, however, he was reluctant to admit that he had heard about her reputation of being a witch. At most, he confirmed that after the wax statue had been found near the altar, he had begun to hear rumors about her reputation.[65]

But his examiners were not ready to let him off so easily and turned to the magical practices that he had reportedly used to escape the binding passion of love, evidently hoping to force him to reveal the source of the magic after they had forced him to describe it. It appears that Andrea had come to believe that his suffering in love had been the result of love magic that had been used against him—that is, that he had been hammered. To overcome this, he had used magic that was to some degree

based on the power of the Church, a fact that deeply troubled his superiors. "This year serving as subdeacon in the Cathedral Church on Holy
Sunday," he confessed, "I took the three holy candles of Holy Saturday
one of which I turned upside down and lit before the image of the
Madonna in my room saying these words, 'As this candle burns and I
have this pain that I have in me [*mi*], so you may have it also in you [*ti*].'
I did not pronounce, however, any name, but rather was sending my
willing [of it] to the person who was giving me the hammer."[66] Such
magic was typical of hammering and antihammering magic at the time.
Reversals of holy objects in conjunction with metaphorical language that
drew out the deeper connections between things named seemed to have
the power to both hammer and turn the power of the hammer back on
the hammerer. Such reversals were often seen by ecclesiastical authorities as calling on the Devil; by reversing normal sacred things, one was
calling on their opposites. In this case, however, the authorities did not
pursue that issue.

In fact they did not even ask Andrea to explain how his magic would
have worked. Rather, they turned to the one thing that to them did not
ring true in Andrea's confession, that he had devised the magic himself,
asking point blank if Lucretia had taught him. Again he replied in a way
that would have covered for her: "I told her about this, but she did not
help me. . . . She did not teach me these words in any way. Rather on
my own I thought them up, believing that I had to help myself to lift this
hammer."[67] Needless to say, his examiners were not convinced, especially given the fact that Andrea had confessed that he had gone to
Lucretia for other, much simpler love magic. They may well have also
found it unlikely that on his own he had thought up such a complex
procedure that was so similar to other forms of magic associated with
women. But having tried to force Andrea to name Lucretia as the source
of his magic repeatedly and without success, they were forced to let the
matter drop and pursue other evidence against her.

Still, some interesting things are revealed by Andrea's evasive testimony. Andrea, in his troubles with love, was quite willing to turn to a
powerful woman for help. Thus we encounter here, rather than learned
clerics instructing women on power and life, strong implications of the
reverse. Here, rather than a masculine written culture informing an
inferior and ineffectual feminine one, we find a priest begging a woman
to teach him how to manage his life and overcome his problems. And
with a nice irony that perhaps misstates the reality of the case, both
Lucretia and Andrea claimed that it was she who took the correct theological and, in turn, high cultural position by recommending that
Andrea overcome his problems by prayer and an appeal to the quintessential protector of women, the Virgin Mary.

Although my suspicion about Lucretia—that she manipulated the
revelation of these things to shift the blame for the wax statue to Andrea

or to distract the authorities from that issue to the more serious matter of Andrea's problems—cannot be proved now, four hundred years later, one last piece of evidence underlines the cleverness with which she planted the seeds of doubt about Andrea and worked to redirect the ecclesiastical investigation. When she gave her almost secret, almost confession to the chancellor of the Cathedral, Antonio Argento, she added toward the end of it a detail that troubled him. She admitted that Andrea had also asked to be helped to regain the friendship of an old "dear friend" whose good graces he had lost. Antonio reported, "Donna Lucretia added that Andrea identified this friend as me." In fact, Antonio at the end of his testimony admitted that this revelation by Lucretia had disturbed him. "When donna Lucretia said to me that the priest had sought some favor over a friend of his, meaning by this me, I felt quite uneasy thinking that he wished to gain from me by this means that which he could not be able to imagine gaining by other means. Still in my heart I calmed myself realizing that God is the one who governs and he rules all things and he who has faith in him cannot perish."[68]

Despite Antonio's faith, Lucretia's confession clearly made him suspect Andrea's friendship and their relationship in ways that even without his revelation of her confession would have weakened one potential supporter of Andrea. Again Lucretia's use of words was creating new realities and a subtle haze of uncertainty that undercut the case against her and fingered Andrea as the significant culprit. In fact, her actions following the discovery of the wax figure suggest that she was carefully sowing the seeds of gossip and more formal words in confession that would flower into a rich thicket of testimony that would change the path of the investigation in Feltre and make her appear an innocent victim of that same *fama* that she was trying to manipulate. Yet for all her cleverness, there was one problem with the case she had created against Andrea: Andrea, according to all accounts, had been the one who discovered the statue near the altar. If he had perpetrated that specific magic, it would have made little sense to point it out to his colleagues and kick off an investigation searching for the person responsible.[69]

The Good Witch as Marriage Broker

Yet in the end, Lucretia may have been telling in all these contexts one very different truth. Among all the accusations leveled against her, one significant one emerges: that she magically forced people to marry against their will. Her daughter put this accusation in a different light, claiming that her mother was called "a witch in Feltre because she labors to make marriages, as she did with messer Bartolomeo Sandi who married madonna Marieta daughter of messer Vettor Scalladria and she arranged also the marriage of donna Pellegrina del Zas with messer

Bernardo in Zas. These marriages she arranged with deliberations between one side and the other.''[70] Every town had its marriage brokers,
people who arranged marriages between families and either collected a
small fee for their services or the more nebulous good will of the families
involved. At times, however, such good offices could backfire on the
marriage broker, especially when the match did not work well or the
partners crossed social or age boundaries in ways that troubled society.

In such instances, it was not hard to assume that some magic or
witchcraft was involved in creating the binding emotions that had led to
marriage. As we have seen with Andriana Savorgnan and as we shall see
when we look more closely at these issues in Chapter 4, it might be more
accurate to say that when everyone was happy with a match made using
magic, there were no complaints and the good witch/matchmaker was a
popular and powerful person. When the matches were seen as incorrect,
crossing class lines, thwarting the wishes of the powerful, or even merely
creating unhappy marriages, the same magic could quickly become evil
in the eyes of the community and was much more likely to come to the
attention of the authorities.

Lucretia's neighbors' complaints about her witchly ways, when read
in this light, take on additional meaning. We see from their perspective a
potentially positive and useful service to the community that had gotten
out of hand and become literally destructive. Giacomo Cambrucio remembered perhaps the most damning incident. It appears his eighteen-
year-old daughter had been courted by a young man whose attentions
she did not appreciate. The young man turned to Lucretia for help. As a
result, according to Giacomo, one day she came to his house and called
his daughter to the door, saying, "If you do not make love with that
man, I would tell you to repent and you will be unhappy with your life."
He continued, "As far as I can remember she [Lucretia] touched her on
the shoulder. The child after that began to cry and complain that her
heart ached. She remained like that slowly dying for twenty months and
neither medicine nor doctors could aid her, until she became like a
statue and died. Before she was always healthy and full of life."[71]

Rather than making a positive match that would have served the
community and its desire to see young women successfully married and
families continued, Lucretia's magic had caused death. Clearly, this undercut Lucretia's daughter's claim that her mother was performing a
useful and necessary social function, but it does not undercut her contention that such a service could be positive if used judiciously. And as
we shall see, whether it was used judiciously or not, it was used extensively both in the urban environment of Venice and in the countryside of
the Veneto. From a slightly different perspective, however, it should also
be noted that once again Lucretia appears to have been trying to use
words here to control the future. With or without magic, she had subtly
threatened Giacomo's daughter, warning her that she should accept the

attentions of her suitor or her life would turn out badly. Given her reputation, the young girl might well have heeded her warning, accepted her suitor, and married him. If that had occurred, presumably Lucretia's magic would have worked again, and if the marriage had worked out her words would have brought a better future, binding passions to continue family and community.

That was not the case, however, and the failure was compounded by the young girl's suspicious death. The testimony of Lucretia's neighbors reveals that this failure and others like it, read negatively, had slowly built into the conviction that she was a dangerous and evil witch. Thus the discovery of Elena Cumano's magical quest to regain her lost husband once again focused suspicions on her. While Elena's father followed more regular masculine paths to regain her husband, it was logical in the eyes of the community that Elena and perhaps her mother would turn to another source of power available especially to women—the marriage broker/witch Lucretia. According to her *fama,* she had forced other marriages; the wax figure under the cathedral altar was just another instance of her powers.

Witch or victim of her reputation, wife or victim of a rake's progress, both Lucretia and Elena remain enigmas. The many-layered tales that they, their supporters, and their enemies constructed create a web of words behind which it is almost impossible to uncover the truth of their deeds. But that web, much like a spider's web, both disguises and builds; in this case, it builds a complex vision of the interrelationship between marriage, honor, and reputation in the lives of women and men in late-sixteenth-century Italy. Moreover, it suggests how some women could use elements of that vision to their advantage, building realities out of certain strands of the social fabric such as honor and reputation to bind their opponents and advance their own causes. Neither Lucretia nor Elena was completely successful in this; both leave the court records still more victims than winners. Lucretia escaped being prosecuted as a witch but undoubtedly was still reputed to be one by her neighbors. Elena remained unmarried, although she did eventually gain money from Gian Battista's family for a dowry and maintenance.[72] But neither woman was a passive victim; each in her own way chose a strategy that attempted to turn the calculus of honor and reputation that society applied to women to her advantage. And in the end, they realized that what the patriarchs of their world held to be "more dear . . . than life itself" could give them a certain leverage even in what appeared to be largely hopeless situations.

3

That Old Black Magic Called Love

Giving the Devil His Due

"[I declare] . . . by means of the present contract that I obligate myself to the prince Lucifer and all the princes of Hell. I call him my Lord and am his slave until the final judgement under the agreement and condition that he grant me a grace: that he make Madonna Paolina di Modesta . . . be inflamed with love for me. So much so that she will have no content, no repose of her spirit or her body unless she is with me. Moreover I pray to those most wise and prudent princes of Hell that they make me this grant. In return I promise my body and my soul at death. I Andrea have written this with my own hand."[1]

So, in April 1590 Andrea Meri, a young apprentice, attempted to sell his soul to the Devil with a formal contract in exchange for the love of his master's wife. Andrea immediately repented, however, and threw his pact with the forces of darkness away, dumping it in the *necessario* (the toilet).[2] Unfortunately, late-sixteenth-century sanitary conditions in Venice were not appreciably better than modern ones; then as now, many toilets emptied directly into the canals. Thus Andrea's contract was soon spotted by neighbors, fished out, and identified as written by him. Andrea's master, informed of the young man's passion for his wife and the strange contract with the Devil, responded to the situation with moderation. After a man-to-man talk, he forgave Andrea. Matters could well have ended there, with Andrea frustrated in love and the Devil presumably frustrated as well, but by the late sixteenth century, as we have seen, there was a third party that had become deeply interested in such matters: the Church.

Theoretically, of course, the Church had always been interested in such Faustian aspirations. But, in fact, aside from a late medieval flurry of heresy prosecution, it had lacked the bureaucracy and the will to make theory reality. With the renewed Inquisition and in Venice with the Holy Office, a much more effective bureaucracy had been created to deal with such issues. And as the Holy Office began to look more closely at what passed for Christianity among the general populace of the Veneto, they were amazed and often horrified to discover the strange twists that religion had been given by the fertile imagination of everyday people. Across Europe, in fact, it became apparent that those people whom the Church had assumed it had been leading for more than 1500 years had not been merely following. Christianity as a popular religion was quite another beast from Christianity as a theological tradition.[3] Unfortunately, the creativity of this range of popular beliefs, the richness of this popular theology, has often been overlooked—too quickly straightjacketed as surviving remnants of ancient beliefs or as simplistic materialist misunderstandings of sophisticated concepts. Certainly such things were involved in this popular theology, but perhaps more interesting and significant was how common people had forged a rich culture out of their experience of the divine in everyday life.

To return to Andrea's contract with the Devil, in his second testimony before the Holy Office he discussed his theological context. He explained that he had found his idea for his contract with the Devil in a book titled *Legendario delle Vite di Santi*, written by a certain Fra Giacomo and printed in Venice in 1585, a copy of which he opened to page 144. There in the middle of the second column he pointed out a discussion between the Devil and Saint Basil in which the Devil complained, "You Christians are perfidious, only when you have some need do you come to me."[4] Andrea correctly saw that the Devil complained because Christians worshipped Christ but came to him for aid; thus, from the Devil's perspective, Andrea as a Christian had to offer something more binding than a momentary prayer or sign of worship. The Devil made his point perfectly clear: "If you wish me to fulfill your desire, make me a contract in your own hand in which you confess to have renounced Christ . . . and in which you agree to be my servant."[5] That was exactly what Andrea did; an apprentice perfume maker of eighteen took his theology into his own hands and, as a result, ran afoul of the Holy Office of Venice.

Andrea's case reveals more than an instance of private theology; it also suggests a range of dangers that love posed for a Christian community and some reasons why the Holy Office of Venice became so concerned with disciplining what we might style that old black magic called love. First, of course, his passion had led him to literally sacrifice his body and soul. For a truly Christian society, that was the ultimate loss. But on a more direct practical level, the disruptive potential of such passion was of concern. Andrea was willing to sacrifice his soul to have his desire; what other, lesser crimes was he capable of? Obviously adultery; he hoped to lead a married woman astray, with the real danger that a marriage and a family would be broken as well. Moreover, Andrea did not ask merely for Paolina; he asked that she have no rest in body or spirit unless she was with him. In other words, he sought to bind her to him and punish her if she resisted. Thus Andrea's contract with the Devil threatened his salvation, his beloved, and some of the most basic institutions of society: marriage, the family, and the Church.

We may smile today at Andrea's encounter with that old black magic called love, but neither Church nor Venetian government were prepared to do so. As a result, the Holy Office was drawn ever deeper into investigating and disciplining such activity. In Andrea's case, however, his repentance mitigated his penalty. After a careful investigation, he was banished from Venetian territory for three years and ordered to recite an elaborate series of prayers every Friday for a year.[6] Actually, his case was rather anomalous. Young men were seldom brought before the Holy Office for such matters. More prevalent among the accused were women, often but not always accused of witchcraft, and ecclesiastics. One might assume that ecclesiastics approached love magic from a more learned tradition and that women represented a more popular tradition. But things were not so simple. Often, as the case of Andrea da Canal in Feltre suggests, clerics learned their magic from women. In turn, a surprising number of the women accused could read and write and were involved in passing on to other women a written as well as an oral culture. Still, a distinction does seem to hold: most male ecclesiastics appear to have been renegades on the edges of the mainstream of the Church, whereas the women involved represented a much broader range of society, although prosecutions (perhaps quite apart from practice) also focused on more marginal females. Moreover, in examining the cases of the Holy Office, it becomes clear that there was a highly articulated discourse concerned with magical power over love that was widely understood and practiced in late-sixteenth-century Venice, and that it was dominated by women and women's networks.

"For This Is My Body"

This brings us to the case of a very interesting woman, the courtesan Paolina di Rossi, and her friend, the priest and friar Felice di Bibona. Their encounter with the Holy Office of Venice in 1588 illustrates well the rich context of the magic of love and at the same time the picaresque complexity of love itself in late Renaissance life. Perhaps the best place to begin is with Paolina speaking for herself. "I am called Paola di Rossi the Venetian. I am married, but I have not lived with my husband for going on five years now. I left him because he felt I was a corrupt woman. . . . I know this priest called Don Felice as he was sent to my home during the last Carnival because he played the lute and sang."[7]

Although Paolina, as she was more generally known, did not go into detail about her life as a courtesan, it is apparent that one of her services was to entertain with dance and song. Don Felice had joined her small group of musicians during the previous carnival season in this context and become a regular acquaintance. Moving on, she was asked if Don Felice "had even thrown beans or committed other acts of witchcraft?"[8] Her reply admitted as little as possible. "I have never seen him throw beans or do other things associated with witches excepting on one occasion. . . . Just before Holy Week I was crying in my room . . . because a noble from the Giustinian family called Gian Battista had abandoned me . . . when Don Felice arrived, he asked me what was wrong. I told him that he saw me distraught because that gentleman had abandoned me."[9] Don Felice said soothingly, " 'If you wish, I will make you happy. . . .' Then he went and got me something wrapped in paper with writing on it which turned out to be the host. . . . On this host there was writing which he told me was the secret. When I saw this I became afraid and hid it in my sewing basket. [Later] I said to my maid Lucia, 'Look at what the priest gave me. He wanted me to give this to Giustinian to eat in his soup.' "[10] Paolina contened to explain that the magic of the host was too frightening to use and that she had decided to keep it hidden in her sewing basket, "even though the priest assured me that it was not a sin to give it to Giustinian."[11]

Others were prepared to testify, however, that Paolina had given the host to her servant to put in Gian Battista's food. Both the servant, Lucia, and a servant of Gian Battista's named Argenta were called to testify. Argenta explained to the Holy Office that one day "this Lucia came to me with a host and gave it to me saying that Paolina had given it to her to put in the broth of Gian Battista. . . . But Lucia gave it to me . . . and said, 'take it madonna Argenta as it will be good to give to your husband.' She said this because she knew that my husband did not want to stay with me."[12] The host passed through several other hands until finally Gian Battista's mother, learning of it, warned him about the love magic that his courtesan was trying to work on him.[13] This brought about the definitive break, with Gian Battista locking his mistress out of his house.

Paolina, however, continued to deny having given the host to her servant, insisting that she had seen immediately that it was a magic too dangerous to use. Her inquisitors changed their tack in the face of this firmness, returning to question her relationship with Don Felice. Asked if she had spoken with the priest in prison, she replied that she had. As she passed his cell, she admitted, he had asked her if she planned to confess. She replied that she would tell the "whole truth." Don Felice, she reported, threatened that he would claim "that she was lying through her throat"[14]—a straightforward-sounding jail conversation between people nervous about their fate. The court apparently took the conversation at face value and went on to other matters. Later they would realize that things were not that straightforward.

The court next asked Paolina if she had ever collected her menstrual blood in a sponge and given it to her servant to add to Giustinian's wine.[15] Aghast, Paolina replied no. Pressed, she remained firm in her denial. But her examiners continued with even more troubling questions: "Shortly before you were arrested, did you skin a bird backwards sticking two needles in the head from in front and two needles in the tail and then go into a dark room and begin to cast spells over the said bird so that the Devil spoke to you?"[16] Needless to say, Paolina denied this firmly under repeated questioning.

For Paolina, that old black magic called love was no laughing matter either. Her accusers, however, had hit on a number of the major themes of magic associated with love. The casting of beans was a staple in accusations of witchcraft, such a staple that one may assume that its meaning was understood by both inquisitors and common people. As a result, it appears to have been frequently included in cases as a reference that proved that one was involved in magic or in a nice reversal denied in such a way as to suggest that if one did not even understand casting beans, one could not possibly be involved with magic.[17] While accusations of using the host for magical purposes were less common, this fits nicely with a more general trend to use holy things to gain special power over others and especially bind their passions. From the host to menstrual blood seems a long jump, but for love the body was at least as important as the soul, and another significant range of magical practice was concerned with special aspects of the body that were seen as sexually significant. Much of this magic played on the perceived essential differences between men and women, and thus is revealing for the basic gender and sexual assumptions of society. And in all of these areas, words played a crucial activating role. It was almost as if the signing and metaphorical nature of language still had a deeper reality that could activate connections between things named. Finally, lurking behind much of this magic was another power, the most dangerous of all in the eyes of the Church and perhaps the most promising of all in the eyes of those fully committed to power over love and sexuality—the Devil.

Placing Don Felice's testimony in the context of late-sixteenth-century prosecutions of love magic provides a good first step toward understanding how such magic was perceived as working and what it meant. Testifying after Paolina, Don Felice described himself and his relationship to Paolina as follows: "I am called Don Felice di Bibona, being a Sicilian from Bibona. In the thirty-ninth year of my life, I am a priest and have been one for twelve years and I have been a monk for fifteen . . . I have known Paolina since last carnival. Frequently I have been in her house and eaten there. . . . Sometimes I sang and played the lute. I think that this Paolina may be a courtesan and as she asked me to write certain things for her there, I wrote them."[18]

His examiners immediately focused on his vague admission about writing something for Paolina. Pressed, Don Felice dropped back to narrate an encounter with two young prostitutes during carnival who had some special prayers and symbols written out that they had been using to bind the love of their customers. They had asked him if such things were licit, and he had replied rather weakly that they were not because they were holy things written in the vernacular. He continued, "Carrying those writings I went to the house of Paolina and falling into a discussion about such things that people used in order to be loved (*farsi voler bene*) . . . I told her that some people take sage leaves and write on them the secret of the Mass. Then they give them to eat to those whom they wish to love them. . . . Immediately Paolina began to suggest that she wanted me to write the secret on a leaf."[19]

One can imagine the attractiveness of such a recipe, especially for a courtesan; a leaf of sage in a lover's food, and his love would be bound. For Paolina, moreover, the timing was right, as at the moment her troubles with her lover seemed particularly trying. What better way to overcome them than use a little holy magic revealed to her by a priest, even a rather questionable priest who sang and played the lute with courtesans? Don Felice claimed to have attempted to convince Paolina to forget about such magic, but faced with her continued pleading, "Finally I suggested that the said leaves of sage were not very practical and that instead one could write on the host itself. . . . I wrote those five words that consecrate the host [*Hoc est enim corpus meum*] but without the intention to consecrate it; nor did I say those words out loud, nor did I even have faith in the deed . . . and I said to her that she would be my ruin."[20] He also warned, "You ought not to do this, but if you do, do it by yourself and do not have your servant do it. For in that case there will be greater scandal than you might imagine."[21] It was a warning that, if followed, might well have avoided the travails that awaited them both.

How this host was to bind the love of her noble is not stated, but it is apparent that, eaten by Giustinian, the power of the central mystery of the Mass would be redirected to secure Paolina's desires. Don Felice's denials that he had said the words required to consecrate the host or that he had actually intended to consecrate it merely underline the point: the power of the Church could be adapted to other, more secular ends magically. Could it be that "for this is my body" written on the host could have been meant to refer to Paolina's body as well as Christ's? If this were the case, we would have an interesting form of metaphor typical of much love magic. As the consecrated host became the body of Christ that ingested cemented love for God in the communicant, so too the host consecrated by Don Felice became the body of Paolina and cemented Gian Battista's love for her by being ingested by him.[22]

Consecrated hosts with the words of the secret written on them are found in other cases, but explanations of why this magic worked were neither offered by those examined nor sought by the Inquisition. A somewhat simpler reading is suggested, however, by a written prayer used in love magic discovered in a young woman's possession in 1590. This prayer began: "I do not see you nor do you see me [just as we do not see] the sacred blood and body of Jesus Christ that is made sacramentally by the hands of all priests. I send it by messenger to your heart so that your every annoyance with me is changed to peace and love for me and so that you are bound to love me just as in this most holy sacrament the bread and wine are changed into the flesh and blood . . . thus I wish that your dislike and unhappiness change into love of me."[23] Here the relationship between lovers who have quarreled perhaps and "do not see each other" is first paralleled with the consecration of the host, where the flesh and blood are similarly not seen. Then, more pertinently, the change that is to be wrought in the heart of the beloved is paralleled to the change wrought in the bread and wine as it is transformed into the flesh and blood of Christ.

Here evidently we see a transformation of something not particularly useful from a religious point of view—bread and wine—into something central—the body and blood of Christ. The prayer calls for a similar transformation from something not desired—the annoyance and enmity of the beloved—to something very much wanted—peace and love. As one change occurs miraculously, so the other is called for. This type of paralleling of things in the form "as such and such happens (often something holy) so should this happen" is very typical of love magic, as we will see. But this was merely a prayer, not an explanation of how the host was actually believed to work its binding magic. Nonetheless, it is at least evident that here holy things were being given a broader meaning in ways that both troubled the Church and ultimately revealed a profound respect for its power, especially in terms of its sacrament of the Eucharist and its deepest mysteries.

The Spiritual Dimensions of Love Magic

Both the host and sage inscribed with the secret are encountered in other cases, but they were only one small facet of the complex use of the holy to magically bind the love of others. Perhaps the most popular form of such magic was the use of holy oil. In fact, it had myriad magical uses that went well beyond love. For example, there appears to have been a long tradition of using holy oil to treat illness by women healers, especially childhood diseases.[24] But to bind the love of another, holy oil was adopted usually in one of two ways, either to touch the person to be bound or to kiss that person. The results were often impressive. People so treated were reported to have fallen completely and permanently in love, and as we shall see, one prostitute noted with eminent practicality that while men bound in this manner could love no other, the woman who administered the holy oil was in no way bound.[25]

The case of a certain Julia, daughter of a boatman, is exemplary. Eighteen years old, she was described as living on her own, "being physically large with a rather big nose and a slightly yellow face."[26] It was also strongly suggested that she was a prostitute or at least a young woman forced by her economic situation to sell her favors occasionally. But Julia wanted to escape this situation and saw marriage as her best opportunity. Thus one evening when the priest, Paolo Amici, was taken by a friend of his, who was one of Julia's lovers, to visit her, he found himself in a troubling situation. Visiting a woman of questionable reputation was no problem for the priest. Paolo treated visiting his friend's mistress as a matter of absolutely no concern in his testimony before the Holy Office—an indifference apparently shared by the clerics who heard his testimony.

But a curious coincidence led to more troubling events that evening. For as they talked, Paolo recognized the young woman of eighteen as a neighborhood youngster whom he had known as a child. She recognized him as well, and an immediate bond sprang up between them. In fact, she asked to have a few words with him in private. Ever correct, Paolo asked and secured his friend's permission to do so and withdrew with her into a private room. There he reported, "She said to me that she wanted to reveal a secret, but that I must not tell it to anyone not even to Messer Antonio [her lover and his friend]. I said 'Go ahead and tell me.' She then opened a chest that was near the balcony . . . took out a box and opening it she showed me a small bottle . . . asking 'Oh dear Monsignor, please look at this and tell me if it is holy oil. . . . It was given to me by a midwife who treats sick children. I paid her a *scudo* for it.'" Paolo continued to explain: "She said . . . that she wanted it for one of her lovers so that he would love her and that that midwife had taught her that touching her lover with that oil he would take her for his wife. I told her that I did not believe that this could be holy oil because not just anyone could put their hands on it."[27] On the availability of holy oil he appears to have been mistaken. It pops up regularly in love magic, being bought, sold, and used primarily by women and priests. And, of course, Paolo was concerned enough about the matter to break his promise to his childhood friend and inform the Holy Office.

Although for some a mere touch with holy oil was enough, the preferred method was the kiss. A friend of another courtesan, Angela Salo, reported to the Holy Office, "This Angela . . . showed Zanetta and me a small bottle with oil in it which was stopped up with cloth that had absorbed most of the oil. To my question about what it was, she replied that it was holy oil that had been given to her by a woman . . . and she explained that if one went to bed with a man and if one had oiled her lips with it and kissed the man then he would have so much affection for her that he would take her for his wife."[28] Holy oil had a particularly attractive side effect, as was noted by another prostitute: "If one wished to oil one's body with this [holy oil] and then have sexual intercourse with one's man . . . he would not be able to leave ever, but one would be perfectly able to leave him."[29] This certainly was useful for prostitutes who wanted to bind to themselves the passions of a regular clientele, and it seems to have been a fairly regular part of their practice, as was a wide range of other love magic. But the use of holy oil was ubiquitous; it was used by wives to hold their husbands and their lovers, as well as by women seeking to marry.

Many other things of the Church were loaded with enough spiritual power in the popular mind to serve for love magic; most common among them were holy water, often taken from specific churches, and blessed candles. In the use of both, however, the magic had a tendency to move beyond adapting Church power to bind passions toward reversing and thus denying that power in order to secure the support of the Devil or his minions for similar ends. As in the case of Andrea Meri's contract, for some the Devil and his allies seemed to offer a promising range of powers. Given a Christian vision that saw the world as essentially corrupt and evil, it was not difficult to go a step further and accept the Devil as the real power in this world. God's power was impressive but irregular; the daily triumph of evil in this world was visible to all and even proclaimed by the Church.

Significantly, most used the power of the Church and the Devil in a more eclectic manner. For them the conflict between absolute good and absolute evil was less meaningful than the search for power over love and the passions wherever it could be found. Thus, they ranged widely across the powers they perceived in the world without necessarily feeling the need to recognize one as absolute. This world was awash with conflicting fields of power; there was no need (beyond perhaps the logic of high theology and the Inquisition) to limit oneself to only one. Paolina's case is exemplary: she was accused of conjuring the Devil with her reverse skinning of a bird at the same time that she was accused of attempting to adapt the power of the central mystery of the Church to hold her lover by feeding him a consecrated host to bind his love.

In fact, the Holy Office often found itself involved in convincing the accused that they were rejecting Christ in accepting the Devil—that is, explaining to people that they must choose between the two. The long, complex case against Isabella Bellocchio is especially revealing in this context. A courtesan as well as a powerful woman with important friends (she regularly ate with friends while held in the Holy Office's jail and even received a proposal of marriage from one of her noble lovers while there), Isabella nonetheless eventually confessed to practicing a wide range of magic in order to win and at times free herself from the love of a young man named Milano. Among other things, she lighted a holy lamp before a tarot card with a Devil on it, boiled holy water in a new pan, prepared a magical potion to put on the door sill of a rival, put salt under the coals of the fire while saying special prayers, buried an enchanted egg, touched Jews with pork in the Ghetto, cast beans, measured cords, and threw chains. Clearly, her magic was nothing if not eclectic.

But her lighting of a holy lamp before a picture of the Devil on a tarot card seriously troubled her inquisitors. They returned repeatedly to the matter, trying to force her to admit its implication—that she had worshipped the Devil and rejected Christ. The give-and-take of her testimony is most suggestive. Her interrogators asked, "To what end did you light that holy lamp before the tarot card?"[30] She replied, "So that Milano [her lover] would come to me, that was my intention that he come." They pressed: "Tell us clearly who made this Milano come." She answered. "Because I lit this lamp before the Devil, in this way Milano would have to come." Trying to close their logical trap, the inquisitors concluded, "You should decide to explain who would make this Milano come and your true intentions in lighting this lamp and if you lit it to honor and pray to the Devil so that he would make the said Milano come."

Perhaps cleverly, Isabella sidestepped the inquisitors' logic. Yet her testimony suggests that she did not see the matter in as dialectical terms as they. "I never understood," she claimed, "that one had to pray to or honor the Devil but only that one must light a lamp to him in order to have that which one desired, that is in this case my lover. Thus I did not light it with the intention of worshipping or praying to him, but with the intention that my lover be made to come." She conceded immediately, however, "I did light it for evil." But this admission did not mean for Isabella that she had rejected Christ for the Devil. "I lighted the lamp before the Devil because I had the will to honor him so that he would make Milano come to me, *but for only this fact and not for any other.* [italics mine]. For if I had intended to honor him in other ways I would not have gone to Mass, nor would I have said other special prayers of mine."[31]

Honor the Devil for that which is the Devil's seems to have been Isabella's logic. But she saw that the Church had its powers as well, and a wise person did not sacrifice the one for the other. In the text Andrea Meri showed to the Holy Office discussed earlier, the Devil put his finger on just this type of eclecticism when he complained that Christians, when they found that their religion could not give them what they wanted, came to him. Yet they remained Christians and were ready to desert him as soon as they secured their desires. In this context, it is interesting to consider for a moment the old paradigm that sees magic as power for the powerless and suggest a slightly more complex reading of the situation, at least in the late Renaissance. Noting that this type of eclecticism was more popular among women and the lower classes, we might consider that magic was a complex and creative way of encountering the world that allowed the cultivation of other ignored powers to be found there by those unwilling to accept the marginality assigned them by social and political conventions. In turn, this creativity underlines a truism concerning the position of both women and the lower classes in Renaissance society: a lack of access to more apparently regular channels of power that made some willing to seek power outside those channels and take it wherever it could be found. Significant in this context was a whole other range of love magic concerned with the domestic sphere, where hearth, kitchen utensils, doorsill, stairs, and bed took on special deeper meanings—as if women had discoverd the deeper powers in the world assigned to them.

But to return to honoring the Devil for what is the Devil's, it should be noted that seeking the Devil's aid in matters of passion was an endeavor that had been aided by the Church's own vision of sexuality. As the Church's position that much if not all sexual passion was the work of the Devil became a more general view, it was a logical conclusion that those who wished to have power over the sexual should work with the Devil. In everyday life, people remained committed to honoring both the body and the soul, but as power over one appeared to be the Devil's and power over the other God's, it was logical that Isabella and others felt they could honor each in his area of competence.

Still, to give the Church its due, Isabella demonstrated an inconsistency in using holy things and the Devil's aid for the same ends. Such inconsistency lends itself to easy accusations about the naïveté and shallowness of popular culture. Reflections of this sort, however, at times suggest more a cultural bias toward tightly structured metaphysical systems of thought than a realistic appreciation for the rich and eclectic creativity of popular cultures that must explain the complex, apparent illogic of everyday life. The latter may lack the aesthetic symmetry of metaphysics, but they do not lack for complexity or beauty, often offering what might be labeled a poetics of the everyday. The point is simply that metaphysical systems that can transcend or ignore quotidian contingencies can afford the luxury of tight structure and achieve the aesthetic of a perfect symmetry. Systems that must deal with the everyday, however, can be tightly structured only at the expense of being applicable.[32]

If we view the magic of love from the perspective of perceptions of power, it is perhaps best to speak in terms of a range of visions that swing from the highly eclectic to the highly structured. At the pole of the highly eclectic I would place most of the everyday people who turned to such magic to help them in their love life; both Paolina and Isabella seem to fall into this category. At the other pole would fall the ecclesiastics of the Holy Office, who, with their much more structured vision, were trying to impose a tighter Christian logic on the situation. For them, Isabella had to worship the Devil and reject the Church because she burned a candle before a tarot card, but to give Isabella her due, we might well sacrifice the musical ring of our title to call this chapter "That Old Gray Magic Called Love." It does appear, however, that there were a few people like Andrea Meri who had decided consciously to reject Christ in order to align with the Devil, but obviously those actually committed to such a course are most difficult to identify in the records of the Inquisition. They had too much to lose before such tribunals to admit their alliance with the Devil, and the court's constant attempt to force those who practiced love magic into such a dialectical mold further confuses the issue.

Even Andrea Meri was not a good example of this latter type, as it appears that his flirtation with the Devil was merely a passing fancy. We might hypothesize, however, that those who had truly rejected Christ and the Church to follow the Devil in order to sustain their systematic vision had to be the most alienated from the everyday order of things and perhaps the most committed to their way of life. Such people, living more on their own and sustained by their beliefs, rather like intellectuals and clerics, could create a more structured world beyond the chaos of everyday life where they could exist with their more ordered and dialectically pure culture. But the price that had to be paid for this was a considerable alienation from the main points of reference of late Renaissance society: family, Church, neighborhood, and/or village. If this hypothesis is correct, a more systematic study, looking for such an underlying structure in testimony behind the structure imposed by the Inquisition's questions, might reveal those truly committed to the Devil if they existed. In fact, in love magic prosecutions there appear to be very few who fit this model.

The Word and the Carta di Voler Bene

In no other area is the eclectic mix of the divine and the diabolic more evident than in the use of the *carta di voler bene*. This little-discussed but very popular type of magic involved anything from an apparently simple prayer written on a piece of paper to elaborate concoctions of signs and spells covering several pages. Their use, however, was simple; like holy oil, they were used to touch the person desired, in that way binding his or her love. When Don Felice referred to the written prayers in the vernacular that the young prostitutes had shown him, it appears that these were *carte di voler bene*. Although he never explicitly called them by any name, it was in this context that he moved on to describe to Paolina easier ways to bind love.

"Oh Lord Jesus, oh you who with great wisdom created the world and came into it where with great suffering you were persecuted to such an extent by the Jews that you were tortured and crucified. Lord Jesus, I ask you humbly in my great suffering, unhappiness, sadness, and tribulations that you help me."[33] So begins the *carta di voler bene* found in a chest left behind by a certain Girolama in 1589. It seems that Girolama had been a prostitute who had secured a promise of marriage from one of her lovers, just what the *carta di voler bene* was supposed to provide. But the *carta*'s power broke down when her lover was informed by neighbors that Girolama was continuing her profession behind his back. He asked her to leave his house. Later, going through a chest that she had left behind, he claimed to have found this *carta* and had come to fear that his love had been bound by his ex-lover.

The beginning of Girolama's reputed *carta* could be hardly more humble and prayerlike, but the text moves on to mix the sacred and the profane, asking that Christ force "my lover to love me with good heart and love me as much as the love of his own eyes. Moreover all those people who would get in the way or cause problems or annoy me are with your powers to be destroyed Lord as you punished Adam and Eve."[34] From lauding the power and suffering of the Lord, to asking for the binding of the love of another, to violence toward one's enemies, the *carta* swings from humble reverence to vindictive violence. Yet in a way, it also swings across a perfectly logical continuum of perceived divine powers, as the *carta* explicitly states that God's powers include creation, his own existence and suffering as a man, and his judgment and punishment of sinners. In this last punishing aspect, typical of most *carte*, it had close affinities with other forms of magical prayers and writings not necessarily associated with love that called for the suffering or destruction of enemies. Testimony often speaks of those who had been hammered (*martellato*) or who had suffered a hammer (*un martello*). These could be inflicted in any number of ways, but often prayerlike words were considered enough. And the results could be quite effective, as the rather pathetic testimony of a number of hammered people vividly attests.[35] Most *carte* included this punishing demand along with the central binding prayer.

Girolama's *carta* also sought God's help in binding her lover to her in the name of a wide range of powers, again suggesting the eclectic nature of most love magic. Invoked, among other things, were the sciences of the world, philosophy, astrology, the grammatical science of Priscian, the holy martyrs, Saint John the Baptist, Saint John, Saint Joseph, the angels of heaven, Saint Michael, Gabriel, the wisdom of Solomon, the holy days of Abraham and Jacob, the law of Moses, the Cross, those priests who say the Mass, the body of Christ, the Mass at Christmas, the profession of faith at Easter, and the Virgin Mary. Behind what may appear at first merely a shopping list of things holy, there seems to be a certain logic. God's power is multifaceted and very present in this world; the macrocosm is ever present in the microcosm. God's power infuses and in a way en-forms the world through the human sciences, through his martyrs and angels, through his holy calender and time, through his Church and its rituals, and, of course, through his human mother/wife. Simply put, God is not a distant abstraction but a powerful figure intimately involved in the world, so much so that even in the logical paradoxes that grow out of that involvement (God as both son and husband of Mary, for example), his great power is confirmed. And significantly for the *carta*, as well as for much other magic, that range of involvement also implies a host of power relationships that can be turned to the purposes of those who understand.

The fact that such *carte* often had a strong theological and learned dimension meant that it was an area where the higher culture of the written word and the educated priest potentially intersected with a more popular one. Girolama claimed that she could not even read her *carta*. She had bought it on faith from a man who guaranteed its efficacy. But that was not always the case, and a surprising number of the women brought before the Holy Office admitted that they could read and write. As we saw in Chapter 1, for example, Cassandra Lizzari, a young prostitute of about nineteen accused of writing out *carte di voler bene* to bind the love of others, proudly claimed that she had read widely, including Petrarch, *Orlando Furioso,* and *The Lives of the Saints,* and that she had written sonnets as well. Beyond the abilities of Cassandra and other women, however, the written nature of these *carte* and their wide use suggest a certain unexpected utilitarian purpose in being able to read and write.[36] A host of women, including a goodly number of prostitutes, wrote or copied *carte,* and still others were busily involved in reproducing and selling this aspect of a small world of written culture that was very significant for love and power.

Once again, such *carte* were not adverse to calling on the aid of the Devil as well as God. In one complex example found in the possession of a priest, apparently designed to bind males because of its references to the phallus of the beloved, part of the invocation called on the Devils of hell. Following more than a page of elaborate lauding of God and asking for his aid, the *carta* abruptly changed direction. "I cast a spell on you N. to bind your love by all the Devils who are within and outside of Hell. . . . I bind all your members, your hair, your head, your eyes and nose, your mouth, your heart and especially your phallus."[37] But interestingly, it then went on to attempt to force the aid of the forces of evil by holy means. "I cast a spell on you all the Spirits of Hell for the lance, for the crown of thorns, for the evil and vinagrous drink, for the cruel death, for the seven words which our Lord said as he was hanging on the wood of the Holy Cross and for the sweat of blood and for those sharp spines which pierced his precious head and for the merits of his Holy Passion that you Devils ought to ignite and place every evil and discord among those who speak evilly of me."[38] Theologically, one might even argue that such use of the Devil was relatively correct, as it was divine power that forced the Devil's aid. But once more, the power mobilized was highly eclectic, as was the case in most *carte*.

Clearly, such *carte di voler bene* were far more complex in form than Don Felice's attempt to write the words of the secret on a host. Yet they shared a common purpose: to bind or tie love. The victims of such magic shared this vision, often referring to their problems as stemming from having been "bound" or "tied." The cases heard by the Holy Office confirm that this was a general vision: victims, accused, witnesses, and inquisitors shared at least this common understanding—certain words could literally bind. Moreover, they could bind in the most basic and aggressive ways, not just women and men, but also devils and spirits and, with a curious anthropomorphism perhaps seldom clearly faced, God as well.

This power of words, largely forgotten today, appears to have been for the premodern period an immense and complex subject that ranged far beyond Don Felice and Paolina's love magic. Still, some suggestions emerge from looking more closely at what the language of this binding magic seems to imply, whether in *carte di voler bene* or in prayerlike incantations. First, clearly the emphasis on the prayer in the Christian tradition (an emphasis that was undergoing a revival at the end of the sixteenth century) had given the word special weight, especially in everyday life. It may have been that in a strictly correct theological vision, words in prayer merely helped one gain the grace of God, his holy family, or the saints—quite an accomplishment in itself. But in the everyday world, when prayers worked, their words seemed to secure action, the action of the divine in that world. That was, after all, a central motivation of prayer. And outside the strict confines of high theology, their words could be seen as powerful for securing a wide range of goals, including love, sex, and hammering.

Moreover, in ritual situations, as exemplified by the Mass, prayerlike words seemed even more potent, as Girolama's *carta*, with its call on the powers of the priests who say Mass, suggests. The priest's words seemed to literally command (we might even say "bind" in a sense very similar to the binding of the *carte di voler bene*) the presence of the Holy Spirit in church. And, of course, at the center of the mystery of the Mass, the priest's words seemed to command the miraculous transformation of bread and wine into Christ's body and blood; they seemed to command God himself to become incarnate. If words could do that, there was nothing that they could not do. That appears to have still been a general vision of the late sixteenth century. And, if anything, the reforms of

Trent, with their emphasis on a verbal Church—catechism, regular at-
tendance at Mass, and a heightened stress on prayers and the rosary (and
a certain deemphasis on Augustinian grace that tended to undermine the
significance of human words)—may have actually accentuated the importance of words.

An ever broader diffusion of the printed word almost certainly was
significant in this as well. In fact, it might be argued and has been argued
that the increased familiarity with written words that printing allowed
undercut the word's special status, making it everyday and literally
mundane. Over the long run this may have been true. But in the sixteenth century, things seem more complex. Magic suggests this, and the
explosion of interest in disciplining words over the century suggests even
more. Among other attempts at disciplining words, especially revealing
are the extremely popular manuals of behavior and manners that gave
high priority to the correct "mannered" use of words; a concomitant
heightened emphasis on the honor dynamics of words; new civic magis-
tracies concerned with the control of words, both swearing (*bestemmia*)
and potentially violent words such as insults; and civic and ecclesiastical
efforts to censor printed words. Only the last was entirely new, but it is
clear that in all these areas the sixteenth century in Italy saw a heightened emphasis on the significance of words. In this whole complex,
perhaps the most important aspect from an elite perspective was the
continued concern with honor in a society increasingly aristocratic.
Honor, of course, was measured by deeds and blood, but it was displayed and evaluated verbally; thus the emphasis on the man who could
speak well, modestly, and with moderation. Family, deeds, money, even
clothing made the man, but the word revealed and measured him. And
at lesser social levels words did much the same, evaluating neighbors
and demarking, as we have seen with Lucretia in Feltre, the good people
from the bad. In a highly verbal society, faith in the word was easy and
reinforced at many levels.

But limiting our discussion to magic, it reveals a range of powers
implicit in the word that was rich and diverse. Returning first to the
words of prayer, crucially such words seemed to somehow link man and
God—the macrocosm and the microcosm. Again there was a theological
explanation that dealt with this linking, as well as complex ancillary
issues such as the relationship between grace, divine omniscience, and
the words of an ordinary person. While Luther rejected that theology in
order to construct or reconstruct another in its place, many everyday
people, it appears, had already opted for other interpretations. A more
popular faith in the efficacy of prayer and the closeness of God almost
certainly lay behind many of the incantations of love magic. One important way of invoking that faith was in forming an incantation in the
same way as a prayer, as if giving words the form of a prayer gave them
the same efficacy as a prayer. In fact, the term *oratione* was often used by

both the Inquisition and those who practiced love magic to label both prayer and the words used for the spells of love magic.

Such interconnections are further suggested by the range of prayerlike incantations used for love magic that seemed to span a continuum that stretched from humble pleas for aid to binding and hammering prayers that forced even God to act. At one end of the scale, many incantations began with a humble invocation of Christ or the Virgin and ended in a similar fashion, even concluding with an "Amen." As such they were little more than specialized prayers that might be criticized only for the ends they sought. Yet even at that level things could be unclear, for it could be very difficult to draw the line between a prayer that asked for a love that would end in marriage and a family and any other prayer. A small step beyond lay the very popular use of regular prayers such as the "Our Father" or the "Hail Mary" with a word or two changed to help secure amorous ends. Also very common and perhaps even less theologically incorrect were the patterned repetitions of prayers, where the pattern was seen as giving extra significance and power to the prayer—not unlike the patterned style of the rosary. At the other end of this continuum would lie specially constructed prayers that bound love and hammered the reluctant or sought to force God, Mary, saints, or angels to aid in such endeavors. And clearly beyond that continuum, but with very similar forms, lay those prayers that called on the Devil or the forces of darkness.

Within prayer, however, certain verbal structures seemed to have been particularly important. First, there was the invocation of aid, which usually made reference to the superior power of God, saints, spirits, demons, or the Devil and, in the case of God, often focused on his commitment to use his power in this world and his voluntary suffering as a man to do so. The verbal acknowledgment of power by those seeking aid from important people is a frequent ritual of power between humans, and between humans and their gods. Such verbal acknowledgments in the Renaissance tended to *honor* the transcendent or the superior person—again revealing the ubiquity of honor dynamics—by acknowledging his superiority and explicitly or implicitly accepting a subservient status as the person seeking aid. But suggestively, the acceptance of subservience seems to have been perceived as virtually forcing the support of the superior power. This was because power was to a great extent determined by relationships; in other words, it was less something imposed from above than a reciprocal set of generally accepted relationships whose web tied all who fell within its bounds to certain obligations, even lords and the Lord. Being below meant being protected from above. Thus, in a way, we might say that the power claimed by such prayers was based upon the rewards due to subservience, the givens of acknowledging one's place in a hierarchical society and cosmos. While mere lords and patrons might overlook this natural order of things, the Renaissance master of words may well have been much more optimistic about the true lord and his holy pantheon responding correctly.

Equally complex are what might be called "metaphors of power" that figure so frequently in incantations. "I bind and pierce the hands and feet of you N. with my love just as were bound the holy hands and feet of Our Lord Jesus Christ so that you cannot love another person in the world excepting M." The form at its most simple is: as such and such happened, so should the thing desired happen; thus in the above, as Christ was bound, so should the beloved be bound. Lying behind that surface metaphor, however, there seems to be a deeper set of resonances, virtually a poetics of divine power and human, for, of course, Christ allowed himself to suffer these things for love, and love is explicitly named as the driving force of the other half of the equation as well. Another salient feature of this form is that the metaphor is usually drawn between normal events in the physical world of everyday life and events with a transcendental significance, that is, events that concern Christ, biblical figures, the saints, the Church, or the Devil and his troop of fallen angels. Thus such metaphors also seem to have worked by verbally evoking at one level another higher and more powerful one, finding, as it were, the power of the macrocosm in its reflections in the microcosm. In this there appears to be a typically realist perspective in the classic sense: reality is a hierarchy where words are superior to the things they name, and words that name the crucial transcendent things are even more superior. Thus by saying true words, words that truly name and thus correspond to the very nature of things, one can draw the power of those words and things down into their more humble re-evocations in the everyday world of human love and power. This was the real power of metaphors and words, a power that modern science and, in a way, a much simpler perception of the order of things have largely delegitimated.

Thus the very naming of the binding of Christ above, the ultimate binding, evoked a parallel binding of the beloved at the level of the everyday, verbally and actually. It seems, however, that the prayer format takes the metaphor a step further, almost seeming to bind God or the power invoked to action, as noted earlier. It might be asked if magicians believed that such metaphors actually bound God or the Devil to act in their behalf. In the end, there is probably no one answer to this query. Yet on one level, the most significant aspect of God's creation and the order of things was that it was chock-a-block with metaphors that revealed the myriad connections between the macrocosm and the microcosm, between the one and the many, between the transcendent and the everyday, between God and man—metaphors that were truly powerful and made the poetics of everyday life extremely significant. Some of the stronger incantations, where the verbal metaphors of power are carefully and aggressively structured, seem to imply just such a binding. They seem to posit a God who is a powerful force to be manipulated, much like any other in a hierarchy of reciprocal power obligations where worship, honor, and deference obligate or at least imply reciprocity. Less forceful incantations tend to emphasize more the traditional invoking or requesting of aid.

Yet another verbal form of such prayers is what might be labeled a "transfer of accrued power." On the surface, this form seems quite simple and rather naive. It asks for power in the name of some superior thing, usually again associated with the holy: "for the lance, for the crown of thorns, for the evil and vinagrous drink, for the cruel death, for the seven words our Lord said as he was hanging on the wood of the Holy Cross, and for the sweat of blood and for those sharp spines that pierced his precious head and for the merits of his holy passion," it is asked that the intended victim be bound in love. The form, then, seems to have implied that in the naming of certain profoundly important holy events, the power accrued through the naming of those true names could be transferred to accomplish other tasks.

Looking more closely, it is suggestive that the great majority of these transfers turn on the suffering of God. A few do focus on divine triumphs, but it seems that God's suffering was perceived as much more potent in pooling spiritual power for the practitioners of love magic. Perhaps miraculous triumph seemed too easy for God and too abstract as well; God's truly impressive spiritual power was made manifest in his voluntary suffering for humanity. Most powerfully, there God had shown his love for humanity, and there almost irresistibly the masters of love felt drawn to Christ's suffering. Again the using of this to bind lovers should not distract us from the fact that the basic vision here was a strong testimony to the underlying strength of the basic Christian vision. In focusing on Christ's suffering for humanity, magicians had incorporated into their magic one of the central mysteries of the faith. Christianity had become with time certainly a more intellectual and aristocratic religion than that of a humble carpenter-savior and his fishermen disciples, but in a popular context it was still perceived as a religion where God had suffered (just like everyday people) and died in this world for even the most common person, and ultimately the power accrued by that suffering could be drawn upon when truly named to influence and perhaps control the more common world of love as well.

In sum the wide range of love magic based upon the power of the divine implicitly reveals the triumph of a basic Christian vision in society. It may not have been the Christianity of Church theologians, but it was a vital, complex religion that intersected with daily life immediately and, in the case of love magic, one might truly say intimately. In that popular religion, the divine was close and the central events of the first time of Christianity were immediate and familiar. But perhaps most important, these things of religion and the relationships they implied between the human and the divine were ripe with power for life. As Christ had shown on the cross and as priests showed regularly in the Mass for God, *carne vale,* the flesh mattered, and it was intimately interconnected with the spirit. In that world, rather than in the dialectical opposites of the intellectuals of the Church and the Holy Office, there existed a much more fluid situation where flesh slid into spirit and spirit into flesh; where the powers of good slid into evil and evil into good; where true words slid into things of power and things of power slid into true words; where suffering became power and power overcame suffering; where God became man and, in a way, man became God. Truly a poetics of the everyday.

Domestic Love Magic and Spatial Relationships

But Paolina di Rossi's encounter with the Holy Office reveals that there was considerably more to the eclectic range of powers that the masters of love could draw upon. Beyond denying that she had attempted to bind her lover using a host with the words of the secret written on it, she also categorically denied casting beans. Don Felice, however, in his first testimony was forced by the evidence presented to take a rather different tack and eventually confessed that Paolina had thrown beans to help him. The context of his confession is interesting, as again it calls up images of a group of priests and friars who lived a more open life than one might have expected in the age of reform following Trent. He was asked if he had ever thrown beans. "Never," he replied. "I know as much about this as about a pig." But the Holy Office was not put off by his bluff. The inquisitors continued: "have you ever had in your possession the beans which are used for throwing?" It may have been that Don Felice was aware that his house had been searched, or it may have been that, as was often the case, one of the minions of the Holy Office had begun to put out some of the evidence that had been gathered against him, for he quickly changed tack, attempting to undercut the case that was being built against him. "In my house," he admitted, "I had two packs of cards, with which one gambles and I kept beans as counters. I played cards with a countryman of mine called Alessandro Siciliano for eight, ten *soldi.* ''[39]

An explanation of sorts and to a degree a clever one, for by admitting the relatively small sin of gambling, Don Felice may have hoped to distract his examiners from their line of inquiry. But the Holy Office was interested in beans, not gambling, and they pressed on, showing him "eighteen beans with a piece of coal, a coin with wax on it, a stone with some [rock] salt and a piece of bread," all wrapped in a piece of paper. They were slowly boxing him in with their evidence, but Don Felice made one last attempt to escape the implications of those eighteen beans wrapped up with other suspicious materials not suited for gambling. "These were in my house," he confessed. "I kept them there where there were the cards and the rest, bound together in this way and it may have been that they were kept wrapped in this paper."[40]

Relentlessly, his interrogators continued. "For what reason did you keep those beans together wrapped up?" That was the problem; beans as gambling counters were not usually kept apart, and they were certainly not kept bound together with pieces of bread, coal, and other objects typically used by those who cast beans. Although Don Felice claimed to know no more about beans than about a pig, both he and his examiners were aware that eighteen beans were often the number used when beans were being cast for magical purposes; in fact, the whole ensemble of materials found wrapped together in his house was fairly standard. Thus Don Felice switched tactics once again and dropped back in his story to explain how he and Paolina had used the beans. "One night," he began, "leaving the house of this Paolina I was assaulted by three men. To find out who had attacked me Paolina gave me these beans bound together. This was so that I could find out who had wounded me. I had two wounds. Paolina threw the beans two times and she told me that they were people who ate and drank with me." He also admitted that there had been another woman, "who was about thirty-six years old who came and cast the beans in the house of Paolina several times. For me she cast them two times, but later she cast them several times for Paolina in relationship to her lovers. Her lovers are Il Giustinian and Il Cremona, at least as far as I know. After we threw the beans at Paolina's house, I took them to my house."[41]

Finally, Don Felice had provided a description of the use of beans. Although apparently some believed that beans could also be used to bind love, in most cases they were used to gauge how people related to each other, especially in terms of friendship and love. Don Felice's attackers or Paolina's lovers: the beans revealed their closeness/love or their distance/hate. The method was frequently explained in the records of the Inquisition. For example, in the case of Isabella Bellocchio, already discussed, she confessed to casting beans in the context of a general magical program of trying to win back the love of her ex-lover Milano. "The reason I did these things was so that this Milano would return to me. Actually I threw the beans to see if he was close to me or not. For this I marked two of the beans, which denoted him and me. Then casting them from my hand, if the two beans were close, it was a sign that he was close to me; if far apart, it was a sign that he was far away from me."[42] Suggestively, Isabella's account of how casting beans worked reveals once again the underlying power of a metaphorical way of viewing the world, but in this case based more on space than on words and with no power implied: as marked bean related in space to marked bean, so the person denoted by one bean related emotionally to the person denoted by the other. Yet words were involved and gave a certain added strength to the metaphor, for the same words were used to describe the physical relationship of the beans and the emotional relationship of the people represented by the beans. *Arente* meant close both in the physical and the emotional sense in Isabella's description of what she was doing, and *lontano* meant far in both senses as well. Thus spatial relationships served as a true metaphor for emotional ones and provided a sign of love or hate.

Isabella's signing beans calls to mind a line from Italo Calvino. In his *Cosmicomics*, he tells a series of playfully metaphysical fables about amorphous personalities who experienced the founding and development of a universe reminiscent of our own. In one of the most suggestive tales, Calvino describes the trials of perhaps the first intellectual. Swinging endlessly through space at the end of a spiral arm of a galaxy, this ur-thinker decided to leave a sign in space to mark his passing, which he would then reencounter a few million years later when he swung by again. But after his long wait, when he returned to the spot, he found that someone had erased his original sign and replaced it with another, which he, true to future intellectuals, found much inferior to his own. This then began a long and emotionally trying war of signs, the ins and outs of which provide a sly commentary on the battles of semiotics. But in the end, the first signer came to realize an important point for love magic in general and the magic of beans: "Slowly as the ages passed living among signs had led to seeing as signs the infinity of things that in the beginning were merely there without marking anything but their own existence."[43] That is what seems to have happened with beans and their relational significance. They reflected an everyday world superinfused with signs and meanings that regularly could be lined up in metaphorical relationships that revealed deeper significances or transferred power from the higher to the lower. The question remains, however: why beans? With the divine or the diabolical, significant associations are relatively easy, as they are widely credited with deep meaning and power and their cultural significations are broad-ranging and rich. But beans, coal, bread, small coins, and rock salt thrown together seem a priori to be on quite another level than God or the Devil.[44]

Beans stand out here. In the popular mind and in the Inquisition's investigation, the casting of beans is the focus of description and naming. Perhaps at one level it was the simple ordinariness of the bean that made its signing potential so rich; its magical properties are encountered in societies from the ancient to the modern. As a basic staple of daily domestic life, it was a sign waiting to be given significance by any passing intelligence, as in Calvino's tale, and the intelligences that passed were myriad and regular. In this context, it is noteworthy that quite a few other everyday items of the domestic sphere had also taken on magical significance. The most similar in appearance was the throwing of chains, when specified, often a chain from the hearth where meals were cooked. The process was again relational and metaphorical. Links in the chain were designated as people, and after the chain was thrown, the distance between the links indicated the state of the relationship.

The hearth was, of course, widely seen as the focus of domestic life; thus, like the bean in a way, it was a sign just waiting to take on wider meaning. And it did. Not just in Renaissance society but in many societies, the hearth has a rich lore that extends well beyond cooking, warmth, and sociability. In Venice and the Veneto it appears that not all the associations were positive. Behind the hearth, for example, it appears that there was a widespread assumption that there lurked an evil spirit, demon, or Devil. Salt was often thrown to the Devil on the hearth, and the sputtering that occurrred when the salt hit the coals was a sign that the Devil had taken it. In the context of hearth and the domestic sphere, pans also took on special meaning. Magical recipes usually were quite specific about the pan to be used if cooking was necessary; not just any old pan would do. Normally, such recipes called for a new pan, and often specified as well that the pan had to be bought in the name of the intended victim or the Devil.[45] Perhaps this reflects a shift in the signifying of the everyday, as the everyday was rejected for the new. Had private property and the new begun to penetrate even the poetics of the everyday?

Used hearth chains, however, were adequate to the task, and they were not employed just to measure relationships. Occasionally they were also used as a form of *martello,* a hammer, to cause suffering for an enemy, a competitor in love, or an unfaithful lover. Isabella Bellocchio, for example, confessed to hitting a hearth chain against the wall to make her lover's heart beat hard. "Concerning the [hearth] chain I hit it against the wall with the intention to make my lover's heart beat hard."[46] Again the verbal symmetry is strong here, even if the spatial relationship seems to have dropped away. Isabella beating the chain against the wall made the heart of the person to be hammered beat hard. Aside from casting beans and beating chains, she also admitted using a wide range of other magic practices associated with the domestic sphere. As noted earlier, she put salt in the fire, although her description is rather different from the norm and her explanation carefully leaves out any reference to the Devil. "Concerning the salt, I took a handful, opened the stove and threw it in. Then I covered it or really put it under the coals with the intention that all the love that I had for Milano ought to be buried under that fire in that salt and thus would be consumed everything that I had in my heart for him."[47] Isabella's explanation follows the already noted metaphorical form and is clear, at least up to the point where one asks what was the relationship between her heart and the salt. It may have been a purely arbitrary association, but the use of salt thrown on the fire was so ubiquitous, and Isabella's magical knowledge was so eclectic and wide-ranging, that it seems more likely that she was strategically leaving out details to make her confession less damaging. Unfortunately, her examiners were not concerned enough about it to pursue the matter. Most other women who threw salt on the fire were equally cryptic, perhaps because, as other sources suggest, this was a common way of rewarding the Devil for his aid.[48] Suggestively, however, much of the magic that focused on the hearth called on the Devil, his minions, or the souls of the damned, especially criminals. Evidently there were resonances with that place in the house that struck deeply and darkly in the consciousness of the time.

Salt, beans, hearth—the power of things in the domestic sphere could hardly be more basic on the surface. But behind the apparent simplicity of adapting everyday domestic things to magic lay an often much more complex culture. Returning to spatial relationships, for example, women were often accused of measuring (*spannare*) the hearth, a wall, or a chord with their hand or their forearm. This was done for many purposes, but as with beans, it often seems to have been concerned with evaluating the relationships between people, using space as the key. Occasionally the ecclesiastics of the Holy Office pressed their inquiry more aggressively, and deeper relationships and connections were revealed. A certain Elisabetta in 1587, for example, confessed, among other things, that she had learned from another woman a considerable range of love magic, including casting beans, saying special prayers, and a great deal of household magic including measuring the wall. "In addition she taught me to take a pinch of salt and measure the wall and say, 'As I measure the wall, thus I measure the heart and mind of said person so that he will come to me and [I do] this in the name of the Devil.' Then I threw this salt in the street or in the fire and I said, 'Now that I have paid you, send him here to me.'"[49] If to measure (*spannare*) is read as meaning to cover the space or to control it by measuring it, the parallel between measuring the wall and the heart and mind of the lover takes on a much richer significance. To measure becomes to control, and once again, we have a metaphor that brings out deeper relationships, but now shapes them as well.

Even without taking that extra step, Elisabetta did associate heart and salt, and paid the Devil with the salt as well at the hearth fire. The choice of either throwing the salt in the fire or in the street for the Devil again implies a certain ambivalence about the hearth: was it somehow perceived as a passageway to someplace else beyond the domestic sphere (like the street) where the Devil could lurk? We might even consider whether it was just salt that Elisabetta was giving to the Devil or whether, in its association with her lover's heart, she was also sacrificing that to win the Devil's support. The symmetry would be attractive, the alliance rather logical—a split of the beloved's heart between the magician and the Devil—but Elisabetta does not take her explanation that far and may well not have been concerned with such logical niceties.[50]

Clearly, however, space, especially domestic space, was very important for magic. The geography of the house was laden with meanings,
signs, and metaphors largely lost today. Along with the hearth, the door
sill and the door were very important, marking as they did the threshold
and the boundary that divided domestic space from community space.
Once again, a large range of magic focused on these boundaries of the
home, especially magic designed to harm. Isabella Bellocchio actually
met her downfall when she decided to attack her rival for Milano's love,
Elena Zamberto, at her door. Isabella, as part of a campaign to hammer her rival, ordered a servant to mark her door secretly with a foul
mixture. Although the ingredients vary slightly from one testimony
to another, most agreed that the mixture stank and was made up of
things primarily associated with excrement, suffering, and death. Elena
claimed to have learned from one of Isabella's servants that the mixture
included "an extract from the root of the stinking fennel, ground taken
from between the columns [the Columns of Justice, where executions
were carried out on the edge of Saint Mark's Square], bones of the dead
taken from San Giovan di Furlani and other graveyards, water of San
Alberto, feces of dogs . . . wolf fat and other things." Isabella had then
instructed her servant to "anoint the door sill and the door [of Elena's
house] in the form of a cross."[51]

This was not the only magic Isabella had used to hammer her rival,
but the impact of the total program was quite impressive. Elena, testifying reluctantly before the Holy Office, reported, "I do not have any
interest in this case at all except for the fact that the first day of this year
at night I came down with a very serious stomach ache and palpitations
of the heart." Her beating heart, of course, calls to mind Isabella's beating of her hearth chain against the kitchen wall to make the heart of her
lover beat. Had she used the same technique against her opponent?
Elena continued, "It was so bad that I thought I was close to death. After
that there continued certain pains in my heart that felt as if I were being
cut into . . . [then] there came over me a feeling so that I could not
stop my head from spinning and I went around in a daze, so that I
seemed to have gone mad."[52] These sensations, which she claimed to
have attributed at the time to natural causes, continued until January 12
or 13, when "in the morning two women knocked at my door and said
that they wanted to talk to me about something that would be to my
benefit. To tell the truth, I wanted to have them told that I was not at
home because I did not feel well. But finally I answered and agreed to
listen to what they had to say. . . . They asked me to forgive them for
coming to my house without being introduced, but inspired by God and
moved by the great things that they knew that Isabella Bellocchio was
doing against me they decided to come warn me. I asked them what
things because I had had nothing to do with this woman."[53]

Her two visitors then explained the hammering magic that Isabella was using against her. It is interesting to note that Elena claimed that this was the first time she was even aware that Isabella existed. And she underlined this by stressing her doubts about the claim of her two visitors that she had been bewitched. "I, to tell the truth, hearing this began to laugh. But this Vienna said to me, 'Signora, this is not a joke; you will have it [the last bit of door-marking magic that Isabella had planned for her] really at your very door, because when what is to be done is done, there will be thrown against your door or your walls a foul mixture.' At this I pricked up my ears as it seemed to me that here they were talking about an insult and a dishonor to my house."[54] As a skeptic, then, she portrayed herself as more concerned about her honor and that of her house—a significant sign of the importance of the door in a broader context—but not yet particularly concerned about the hammering magic that had been used and was planned for her.

But following Isabella's arrest, an arrest reportedly punctuated by Isabella's throwing some of her magic down the toilet and some of it into the canal, Elena's illness suddenly broke and she regained her health. Ironically, however, where Isabella's magical campaign left off, the power of her friends in high places appears to have taken over. Although they could not keep her from being arrested and held by the Holy Office, they did see to it that her stay in jail was as pleasant as possible. As noted earlier, she regularly entertained in jail, inviting unspecified noble males to share her repasts and even frequently dining with the head jailor. Elena, in contrast, although recovered from her mysterious illness, found herself thrown in jail. Her imprisonment was motivated by the charge that she had paid the officers who had arrested Isabella to claim falsely that they had found the latter destroying her magic when they came to arrest her. Where the truth lay in this web of claims and counterclaims is virtually impossible to say, but it is clear where the power lay. Although in the end, Isabella confessed to using a wide range of magic and received a stern sentence, including a long jail term, she quickly arranged a deal that allowed her to contribute a considerable sum to pious causes and be freed. Elena and the captain of the watch, however, languished in jail for at least another year, petitioning to be released on the grounds that the case was over and Isabella had confessed.

Doorstep magic less clearly described, but with a related emphasis on metaphors of public and domestic, was frequently reported. For example, a Greek woman named Angela, who styled herself a dancer but appears to have been a higher-level prostitute or perhaps even a courtesan, had her doorstep washed every new moon with holy water by another Greek woman. Several neighbors testified about the wide range of love magic used by this Angela in her trade, including casting beans, making potions with the hearts of animals, wearing special amulets to attract men, and wearing a piece of the rope with which criminals had been hung. One neighbor described the doorsill washing briefly as follows: "A Greek woman, Betta the Fat, came to the house of this Angela every new moon to wash the door with holy water."[55] Another explained, "I know that this Betta the Fat went about anointing doors, that is washing them. She also washed the waists of women [with holy water] so that [Angela told me] men would run after them."[56] The door, this time anointed with the holy rather than the foul, brought love rather than sickness. The apparent reversal may not be as symmetrical as it seems, but clearly doors were of great significance in the magical space of the home.

As one might expect, another point in the geography of the home that was central for love magic was the bed. Magic there could act with unique immediacy, for then as now, the bed was seen as a primary place for sexual activity. In fact, "to go to bed" with someone was already an indirect way of referring to sexual intercourse without necessarily implying that that sexual intercourse took place in bed. A rather humorous indication of the potential power of the bed comes from a certain Lucretia. About forty years old, she was the wife of a carpenter and was having problems with him. She explained to the Holy Office, "I said to my confessor outside of confession that my husband was making me a poor companion and that I was afraid that he had been bewitched as he was fooling around in the house of Caterina and Rosa, both women of evil reputation. He [my confessor] told me that I ought to look in our bed to see if there was anything there and if there was I was to bring it to him. I did what he said and I found [there] millet, sorghum, spelt, laurel, wheat, apple seeds, seeds of flowers from every month, peas, husks of sorghum and small bones that seemed to be from babies, coal, stockings, rocks of several types, pieces of wood of various kinds, and two nails plus two large needles one with the head the other without as was the case with the nails, needles with hard heads one of which was for sewing, whistling bones, and other things."[57]

It is tempting to remark facetiously that if her marital bed was so full of extraneous material, it is not hard to imagine why her husband found other beds more comfortable and attractive. But such uncharitable thoughts are not really fitting, as this type of report was not uncommon: beds were frequently loaded with magical materials designed to either bind or hammer for love or other motives, as was the case in Feltre with the bed of Zuan Vettor's father. In this instance, both seeds and penetrating things stand out, and while their exact significance is not spelled out, both seem evidently related closely to sex and love. The broken pairs of nails and needles (one with a head, one without) also suggest again a metaphorical kind of hammering magic to break apart the couple. Interesting as well is the fact that Lucretia's confessor both knew enough about magic and evidently believed enough in it to suggest that she search for such magic in her bed. Of course, the evidence on this is hearsay and clearly not from a disinterested party. But whether Lucretia's testimony is true or not hardly matters; even as a lie, it was told as something that could be believed by the Holy Office and apparently was.

Along with the hearth, the door, and the bed, domestic magic also exhibited a fascination with the space under the staircase. References are vague, and it may be simply that this was a place that, because it was out of the way, was handy for carrying out activities of a questionable nature like love magic. But because it was out of the way it was also frequently used as a toilet, especially in homes that had not yet created a special space for such necessities. It may be, however, that this place had deeper meanings, as it literally underlay the space that connected one level of the house with another. Rather like the doorway, the stairway served as a boundary, but in this case between the downstairs and the upstairs. As domestic space became more diversified, with living and sleeping areas separated, the stairwell may have taken on a special significance, connecting the more public space of living rooms with the more private space of sleeping areas.[58] It would be interesting to see in a broader investigation of domestic magic if, as the geography of the house became more complex and diversified, the magical significance of domestic space evolved and developed a corresponding complexity.

Urban space was also important for magic. In that larger space, graveyards and churches were especially significant for their ability to provide a passage from the urban world to a broader spiritual cosmos. The familiarity of Lucretia in Feltre with the sacred space of her churches found many parallels in Venice. And as we have seen earlier, a whole range of love magic turned on sacred signs and rituals, many of which gained special power by being reenacted within the highly charged spiritual spaces of a church. Also as noted earlier, a church was one quasi-public space where women could move with relative freedom and without loss of honor, thus making its magical powers more accessible. Graveyards were another matter. Isabella Bellocchio's hammering magic for her rival's doorstep included, among other ingredients, ground that "she had taken from between the Columns of Justice, [and] bones of the dead taken from San Giovan di Furlani and other graveyards."[59] Most women, however, preferred to send others to collect the bones of the dead or earth from the grave to be used in mixtures for love magic. Both were often used in conjunction with prayers, at times quite elaborate, designed to force the aid of the dead in the hammering part of love magic. The use of urban space also suggests that at least some of the lessons that the rituals of state were designed to teach to the populace were actually being learned. The incorporation of earth, blood, and even the hangman's rope from the traditional place of execution in Venice for hammering magic implied an acceptance of the state's vision of executions, at least to a degree. Usually the damned souls of those executed were called upon or forced by the magic to provide the hammer to drive a lover to the person desired. Behind this apparently stood an acceptance that the people executed by the state were truly criminals, truly damned, and thus capable of being called upon to do the hammering necessary.

One thing stands out in this magic drawing on things from outside the home: aside from that done in churches, most of it was actually done in the home, merely drawing on the power of the outside world. Moreover, when it was done, this type of magic often was refocused within a domestic context. Bones of dead criminals or earth from their graves might be combined with a range of other ingredients to be cooked over the hearth fire with prayers that called on God, the Devil, the spirits of the damned, or other evil spirits to bind love. Such typical eclectic mixing makes it difficult to gauge in any statistical manner the relative proportion of magic that might be labeled domestic as against the magic that drew on the space beyond the home. But a reading of the cases from the second half of the sixteenth century in Venice makes it clear that domestic magic was far more important, and even magic from beyond the home was often given a domestic dimension.

Nonetheless a practice reported from the seventeenth century, apparently reflecting usage in the late sixteenth century, shows that civic space could be used outside the home at times and in very structured ways. Ruth Martin relates that in a case of 1615, a certain Bellina Loredana was accused of taking a young girl with her along the customary path of ritual executions in the city, reenacting in reverse an execution. The girl metaphorically became the criminal in this magic in order to bind the souls of executed criminals in the service of Bellina. Several people testified about this, but Alvise Ongaro provided the most complete account: "She seduced a young girl with her diabolical plan and on a Thursday when the moon was waxing at midnight the aforesaid Bellina Loredana took this girl to the *Giesiolla* [a little chapel] in San Marco where they hold those who are to be executed and tying her hands [the young girl's] behind her and having previously arranged to have a gondola waiting they left that place and went to the *riva* where they got in the boat and were taken to [Santa] Croce where they got out. [There] the old woman imitating the executioner pretended to cut off the right hand of the girl. She then made her walk backwards down the exact street that those who are to be executed follow until they arrived between the two columns in San Marco. Once there she placed the girl as criminals are placed and the old woman acted out her execution conjuring and pronouncing those devilish words and characters known only to her to force souls, or more accurately, devils, to talk to them. But she was disturbed by some boatmen . . . who seeing her act in this way . . . called out 'Hey witch, we see you! Hey witch, we see you!'" Although Martin reports this aspect of Loredana's magic in the context of a discussion about commanding the aid of spirits for gambling, it seems likely that this magic, in reversing the spatial order of the execution of criminals, sought to gain control over the souls of those criminals or the evil spirits with whom they associated after their execution. With the aid of such beings, as we have already seen, hammers could be activated with impressive efficacy for many uses, and Loredana, in fact, was accused of having been involved in a wide range of healing and love magic.[60]

Spatial relationships, whether in the urban sphere, in the domestic space, or in more prosaic areas like the distance between beans or the links in a chain, were clearly important for love magic and suggest in their frequent domestic context the central role of women and women's networks in love magic. They also suggest the complex culture and rich imagination that women had built around the spaces that across the Renaissance had been assigned to them with increasing rigor and insistence. The home may have already become a prison for some, but the prisoners had quickly opened with their culture breaches in the walls that confined them. And while to the modern eye that culture may still seem weak and peripheral, it would not be wise to give in too quickly to such sentiments, for the documentation that survives tends to reveal only a small portion of that world, and not from the best of lights. Nonetheless it reveals clearly that that culture and the powers that went with it were taken very seriously by the society at large; that people, including the intellectuals who staffed the Inquisition, viewed those powers as real and dangerous; and that, in fact, passions were bound and people both loved and suffered as a result of those powers discovered by women in the domestic sphere and beyond.

The Body and Love Magic

If space was rich with meaning for love and sex, the body was even more so, especially those parts of the body perceived as central to the intense emotions of love and sex. Much of this magic was frankly phallocentric, as one might expect in a society where the active, the powerful, and the male were all centrally associated with the phallic. But significantly, because women played such an important role in this magic, it also drew heavily upon what was perceived as quintessentially feminine: fertility, birth, menstruation (seen as closely related to both fertility and birth), and a woman's "nature" or "shameful parts," that is, genitals.[61]

We have already seen that Paolina di Rossi was accused of having her servant put her menstrual blood in the wine of her lover to attempt to bind his love. As this blood was, according to medical theory (and apparently popular perception as well), the material base of the female seed and the foundation of the flesh of future children, it was a uniquely powerful sign of a woman's fertility and thus highly suitable for a magic

that, as we have seen, placed great weight on signs. Implicit here, however, was another victory for formal theology, for this type of magic
suggests that its women practitioners perceived their "femaleness" as
centrally reproductive. Menstrual blood as a primary magical sign of
femininity, at least in part, recognized the Church's vision that women
and their sexuality were aimed at the reproduction that the Church held
was the first purpose of sex. In contrast, other areas of the female body
that could potentially be considered centers of erogenous pleasure or
power were largely ignored. Thus the womb and the genitals as the locus
of birth figured regularly, but breasts, thighs, or other areas of potential
erotic interest were largely overlooked.[62]

One must be careful, however, not to fall into the trap of accepting
such a clear association merely at the level of Church doctrine, for with
only a slight twist, the emphasis on reproduction and fertility could have
a much more aggressive and power-oriented reading. Rather than being
doomed to give birth in suffering and pain, as in the Genesis account of
the differentiation of the sexes, reproduction could also be seen as a
tremendous power that only women enjoyed. Women, like God, gave
life to humanity, and in a culture that was highly sensitive to metaphors
that seemed to reflect macrocosmic and microcosmic aspects of the same
power, reproduction had the potential at least to be an extremely potent
metaphor of power, making those who possessed that power in a way
gods among men.

For the male there was some reference to reproduction as well, but it
was only a small part of a larger range of body magic that went well
beyond the reproductive. A good example of a strong reproductive metaphor, however, can be seen in the case of Splandiana Mariani, who
confessed to putting semen in the wine of people whom she wished to
bind in love. She admitted that she had also used holy oil, beans, and
special prayers to the same ends. But a neighbor's testimony provides
perhaps the best reproductive rationale for her magic, as well as an
interesting perspective on sexual values. She reported that she had
learned that this Splandiana "gave to diverse people to eat some semen
or come [*spelma o sboradura*] from the man and from the woman soak-
ing this up with a handkerchief . . . and putting the said filth [*spor-
chezzo*] in a flask full of wine and giving it, that filth, to drink to whoever
she wished so that that person would desire her and feel for her a great
love."[63] Here both male and female "semen" are seen as powerful. Also,
there is a telling value judgement revealed obliquely in the reference to
this "semen" as filth. It may have been a given that both male and
female "semen" were necessary for reproduction and birth. Thus they
were powerful for magic and to be respected, but at the same time they
were seen as filth. Power, filth, and reproduction seem not to fit well
together logically in this vision, but, of course, society today is not

without similarly illogical layerings of meaning in its vision of reproduction and sex.

This case reveals in another area of magic not directly associated with love the strong reproductive nature of magic associated with the female body. Splandiana also admitted that she had adopted a widely used form of magic that called upon young virgin girls to look into a flask and call upon the White Angel to discover lost or stolen property, already discussed in regard to Veronica Franco. She had been robbed of "pearls, jewels, and other precious things," and thus, "wishing to know who had stolen these things from me, moved by this desire and the memory of a relative [a woman], I agreed with my mother to look into the flask [*inchistara*] calling up the Devil to reveal the thief. That magic is done as follows: one finds a pregnant woman, two virgin girls and you put them in a well closed room. Then in a hand-washing basin in which there is a wedding ring of a true and legitimate marriage you put a flask full of holy water on the top of the ring. Then the pregnant woman and the virgin girls all kneel with a blessed candle in their hands, calling upon the Devil in the name of the White Angel, calling him Saintly Angel, [they] look in the flask [to see the thief or to see where the stolen goods were hidden]. In this way I was able to regain the stolen goods."[64] The reproductive imagery of this magic is particularly strong. Pregnant women and virgins—the two poles of the power of fertility, one totally potential, the other totally actual—pray before a true marriage ring, the midpoint, one might say, between their states. "True and legitimate marriage" traces the correct path from the virgin state to the pregnant state. This again is a very Christian vision of marriage, sex, and reproduction, at least until the Devil is called in to identify the thief. The symmetry here is exceptional: physical, in the various physical states of the women involved; spatial, in the arrangement of bodies and symbolic things; and even verbal. The range of that verbal symmetry is suggested by the prayers briefly reported in many cases. The virgins usually prayed, "Holy Angel, White Angel, for your Holiness, for my virginity show me who has taken _____ [the thing stolen]."[65] Purity is metaphorically overlapped with purity here to generate the power to gain the White Angel's aid in forcing the absolute opposite, the Devil, to show them in the flask a thief.

The power of virginity and purity that we see in the prayer to the White Angel seems to have had little resonance with the magic that focused on male bodies. For men there appears to have been, in magic at least, little sense that the presexual or asexual was powerful. The phallus's power was in its use. And in this case, the Christian theological vision that valued chastity for both men and women seems to have been overlooked, much as it was in daily life. For the women and men who practiced the magic of love, the essence of the male and his power was the phallus; thus we encounter a host of practices that refer to the phallus either directly or metaphorically. An interesting Venetian case from the fifteenth century refers to a Greek woman binding to her a noble lover, by, among other means, measuring his erect phallus with a blessed candle that was later burned in church in the name of their love. Again, here as in the measuring of other things, the measurement seems to reflect an attempt to bring the measured thing under control. The mixture of the sexual and the sacred is by now familiar, and the mirroring/measuring of the phallus/candle takes this metaphor to a nicely significant binding conclusion.[66]

Negative examples are also particularly revealing for the place of the phallus in love magic. Certainly in Feltre, Elena Cumano and her associates, in trying to bind the love of Gian Battista Faceno, were ready to use the phallus as a central part of their magical strategy. Their wax figure was laden with needles, but the focus of their damage was the heart and the genitals. In fact, Elena's problems in securing an adequate wax statue underline how important the genitals were. It will be remembered that at first her order for a statue had been filled with a standard commemorative wax one without a phallus or testicles. This was sent back immediately, with orders that for this commission genitals were necessary. What for the funeral imagery of a man was unnecessary for love magic was central.

Verbal hammers that were aimed at males also often focused on the genitals, attempting either to bind them or to destroy their value by making them nonfunctional. Males frequently attested to the power of such measures, remarking ruefully that they were "broken" [*guasto*] in a sexual sense by the spells or hammers of neighborhood witches or magicians. Clearly, in a very phallic world of sex, power over the phallus gave one power over the sexual man. Most frequently, however, this was expressed metaphorically by things that represented the phallus rather than directly. In a brief case against the prostitute Diana and her mother, Faustina, who practiced in the house of prostitution owned by the noble Marco da Riva, both women were accused of having committed "diverse witchcraft such as throwing beans continually . . . for every sort of person making of this a public occupation. They also put live eels under the coals of the fire with needles in the head and the heart. Moreover for some time they kept in their house a priest who gave them holy oil with which they kissed their clients."[67]

Here in the context of a familiar range of magic designed to measure and bind love, we find phallic eels being stuck with needles in the head and heart and placed under the coals of the fire. Were these eels, like the salt, placed under the coals of the fire, being consigned along with the phallus of the victim to the Devil? At the least, it seems clear that this magic was designed to hammer males through the transfixed eels, whether the Devil was involved or not. Also, the accusation seems to involve a total sexual package—a nicety that apparently escaped the Holy Office, for they did not pursue the case. That program would have used the casting of beans to determine if love was felt and how strongly, holy oil to bind love, and the mutilated phallic eels to hammer the reluctant.

Beyond the male phallus, perhaps the most popular part of the body for magic was the heart. As we have already seen, the heart was frequently also bound or hammered verbally, but the process could be more concrete. Often animal hearts were used as a metaphor for the human heart, and they were especially popular in the brews and potions of the magic of love. The case, already discussed briefly, of young Elisabetta Giantis, who measured the kitchen wall, is particularly full of magic that used the heart and was aimed at controlling people by controlling their hearts. Elisabetta confessed, "In addition this Betta taught me to take the heart of a bird and with some sage, salt, and a small measure of oil to put them on the fire all together in the name of the Devil in a pan bought in the name of the Devil. When I put it on the fire I said that I put all these things in this pan in the name of Martino, my love, and that it must happen that these things go to his heart in the name of the Devil and that he cannot sleep nor eat nor have any rest until he does my will."[68] The symmetry here is to a degree clear. The heart of the bird mirrors the heart of the man. The words, the mixture, and the Devil make the cooking of one bind and hammer the heart of the other. Once again, the eclectic nature of this magic comes through strongly, although exactly how its various aspects interacted would be difficult to disentangle without a clearer explanation from Elisabetta. The words too are familiar, as is their form, with their metaphorical and hammering elements most evident.

There may have been another element as well, less immediately apparent. Hearts used for such magic were often from large, powerful animals associated with masculinity such as bulls. But the hearts of birds were also popular—if anything, more popular. Perhaps it was simply that bird hearts were a convenient size for cooking in potions and easy to obtain. Certainly in many societies, birds are not seen as particularly powerful or masculine; as symbols they tend to attract meanings more in the areas of freedom, transcendence, and etherealness. And magic to bind could have built on the contrast or reversal between the free heart of a bird and bound hearts. Unfortunately for this interpretation, the prayers said while preparing such potions do not refer to such a relationship, even if certain *novelle* like Boccaccio's clever little tale about the trapping of the nightingale does seem to play on such a freedom–bound dichotomy using a bird metaphor. But, of course, that tale is early; perhaps more tellingly, the core of the metaphor that made it work was the double meaning of "bird" [*uccello*]. Across the Renaissance and on to the present, *uccello* in Italian has been a popular euphemism for the phallus; thus, the use of the hearts of birds had the potential to create resonances with the male body at two levels—the heart and the phallus—both seen as extremely significant in love. It is unclear if Boccaccio was playing also with a magical metaphor in his tale, and it is equally unclear if Elisabetta in her magic was playing on this extra dimension of her bird heart. But other cases, especially those that feature needles in the heart and a prayer not to allow the victim to have sexual intercourse with others, seem to reflect such an association fairly explicitly.

Returning to hearts, Elisabetta's magic is noteworthy because, for all its wide eclecticism, it focused on the heart, revealing a strong sense that the heart was central in love. For example, just before she confessed to preparing a mixture based on the heart of a bird, she related that her teacher in magic, Betta, "made me say thirty-three Our Fathers for the meanest soul that had been executed and when I had said the thirty-three Our Fathers she had me say these words, 'I have said thirty-three Our Fathers for the meanest soul executed, so that it will leave where it is and go to the heart of such and such, so that he cannot sleep nor eat nor find repose until he does my will.' These Our Fathers I have said several times whenever I had the whim. She had me say these Our Fathers with my hands behind my back walking through the house with all the doors open."[69]

Several things stand out in this description, but centrally it is the heart/soul nexus that creates the essential hammering. Also noteworty, however, are the reversals implied in the saying of the "Our Father," which are found in several other cases as well. First, a specific number of repetitions—thirty-three in this case, perhaps associated with the length of Christ's life before his execution—could give the most common of prayers a special meaning. If the thirty-three prayers with their number were to call attention to Christ's crucifixion, we could have a particularly telling reversal: Elisabetta would have been using the Lord's Prayer in a number that reflected his execution as the most perfect man to call upon the most abject of criminals also executed to come to her aid. Whether or not this was the case, the metaphorical magic was potent and designed to redirect prayer toward less licit ends. And, of course, the manner of saying the prayer—while walking rather than still, with hands behind the back rather than in front and with the doors of the house open rather than closed—implied a series of reversals that transformed the power of prayer and allowed it to move not God or his saints, but less seemly characters like the meanest criminal executed to help in the more negative goals of hammering a reluctant lover.

But perhaps Elisabetta Giantis's magic of the heart that was richest in bodily significance and reversals was the following: "She [Betta] also taught me that I should undress fully nude both having bought and said [that I bought] a candle in the name of the Devil. Then [having lit the candle] I should turn my face to the shadow [created] and say 'I have undressed myself and you dress yourself' and also say 'good evening my shadow, my sister you go to the heart of so and so.' Then I took the candle from behind me and I said, 'I understand that one must pay the Devil.'"[70] Almost the poetry of black magic, Elisabetta's candle once lit created her dark sister, her shadow thrown by its light dedicated to the prince of darkness. Her undressing demonstrated to her opposite, her shadow sister, that the latter should dress. Dressed, she was ready to go forth and do the business of Elisabetta, who in undressing had sacrificed her power to go out into the world. In a world that required women to be dressed to exist publicly, had she sacrificed her public being to her shadow? This shadow sister, created and empowered by an alliance of Elisabetta and the Devil, and Elisabetta's literal self-sacrifice was empowered to go forth and bind the heart of her lover. Of course, even such poetic power had its price: Elisabetta promised the Devil that she would pay him his due in return for control over the heart of her lover.

At the end of her examination, the inquisitor asked her a very interesting question: "Did you have faith and belief in all this witchcraft?" She responded with an answer less poetic than her magic, but one that makes her seem very human. "When I saw that my lover came I believed in the witchcraft and that the Devil could change his will. But when he did not come I did not believe it worked. Yet when he came I believed that behind it lay the Devil who had reversed [my lover's] will to make him come to me and actually I know that he came to me many times when I did that witchcraft."[71] Beyond the simple ring of honesty in her statement, there lies a familiar, seemingly practical and empirical approach to life that appears very modern after the alien mix of her magic. And behind that also lies a familiar feeling of human insecurity in the face of love: Elisabetta, even to her own detriment before the Holy Office, continued to see her lover's visits as being forced upon him against his will by the Devil, his passions bound to her by magic. Her own attractions, the success of her relationship with her lover at whatever level it may have existed—all of these things seem nonexistent in her vision. It could be simply that this was the case: her lover, Martino, came to her all those "many times" simply because he had been bewitched and bedeviled; but Elisabetta appears also to reveal a deep insecurity and lack of self-esteem in her relationship to her lover that seem to have bedeviled lovers in various forms as long as there has been love.

Magic that worked on the heart was ubiquitous, whether it utilized a sister shadow, words, or the actual hearts of animals. But using parts of animals as a parallel to or a metaphor for parts of the body went well beyond using hearts. Earlier it was noted that while the phallus was a particular focus of love magic, female genitals were less often referred to. They were seen at least for magic primarily in a reproductive context.

But occasionally, in using the body parts of animals, love magic seems to have leaped this barrier, as if somehow using female animals allowed magic to express things that could not easily be expressed directly in relation to a woman's body. The case of the Greek courtesan Elisabetta, discussed briefly earlier, involved accusations by her neighbors that she used such magic. As she was not very popular in the neighborhood their testimony is not particulrly trustworthy, but it is revealing about what appear to be the extremes of accusations. One neighbor, asked if she had a good relationship with Elisabetta or any of her friends, remarked, "My Lords no. I do not even talk with her or her friends because they are not meat for my teeth. They are too evil those women."

The main focuses of body magic were three: one sexual—the phallus; one affective—the heart; and one reproductive—female genitals along with menstrual blood. Other parts of the body were also referred to especially for the hammers of the *carte di voler bene*. There, as one might expect, along with the heart the eyes figured prominently; love and attraction were both emotional and visual. Lips were also important, at least for making holy oil work. Touch was important in the same context and crucial as well for the *carte di voler bene*. Letting down one's hair, much like undressing, seemed to empower the body by reversing or undoing its normal state, perhaps playing on binding and unbinding metaphors. Finally, measuring magic often called upon the hand or the arm. But in these areas of magic the power generated by metaphor did not come so much from the bodily part itself as from other central relationships. Thus in these instances, it was less magic of the body than magic that made use of the body. Such a distinction may seem too fine, but it seems warranted by the cases themselves and helps reveal more clearly the central perceptions of the phallus and female reproduction in love magic.

Of course, frequently the practitioners of love magic preferred to mix their magical forms in a manner that suggests that they were prepared to use all the forms of magic that they perceived as available in their universe. Paolina di Rossi's examination reveals this well. The last accusation leveled against her was that she had had her servant buy a bird in the name of the Devil. This bird she had then secretly skinned from back to front [*al rovescio*] and stuck pins through its head and the lower part of its back. As she did this, she said certain prayers to the Devil, who according to the accusation against her replied rather cryptically but in a frightening voice to her pleas for aid. Paolina repeatedly and strongly denied that she had done this. Her friend and fellow accused, Don Felice, also claimed to know nothing about such magic. In the face of such firm denials and without other evidence to follow up, the Holy Office let the matter drop. But for us, whether or not actually Paolina did mutilate a bird in this manner matters less than for her and the Inquisition. For us the accusation reveals once again a poetics of the everyday and magic that makes excellent sense given the discourse on the magic of love that we have merely begun to discover. Her bird bought in the name of the Devil appears to have been a metaphor for the phallus of her noble lover, Gian Battista Giustinian. The needles and prayers to the Devil were to bind Giustinian and to hammer him as well if the binding did not work. The consecrated host in his food and her menstrual blood in his wine would draw on her body and Christ's body to the same ends if the Devil failed her. She could evaluate the progress of the whole program with the casting of beans. In sum, false or not, the accusation against Paolina reveals virtually the full range of that old black magic called love. She supposedly drew on the Devil, the divine, spatial relationships, her body, and her lover's body as well to bind love, redirect it, and punish when it was misdirected. And while even in the tale told against her that magic clearly failed to bind Gian Battista Giustinian, it may be in the end that it did not entirely fail her.

The Other Love Stories of Paolina di Rossi

For although Paolina's trial was concerned with magic, intimately inter-twined with her love for Gian Battista Giustinian were two other love stories, equally unhappy and revealing and worth briefly retelling. The first as it came to light towards the end of the investigation was so obvious that it was surprising that it had not been discovered earlier. Simply put, Don Felice loved Paolina. She knew it as did he. This came out when the Holy Office decided to get behind the confessions of both to see if they were hiding even more serious crimes. Such suspicions had been briefly touched earlier when Paolina had been questioned about conversations with Don Felice in prison. As noted, her reply about a small argument over telling the truth had satisfied her examiners and they had let the matter drop.

Towards the end of June, however, after examinations had gone on for two months, a fellow prisoner, the priest Sebastian Meliori, was brought in to testify. He related that before Don Felice's first testimony one day passing his cell Paolina had asked him to contact Don Felice. "She asked me to tell Don Felice that now she would learn if he really loved her and that he should take on himself the responsibility. Those precise words I wrote on a scrap of paper for Don Felice."[72] Simply put, she had asked Don Felice to prove his love for her by taking the blame. In that light his testimony takes on new meaning. By the end, having rejected some early admissions, he had confessed little beyond using beans and that he had given her a nonmagical host. The rest of the accusations he steadfastly rejected, suggesting strongly that Paolina understood nothing about magic.

That he had proved his love was made clearer yet by his firm refusal to admit any attempt at a cover-up. Even though the note written by

Sebastian was found among his belongings, he claimed to know nothing about it because he asserted he could not read very well. Unconvinced by such a feeble alibi, the Holy Office decided to use torture to try to force him to confess. But even under torture Don Felice refused to implicate his love. Paolina, untortured, also maintained her defense—there had been no cover-up; she had accepted the host but decided not to use it; about beans and other magic she knew nothing. If it was not her magic that had made his love so strong, she could at least believe that it was and see it finally as having worked for her.

The Holy Office was stalemated. Without a better case against her they decided that torturing her was not warranted; thus in the end they ruled that as an example to other women to avoid magic she was to be banned for six months from Venice. She was also ordered to confess regularly and say a series of prayers daily during the banishment. For Don Felice, however, their penalty was more severe. Clearly they felt he was covering up serious crimes and he had confessed enough about his irregular life to warrant a major penalty. He was condemned to perpetual imprisonment; a heavy price to pay for love.[73]

The last love story of this case involved the servant of Gian Battista Giustinian, Argenta, who had provided the Holy Office with some exceptionally detailed testimony about Paolina's magic. Her love came out in the context of a series of late examinations that the Holy Office heard; as the servants involved were so central in the transfer of the host, a closer inquiry into their relationships with their masters seemed in order. It was a fruitful tack to take. Salvatore Samater, a young singer and musician, provided new light on those relationships and also another perspective on the cultural life of a courtesan. He began his testimony by explaining how he had become involved, "I have known this Paolina for more than a year, as I was called upon by a musician . . . who asked me to sing with him, his friends, and a woman before the mother of signora Paolina, so I went. One of them played the clavichord that is his master named Zuane and Julio the barber played the lute. . . . I sang improvising my songs in praise of her mother."[74]

Under questioning about who might want to harm Paolina, Salvatore slowly wound his way back to her servant Lucia and to Giustinian's servant Argenta: "This past Lent on the Fourteenth or Fifteenth. . . . I was visited by this Sicilian priest [Don Felice], who lived in the same house as me. . . . [He asked] in the name of Signora Paolina, who was at the house of the Giustinian family on the street of the Ca D'Oro, if I would go and sing there." At first Salvatore refused, but when Paolina sent her maid to beg him to come, "I went and sang a little." Afterwards he walked Paolina home and as they were walking asked her why Giustinian's maid Argenta had not been at the performance. He reported that Paolina had replied, "We had a fight and I have written to Giustinian that I want him to send her [Argenta] away."[75]

Certainly Paolina, as a threat to her livelihood, might have merited Argenta's animosity, but the matter went deeper. Salvatore continued: "About four or five days later I encountered Lucia, Paolina's maid, in campo San Felice and asked her where she was going. She answered, 'I am going to the house of Giustinian to get a flask of wine for the Signora. Come along with me' So I went . . . and she made me wait at the door. . . . Finally she returned carrying the wine and I asked why she had been so long. She replied that she had been talking with the maid of Giustinian [Argenta] for a while. . . . She told me how that maid had said to her that she would have gladly put poison in the wine. And in the same vein she told me that I ought not to go to sing under the balcony of the Signora. Also she told me that she, Lucia, did not want to stay with the Signora. I asked, 'Why?' She replied that Signora Paolina wanted to beat her . . . and thus she wanted to run away at any cost."[76]

Salvatore's testimony reveals the animosity for Paolina of both her servant, Lucia, and Giustinian's servant, Argenta. The context of Lucia's animosity is clear and confirmed by others. Most of those called to testify regarding this pointed out that Lucia, who by this time in the case had disappeared, had fought frequently with her mistress, spoke evilly about her, and had been anxious to leave her service to avoid further punishment. From this perspective it is significant that in the case against Paolina, it was Lucia who claimed to have been instructed by Paolina to bring the host to Gian Battista's house; and perhaps even more significant that she had claimed that she turned it over to Argenta to put it in his broth. Of course it may have been that Salvatore's testimony was a lie designed to suggest that Paolina had been framed by her servant and Argenta. But its wide support among neighbors and others called to testify suggests an underlying animosity between the women.

At first, Argenta's animosity, however, is harder to explain. Finally a neighborhood woman, Angela, wife of Dominico Toscano, who went about with both servants, provided a rationale: "I know that the said Signora Paolina is an enemy of Argenta, servant of the Giustinian family. I heard that they fought. . . . This Argenta always spoke evilly of the Signora saying that she was a whore; that she was a fate; and that she was a ruined fate as well as other things that I would be ashamed to say. . . . One evening this Argenta told me that she had fought with the said Paolina and she said that if she came into the house again she wanted to throw burning oil on her face so that she would never again have the face of a Christian. Moreover [she admitted that] she had a great hate for her and that if Carnival had been longer she would have arranged a showdown so that she would have remembered her every time she looked in the mirror."[77]

Obviously no love was lost between these two women. According to Angela, Argenta even showed her the poison she had bought to eliminate her enemy once and for all! Finally virtually as an aside she revealed the reason for all this hate and, not surprisingly, it was that same passion that so often bound people together in the renaissance vision of things—love. "I believe that this Argenta was in love with Giustinian even if she was old,"[78] she informed the Holy Office. It appears that while Gian Battista Giustinian was living in Padua (he had only recently returned from there to Venice) Argenta had been both his mistress and run his household as if it were her own. Separated from her husband, a humble boatman, she had discovered in Giustinian a master who in many senses she found difficult to lose to the Venetian courtesan Paolina di Rossi. It is suggestive to note that during the course of the investigation, as this broader context became known, donna Argenta was let go by the Giustinian family—perhaps a tacit admission of the relationship and the loss of honor it entailed for the Giustinian family when it became public. By the end of the case she is referred to as Gian Battista's ex-servant.

Also it is very interesting to reread her original testimony against Paolina in the light of her love. Only she reported in detail the final separation of Gian Battista and Paolina, after he had been warned about her attempted love magic. With what satisfaction the words of that evening must have remained in her mind. She remembered: "The following Wednesday at about the fourth hour of the evening, Paolina came to knock at the door of the said Signor Gian Battista. Signor Gian Battista said, 'What do you want? Go about your business. I don't want you in my house anymore.' Paolina replied, 'Why my dear? What have I done to you?' Signor Gian Battista answered, 'You know well what you have done to me.' Paolina pleaded, 'Open up so that I can at least touch your hand.' Signor Gian Battista said to her, 'I don't want you to touch my hand or even my feet.' Then Paolina left and returned to her house."[79]

Three loves that failed then: Paolina di Rossi's for Gian Battista Giustinian, Don Felice's for Paolina, and Argenta's for Giustinian again. It might seem that that old black magic called love had little to offer, if none of our lovers could make it bind passions as they wished. Nonetheless, it was central enough in the lives of these people that it provided a crucial focus for their intrigues and passions. In this, the cases of the Holy Office suggest that they were little different from a wide range of other people at the end of the Renaissance. To understand their world one has to understand this central discourse of magic and passions bound. It was a discourse that built out from a world where the macrocosm suffused the microcosm with power and meaning, metaphors, and signs—a world replete with a rich poetics of the everyday that played across the holy and the unholy, space, the home, and the body. And centrally it was a world where the power of Christianity had a strong influence at many levels now lost. The popular faith of many led them to adopt the signs and words of the Church to gain power. In turn it was a world where the Devil was a strong presence. In matters of passion he could be utilized as just another force or worshipped as the true master. But significantly most seemed willing to mix the things of the Devil with the things of God to create a richly layered, eclectic old black magic called love.

4

The Women Priests of Latisana: Apollonia Madizza and the Ties That Bind

Is any among you sick? Let him call for the elders of the church, and let them pray over him, anointing him with oil in the name of the Lord; and the prayer of faith will save the sick man, and the Lord will raise him up; and if he has committed sins, he will be forgiven.

James, V, 14, 15.[1]

And he called the twelve together and gave them power and authority over all demons and to cure diseases, and he sent them out to preach the kingdom of God and to heal.

Luke IX, 1, 2.[2]

Defenders of the Faith in Latisana

More than twenty years ago, in his well-known book *The Night Battles*, Carlo Ginzburg noted that in the countryside of Friuli in northeastern Italy at the end of the Renaissance, the clergy of the Catholic Church were not alone in their defense of the faith and the faithful from the forces of evil. A number of peasants had taken up the battle as Benandanti, good Christians, who on certain nights of the year went out to fight the minions of the Devil to secure good harvests and, by implication, defend the material and spiritual base of rural Christian society. Ginzburg chronicled how the ecclesiastical authorities attempted to con-

130

vince their "allies" (at least from the Benandantis' perspective), that they were being tricked by the Devil and that, rather than Benandanti, they were *Malandanti* or worse—witches and warlocks.

But the Benandanti were not the only other defenders of the faith in the countryside at that time. In fact, it might be argued that neither they nor the official clergy were the primary proponents of Christianity there. Religion in rural areas like Friuli and much of the Veneto was still largely in the hands of women—priestesses, not priests. Certainly priests, monks, sacraments, the rituals of the Church, and its calendar of feast days and celebrations had long penetrated the countryside, but because a male hierarchy would eventually dominate religion even there, we should not be blinded to the fact that for more than a millennium their control was often highly problematic. With the late sixteenth century and the Catholic reform movement, this feminine Christianity was challenged by the masculine hierarchy that we assume dominated premodern Christianity. But to truly win male dominance, the Church required education, discipline, and considerable repression as well, and in isolated rural areas like Friuli things moved slowly.[3]

One of Ginzburg's central cases had as its protagonist a cowherd, Menichino della Notte, from Latisana, who in October 1591 testified before the Commissioner General of the Venetian Inquisition: "Giambattista Tamburlina . . . informed me that he and I were Benandanti and that I had to go with him." Although he claimed to have rejected Tamburlina's call, "a year after these conversations I dreamed that I was in Josaphat's field, and the first time was the eve of St. Matthias, during the ember days; and I was afraid." Against his will he had joined the Benandanti: "I had the impression there were many of us together as though in a haze but we did not know one another, and it felt as if we moved through the air like smoke and that we crossed over water like smoke; and the entrance to the field seemed to be open."[4]

That field smelled of "flowers and roses," but it was not the field of the witches' sabbat and perverse pleasures, as his inquisitors feared. Rather, it was the scene of regularly repeated battles between the forces of good and evil: "we fought, we pulled each other's hair, we punched each other, we threw each other to the ground and fought with fennel stalks." The goal of these battles was to defeat the forces of evil, ensure good harvests, and "preserve the faith."[5] As fascinating as Menichino's account is for us, and as disturbing as it was for his ecclesiastical examiners, significantly, as Ginzburg noted, it was merely a sidelight of a much broader investigation centered on the little town of Latisana—a small agricultural and transshipment center at the southwestern edge of Friuli. In fact, although mentioned briefly earlier in the case, Menichino was called in to testify only on 16 October 1591, well after the first sentences had been handed down in the broader trial and more than six months after local authorities had begun their investigation.

The original accusations, the vast majority of the testimony, and the Inquisition's concern focused on another group of people, who, if they did not quite see themselves as defenders of the faith, did see themselves as controllers of its powers in everyday life: the women healers, signers, and love magicians of Latisana. To list their individual activities, however, diminishes the real significance of their powers, based so intimately on the popular Christianity of their community. Priests might dominate the sacraments. They, along with monks and nuns, might dominate in pooling spirituality in some abstract manner for themselves and society. But on a day-to-day basis, Christ and his powers entered the rural world of Latisana through the women of that little town and its surrounding countryside. And tellingly, they knew it, their men knew it, even the local priests knew it. Of course, in a way, the ecclesiastics of the Inquisition knew it too; that was why they ignored Ginzburg's Menichino for six months to focus on the women of Latisana. Benandanti were a troubling but limited problem. The power of rural women over things sacred was not—and the reformed Church wanted no women priests.

The women of Latisana were brought to the attention of ecclesiastical authorities by an outsider, the priest and Capuchin friar Pietro di Venezia, guardian of the monastery of Santa Caterina in Roveredo. He had visited Latisana to preach the Lentin sermons in 1591. But he had been troubled by what he found there: "This past Lent, I preached in Latisana," he reported to the Holy Office of Venice, "and on many occasions I had indications that there were several people suspected either of witchcraft or magic as I wrote to his eminence the Patriarch of Venice."[6] What to Pietro was witchcraft and magic, and thus evil, was not so clearly evil to the people of Latisana. It was true that some of the women of Latisana were perceived as using evil powers for evil purposes, but in most cases things were far less clear.

What is clear is that many of the women Pietro labeled witches found their powers in what might be called a "popular" Christianity, a Christian culture that surrounded them, was integrated with their everyday life, and was literally theirs. This popular Christianity offered a wide range of techniques that could be used for the crucial necessities of life in Latisana: healing, joining people in matrimony or friendship, and thwarting evil. For the villagers of Latisana and presumably for many other rural villagers of premodern Europe, Christianity was not merely a religion of priests, churches, and formal sacraments; it was a religion of daily life intimately intertwining the transcendent with the social and private life of the everyday. And women were its priests.

Pietro, trying to cast such activity in Latisana in as negative a light as possible—in this he was in perfect step with the reformers of the Church—warned that love magic predominated there and was used as much to create "hate as love especially between husbands and wives."[7] In other words, love magic, rather than being used to bind marriages together, was being used to break them by sowing hate between spouses. What might well have been seen as a positive force from a different and more sympathetic perspective—the power that brought people together—Pietro had turned on its head. Of course, he was not so much being clever in this as following the standard logic of ecclesiastical authorities.

But the logic of the eventual winners should not blind us to the fact that there were other possible logics: love, the tie that binds both in marriage and, more broadly, in the more intimate premodern vision of community, if fostered in a positive manner, could be a potent force for good in society. In *Gli Asolani*, written early in the century by Pietro Bembo, the famous love poet and future cardinal presented a dialogue on the values and dangers of love. It began with a cutting attack on the negative aspects of love that in many ways prefigured the attack of the later Pietro di Venezia. But on the second day of the dialogues the interlocutor, Gismondo, came to the defense of love, providing not so much the reasoned argument of a humanist as a commonsense defense. As part of that defense, he presented a history of the development of civil society that would have made perfect sense to the women who practiced the binding magic of love in Latisana. "Surely, if our parents had not loved one another," Gismondo began, "we would not be here or any-where else. . . . Nor, ladies, does love merely bring human beings into existence, but it gives a second life as well—or I should rather call it their principle life—that is the life of virtue, without which it would perhaps be better not to have been born or better to have died at birth. For men . . . would still be wandering up and down the mountains and the woods, as naked, wild, and hairy as the beasts, without roofs or human converse or domestic customs, had love not persuaded them to meet together in a common life. Then abandoning their cries and bend-ing their glad tongues to speech, they came to utter their first words. . . . Little by little, as men lived in this new way, love gathered strength, and with love grew the arts. For the first time fathers knew their own children from those of other men, and grown-up children hailed their fathers, and the delightful yoke of holy marriage bound man and wife together in shamefast honesty. Then villages were newly filled with houses, and cities girt themselves with walls for defense, and laws were made to guard praiseworthy customs. Then friendship, which clearly is a form of love, began to sow its hallowed name through lands already civilized [*dimesticata terra*]."[8]

Love led thus through marriage to civilization—civilized lands were literally lands *dimesticata*—and was responsible even for language. But marriages, as we have seen, for all the Church's insistence that they be a matter of free will, frequently were anything but that. Family and com-munity were expected to be intimately involved in the building of a form of love that would reinforce the marriage bond and the bonds of com-

munity. Crucially, in that context, love magic could be used as a significant tool in the continuing struggle to maintain society by constructing
family solidarities through love and marriage. Lucretia, the witch of
Feltre from Chapter 2, provides an excellent example of this. She saw
herself, and so did others, at least for a time, not as a negative force in her
world but as a positive one who marshaled a wide range of powers to
bind together people in the positive sene of binding that created community.

     Certainly Latisana, as well as much of the Friuli that bordered it, had
a great need for such magic. In a report on the region presented to the
Venetian Collegio (a powerful central executive committee of government) by three syndics delegated to investigate the area's problems, they
noted that much of the land of the region was poor, uncultivated, and
abandoned, and hypothesized: "The reasons for this are explained by
different people in different ways. Some hold that the desire to avoid toil
which has at present become the nature of the populace means that the
men willingly leave the labor of the fields to the women and they concentrate on cards, bars, and litigations because they are highly liti-
gious."[9] They also suggested that many had fled to the cities, where they
could earn more money, abandoning their families, and that others had
left because of debt, the ravages of war, recent years of bad weather, and
to avoid military levies for galley duty. A little magic that solidified the
ties that bound society together would seem to have been ideally suited
to the territory, even if the Venetian syndics did not see fit to recommend
such magic to the Collegio.

     Latisana apparently shared most of these problems and others par-
ticular to its rather unusual status. It was described briefly in another,
much more specific survey of the region prepared in 1548 as "Latisana, a
land on the Tagliamento about a half day distant from where it enters the
sea and about 22 miles [35 modern miles] from Udine [the main city of
Friuli]. It is ruled by the magnificent Vendramin family [Venetian no-
bles] who bought it from the emperor."[10] This survey estimated the
population of most of the towns and villages of the area, but unfortunately, perhaps because of Latisana's quasi-independent status under
the Vendramin family, no estimate was included for it. Still, we can
hypothesize its size by noting that the largest city in the area in 1548 was
Udine, with 12,700 inhabitants. The other "large" towns in the region
had populations in the 1500 to 3500 range. Latisana may have fallen
into this category, but given the general demographic decline in the area
in the second half of the century and Venice's rather relaxed attitude
about its anomalous status under the Vendramin family, if it was to be
numbered among the "large" centers, it probably fell toward the bottom
of that category, in the 1500 to 2000 population range.

     Curiously, there is some reflection of the way in which the town was
treated by the Vendramin family as virtually their private property in the

second half of the sixteenth century as well. On the more positive side, there is the will of Zaccharia Vendramin (undated, but apparently from shortly before his death in 1563), who had been Procurator of San Marco and clearly a major figure in Venetian political and economic life. He left numerous charitable bequests for Latisana and its surrounding hamlets, including orders for the building of two small churches and their part-time staffing with priests paid for from his estate specifically to improve religious life there. Very interestingly as well, he left the part of that land that had been personally his—evidently ownership had been divided within the family—to "my most obedient daughter Elena, who I wish to be able to run it as she wishes during her life."[11]

On the negative side, in 1589 a number of the leading families of the town were so upset with the high-handed ways of the Vendramin family that they filed a formal complaint with the Venetian Council of Ten about another Zaccharia Vendramin, son of Bartolomeo. He was accused of a host of misdeeds, including surrounding himself with *bravi* and *banditi*, terrorizing the local populace, and running roughshod over the Venetian Capitano in the town, who theoretically was still responsible for justice there. It was also claimed that both Zaccharia's wife and her mother practiced evil forms of witchcraft and were responsible for many of his misdeeds. Zaccharia, it was even suggested, lived in Latisana only to avoid the stigma of living in Venice because his witchly mate had been a courtesan. Was Zaccharia then a rural Marco Dandolo and his wife another dangerously powerful woman like Andriana Savorgnan? Unfortunately, the Council of Ten's typically cryptic records do not allow us to know.[12]

What is clear is that although the Friuli in general and Latisana in particular might have had need of love magic, Paolo di Venezia was not the only one who recognized its negative potential as well. Like Andriana Savorgnan, it could create matches that threatened the community and divisions that could tear it apart. From the community's perspective, that may have been the real divide between good love magic and evil. Magic that was perceived as binding to a community's ends was good; magic that did not was bad. Thus Pietro di Venezia, by stressing that the magic of the women of Latisana concentrated on breaking marriages rather than forming or strengthening them, may also have touched the concerns of the community. Without pressing too far, however, it is evident that the question who controlled the binding of love was crucial in the late Renaissance, and Pietro, by making this one of the focuses of his accusations, touched a significant concern of society as well as of the Church.

Pietro's last major charge was that the women of Latisan had cured illnesses by "signing." This type of magic has been encountered already, and it was an issue often considered by the Holy Office of Venice. In fact, it was an issue that had created theological problems for that body, especially as signing was so intertwined with a popular Christianity that stressed Christ's suffering and love for man, Mary's intercession for humanity, or the help of saints. But by the time the Inquisition came to Latisana, the theology had been largely worked out. It had even begun to penetrate the consciousness of some of the women of Latisana, who claimed to have curtailed their use of the holy to cure at the behest of their confessors. Still, most women who made this claim asserted that they had done so more out of obedience than because they agreed with their confessors' evaluation of their practices. And when examined more closely, many admitted that when pressed by neighbors, relatives, or people in need, they had slipped back to the use of their old religious cures. It was simply hard for these women healers to see how cures effected with the help of God, the Virgin Mary, or saintly intermediaries could be evil; thus, even as they submitted to the will of the Church, they could not help pointing out that they still did not see its logic.

Logical or not from the perspective of healing, the Church's logic was impeccable from the perspective of power. There was to be only one master of the spiritual power of God in this world: the Church itself. The Catholic Church had no intention of aggressively fighting the "heresies" of competing churches, only to concede power over the spiritual to healing magicians, especially female ones. Yet it was precisely in the area of signing to heal that the Church faced highly visible and compelling competition. The miraculous cures of local healers provided a difficult contrast to the miraculous Church and its sacraments, especially at a time when the latter were being challenged. The transformation of the bread and wine into the body and blood of Christ or the power of holy oil to transform the very nature of a person, living or dead, had a great impact even on popular religious perceptions—as we have seen with love magic. Still, this was a period of emphasizing but at the same time withdrawing these miraculous powers under an ever tightening discipline in competition with reformation churches that had called into question Catholic "excesses," particularly in this area.[13] In a way, therefore, the Church withdrew the Holy Spirit back within its hierarchy: popular saints were curtailed, miracles were investigated rather than celebrated, even icons ceased to weep, and popular Christian magic was denied its Christianity. Thus, ironically, at the same time that the Church was trying to contain the spiritual cures of women healers, by withdrawing its own spiritual powers within a more clerical and disciplined frame, it heightened the attractiveness of such competitors and rendered them more threatening because they did seem to have access to the spiritual.

Certainly in this context, the Inquisition's rejection of the aid provided by Menichino and his fellow Benandanti gains additional meaning, but the Inquisition was far more concerned with the women of Latisana. Menichino battled primarily to control the harvests, clearly a contest between good and evil with material results of significance for rural society. The Church by the late sixteenth century, however, harbored few claims to be a fertility religion; thus, Menichino's power over the harvest was largely overlooked, while the Inquisition focused on the question of whether or not he and his peers worshipped the Devil on their rose-strewn battlefield. The women of Latisana, in contrast, were attempting to control love, marriage, friendship, and health in their village by manipulating the spiritual powers of Christianity. If, with the help of God and his saintly intercessors, these women could manage the spirits and bodies of their peers at the most crucial moments of private and community life, how could priests compete? That question was made more telling yet by the fact that while priests were often poorly educated outsiders, at times even marginal to the community, the women priests of popular Christianity were normally integrated into the community as wives and mothers and perhaps even as the matriarchs of women's networks. In Feltre, as we have seen, the priest Andrea da Canal, in a virtually perfect example of this situation, went to Lucretia, matchmaker, healer, love magician, and reputed witch, for help with his physical and spiritual problems.

In Latisana, Pietro di Venezia reported to the Holy Office that his activities had led to the arrest and incarceration of one witch: "and as a result one woman was imprisoned by the Capitano of Latisana, who from what I have heard escaped."[14] Certainly that escape added to the presumed guilt of Apollonia Madizza, widow of Jacomo di Jaco, who Pietro did not even name in his denunciation. And it appears to have underlined for the Holy Office the necessity of looking more closely into Pietro's denunciation. Within a month, having been called to Venice by that body, Apollonia voluntarily came before them and became the first focus of their inquiry into the magic and witchcraft of Latisana. After being questioned briefly about her imprisonment and escape, the Holy Office turned to their primary concerns, asking: "In Latisana are there many women who enjoy making people fall in love and how do they operate and have you been involved in such things?"[15] Apollonia, even though she had come in voluntarily, answered with care. Adopting a tactic used often, she admitted knowing women who had practiced love magic but avoided implicating anyone from Latisana by naming only two women already dead.

But in her first response there was more than evasion. The Holy Office had asked if she knew women who "enjoyed" doing love magic. Apollonia shifted the verb, intentionally or unintentionally, but tellingly in her response. Her interrogators were seeking evil women who enjoyed a power that was illicit, but Apollonia presented her deceased compatriots in another light: "in Latisana there was the Panzona and another woman called Catarina Faura who both made their living by making people be loved by those they wished to have love them." From a dangerous pleasure in power over love, Apollonia attempted to shift the discourse to a question of women's work and, moreover, work that helped to secure people's desires. Yet she seems to have heard the extra query in the Inquisition's question, for she continued: "I do not know if there are any in Latisana [today] who enjoy doing those things."[16] Perhaps, in fact, her interrogator's use of the word "enjoy" gave her an easy out because, as we shall see, Apollonia did actually know many women who worked at love magic as a profession rather than enjoying it as a perverse pleasure.

That may be reading her testimony too closely; still, having construed love magic as a profession, she could eventually admit that she had worked at it and also had taken pleasure in her work. At first, however, she denied under questioning any knowledge of it. Her work, she confessed with evident pride, focused elsewhere: "I enjoy practicing medicine and making recipes for healing the stomach and illnesses of the womb. Many people came to find me so that I could treat them. For illnesses of the womb I used a medicine made from nutmeg, cinnamon, cloves and other spices. So according to the particular illness, I gave people the remedies by themselves without saying any words or without making any signs whatsoever; but I gave them only the medicines that their illnesses warranted."[17]

Apollonia claimed, then, to not be a practitioner of magic and certainly not of popular Christian magic. Rather, she portrayed herself as a healer especially dedicated to the illnesses that afflicted women, and a successful one at that. Her last careful qualifications of what she did not do suggest, however, that Apollonia was no innocent folk healer ignorant of the things that the "higher" culture of the Church feared in popular medicine. For although she avoided the issue, by pointing out that she only used simple concoctions by themselves, without words or signs, she was assuring her questioners that she was merely a healer, not a priestess. The words that she claimed she had not used were prayers much like those used in *carte di voler bene* designed to gain the aid of the holy to cure. In turn, the signings that she claimed to have avoided were various forms of crossing and laying on of hands to heal. Tellingly, Apollonia's distinction suggests that already, even in rural Friuli, some people were aware of the distinction that the Church was trying to establish between medicine and magic. Medicine was to be corporal and mechanical; magic went beyond the corporal to the spiritual. Thus it was illicit, as the latter was the domain that the Church was staking out solely for itself. Here again we find the Inquisition, rather than working against the development of modern science, actually working for it by pressing to eliminate the spiritual from medicine, reducing the latter to simply a material issue.

That Apollonia was aware of this distinction in 1591 brings us face to face with another interesting aspect of this case. At first glance, she might seem to be the quintessential victim of witchcraft prosecutions: a middle-aged widow living on her own in a small town fairly distant from the more cosmopolitan cities of the early modern period. Yet that characterization of witches that has fueled so many general theories about witchcraft dissolves with a closer look at this fascinating and knowledgeable woman. For Apollonia was a clever, dynamic widow who moved with relative ease about the countryside and on to Venice, where she was known even in some noble households. Moreover, in her hometown of Latisana, although she had her enemies, she was well connected and respected, especially within the networks of women who readily turned to her for help. How many other middle-aged widows who have been lumped into standard generalizations actually fit Apollonia's model warrants consideration and further research.

An Escape from Jail and a Stereotype

Apollonia's escape from jail provides more concrete information on her broader experience and on the dynamics of family and community in small-town society. On the morning of Saturday, 27 April, the door to the room in the communal palace of Latisana where she had been held in chains for twenty-eight days was found broken in, and Apollonia was gone. An investigation began almost immediately and the first depositions were taken the next day, Sunday, in the home of the Capitano of Latisana. First examined were some neighbors of Apollonia, who reported seeing her brother, Antonio Madizza, walking back and forth in front of her house, energetically discussing something with her son Tonino the day before the escape. After the fact, these women speculated that the discussion had concerned plans for Apollonia's escape. But such suspicions were not enough for the Capitano, and when pressed, they admitted that they had not actually overheard what had been said. Still, in the context of these speculations, Sensa, wife of Tonigucci, was asked where Tonino lived and replied: "He lived over there a little beyond the Church not far from the house of Apollonia."[18] In other words, this widow and her son had enough wealth to live independently, each in his or her own dwelling. Apparently Apollonia also lived separately from her brother, even though the public assumed that they were close and that he was a probable leader in planning her escape.

Another early testifier was Paolo de Casteon, who appeared anxious to supply information, perhaps because he also felt implicated as a relative. He provided the first concrete lead, volunteering that that very day Antonio Madizza had come to his house, "and he confessed to me that the night before last about the third hour of the night Gasparo, son of the said Apollonia, came to ask Antonio to go with him to break Apollonia out of prison." When Antonio refused, Gasparo had gone ahead on his own, "and moreover," Paolo concluded, "it is being said publicly that it was Gasparo who released Apollonia from prison."[19] The public acceptance of Apollonia's son Gasparo as the sole culprit was good news for Antonio, if true. Because he was her brother, public *fama* was ready to blame him, and his suspicious public conversations with other relatives the day before the escape did little to undercut such speculation. Brothers were still perceived as playing a significant role in supervising the honor of their sisters even after marriage. When they became widows, that responsibility normally increased. Even Gasparo's reported calling on his uncle's aid probably fit within that context.

Antonio Madizza, then, clearly had an interest in shifting the blame to his nephew. In his testimony on Sunday, he elaborated on his conversation with Paolo, implicating two additional relatives.[20] In his second examination, however, Antonio revised his account, providing what would become the standard tale of Apollonia's family and their supporters. When asked on Tuesday to confirm his earlier testimony, he requested that the transcript be read to him so that he could correct it. He then clarified: "What you have read to me here is true except that after my earlier testimony, I talked with Gasparo, my nephew. . . . He said to me that it was true that he had broken his mother out of the prison or the palace. In fact, however, Jacomo Committo was not with him. . . . Rather he found by chance a vagabond that day . . . a foreigner . . . and with him alone holding the light [he] broke Apollonia out of the palace."[21] Gasparo, then, had acted virtually alone. That, suspicious as it might seem given Antonio's earlier story, and the unlikely, unknown foreigner who perhaps had to be substituted for relatives to make the mechanics of the escape make sense, made a good story from the perspective of Apollonia's family and supporters. That was especially true because Gasparo was a soldier who lived in Marano, a town beyond the jurisdiction of Latisana, which made him ideal for shouldering the blame if blame was to be assigned.

Even Apollonia was rendered less culpable in the escape by an interesting detail that Antonio added toward the end of his tale. "Gasparo also told me that his mother began to cry when she saw that he wanted to break her out of prison saying 'I do not want to leave because we all will be ruined in the world.'"[22] Escape would ruin her reputation; thus, even she was reluctant to become involved. But there is more to Apollonia's reported lament, for tellingly, she did not say, "I will be ruined"; she said, "we all will be ruined [*saremo tutti rovinati*]." Who that ''*tutti*'' referred to is not specified, but it implied that Apollonia (or Antonio speaking for her) had in mind a larger group than just herself and Gasparo. In those simple words is a vision of her situation that sums up well the fact that Apollonia, with her extensive family connections, was not the isolated, defenseless widow of modern witch lore.

The family defense that focused upon Gasparo, acting alone, was still being maintained when Apollonia testified before the Venetian Holy Office in June. She, however, went out of her way to make it clear to them that Gasparo had no intention of interfering with that considerably more powerful body. Gasparo could shoulder the guilt for the escape from the prison of Latisana. If the issue were to be pursued by the secular authorities there, he lived beyond their limited power. But the Holy Office was another matter. "Gasparo came alone to the prison," she maintained, "and he broke the hinges on the door and knocked it in. Then he came in and broke the chains where I was held and he took me with him and he was alone. . . . Then I went to Pescarola thus leaving the jurisdiction of Latisana. But having been called by this Holy Office, I left there to come here to explain myself and to be obedient. Moreover, I know that my son knows that I came here, because actually he persuaded me to come."[23]

Clearly to be taken with more than a grain of salt, Apollonia's testimony provided the final version of the family's tale of her escape. She even put Gasparo's guilt in the best possible light by pointing out that she had been held in jail for twenty-eight days without charges at considerable expense to her family. Without any end in sight to that imprisonment, Gasparo had freed her, albeit against her wishes and with considerable loss to the family's public reputation, with an impatient violence that his more cool-tempered relatives had rejected. In the end, Gasparo was to be perceived as a hot-headed soldier who broke down the door of his mother's prison to free her from a confinement that seemed neither just nor susceptible to correction. And, of course, when the unquestionable power of the Holy Office came into play, even that hot-headed son respected their authority and "persuaded" his mother to trek down to Venice to turn herself in.

Stated so baldly, Apollonia's tale of her escape hardly rings true; its economy and its rather heavy-handed attempt to paint all involved in the best possible light seem too clever. Still, it might be wise not to rule out all well-constructed defenses as lies. Whether fact, artful fiction, or bold lie, behind this defense several things are clear. Apollonia moved with relative ease about the Veneto, was well connected in Latisana, and had a fairly sophisticated understanding of how the broader world around her worked—even its legal institutions, including the relatively distant Holy Office of Venice. Like Lucretia of Feltre, Apollonia appears to have had the kind of understanding that would allow her in more normal times to manipulate the earthly powers that be, even as she was attempting to manipulate those that stood beyond this world. And once again here, if Apollonia and her supporters were lying, paradoxically their lies may hold many significant truths about the late sixteenth century.

A Witch's Reputation and the Church's Confession

Recalling Lucretia of Feltre highlights another central aspect of Apollonia's case—her concern with reputation and that of her family, already encountered when she expressed the worry that fleeing jail would ruin "them all" in the public eye. Actually, her concern with honor and reputation, along with Pietro di Venezia's formal complaints, played a crucial part in the creation of a furor about witches in Latisana. And one of the keys to that concern was another significant aspect of the Church's offensive following Trent—the more aggressive use of confession to mold and discipline the Christian community.

Of course, from early on, confession had ideally been an important mode of disciplining the faithful. One might even argue that it was an important and largely unrecognized tool in restructuring the mental processes of Christian Europe, or at least its elites—emphasizing as it did an inner evaluation of individual outward behavior. How significant that emphasis was in a society more accustomed to think of evaluating deeds primarily in the context of family, group, or community, it may well be impossible to ascertain today. But given the limited frequency of confession in Europe before the more urban society of the Renaissance made it more accessible, its impact was probably limited as well. Thus it may be that the inner reflection on the relationship between individual deeds and will encountered so forcefully in Augustine and later in Luther (which seem so closely to reflect the type of mentality that confession should have encouraged) actually had very little impact until the urban piety of the Renaissance, with its stress on frequent confession, empowered confession. If that were the case, the urban nature of the Renaissance may have influenced the Reformation and the Catholic reform that paralleled it in yet another way, by beginning finally to make the disciplining potential of confession real.

With the more aggressive penetration of the Church into the countryside, even in relatively isolated places like Latisana, confession played an increasing role in the life of people. And although it did not leave the rich records that the Inquisition did, it too was a significant factor in restructuring the Western world view and, if not eliminating, at least curtailing, the women priests of Latisana. To a great extent, Apollonia's confrontation with ecclesiastical authorities began in confession motivated by her personal sense of honor as a Christian. In her second testimony, Apollonia explained that her problems with the Church had begun when she had gone to confess to Gasparo, the priest from Latisanotte. Her desire, she claimed, was to use the confessional to get her life in order and clear up her reputation. "I kneeled before him [the priest] and said: 'I am Polonia falsely known [*infamata*] as a witch, a practitioner of witchcraft, of herbal magic and many things. I ask that you give me a hand in examining my conscience, because I wish to escape from such great sins. And if I am doing anything that one should not do you must warn me so that I will not do it again.'"[24]

There may well be more than contrition here; for *infamata*, Apollonia may have been trying to use confession to learn more than what acts were sinful. Confession was also, in a way, a public event where her reputation (*fama*) could be defended or even restored. How that often happened her narrative makes clear. Ideally, after her confession, the priest, Gasparo, should have allowed her to do penance for her sins and receive communion. While the penance prescribed may have been private, normally it was not, as a person praying in church after confession was highly visible in a small community, and if not, it was perfectly permissible to discuss with neighbors a penance imposed to make it public and demonstrate that there had been a reconciliation with the Church. That was only the first step; more public yet was communion, a ceremony whereby the community could see that a person had been accepted within the fold. What this could do for a woman *infamata* as a witch should not be underestimated. Essentially a public ceremony demonstrated that in the eyes of the Church one was not a witch or any of the other things that Apollonia had been accused of being by rumor. Thus she could use confession and communion as allies in her quest to regain her lost reputation and honor; in fact, she and others used the new and more visible Church following Trent, especially confession and communion, as tools for legitimating their recognized powers and defusing potential criticism or rumors of malpractice.

Certainly this was the case with Camilla Orsetta, a well-known Venetian healer in the 1580s. A certain Fioralisa testified before the Inquisition late in 1590 that when her daughter Andriana was suffering from a wasting disease, a friend had recommended that a local woman be called to cure her. As was often the case, this woman tried to treat the illness without even seeing the child by working with a sash from her clothing. But the three-year-old's condition did not improve; in fact, it got worse. Fioralisa then decided to take her child to the much better known Camilla, famed for her ability to sign (that is, cure by making the sign of the cross over people in conjunction with saying prayers and giving remedies). Camilla diagnosed the child as bewitched and asked a high price for signing her, ostensibly because the signing, to be effective, would require expensive herbs. Fioralisa agreed to pay, and shortly thereafter, Camilla came to her house to begin the cure. But Fioralisa's description suggests that she was both concerned about Camilla's reputation and quite sensitive to her child's behavior, for she reported: "When this Camilla came in, my little child began to look at her fixedly without saying a word; therefore I said immediately to this Camilla, 'Madonna if the things that you use are of the Lord, sign the child; if not let her be.'"[25]

Camilla's response was both reassuring and revealing. According to Fioralisa, she replied "that her cures were good and that *she still went to confession.*"[26] A neighbor present, who had also had her child signed and cured by Camilla, remembered virtually the same reply: "She answered that they were good things [her cures] and that she confessed them to her confessor. I did not hear the confessor's name, but the mother of the child [Fioralisa] told me it.''[27] Going to confession was then, for Camilla and her clients, a kind of warrant of the legitimacy of her medicine and thus of her reputation as a good and safe healer. Fioralisa's unease, reinforced by her child's apparently unnatural reaction to the presence of Camilla, had triggered a challenge to the healer that she overcame using confession as her guarantee. The whole confrontation was probably motivated by the fear that those who used evil means to cure could use them to harm as well. In the end, when her child died, Fioralisa returned to her earlier suspicions and denounced Camilla. But in the beginning, her own uncertainty and her sense of her child's wariness were overcome by the reputation that attending confession provided. Given Apollonia's situation in the much more intimate confines of Latisana, continued public confession, penance, and communion were most useful assets for her reputation and her practice.

If that was Apollonia's primary goal in going to confess, things could hardly have gone more awry. "I began to say [in confession] what I said above," she reported, "and this priest said to me that I should hurry up because he had to confess others. And thus he absolved me.''[28] To that point things had gone as planned, but Apollonia's next remarks suggest (although they may be self-serving) that she was truly interested in her soul as well as her reputation. For rather than taking her absolution and running, she remembered that she had not confessed everything. Thus, although she wanted the restoration of honor that confession, absolution, and communion promised, she wanted those things legitimately and returned to confess the rest. Things quickly unraveled. For when she returned to the priest, "immediately he began to scream loudly, saying to me, 'Go away, keep signing, but the things of God have always been God's.'''[29] Most important, he publicly refused to hear the rest of her confession.

Apollonia's understanding of that public refusal is significant. "And because there were women and other young people there to hear these things, they began to spread the rumor saying that the priest had thrown me out and that I was a witch." She went on to detail one encounter that confirmed her fears and again reveals the powerful impact of rumor and reputation in her small community. "A son of messer Zuan Riviera who lives in Latisana was walking around with another youngster and he said to his companion, 'see that woman, the priest kicked her out and he did not want to give her penance because she is a witch.' And I turned around and said to him that he was lying because I was not a witch and I had been absolved.''[30]

But public denials were not enough, as Apollonia was all too aware. Thus she took what was a very dangerous option, but perhaps one of the few open to her for regaining her reputation. She went to Pietro di Venezia, who was preaching in Latisana at just that moment, to explain her situation, confess, and attempt to gain absolution. Given his suspicions about witches there, she had made a grave miscalculation. "We were three women, that is my sister, who made the first confession. Then I went. I kneeled before the Father Preacher and I said to him 'Father I am that Polinia [who has been] so defamed as a witch and user of magic herbs. I beg you to be willing to carefully examine my conscience and if I have any sin or if I do anything that should not be done tell me so that I will not do it again. And give me my due penance."[31]

Back to square one, Apollonia found that after her complete confession, Pietro di Venezia also refused to give her penance. This, as she explained to the Holy Office, was for essentially technical reasons. As she had left out sins in her earlier confession before another priest, Pietro did not feel he could give her penance and absolution until she was reconciled with her confessor. Thus Apollonia left Pietro without doing penance, a fact that once more was not lost on her neighbors and fellow inhabitants of Latisana, who were already gossiping. Apollonia again emphasized this point to the Inquisition, complaining that "for this reason throughout the whole of Latisana there grew the rumor [si leva una fama] that the preacher did not want to absolve me because I was a witch."[32]

Ironically, this occurred even though Apollonia followed Pietro's orders to the letter. She did return to her original confessor and did become reconciled with him. In fact, that very morning after having confessed again to him, she did penance and received communion. But it was too little too late. Having been twice publicly rejected by priests and already having a questionable reputation, matters had gone too far for a quickly done penance and communion to undo the fire of gossip and her growing negative fama. Again Apollonia eloquently evoked the situation: "a box of witchcraft things [stregamenti] were brought in to him [Pietro di Venezia] and the blame was placed on me. And because all the people were whispering against me, I did not even have the courage to go to hear his preaching, because when the preacher spoke of witches all the people turned to look at me."[33] Of course, this was exactly the moment when Pietro, having become aware of what he saw as the widespread use of magic and witchcraft by the women of the town, was aggressively preaching against just the evils that public fama had laid at the feet of Apollonia. And it is not out of the question that he saw Apollonia as one of the chief culprits, or perhaps even as an ideal vehicle for bringing the problems he saw in Latisana into public focus and more forcefully before the eyes of his superiors.

Apollonia, on the other hand, appears to have concluded that her reputation had no chance without the preacher's public support. Thus she returned once more to Pietro to try to work out a settlement that would save her reputation and satisfy him. But Pietro, reading only a little into her account, appears to have been carefully unresponsive. Talking with him, she repeated her problem, emphasizing again that because she had not been given penance the first time, gossip and rumor had labeled her a witch and destroyed her *fama*. Pietro cut her off, saying, "Madam I do not know you; I do not know who you are."[34] Finally, however, Pietro did seem to offer some hope of a solution. He asked her to swear on an open book to tell the truth about her deeds. Apollonia claimed that she thought that this was yet another confession, but it was not.

He then asked her a series of questions about various forms of magic and witchcraft that apparently he had by this time become concerned about in Latisana. Most of the activities she denied, claiming to not even understand what he was saying. She did admit, however, to using two special prayers in healing, the same two that she had previously confessed to him. When she recalled that they had discussed them in confession, she reported that he said, "Do not speak to me of confession. Instead tell me again." If her report was accurate, Apollonia should have been put on her guard. Instead she continued, "So I told him those prayers which I had said and he wrote them both down."[35] Apollonia's guard was further undercut by the priest's promise to speak about her when he preached that Sunday. He even asked her to come to hear what he had to say. On Sunday, in fact, he preached a sermon about the witchcraft of three noble women using cats. Although Apollonia claimed not to have understood what he was talking about, she did hear one reference to poor women who were falsely rumored by people to be witches. This she took as referring to herself, concluding, "thus he did me a small favor."[36]

If it was a favor, it was both small and his last, because the very day that she had talked with him, Pietro had given his transcription of her prayers to the Capitano of Latisana. Shortly thereafter she was arrested, whether at his orders or because of complaints that grew out of his preaching against witches or the fire storm of rumor that had grown up around her is unclear. Imprisoned in chains, Apollonia apparently was still not convinced that she had lost all hope with Pietro. She explained to the Inquisition that she thought that the preacher had had her placed in chains as a form of penance. Thus, after a while, she sent her son to tell him that she had fully repented and realized that she was "the greatest sinner in the world."[37]

Her expectation was that once her repentance had been deemed adequate to her sins, she would be released; thus her readiness to portray herself as a major sinner should have signaled to Pietro that she was approaching true contrition. But Pietro was already preparing his denunciation of the women of Latisana, and Apollonia perhaps served his purposes better in jail as a witch than as a reformed sinner—especially as he may well have had serious doubts about her reform. Be that as it may, rather than coming to jail to evaluate Apollonia's contrition, he turned away her son and shortly thereafter left town. Without much hope of regaining her lost *fama* as her days in jail stretched on to twenty-eight, escape and leaving Latisana must have seemed a better and better option. Her plans of reestablishing honor and reputation through confession and communion had failed.

Given the nature of the records, it is not clear what role true repentance played in this sequence of events or even at what stage Apollonia had made her decision to try to use the Church to reestablish her honor and reputation. What is clear, even though everything went wrong for her, is that a woman who knew how the Church worked could use confession to her advantage in normal times. Certainly one would want to look at a much wider range of material before accepting this hypothesis, but still it is worth considering that the often reported closer relationship between women and the Church in Catholic countries may have been based in part on the way in which women could build their honor and reputation through the Church. This might seem a forced interpretation, but it is especially interesting when one considers that in almost every other way, a woman's honor and reputation were in the hands of and at the mercy of others. Of course, Apollonia's case reveals that ultimately, even with the Church, this was the case. But "ultimately" is a most important qualifier, for normally priests had little option but to accept claims of repentance and contrition. A priest might examine the conscience of a sinner; he might press for a deeper awareness of the magnitude of the sin and the need for sincere contrition; but absolution, penance, and confession must have seemed virtually assured, especially in the countryside before Trent. In many ways, the relationship between priests and women in the countryside may have been a nicely symbiotic one, with women using the priest to ensure their reputations, and often the things of priests as well, to extend their power; and the priest, in turn, using the recognition and support of women to penetrate the families of a community.[38]

Women Priests as Healers

In Apollonia's testimony before the Holy Office, beyond the immediate concern with her escape, questions focused on three areas: love magic, magic used to find lost things, and magic used to heal. While all three were quite prevalent in Venice, in Latisana women were more willing to admit the first and the last, and seemed less interested in or aware of the use of magic to find what had been lost or stolen (perhaps because in the more personal setting of a small town, things as well as people tended to be kept track of by neighbors and family). Apollonia, as noted earlier, seemed most willing to discuss her medical practices. In this she was similar to many of the other women of Latisana questioned. Women's illnesses were a particular emphasis of their curing, as were childhood ailments. It seems, however, that women were perceived as having a more intimate and immediate relationship with the body across the board; thus, they had the ability to heal most of its ills. Their medicine might appear at first sight to be a rather strange mix of religion, folk cures, and sympathetic magic, but once again we must be careful not to underestimate its intellectual range, its ability to heal, or its poetry. Crucially in the context of the late Renaissance, this syncretism touched many of the bases that promised power over the body and, ultimately, health.

Both the range of the illnesses treated by women in Latisana and the focus of that treatment are significant. Beyond Apollonia's treatment of problems of the stomach and the womb, we find women there treating fever, headaches, measles, sun stroke, bleeding wounds, bloody noses, broken bones, various skin diseases, and diseases whose symptoms made them appear to be skin diseases, as well as gout, persistent coughs, worms of various types, eye problems, epilepsy, depression and melancholy, a range of wasting and digestive diseases that affected babies and young children, and, of course, those who had been *fatturato,* or bewitched (the ever-present catchall diagnosis when others seemed inadequate).

Most prevalent in this wide range of rural ailments were childhood diseases, which, with their seemingly rapid weakening and wasting away of a child, could easily be interpreted as something more than a simple illness. Ailments of the womb—a catchall category for numerous problems that affected women—were also very common, although the Holy Office was less interested in these cures, perhaps because they seemed less likely to involve witchcraft or perhaps because mature women and their ailments were seen as less significant. Skin diseases and headaches were also, not surprisingly, very prevalent. Syphilis, seldom referred to in Latisana, probably lay hidden behind some of the eruptions and rashes that seemed endemic there. Broken bones, bleeding wounds, and simple bloody noses were also common, reflecting the physical nature of rural work and the prevalence of everyday violence in the countryside.

More surprising perhaps were the significant number of cases involving depression. Some of these may have actually been the final stages of adult diseases that had so weakened the stricken persons that they were perceived as having fallen into a deep melancholy. Usually such people were described as listless, emaciated, and without appetite; death often quickly followed treatment. This made depression rather dangerous to treat. For much as with childhood diseases, it was easy to associate the symptoms with witchcraft, and an unsuccessful healer could find herself quickly relabeled a witch. There were, however, cases of melancholy that seem more analogous to depression, and these seem to have been especially prevalent among women. Given the often hard tenor of rural work, childbirth and rearing, and family life in the countryside, it may be that these cases would not be hard to understand either if we had more information. What does seem clear is that the women healers of Latisana moved out from a nexus of diseases that focused on reproduction and childrearing but included the everyday concerns of the body as well. And at times, they even moved in areas beyond the body, treating the spirit for melancholy and, of course, for love as well.

The most prevalent element in the healing arsenal of the women of Latisana, and of Venice as well, was signing [*segnare*]. In her second examination before the Holy Office in Venice, Apollonia was again asked, "how did you cure the sick that came to find you?" Her response began in a most unexceptional way: "I gave to the infirm many medicinal remedies [*remedii medicinali*] and I then knelt on the ground and said seven Our Fathers and seven Hail Marys." But then her account, without losing its Christian tone, began to slide into areas that were more troubling to the Inquisition: "and then I signed over the person 'In the name of the Father and the Son, and the Holy Spirit. Amen.'"[39] What Apollonia was referring to was the most basic form of signing, which seems to have been drawn from or at least played upon resonances with the way people crossed themselves. As she described it, it might seem a quite harmless appropriation of a common Christian gesture. But of course, it was one thing to cross oneself and quite another to be crossed by someone else. Done by someone else, the gesture implied something given, and in a society unusually attuned to the subtleties of gesture, that distinction was not lost on the Church or on our healers and their clients. Thus Apollonia's seemingly innocent remark immediately focused the interrogation on the religious nature of her cures and the claims that she made for her medicine in Christian terms.

Signing and la Draga

Of course, Apollonia's inquisitors heard more easily what it is difficult for us to hear in her admission, because they had been attuned to hear it by earlier, more open—and, from their perspective, dangerous—testimony. The case of la Draga provides a rich example. One of Venice's most famous healers, widely known for her cures and long remembered after her day, she was active from midcentury to the late 1580s. Her real name was Elena Crusichi, but she was widely known as la Draga because that was the name of the most active of the spirits that lived inside her. Brought before the Inquisition twice, her testimony reveals her as at once a clever, masterful person and one who occasionally painfully disintegrated into multiple personalities that she and those around her attributed to the spirits that possessed her. It appears that the Inquisition had great trouble deciding what to make of this woman who flitted so unnervingly among personalities.[40] Exorcism may have seemed the correct response, as it made little sense to punish a body already the victim of evil spirits. The Inquisition's records provide little clue to what they decided beyond demonstrating that their investigations had little impact on her healing. In fact, la Draga was often a significant point of reference in other cases. Many knew her as a healer and signer, and many admitted that they had learned aspects of their magic from her or her disciples.

What we do know is how la Draga claimed to sign, for in her lucid moments she was quite willing to share her techniques with the Holy Office, techniques that had strong resonances with other signing in Venice and the countryside. In 1571 her interrogation before the Holy Office began with a question about her work. She replied, "I spin linen thread on a wheel and I have lost the use of my right side [others would suggest that this was the result of a battle that she lost with the demons that inhabited her body] and I have been blind now for thirty-three years. By the grace of God when someone brings me some shred of clothing from some child when I touch it immediately I know what its illness is."[41] The Inquisition, of course, wanted to know more about her cures, and la Draga obligingly responded with a virtual guided tour of the repertoire of a signer.

"When I am brought," she answered, "a child or even its swaddling I know if it has been eaten by witches or if it has some fear [*spasemo*] upon it. If it is bewitched I go and get six hearts of rue and five of southernwood and five of wormwood and five of lady's mantle and five cloves of garlic. And as I clean them I say five Our Fathers and five Hail Marys in honor of the five wounds of Messer Jesus Christ. I take, as well, some of the coals left from the fire of Christmas eve and I pound all these things between two pieces of marble. Then I pour over two soldi's worth of oil of the laurel and with this mixture I want the child to be oiled in the form of a cross starting from the arm and [going to the other] end of the body. Saying [as I do so] 'In the name of Christ and of the glorious Virgin Mary and of the Holy Trinity that the Lord be the one who liberates you from this disease.' And this oiling one does on the third Thursday of the moon or actually the last. And when Sunday comes I do the bath. [For this] I take a little water boiled with the coals [*lissia:* water used for washing clothes] and mix with it the remains of the earlier herbs used and as I oiled him in the form of a cross so I wash him in the form of a cross. Once washed I have this child sleep between two people. And when I have finished the washing and the suds have disappeared, I have the water from the bath thrown in the canal, saying, 'As this water goes away to the sea, so too goes away and runs off all your sickness.'"[42]

More rich than most accounts, la Draga's description nonetheless included the basic elements common to most signing rituals when the patient was present: the oiling of the body, its marking with a cross or crosses, and prayer. Such oiling, as we have seen, could move in several directions at once. La Draga's oil was quite complex in its formulation, and its medicinal qualities in the modern sense, that is, its chemical properties, may have actually had some effect and been intended to have some effect. Oils were also used frequently in a sympathetic way. What the oil represented in nature was another form, usually a higher one, of that aspect or part of the body that would bring the body back to harmony. The oil drew the underlying power from the thing in nature and transferred it to its parallel in the body, reinforcing and strengthening it. Although it is not clear that there was this dimension in la Draga's oil, it is suggested that this was the case in the later washing ceremony that she described and that is found in several other cases as well. The throwing away of the wash water with the last of the original herbs in it suggests that some sympathetic relationship would throw out the disease with the water. That hint is made explicit by the prayerlike refrain "As this water goes away to the sea, so too goes away and runs off all your sickness." Also, perhaps the use of washing water made in the same fashion as the regular water used for the wash by women implied that women could wash away sickness as they could wash away the dirt in clothes. Finally, oils were made more powerful by their association with the holy. Sometimes this was done directly, as when holy oil was used for the oiling or holy things were used in the preparation of the oil; but most commonly, this was achieved by applying the oil in the form of a cross and accompanying the application with prayer.

This crossing part of the ceremony recalls the sacrament of extreme unction and in a curious way harks back to healing practices that appear to have been associated with the early Church. The modern form of extreme unction involves a much more complex series of crossings over the body of one gravely ill, but even the close association of the sacrament with last rites and death has not entirely replaced the earlier association of the rite with healing. Theologians, in fact, can still refer to cures that result from the rite as not miraculous but a normal association with the efficacy of the sacrament.[43] But in the early Church, recovery from illness was a normal concomitant of the forms of unction out of which extreme unction developed, and references to such healing are to be found scattered throughout the Bible. Perhaps the most significant text was the one with which this chapter began from the book of James: "Is any among you sick? Let him call for the elders of the church, and let them pray over him, anointing him with oil in the name of the Lord; and the prayer of faith will save the sick man, and the Lord will raise him up; and if he has committed sins, he will be forgiven."[44]

There is no crossing in this text, but la Draga for the rest of it was not far from having reenacted James's call, adding the later crossing that she and her peers probably saw as working in the same way as the sacrament. Obviously the Church was not anxious to accept such a logic, for it feared that such practice once more put powers and rites that were sacramental in the hands of the laity. In fact, post-Trent readings of James tended to interpret "elders of the church" as "priests" to avoid what by then was seen as a dangerous misreading. But that notwith-standing, a quick perusal of early saints' lives reveals that without being priests, they often healed much in the mode of James and la Draga,[45] and if such healers now would be priests, ironically women would be too.

It should be noted that there is a deeper overlap between the practice of la Draga and the Church. Just as the oil used for extreme unction was ideally to be blessed by a bishop on the Thursday before Easter, so too la Draga prepared her oil on a special Thursday determined by the phase of the moon. In addition, the Thursday before Easter was the evening of the Good Supper; Friday was the Passion; and on the third day, that is, Sunday, Christ rose from the dead. For la Draga, on Sunday the sick child's body was to be washed and freed from disease. Such timing may be merely accidental, but it is suggestively parallel. These parallels, how-ever, should not mask a point worth considering: scholars are often anxious, when discussing paganlike practices found in the late Middle Ages or early modern period, to assume that these reflect an enduring substratum of pagan belief in Europe. Reversing that truism, here we might argue that we are discovering a hidden substratum of early Chris-tian beliefs. And we might even continue to posit a reemergence of a primitive Church in the early modern period out of a folk culture where it had continued for more than a millennium.

Certainly such a claim would be stimulating, but perhaps we should take the easier and more logical path of accepting multiple origins of certain very basic ways of looking at the world. Health and religion are often perceived in ways that overlap, and thus power over the one tends to create and re-create structures of perception that suggest power over the other. The significance of the rhythms of time is also a perennial source of speculation at all levels of culture. Thus closely related forms of magic or belief may well be frequently re-created rather than requiring the hypothesis that they somehow managed to endure hidden across the centuries. And that is particularly true when people are unwilling to accept the everyday as merely the everyday; when, that is, they insist on finding their world rich with metaphor and deeper poetic meanings—when oils draw power from the holy and what it represents, when wash water becomes truly cleansing, when signing with a cross becomes truly re-forming—the poetics of the everyday is capable of re-creating mean-ing, power, and health as well.

The Dangers of Signing Babies

Signing babies, however, was a risky business. When they recovered, a woman was a healer. When they died, things became more problematic. That was especially the case because it was assumed in the popular imagination, both in Venice and in the countryside, that witches somehow consumed babies, and the frequent wasting diseases that struck young children often were attributed to witches "eating" them. This is particularly interesting because there is little sign that the Inquisition or the Church was pressing this vision of witches in the area. If anything, the Holy Office seemed anxious to avoid such accusations and, when confronted with testimony alluding to this situation, seldom followed up on it. The investigation of Apollonia, however, suggests how such fears could be kept alive by healers themselves and at the same time reveals another particularly prevalent form of signing. Early on in the collection of testimony in Latisana, a widow named Antonia informed authorities that "this Apollonia signed a daughter of mine. She signed the swaddling measuring it with her forearm and the span of her hand to see if the swaddling expanded or contracted. After she signed it she gave me the swaddling and I wrapped the baby. But I do not think the swaddling worked. Rather this Apollonia said that my child was being eaten by witches. She said by two witches."[46]

Here the nature of the signing is different. Rather than actually signing the child itself, Apollonia had signed its swaddling. This technique was a common one both in Venice and in the countryside. It may have been that this was merely a practical way of avoiding the early modern equivalent of the house call, as it obviated the necessity of traveling to the sick child. But it seems to have worked in a slightly different way from signing in person. First, it tended to use clothing intimately associated with the body of the afflicted, whether a child or an adult. For children, swaddling was particularly popular. For adults, who were also frequently cured in this way, a belt, cords (used like a belt or cinch), a garter, or some garment worn against the skin were among the most popular. Often these objects seem to have been treated like an extension of the body. They were signed with the sign of a cross, prayers were said over them, and then the person who had brought the garment was instructed to have the person being treated wear it.

Apollonia, early in her testimony in Venice, admitted readily that she had signed cords and clothing brought to her. "Yes sir, many times I was brought at home some cords or other piece of clothing of the sick when they were far away and I could not go to them. Over the said cord I would make the sign of the cross saying, 'In the name of the Father and the Son and the Holy Spirit.' And I would say a prayer over them, which is this one: 'In the name of God and the Virgin Mary who puts her hands before mine. Six saints are on earth who will not help you and three are in heaven who will help you Gasparo, Marchio and Baldisser [the three magi who visited Christ], thus you are called—and I say the name of the sick person—Catherine, thus you are called and I sign you against the evils of witchcraft, against the evils of bad encounters, and against the evils of the evil eye. And then I make the sign of the cross [saying], "In the name of the Father and the Son and the Holy Spirit.'"[47] Leaving aside for the moment the prayer used, here Apollonia was clearly using clothing as an extension of the body of the sick. It is interesting to note that although various forms of clothing were used and Apollonia herself pointed out that any clothing would do, there seems to have been a preference for clothing that bound, such as belts, garters, swaddling, and cords. One might speculate that this fit well in the context of much popular magic that worked with binding and unbinding. It appears that those things that bound in everyday life were seen in a sympathetic way as being particularly powerful for creating binding forces that made magic work.

Returning to Antonia and her ill child, she made little mention of Apollonia's signing it in the form of a cross. What stuck in her mind and became prominent in her testimony was the healer's measuring—*spannare*—of her child's swaddling. It is highly probable that Apollonia both measured the swaddling and signed it, and that Antonia was so concerned about the results of the measuring that that became the focus of her recollection. Apollonia later explained to the Inquisition the significance of measuring cords or clothing: it was a kind of diagnostic tool. "When I was brought some cords I measured [*spannavo*] them with my hand and sometimes with my arm and I told them what seemed to me [right] that they were more or less ill. And this I decided on my own because I asked them how they felt. . . . Then I decided on my own and I gave them those remedies that fit the illness."[48] Measuring, then, was used more for evaluation than for curing, much as in love magic, measuring was used to determine relationships, although in both cases it appears sometimes that one slid into the other. The transition from one to the other may not have been that difficult, as ultimately both measuring and much magic were based upon recognizing the deeper relationships between things, and space was one of the more important fields in which those relationships could be observed and manipulated. Still, at its core, most measuring was designed to observe.

Significantly, Apollonia admitted that her measuring was a sham. In her testimony she portrayed it as a performance that went with and covered a more serious evaluation of the patient's illness, almost as if a simple diagnosis was not enough to convince the patient that she could cure. Measuring projected diagnosis into a world that promised more; thus, it helped to empower cures. In turn, we might conjecture that because her cures worked, *spannare* must have seemed effective. Still Apollonia claimed that she was misleading her patients. "I told them some lies in order to earn something to live on. Thus above the cords I said that first prayer which begins, 'In the name of God' [quoted above] and to tell the truth in measuring the cord I made it get longer or shorter as it seemed to me. But it all seemed a silly thing to me. Still I did say to the sick person that they ought to pray to God and say some seven, some fifteen Our Fathers and fifteen Hail Marys so that the Divine Providence would look after their sickness."[49]

It would be easy to conclude that Apollonia was admitting that she was a charlatan, deceiving her patients with mumbo-jumbo in which she had no faith to earn a living. That, however, would not undermine the central point that signing and curing were very important in everyday life and that they empowered a significant group of women in the late Renaissance. But given this, and the fact that there was no shortage of charlatans abroad, I would still suggest that Apollonia, like many of her fellow healers, was too serious about her practice and too rich in lore to be written off so easily. Even her admission that she did not believe in her measuring may have been an attempt to downplay an aspect of her practice that the Holy Office had shown itself to be more concerned about. While healing, especially if the cures were done using Christian things in a way that was deemed misusing them, required discipline and correction but seldom harsh penalties, the ability to know the future or things that were not known openly was much more suspect. It suggested an alliance with evil forces, and in this light, Apollonia's assurance that she measured using the prayer "In the name of God and the Virgin Mary who puts her hand before mine" may take on additional significance, as it gave her diagnosis a Christian context. But that prayer, with its reference to the three wise men and curing, really did not fit very well in the context of measuring to diagnose an illness; thus it may have been that Apollonia's true dishonesty was in trying to downplay her craft in this area by claiming to be a fraud.

Whether sham or effective magical tool of diagnosis, Apollonia's measuring worked at least in the mind of those who had gone to her. For Antonia, who had had the swaddling of her child both measured and signed, the diagnosis that her child was being "eaten by witches" was correct. After describing that diagnosis, she recalled, "I don't know anything else except that at least four years ago Clara del Zamparo, who lives in the group of houses outside the wall touched with her hands my child, who you see here before you [the child apparently had recovered and had come with her mother]. And she said, 'blessed be this little mouthful [*boccolina*], sweet little child.' From that point on the child was always in decline sometimes with a fever, sometimes vomiting a foul substance like chalk. Moreover the child told me that at night something came over her stomach like a little dog and thus as a result when she saw little dogs a great fear came over her."[50] Clearly in this mother's eyes, Apollonia's diagnosis had been accurate; warned by Apollonia, she had no trouble identifying at least one potential witch who seemed to have enjoyed the "sweet" "mouthful" that was her daughter. And although she claimed that she did not believe the signed swaddling had had any effect, her daughter had escaped the witches that were eating her to come before the Holy Office with her four years later.

Antonia's recollections suggest another way of deflecting the suspicions that could develop around a healer if too many signed babies died; one could, as part of the diagnosis, immediately implicate others as the cause of the affliction. Needless to say, this was a double-edged sword, for while it protected the healer from accusation in a particular attempted cure and helped create business by reinforcing the assumption that there were abroad evil women who "ate" babies, by reinforcing those assumptions it also helped keep powerful women like healers under suspicion. Moreover, it did so without the need to have others like the Inquisition impose such ideas from outside; the regular diagnosis of suffering children as the victims of other powerful women fed the fear.

A Diversified Practice and Holy Tales

Another way of defusing or at least limiting the potential for negative *fama* in signing was to vary one's practice to avoid an overconcentration on signing babies, thus avoiding too strong an association with what were, given the demographics of the period, risky cures. La Draga, for example, signed for a spectrum of other illnesses, most of which were considerably less lethal. Headaches were a specialty that she signed in a rather poetic way. "For headaches, I sign over the head three times in the form of a cross and say: 'In name of the Father and the Son and the Holy Spirit.' And I say the following words: 'In Bethlehem there was born a child, his father was a saint, his mother was a saint.' Then I say three Our Fathers and three Hail Marys, thus in a cross [here she may have been showing the court how she did this] in praise of God and the Virgin Mary and the Holy Trinity. [Then I say,] 'that the Lord will free you from this illness.'

"And I put three blessed olive leaves in the middle of the forehead and say these words, 'Saint Lazarus was on the mountain holding his hand on his forehead when the Virgin Mary passed by and said, 'Lazarus what is wrong with you that you hold your head like that?' He answered, 'Oh sweet Virgin Mary, my head hurts, my heart dies.' The Virgin Mary replied, 'Lazarus go up on the mountain and take three leaves of olive and put them on your forehead in the form of a cross saying, 'In the name of the Father and of the Son and of the Holy Spirit' so that this illness leaves you. And make the sign of the cross three times [for each member of the Trinity] which makes nine times. Then, making the sign of the cross on the forehead, I say, 'I sign you evil for the Savior of the world, for the sign of Tau, for the beard of Christ, for the milk of the Virgin Mary.' These same words one says as one signs every part of the head with crosses finishing on the forehead. And when I have finished signing I say, 'Jesus of Nazareth in this forehead, blood of God in this mouth, and the power of Christ in this breast.'"[51]

In this signing oil was absent, perhaps replaced by the olive leaves suggested by the story of Lazarus and the Virgin Mary. Such legendary tales are found widely in Italian folklore and across a wide span of time as well. The Venetian Holy Office, however, only occasionally encountered them in accounts of healing. But when they did, one glimpses a much richer culture that probably stood behind many popular curing techniques. These *historiole,* as they were called, seem to have served both as mnemonic devices for helping the healer remember the often complex prayers that went with cures and as illustrations for those being cured to help them understand the power that stood behind the treatment. Thus la Draga, in the midst of signing and prayer, enlarged the context of her cure by narrating its sacred origins. She as a healing woman was following the example and advice of the Virgin Mary, the most powerful and perfect woman in the Catholic pantheon of women; thus she became virtually a woman priest of a supernatural woman. Moreover this moment of legend at the heart of healing underscored the Christian nature of her healing; no witchery or devil worship was needed. And tellingly, Mary's advice was motivated by her motherly concern for Lazarus's suffering and was given in the familiar tones of dialect: *che astu* [what is wrong with you?], *tuo* [take], *fazzando* [making, saying]; the result was a warm, motherly Christian cure taken from the first time of Christianity and set in a familiar Venetian verbal and emotional setting. La Draga brought religion literally home to her patients and, multiplied by many women healers, the result may well have been a rich poetics of the everyday and a significant other type of Christianity.

But la Draga did not stop there, for her last line about the power of the Trinity being transferred into the body of the person treated had a tale behind it as well. She began: "It is a long story to relate, but when I tell you, you will be made to understand great things of the mystery of God."[52] La Draga was so much the priest of her Christianity that she had apparently little fear before the Inquisition and was fully prepared to instruct them in the mysteries of the faith. There is almost a colleciality in her tone that suggests alliance rather than conflict.[53]

"When our Lord returned to this world," she continued, "the Apostles were all together in a boat. And talking among themselves they wondered, 'We would like to know what was the greatest passion of Christ when he was in this world.' The Lord came to them and he said, 'My sons, what are you chattering about?' They replied, 'Lord, we are chattering because we would like to know what was your greatest passion in your martyrdom.' He responded, 'I did not suffer any martyrdom crueler than when I was taken down from the column where I had been given 6666 lashes and had the cross put on my shoulder. This brought forth three knots [on my body] and I thought I would then pass from this world to the next. . . . Learn from this, for you must go through the world preaching my faith and you will encounter those who will drive you crazy and criminals, heretics, Jews, and assassins. But be patient: for in this world you will suffer but in the next you will have paradise at my side. I want you to say every morning and evening three Our Fathers and three Hail Marys in praise of God and the Virgin Mary and the Good Angel who accompanies you. And always make this sign: 'Jesus of Nazareth in this forehead, blood of God in this mouth, and the power of Christ in this breast.' Always I will leave you a piece of my cloak, thus in heaven as on earth.''[54]

In this little story, as la Draga promised, there is virtually a popular theology. Rather than sin and redemption, it focuses on the suffering of daily life in the common world where Christ and the apostles lived, not as nobles or members of the elite but as the oppressed. It speaks of the resignation necessary to endure suffering with the hope of eternal life at the side of Christ. This is not a humanist or an elite theology, but one for common people who live a life of suffering themselves and for whom acceptance (or resignation) is an important precept.[55] But the tale is not only about resignation, for as with Christ's promise at the Last Supper that formed the basis of the sacrament of the Eucharist, here Christ promised a piece of his protective cloak in this world to help people get by and, in a way, to give them some of his protective power on earth— when the correct prayers were said and signs made. La Draga did just that to cure, not as some simpler form of medicine, not as some watered-down form of Christian healing, but as a representative of Christianity who could teach even the Holy Office about the close relationship between the divine and the human, between sacred time and the everyday, and about the healing possibilities implicit therein. As one might expect, however, her culture was largely lost on theirs, and with a nice irony, rather than question her further after her theological excursus, they sent her back to her cell and retired themselves for the night—to dream of a different God, a blond noble who did not speak Venetian dialect?

Latisana also had its tales that stood behind the prayers of signing. In fact, Apollonia's mother, Maria, related to the ecclesiastical authorities there a *historiola* of her own. "When I was a child," she told them, ". . . while I was learning spells, I learned this: I was told that one day Messer Jesus Christ [who] was poor and went searching through the world dressed as a pilgrim went to stay in a house where there was a wife and a husband alone with a child. The husband gave him lodging against the wishes of the wife. Messer Jesus Christ went out of the house and the husband in a short time put together for him a bed of straw. But the woman out of anger wet the straw with water without the husband knowing. Messer Jesus Christ went to bed and tossing and turning he found it wet; so he slept on the edge and kept quiet to avoid causing a quarrel between the couple. Thus he slept as well as he could in the room where there was a bow and an arrow. The next morning Messer Jesus Christ left early. Immediately after he left an attack of hysteria came over the child. The wife said 'Oh my God [who knows] if that wanderer knew some remedy for this sickness.' The husband said, 'Go after him and ask.' This woman ran after him and catching him she asked if he knew any remedy. He answered, 'Yes.' So they returned and he healed the child with the following words: 'Between the bow and the arrow be well now, now; the man [is] good, the woman bad, and the straw wet. As the sickness came over you, so shall it leave. In the name of the Father, and the Son, and the Holy Spirit. Amen.'"[56]

As was the case with la Draga, this tale was used to explain one of the prayers Maria used for signing and seems to have also served as a mnemonic device. Once again Christ was put in a familiar, human scene that played on themes of marital discord and hospitality. Earlier Maria had reported a brief prayer that at the time had seemed to make little sense, describing it as the main prayer she used when signing hysteria and other ailments, including children's diseases: "Be well now, now; the man [is] good, the woman bad. As this sickness came over you, so shall it leave. In the name of the Father and the Son and the Holy Spirit. Amen."[57]

Apparently her interrogators had found that small prayer by itself to have little meaning and had not asked for any explanation. We know the longer story that stands behind it and gives it a richer meaning only because later, in the context of discussing how she learned to sign, Maria recalled that as a young girl she had gone to spin at the house of a certain Agna. There she had begun to learn in addition signing and the broader Christian culture that empowered it. Her interrogators were still not particularly interested in this context of her signing, but Maria's testimony, much like la Draga's more aggressive explanations in Venice, should serve as a caution that even though the material that exists reveals a very complex and rich world, we are still just at the edge of it. And crucially from that edge we must be very wary of underestimating its intricacies and logic, if we would understand it at all.

Signing was also used in Latisana for headaches, although few women were as detailed in their testimony as la Draga. Margarita di Latisana, who was brought before the Venetian Holy Office shortly after Apollonia, but clearly as part of the same general furor stirred up by Pietro di Venezia, began her testimony by admitting that she cured headaches with prayers and signing. "For headaches," she related on 13 August 1591, "I normally put a hand on the forehead of the patient touching with my fingers the whole span between the temples and I say, 'Headache you are to be undone as Judas was undone [for his deeds] against messer Lord God.' This I followed with three signings with the cross on the forehead saying, 'In name of the Father and the Son and the Holy Spirit.' If one can say this prayer three times all in one breath, it has more power. And it cures more rapidly when one has a great headache."[58] Although the theology is different here and apparently less developed, the sympathetic aspect of the signing is more evident. The headache was to be undone as Judas had been undone. This sympathetic prayer, as we might call it, in a way grounded the more abstract and perhaps more formally correct invocation of the Trinity in a brief, well-known Christian event that demonstrated the ultimate power of God.

Margarita's signing relied heavily on this type of technique, as did that of many others. For example, her cure for a bloody nose utilized a particularly powerful moment of the Christian tradition to give meaning to another sympathetic prayer. "In order to stop a bloody nose, I put my fingers on the nose and say this prayer, 'Blood stay strong, as Messer Jesus Christ stayed strong in his death. Blood stay in your vein, as Messer Jesus stayed in his passion.'"[59] Again prayer, sympathetic magic, and story overlap to reinforce the request for divine aid in binding blood as the Lord had bound his passion. The Inquisition did not ask, however, one very significant question—one that seems more evident after earlier discussion of similar types of prayers in love magic and particularly in the *carte di voler bene*. Were these sympathetic prayers merely a reminder of God's power that was being called upon to help cure, or were they, with their formal structure, so similar to the structure of magic that bound actually designed to force God's aid in some way? Between asking God or forcing him, needless to say, theologians and inquisitors would have seen a great gulf. But once again, for healers, positing such a dialectical vision may be inappropriate. If God helped, that may have been enough, and if the structure of prayer based on sympathetic magic had some deeper power, so much the better.

In fact, it might be more accurate to rephrase the question in terms of the popular perceptions of the sacraments, especially the Eucharistic ceremony or extreme unction. If those sacraments brought the divine into this world each time they were carried out, was not God in some way being forced by prayer and ritual to comply with a human's will? Of course, the theological answer is "no." But that "no" is based on a series of fine theological points that are neither evident nor particularly compelling without a certain cultural set. From another perspective I think shared by many healers and their patients, God's powers in this world were available through a range of "sacramental" activities much wider than that offered by the formal Church. Trent may have reconfirmed the tradition of seven sacraments and male priests, but Trent was just reaching the countryside at the end of the century, and even in the cities the theology of Trent may not have been enough for popular religion.

Another prayer for staunching the flow of blood, in this case from wounds, reveals well the way sympathetic magic prayers could slide over into *historiole* or holy tales. This prayer came to light in an examination that developed out of Pietro di Venezia's preaching in Latisana. A servant named Aloysia, after her master had told her about one of Pietro's sermons announcing that those who signed were excommunicated, decided to come in and confess her practice of signing for wounds. She confessed that she healed wounds by saying, "The Holy Night that Our Lord was revived, he did not wish that there be any wounds nor even blood" and then "the Holy Night when Our Lord was laid out, he did not wish that there be any wounds nor even blood; the Holy Night that Our Lord was revealed he did not wish that there be any blood or wounds. In name of the Father and of the Son and of the Holy Spirit." "And with three pieces [of cloth] that I had signed with these words," she continued "I covered the wound and blood. And I put the pieces over the wound in the form of a cross."[60] Here we have again a central moment of the Christian myth elaborated as a story recited during signing. It also exhibits the sympathetic form, even though the "as . . . so too" format is not explicitly stated. It is certainly implied: as Christ wanted no wounds or blood at those specific moments of great significance, so too Aloysia asked for (or perhaps demanded) no wounds or flowing of blood any longer for her patients.

But if these cures at one level may have forced God's help, much as sacraments seemed to, there was also a sense that certain people were better at signing and making their curing prayers work. We have already noted that la Draga was relatively famous in Venice over a significant span of time for her cures and was still referred to after her death as an important healer. Her possession by spirits certainly added to her charisma as a healer. Yet it also created problems for her claim that her magic was Christian, as her spirits clearly were not. Even nonecclesiastic contemporaries sensed this logical contradiction. And other healers who claimed the aid of spirits like Apollonia in Latisana faced similar suspicions, especially when their cures failed. Still, such healers tended to see their magic as positive and Christian even if they were inhabited and aided by spirits and demons. Again la Draga revealed this well, even as she also revealed that her primary spirit, the Draga, could be very nasty at times. During her second testimony of 14 August 1571, as she was describing a cough medicine that she made for children based on a syrup of sage, rue, and wine boiled together and then dissolved in honey, "she was overcome by a great burp and then began to grind her teeth and scream, saying many obscene things. She threw herself on the ground with great rage in the typical manner of those vexed by demons. Whence having seen these things the inquisitors ordered her taken to her room wishing to continue [later their examination]."[61]

Three days later, interrogated at home (perhaps as a concession to her condition) and with her demon under control, her testimony once again suggested an everyday life suffused with the holy. Every morning, she instructed her questioners, it was wise to say the following prayer to avoid "evil or accidents": "Lady Saint Mary the gentle one, watch over and protect me your servant N. from evil people, from strong iron, from sudden death so that in water I do not drown and a sorry death avoid. With the arms of the Lord I am well armed, with the veil of Lady Saint Mary I am well veiled so that I can go well and return well as Lord Jesus did from the river Jordan. By water, by land, by sea, by ship, by all the ways, both means and path[es]. Oh true body of Christ most sacred, Son of the Virgin Mary, You consoled Martha and Mary; You brought back Lazarus from the shadows. Put me, I pray, on the good path. To Mary you gave grace. To Magdalen you gave the pardon. To your most sweet Mother you gave most great love. Thus I ask you, true body of Christ, make me this grace and this gift for the merits of your Most Saintly Passion that You protect me from Justice, traitors, and evil companions. Amen.''[62] This prayer was to be said three times each morning. Moreover, before going out the door, one was to say each time: ''Christ before and me closely behind on the cross of cypress. May I encounter the same problems out in the street that Christ found within the Body of the Virgin Mary.''[63]

Possessed by a demon, perceived as giving additional power to her magic, la Draga nonetheless lived a life infused with the holy in a particularly poetic form, both in her healing and in her everyday activities. In la Draga's daily prayers, however, there are some suggestions that she was using Christianity even more aggressively than she was prepared to admit. For example, in her morning prayer the references to the ''true body of Christ'' might be taken to refer metaphorically to Christ's body to stress his common humanity, just as references to the Virgin stressed her gentleness and compassion. But, as we have seen, the host was a frequent aspect of the magician's arsenal of holy things and consecrated hosts were especially prized. Could la Draga's prayer have been said over a consecrated host, thus giving its appeals to the true body a much more direct and powerful significance? The prayer certainly seems to suggest that, but again her interrogators did not choose to follow up on the hint or did not see it, perhaps distracted by her poetic prayers and complex personality.

Returning to the relationship between her demon and her Christianity, even la Draga was acutely aware of the problem. For toward the end of her testimony that day at her home she explained, ''After I have taken communion, which I did last on the day of the Glorious Virgin Mary, this awful beast which I have on me [*che ho adosso*] gives me so much pain that I feel like I am finished. He eats my guts and destroys my legs, my throat and he takes my memory and he does not let me eat and he wishes to kill me and I hide the knife.''[64] A high price to pay for her special powers, perhaps, but more centrally a testimony that reveals her awareness that her spirit was a demon and no friend of Christ's body. Unfortunately for our curiosity about the relationship between her Christian cures and her anti-Christian demon, as she was continuing with her monologue and was beginning to pull various holy objects out of a trunk where she had them stashed, she noticed a group of women arriving and literally dismissed her interrogator or interrogators.

''Come back another day,'' she said, ''and I will tell you all that I know and that which is good I will teach [you] and that which is not good I will never say again." The notary described what followed: "And while I was there in her house, I saw a group of women who had come to talk with this Elena [la Draga]. I asked her why these women had come and she replied, 'These are my old friends who come to tell me their troubles.'"[65] Here we get a sense of the powerful Draga with her circle of friends meeting at her house, and we see once again the contours of a rather different world of power and religion, where ecclesiastical authorities are dismissed with disarming ease, where demons in one's body and lack of status do not hinder overmuch, and where a notary of the Holy Office can be dismissed with a promise that at some vague future date the ecclesiastical powers that he represents will be taught what is good in a different Christianity. It would be several years before she was questioned again.

It should be noted, however, that from la Draga's perspective, her relationship to the Church was not one of competition so much as cooperation. Her religion did not require conflict with that of the Church or hegemony over it. In fact, from her perspective, her religion and that of the Church were merely two faces of the same phenomenon. In a practical way, she and women like her could draw strength from the sacraments of the Church both spiritually and materially. And at a higher level, as the Church represented a power that was also her power, the more effective and visible the Church was, the better it was for her. In this logic, needless to say, there was one major flaw. It assumed that the Church felt the same way about her that she seemed to feel about it. That was not the case, even if the Holy Office, rather than pursuing la Draga any further, let her case drop. In the end, for all her obvious atypicality, la Draga reveals a popular piety and Christianity that warrants closer study for its impact not only on everyday life but perhaps also on elites, especially in the areas of reform ideology and piety.

Reputation, Good Hands, and Licenses

La Draga's apparently all too close relationship with her private demons may have helped to give her a greater reputation as a healer. But demons were not necessary. Some people simply had what could be called charisma, the knack, or the touch, and were better healers than others. This suggests that signing did not work in a merely mechancial way; either as magic or as medicine, the person who signed could also be important. Apparently this was such a given, however, that it was seldom explicitly stated. But occasionally testimony refers to the reputation of a healer or even the healer's hands in a way that suggests the importance of reputation in signing, as in so much else in the late Renaissance. We encountered this concept earlier in the account of Fioralisa, where she recalled that when the first attempt to cure her daughter failed, she turned to the famous but also frightening power of Camilla Orsetta. La Draga's reputation was so great that it was even passed down through her family; both her daughter and her niece followed in her tradition. In Latisana, Apollonia had also followed in the footsteps of her well-known mother. Of course, in family traditions of healing, the quality of the curing technique almost certainly played a part as well. But once again, reputation enhanced power. A Venetian healer named Benetta provides a fine example of the value of good hands. On 12 January 1592 the "lady Gaspara, wife of lord Christopher" explained to the Holy Office how she had become involved with this Benetta. "A most great sickness had come over my husband," Gaspara reported, "and he had been in the hands of the doctors and had received many medicines, but he did not get well. One day I was in a group of women and talking together about his sickness, I was asked if he had been signed by anyone. I answered 'no.' A woman told me that in the Church of the Frari there was a woman [called] Benetta . . . who signed and *had good hands for signing.*"[66]

Gaspara, following the advice of her friends, sent her husband to Benetta, who cured him. Apparently she and her husband were so impressed with Benetta's "good hands" that they, in turn, sent her husband's brother, Pietro, to her as well. In fact, they probably would have continued to send friends and relatives to Benetta and build her reputation, just as it was built for other healers, if it had not been for the fact that Pietro had confided in confession that he had been signed and cured. His confessor refused to give him absolution until he informed the Holy Office; thus, both brothers and Gaspara had voluntarily presented themselves before the Holy Office to denounce Benetta. There may have been more involved in their denunciation, but the point remains: no one who testified saw Benetta's magic as mechanical. Her hands and their reputation were crucial. And tellingly, Benetta's hands signed and cured where doctors and medicines had failed.

Benetta, after being examined by the Holy Office, was released with a warning not to practice anymore. But there was an added proviso: she was not to claim any longer that she had special license from the Church to sign. Benetta was not alone in this type of claim. A number of women, perhaps not finding confession and public communion enough to prove the holiness of their signing, also claimed to have been licensed by the Church to carry out their healing. Gaspara reported, "She [Benetta] said to me that she had had a license and that she had the authority to sign, but I do not know from who as I do not remember."[67] Benetta confirmed before the Holy Office that she regularly made this claim, revealing in the process an interesting way of taking advantage of even being called before the Holy Office. It turns out that Benetta had been called in by them once before. After being questioned, she had been released—technically, in the terminology of the tribunal, *licentiata.* But being *licentiata,* that is, "released" had another meaning as well: being licensed to practice. And although that clearly was not the Holy Office's intention when they released someone, there were enough ambiguities about the process that it could have been interpreted as a licensing. When signers were called before the Holy Office, they were examined about their practices and often specifically about the holy aspects of their craft. If something was found wrong, they were instructed not only to stop the practice but usually also to do some form of public penance to atone for their misdeeds. In this judging of practice the Holy Office was rather like a guild court; holy healers accused of spiritual malpractice were examined, and when they were released (*licentiata*) their practice could be seen as having been confirmed and licensed (*licentiata*). In this way, a successful encounter with the Inquisition could be even better than confession and communion.

Benetta may have been merely clever, but even as cleverness, her explanation of her licensing suggests this ambiguity well. Before the Holy Office she too talked freely and proudly about her signing and healing techniques, faltering only for a moment to admit that she had considered giving up signing. The inquisitor who had listened with patience up to that point could not resist what appeared to him an obvious self-contradiction and asked, "Why do you not want to sign anymore? Are you [actually] aware that you are doing evil?" What follows leads one to question who was leading who in the give-and-take of this interrogation. The stereotype, of course, is that inquisitors led ignorant, uncultured people of the lower classes into confessing what they (the inquisitors) wanted to hear. And there is truth in the stereotype, at least to the extent that at times they did lead people to confess things that they (the inquisitors) expected to hear. But often the people examined were neither ignorant nor uncultured, and some were also quite capable of turning the thread of the interrogation in directions that were significant for them. And many women labeled witches were clever masters of words who were used to verbally shaping reality to their ends; thus Benetta replied, "If I were to have a license I would practice [signing], but if not I would not." Suddenly she had shifted the discussion from her cures and knowing whether or not they were evil to her pious intent to do only what the Church licensed her to do. Benetta went on to clarify: "I was once before called before this Holy Office and was examined for these same prayers and these same signings that I do and I was licensed [*licentiata*]."[68] Even though they had heard in earlier testimony that she claimed to be licensed, it appears that the Holy Office simply did not hear what she was saying. They continued doggedly asking what the Inquisition had said to her earlier.

Benetta had explained to the Holy Office how she got her license; but apparently all they could see was that if they pushed her harder, she might admit that she had already been told that her signing was wrong. In a way, she and her interrogators were ships passing in the night of diverse cultural expectations. And, in fact, at first Benetta seemed a bit put off by the lack of comprehension, responding quickly, "I do not remember what was said to me by this Holy Office."[69] Under continued questioning, however, Benetta appears to have understood that she would have to respond to the inquisitor's lead. Cleverness was not enough; she could lead her interrogators, but in the end, if they would not follow, she had to give them something on their line of questioning. Nevertheless she had been before them before and knew what they wanted. Thus she satisfied them with what she may well have believed as well: "I told them that I had faith in the words of the Majesty of God and not in myself." But in giving the Holy Office an answer that related to their question and showed that even if she was mistaken she was still a Christian, Benetta had turned the tables slightly. Rather than giving them the confession they wanted—that she had previously been warned about the errors of her healing—she painted a vision of that healing as completely orthodox.

Apparently content with that, her interrogators turned to other matters and shortly thereafter came to *their* question about her licensing. They asked, "Did you in the signing that you did, claim to have license and authority [to do so] and from whom?" One wonders how Benetta received this question when, just a few minutes before, she had answered it. Still she took the opportunity to respond again: "I said clearly to those who came to me that I had been here [before the Holy Office] and that I had been *licensed* and that [signing] had not been prohibited to me. And I believed I had this authority to sign."[70] The Holy Office may have heard what she was saying this time, but they took the matter no further. And in the end, after lecturing her sternly about mending her ways and avoiding superstition, ironically once again they "released/ licensed [*licentiavit*] the said Benetta with the admonition to in the future abstain, having been warned."[71] Had they unwittingly once again licensed Benetta to cure with her talented hands?

The Ties That Bind and Women Priests in Latisana

Apollonia in Latisana appears also to have been once regarded as a talented healer. But she was more, as were many of her peers, for although the case constructed against her and a number of other women there did not really concentrate on it, it is important to remember that in the beginning, Pietro di Venezia had been very concerned about the love magic of the women of Latisana. From his perspective, such practices were most harmful, turning husbands against wives, breaking up families and friendships as well. It was almost as if these women had in their hands the power to dissolve the bonds of love and friendship upon which society was built. As we have seen, however, there was another way to envision these powers: they could be construed as literally creating the ties that bound, the affections upon which family and social networks were built.

Once more, Apollonia appears to have been a master in this area and recognized as one. Nicolo Romaneto, labeled *dominus* (lord) by the notary who recorded his testimony, came in early in the investigation in Latisana, "having heard last Sunday . . . the sermon in the Church of San Giovanni that those who know of witchcraft or other similar things should reveal them." He recalled, "it is fifteen years ago [he would have been seventeen at that time] that I was in love with a sister of Battistella Grotto. Wishing to have her love me, I went to Apollonia, who made flowers, and I bought some to send to my love. And in that way, lamenting that I doubted that my love loved me, that [Apollonia] said to me that she wanted to teach me how to make her love me. Thus she asked me to give her a garter or even a tie of her clothing. I found such a tie and a garter, but she signed the garter first. She measured it with her palm to see if it got longer or shorter, saying some words quietly that I could not hear. Finally she gave me the garter that she had signed and I tied it on my right leg if I remember correctly. Every time that I went to this Apollonia I had the consolation of taking it off and putting it on. Then she said to me that it would be more effective to sign a tie. So I found a tie and she measured it with her palm like she had done with the garter [but] making certain knots. Then she taught me that at night I had to tie it on my bare leg saying these words which she taught me, "I tie [*ligo*] and untie [*non ligo*] this tie [*legame*], but I tie [*ligo*] the heart and the mind and the emotions of Jacoma, that she may not ever have happiness, neither eating or drinking.'"[72]

It appears that Nicolo, after fifteen years, did not remember too clearly the prayer that was to go with his tying and untying of the tie. The "as . . . so too" parallel so crucial in this type of magic that clearly stood behind the prayer seems to have been partially forgotten. Also there is the vague memory of a *martello* that would allow Jacoma no happiness, but Nicolo recalled no release from that hammer in return for the love that was obviously the reason for the magic.[73] After claiming that he had done all this with the unthinking ways of a young man in love and that it had not worked, he continued: "I gave to this Apollonia several times money with which she promised to buy some oils to oil the door of the house of my love. Finally she told me that she had done it and said as well some words which I do not remember. And she told me she said this prayer so that my love would love me alone and no one else. I didn't know at that time that I was doing evil, because I did not do it for an evil end but only to take her for my wife."[74] Self-serving perhaps, but this testimony reveals nicely the other side of love magic: Nicolo sought from Apollonia aid in constructing the very tie that bound society together and, as is so often the case, even the language and forms of the magic used to attempt to secure this were based on ties—the one thing that Nicolo remembered clearly from fifteen years before.

Without repeating all that has been discussed already in relation to love magic in Venice and Feltre, Apollonia's use of love magic in Latisana reveals again the ubiquity of certain practices and the centrality of love magic even for healers. This is not at all surprising, for many of the practices of healing were paralleled in love magic, both in Venice and in more rural areas. The use of prayers and signing were common to both; the case of Nicolo merely recalls what we have already seen elsewhere. But Apollonia adds some detail to our picture of love magic that may reflect the rural context of her magic. And that, in turn, suggests that while there were clearly great continuities across the Veneto in such practices, there was also the possibility of considerable variation—variation, I would suggest, that could have been easily reproduced across time and space without having to claim some kind of transmission. Simply stated, given the necessities and logic of rural life and love magic, certain themes were likely to recur over and over again without having to posit an enduring substratum of belief or a complex history of the passing of such beliefs from community to community or individual to individual.

At the beginning of her testimony, it might be remembered, Apollonia had denied any knowledge of love magic and had turned her testimony toward her healing. Her inquisitors, however, came back to the topic, and eventually she was led to admit that she had done such magic. But she did so only on her own terms: "I never taught anyone to bind, because I do not know such things, but rather to free people, because I have a license from my confessor."[75] Nicolo's testimony, along with that of several others, creates doubt about her claim, but we see that even Apollonia claimed her form of licensing and, more important, she took the tack that her magic in this area was entirely positive.

She continued: "The technique that I used for unbinding those who cannot have intercourse with their wives is as follows: for some, I have them put under the bed the blade of the plow, that is the metal with which one plows the field; for others I have them put [there] the hoe and the shovel which are used for burying the dead; for others I have them take a ring with which a young virgin was married and which has been placed in holy water, then they must urinate through this ring."[76] The use of the blade of the plow as a symbol of masculine potency is a fine potential example of the recurrence of symbols. Plowing as a metaphor for sexual intercourse can be found in virtually the earliest written texts we have and, of course, is still used metaphorically in that sense in many cultures and languages today. But one does not have to turn to a theory of *longue duré* or of transmission of culture to explain this. In societies that associate sexual intercourse with the male penetration of the female and understand that this often leads to pregnancy, the parallels with plowing the fields to make them fertile are myriad and ubiquitous. Thus, although it is perfectly possible that Apollonia's lore was passed from mother to daughter for generations, even passed somehow in the manner Ginzburg has described for witchcraft, itself evolving slowly from ancient times,[77] it is equally possible that the parallels between plowing and intercourse and their implications for sympathetic magic were discovered independently numerous times in many different cultures.

The meaning of the hoe and the shovel from the graveyard are more problematic, and one might be tempted by a Freudian eros/thanatos dialectic.[78] More probable would be a reading that draws on a Bakhtinian theme—the carnivalesque vision of the late Middle Ages and early modern period that saw life being brought from death. The hoe and shovel of the gravedigger in that context might be seen as both burying and giving new life, for the dead body, once buried, gives new life. Here the "as . . . so too" form would work nicely as well, for as these tools bring life from death, so too Apollonia's magic would bring life from the death of impotence brought on by being bound by magic.

The last magic, based on a wedding ring, seems the most obscure. Certainly the power of rings and their symbolism is ubiquitous, and virginity, holy water, and marriage add potent additional layers of meaning at least potentially to the mix. But how the mix was actually supposed to work is difficult to narrow down without some clue from Apollonia. Unfortunately, she provided none. But the difficulty in reading this part of her magic should also remind us that our other readings are only hypothetical ones; for it may be that what seems evident to us was not evident to Apollonia and her customers, and that they saw quite other meanings in what they did, meanings that are as lost on us as the significance of urinating through a virgin's wedding ring.[79]

Be that as it may, Apollonia was clear about one thing: her magic worked. "These were three approved remedies [approved by her confessor, who had given her a "license" to use these cures]. I cured a goodly number with these remedies." But even she at times had need of advice on a difficult case, and once again we see clearly the passing of information between women in Latisana. "There was one among the many, who had been bound for more than a year." she continued. "I could not cure him with the remedy of the plow or the wedding ring. Dorothea Giandola from Latisana asked me if he had been cured. I replied 'no.' She, therefore, taught me the cure of the hoe and shovel, saying that she remembered that her mother who was old said that this hoe and shovel were good. This was probably a little more than a year ago."[80]

Although Apollonia stuck to the story that she did not bind anyone, under pressure she finally did admit supplying, as a "joke," some pseudomagic for the local perfume maker, Mario Roma to use.[81] And after further reflection she confessed, "once there came to me a woman named Catarina, who was kept by a priest named Battista from Latisana and she said to me, 'Dear Apollonia do me a favor and bind to me the priest so that he can not go to other women.' I told her that I did not know how. But she pestered me so much that I promised to do it and I had her give me some bread. But really I did nothing. A few days later this priest stopped me in the street and said to me that I ought to leave his house alone and that I should avoid witchcraft. I said to him, 'My lord friend, do you have problems in your life?' He answered 'no' and that he did not fear witchcraft either."[82]

Perhaps here was another factor in Apollonia's problems with the Church, for thinly veiled behind this conversation, at least as she portrayed it, were both a threat to a local priest and a virtual tweaking of his pride with her seemingly innocent question "do you have problems in your life?" His reported response seems to have attempted to turn the tables on her by warning her that he was not afraid of her magic and that he had the power to label her a witch. This probably is reading too much into a conversation disclosed to the Inquisition by an obviously not disinterested participant, but at the least it reveals that Apollonia's relationship with one local priest was not good—something already noted. Here, perhaps from a self-serving perspective, we once again see how she had lost support and fallen into a position where the accusation of evil witchcraft could be laid at her door.

But, of course, Apollonia did not see it that way. She was a healer, and she came from a family associated with healing. Other women referred to her as the source of their knowledge, and she, like la Draga, even claimed to have had supernatural contacts that helped her with her healing magic. Under questioning she admitted, "I said to the people that came to me that I had dreams with a fairy in them. And that she told me certain prayers. And it is true that at times I had dreamt about a fairy who seemed to me to grow very large."[83] Unfortunately, for knowing more about this fairy, the Inquisition appears to have been uninterested in this claim, and rather than pursuing it went on to other matters.

Perhaps more important than her fairy for her trade was her mother, Maria, who was also reputed to be one of the leading healers in Latisana. As the furor wound down, Maria was called before local authorities to be examined about her magical practices, as noted earlier. She admitted freely to signing but claimed to have stopped about a year before, when she was warned by a priest that it was against the faith. When asked who had taught her, she at first tried to avoid the question by replying that she had learned so long ago that she could not remember. Pressed, however, she took the other easy way out by claiming to have been taught by a certain Agna, aunt of Picco, who was long dead. She did, however, admit to teaching her children: "I taught this [signing] to my children and to some others, but I do not remember who. Among my children I taught Tonio, Catherina and Pollonia."[84] Maria, like many others, while ready at least in appearance to testify about her signing, was much more reluctant to name others who signed or who had been taught to sign. In fact, after naming her own children, she quickly added that the only one who she thought might have used the knowledge was Apollonia. And, of course, when she made this admission on October 24th 1591, she was not telling the authorities anything they did not already know, for Apollonia had already been tried and convicted for her signing.

But Apollonia and her mother were only the centerpiece of a much larger group of women who practiced healing and love magic in the small town. The investigation spawned by the preaching of Pietro di Venezia revealed at least four other major practitioners who were generally known as healers and frequently referred to in testimony: Fiore Carattiera, the widow of Gasparo Vicentino; Franchescina, wife of Menichi Jacobi (and widow of Gasparo Bevilacqua); Margarita called Margariton, wife of Nicolo del Gobbo; and Giovanna Tamburlina. Giovanna was the only one not brought in to be examined by ecclesiastical authorities, apparently because she had left the area. The other women all readily admitted that they had signed and healed, and all claimed that they had thought such signing was a good thing, as it used Christian powers to heal.

Fiore, it appears, was Apollonia's main competition, and it may have been that her continued success in healing gave her the reputation that Apollonia lacked at the moment when things came to a head. She was referred to in at least ten testimonies, usually in a positive light, as a healer whose cures really worked. Before the authorities she too showed that she understood their concerns, quickly admitting and apologizing for her signing and expressing a ready willingness to give up any practices that were deemed incorrect. Margarita, in turn, appears to have been a quite mobile woman, like Apollonia, and actually showed up in Venice shortly after Apollonia to be examined there. All the other major women were examined in Latisana by representatives of the Inquisition empowered to hear testimony and assign penances and punishments as they deemed necessary.

But with these six major figures, they had just scratched the surface of the healers and love magicians in Latisana. Twelve other people, ranging in age from twelve to their mid-sixties, also came before the authorities to accuse themselves of signing. This group even included three men: Pasqualino Vio, a sailor; Nicolo Ramanetto; and the perfume maker, Mario Roma. Mario claimed to have used love magic as a joke to create amorous problems for a friend, and perhaps because he was a fellow male, the authorities accepted his rather unlikely story and let him off with hardly a warning.[85] Behind this group at least another twenty people, almost all women, were named as having taught or practiced signing and love magic in Latisana, but they were not questioned. Some, of course, were the ubiquitous dead compatriots who allowed one to name the names that interrogators demanded without actually revealing the names of neighbors or fellow healers. Others named may have moved on. But still it seems clear that a number of the rest were ignored by the Inquisition.

We might speculate that as the extent of the phenomenon became apparent and as it became evident to the authorities of the Church that these practices were not driven by devil worship or major heresy, it became clear that education and discipline were better suited to deal with the problem. From that perspective, using university-trained theologians and the relatively complex apparatus of the Inquisition may have seemed too costly and time-consuming given the extent of the problem. Also, of course, they had made their point about these practices by examining and publicly punishing at least some of the main women healers of the town. But perhaps most important, as the testimony and the cases themselves revealed, the publicity generated by aggressive preaching and the examination of the women of Latisana, plus the energetic use of confession to instruct, seemed to have had quite an effect. Most of those who accused themselves had been alerted to their misdeeds either in confession, by hearing sermons, or by hearing about one or the other. In turn, even the most intensive practitioners of signing seemed ready to mend their ways and accept the Church's position. Given all that, it may have seemed sensible to leave Latisana to the local Church.

But the women priests of Latisana were too central to rural life, too necessary there, to be beaten out by a local Church that for all the reforms of Trent remained relatively poor and had great difficulty providing high-quality priests over the longer periods that it would have taken to truly disempower women healers and love magicians. It may have been that the efforts of the Church at the end of the sixteenth century and on into the seventeenth finally undermined women as the true masters of spiritual things in the countryside. Women priests would not exist, but their spiritual and physical power over the bodies and hearts of their community did go on. And it is important not to let the perspective of the eventual victors in this struggle cloud our understanding of the true merits of the system or systems of the losers. For it seems clear that in many ways the total package that the women priests of Latisana provided suited the needs of their community well. Their theology was closely attuned to the world of everyday life, both its problems and its poetry. Their prayers and rituals, quasi-sacraments it appears, dealt with the needs that were central to community life: love, sex, friendship, marriage, hate, strife, life, and death.

We might even argue on one level that in conjunction with the formal Church and the local clergy, their ministry offered an ideal package for a rural community. The priest offered the ultimate things with the sacraments that allowed one to enter the Christian world with baptism, remain in it with the Mass and the Eucharistic ceremony, and gain eternity in it after death with extreme unction. But in between and in the everyday—a much more spiritual and otherworldly everyday than is often assumed for rural society—women priests ruled with a popular Christianity that bound people in love, friendship, and marriage and could break them apart as well. At this level they created the very cement of society. In addition, in a way that was at once negative and positive, some of them could also be the tools of vendetta—negative, evidently, in their ability to hammer others in the name of vendetta; positive, perhaps, in the promise that they offered that even the poor had the power to punish those who mistreated or dishonored them. Beyond this they healed. And, of course, they healed not just the many illnesses of the body, but also those of the spirit and the heart. Through all of this they moved with a Christian theology of their own, clearly less systematic and metaphysical, but nonetheless, from what we can see of it through the distorted and often uncomprehending lens of the Inquisition, poetic, human, and effective, and at times violently vindictive. It was, as we have seen, a theology that sought less to explain the mysteries of the faith than to use those mysteries to draw the divine into the everyday in useful ways.

As a form of cooperation between women priests and a formal Church, it appears that the spiritual life of Latisana had worked quite well. When the Inquisition came to Latisana, they found a community that lived a form of Christianity deeply integrated into everyday life. Even simple daily acts had been given significant spiritual content. And the main events of life were rife with spiritual implications that were not only realized but acted upon. This little town was not mired in the material; rather, there as elsewhere, I would assert, the material and spiritual interacted in a vibrant and fertile mix that could change rapidly and that deeply affected the life and culture of that society.

Still, for a moment, the greater powers of Church and state in the late sixteenth century entered the world of Apollonia and her fellows. What they found troubled them enough to mobilize the Holy Office of Venice and local authorities to try not so much to stamp it out as to work it out of society with teaching and discipline. And as we have seen, they found an apparently willing group of women, women who had seen themselves as Christians and allies of the Church all along, and were thus ready to confess and be reintegrated within the Church. This was, of course, putting the best face on things. But the stern logic of the Church was never the logic of the women healers of Latisana, and thus the willingness to confess and continue healing may not have been as duplicitous as it seems.

As a result, when Apollonia had admitted her guilt—confessing that she had measured cords, saying prayers over them in order to understand illness; signed people in order to heal them; unbound bound people so that they could have sexual intercourse with their spouses;

and taught people to bind in love—she was termed only "lightly suspected of Apostasy from the Catholic faith." In order to lift all suspicion,
she was ordered to "abjure and detest every and each apostasy from the
Holy Catholic Church and in particular the above named superstitions
named and confessed." This done, all other penalties and sanctions of
the church would be waived, with, however, a set of pertinent excep-
tions. "In order that there be lifted from you every suspicion and scandal
that has surrounded you in Latisana, we order you also to repeat your
abjuration . . . in that place. That done for three feast days in a row
thereafter you must stay with a candle lighted in your hands kneeling in
the main Church while the main Mass is celebrated. Moreover for a year
every Friday you must say a rosary to the Virgin Mary before this blessed
Virgin. And for the present you may not live in Latisana or in Marano,
but in Pescarola in the place given you to live."[86]

A far cry from the penalty one might have expected, it was actually,
with its limited form of exile, more stern than the penalties given the
other women of Latisana and healers in general in Venice and the Veneto. But that should not mask a significant point. This penalty reintegrated Apollonia in the Church and, once the exile was over, in her
community. From the Church's perspective it was supposed to provide a
lesson, and it may well have done so for a while at least, but ironically,
from Apollonia's perspective, after a long and difficult series of problems,
what she had set out to accomplish with confession, she had finally
accomplished in Venice before the Holy Office. They had proved that she
was not a witch, and they provided the means and the public forum for
demonstrating just that to all of Latisana in the main church during the
main Mass. It may be that she never cured again and never helped
people find or refind love, living out her years having denied her tradition and culture as the Church demanded. But Apollonia was such an
interesting and masterful woman that one would like to doubt that, and
it is not hard to imagine her having mended her fences with local ecclesiastics and peers, returning to a slightly more discreet practice with the
"license" of the Holy Office of Venice. What we do know is that the
women healers of the Veneto and Friuli went on and continued periodically to attract the attention of the Inquisition.[87] Apollonia would
have been pleased.

5

"The Fortune-Telling Friar": Fra Aurelio di Siena and the Wages of Sin

Three Marriages

Marin Sanuto, the famous Venetian Renaissance diarist, in his memoirs noted briefly toward the end of that massive recording of all that he deemed fit to remember of his age: "On this day [10 August 1533] there was made and completed the marriage of Bianca my natural daughter with Anzolo di Gratariol son of Messer Alexandro, the physician. It was a handsome and honored marriage because at the ceremony there were a goodly number of senators and my relatives as well."[1]

This daughter and her marriage may come as a shock, for scholars have recently begun to suggest that Sanuto was an example of a Venetian patrician whose continuing homoerotic interests had hindered his political career. Given his family background, his interest in and commitment to the political life of Venice, and his assiduous efforts to obtain office, Sanuto's lack of success in politics has always been difficult to explain. Thus the letter of Gianbattista Malatesta written to the Marquis of Mantua in 1529 seemed to explain a great deal. "Sanuto is very much the gentleman," Malatesta wrote, "but when he has spoken three times with a person, he comes before one as if to impale him. He is learned and would have a great reputation in this state if it were not for this vice. I once had a servant that he gave three *mocenigi* a week, but [for this] he had to run the lance three times. He is very well known in the art [*mestiere*] here."[2]

The rulers of Venice were unusually wary of sodomy and were especially concerned with more mature males who continued to find in adolescents or, worse yet, other men their preferred sexual contacts. At one level this was a moral concern, as the rhetoric of the many laws passed against sodomy in the fifteenth and sixteenth centuries underscored. But closely related to such moral concerns was a political one. Fearful of any organizations, formal or informal, public or secret, across class lines or age distinctions, that might organize male power in dangerous ways, the rulers viewed sodomy as posing a threat of secret cabals based on passion. The regular passage of a wide range of laws designed to limit male association across age and class lines suggests just how seriously authorities viewed the matter.[3] Thus when Malatesta seemed to allude with a certain irony to Sanuto's predeliction for "running the lance" with his young male servant, it seemed likely that his sexual orientation might explain his curious lack of success in Venetian politics.

Yet even with an illegitimate daughter, there may be some truth to the hypothesis that Sanuto's sexual orientation hindered his career. Perhaps Sanuto, like many other Renaissance men, enjoyed the sexual companionship of males as well as females. Of course, it should not be ruled out that Malatesta was merely indulging in a typical insult of the time that had little relationship to Sanuto's sexual tastes. But be that as it may, the one thing that is clear is that Sanuto was not a homosexual in the sense that is sometimes used today: that is, a male whose sexual interests are focused exclusively on other males. And that is underlined by the fact that his daughter, Bianca, was illegitimate. For Bianca was not the product of an arranged noble marriage, a child produced out of a sense of family obligation. Sanuto's family had not chosen a wife for him and demanded that he produce heirs, overlooking his own sexual preferences. No, he had kept a mistress, presumably because he found her sexually attractive, and it appears, as we shall see, that he kept her in his house for at least twenty years, even if, it seems, she did not make it into his massive diaries.[4]

Almost forty-six years later, in 1579, another marriage that might seem light years away socially was being frustrated by the Holy Office. At least this was the complaint of the friar and priest Aurelio di Siena. While he claimed to be from a noble Sienese family, the Stichiano clan, his complaint was not about a marriage in that family, but in his *famiglia*, the group of people that a head of household gathered around himself, including regular family, retainers, and servants. As one might expect, this cleric's *famiglia* in 1579 was quite small, but not for the reasons one might think. In fact, earlier, his clerical status had not kept him from having a substantial household in a fairly large home that he rented in Venice. By 1579, however, Fra Aurelio was an old man, at the least in his seventies. Moreover, he was being held in jail by the Holy Office, which had confiscated most of his wealth, and that was the basis of his complaint.

It seems that he had been loyally served for more than a decade by a servant named Dorothea, whom he had promised to dower when she was ready to marry as part of her reward for that loyal service. Such arrangements were not unusual, often being contracted for young girls by their parents at an early age as a way of ensuring them a small dowry when they reached marriageable age and freeing a family from the necessity of providing for another mouth, especially another female one.[5] Such arrangements were also attractive to masters because in this manner young servants were bound to the *famiglia* by the promise of a dowry, the key to their honorable marriage.

From jail, then, Fra Aurelio petitioned the Holy Office, asking to be freed so that he could pursue his litigations against a certain Antonio Contarini. Contarini, he claimed, owed him several hundred ducats, which he refused to repay. Fra Aurelio had contacted a lawyer, but the latter had pursued the matter without sufficient aggressiveness in the friar's eyes. Upon his release, he planned to take Contarini to court and secure the repayment of the debt, not for his own monetary needs—those, he humbly noted, were limited—but in order to be able to give his servant, Dorothea, the dowry that she deserved. Marriage with a good dowry would allow her to escape the life of poverty and questionable honor that otherwise awaited her, and the friar, like a good *pater familias,* wished to fulfill his promise.

Two marriages forty years apart across the watershed of the Council of Trent, across a considerable social and economic gap, underline the continued importance of the marriage bond for women who would be placed in licit society. And in both cases that placement was rendered more important for those women by their marginal status in late Renaissance society. Bianca Sanuto, although the daughter of a highly visible Venetian noble from an important family, was illegitimate. The marginality that entailed is revealed obliquely by the satisfaction with which her father reported that senators and members of his family attended the wedding dinner and that he had managed to secure a wedding with a physician of good family. Fra Aurelio's goals for his charge were much lower, but again they aimed at taking a marginal woman (a servant without a dowry of her own) and giving her a chance to marry.

A third potential marriage of considerably more social note in 1543 ties all these marriages together: a planned marriage between the major noble families of the Corner and the Soranzo. It seems that Fantin Corner had been suggesting to Pietro Soranzo for some time a marriage alliance. Finally, Corner had offered one of his daughters; Soranzo had been encouraging, and negotiations had begun. All might well have proceeded in a typical fashion for the nobility, with a dowry contract

worked out between the male heads of the families, followed by a be-
trothal and an elaborate marriage, if it were not for the fact that there
was another very important player in the marriage market in 1543:
Cardinal Pietro Bembo. As is known, Pietro Bembo, before he began his
ecclesiastical career and took vows of chastity, had done quite a bit more
than write love poetry and theorize about love. His affairs, real and
perhaps imagined, were widely known and commented upon, especially
when he was linked with figures like Lucretia Borgia.

But as he entered middle age, Bembo, although not prepared to
marry, had apparently given up his wide-ranging and at times dangerous liaisons to settle into a relatively stable relationship with a Roman
courtesan known as La Morosina (Faustina Morosina della Torre). That
relationship had begun perhaps as early as 1513, when she was sixteen
and already working in Rome. In the 1520s they had settled together in
Padua, after Bembo had taken his ecclesiastical vows of chastity, and in
short order the couple had three children: Lucilio, born in 1523; Tor-
quato, born in 1525; and Elena, named probably after his own mother,
born in 1528. Bembo and La Morosina stayed together until her death in
1535.[6] After her death, Bembo followed other passions but stayed loyal
to their children, in 1543 securing permission from Pope Paul III to leave
the papal court to return to Venice and Padua to arrange their affairs
there. One of the main affairs he wished to settle he reported in a letter to
his close friend, the Duchess Leonora of Urbino: "I was in Padua and
Venice almost all this summer in order to marry my Elena and with the
grace of Our Lord I married her to a good gentleman."[7] In those
summer-long negotiations, one of his choices had been Pietro Soranzo.
But that, of course, put a crimp in Fantin Corner's designs on Soranzo as
the match for his daughter.

As a result, Corner turned to a friend whom we have already met,
Fra Aurelio di Siena, asking for his help. He wrote to a much younger
Fra Aurelio (then in his mid-forties), seeking a special favor. It seems
that at this time Aurelio had quite a reputation as a teller of fortunes in
Venice; he was widely known as the "fortune-telling friar" (*"il frate
della ventura"*), and many of the most important people of the city came
to him for his advice about what the future held in store for them,
including both Soranzo and Corner. Essentially Corner asked his friend
Fra Aurelio to help him by adjusting the future to fit his marriage plans:
when Soranzo came to ask him about his future, the friar was to advise
him not to marry the cardinal's daughter, but rather Corner's.[8] Did the
fortune-telling friar alter the future? Perhaps he did. Unfortunately, the
Holy Office, which shortly thereafter began to investigate how he told
the future and the very large profits he seemed to have made doing so,
was less concerned with how he might have controlled the future in
predicting it than we. We do know, however, that Cardinal Bembo in
the end did not marry his daughter Elena to Pietro Soranzo, for in

October 1543 he married her to another Pietro, Pietro Gradenigo, a Venetian noble of some intellectual pretensions and good family, apparently at considerable expense.[9]

A Friar's Reputation

How, one might well ask, did this fortune-telling friar get in the middle of the marriage negotiations of such important people? What were the ties that bound him to such men and they to him? These questions become larger yet when we get to know our renegade priest and friar a little better. For Friar Aurelio, in a checkered career, had moved rather rapidly through at least three different holy orders, breaking his ties to each, finally to live on his own in a large house rented from the noble Zen family. One of the first testimonies that described Fra Aurelio to the Holy Office in 1543 captures the negatives of his background well. Although undated, this testimony from the friar Bernardo da Verona, prior of the monastery of San Sebastiano in Venice, probably was heard in November 1543, along with a number of other dated testimonies from clerics that follow it in the transcript. After carefully reading over the list of accusations against Aurelio (which have not been preserved), Bernardo began: "certainly a while back when there was made public an admonition concerning witchcraft and spells . . . I considered denouncing this most evil and infamous man [Aurelio] in order that he be punished and castigated for his evil deeds."[10] Fortunately for Aurelio, Bernardo was too busy with other concerns to denounce him, even as he wondered "how the most illustrious Signoria of Venice could allow such a disease [*morbo*] in the city which not only should be banned . . . but even deprived of his life." The use of disease metaphors for Aurelio calls to mind similar metaphors used for prostitutes, but Bernardo's rhetoric was considerably harsher. This disease required more than isolation through banishment or confinement within certain areas of the city; it deserved a sentence of death.

We might well ask why Bernardo was so set against Fra Aurelio. Without being asked, however, he explained. "I have known Don Aurelio for about twelve years because he was a friar in our order and he went by the name Fra Marcello." There were early indications that Fra Marcello would not work out as a friar, Bernardo recalled: "One day there came a man from Siena who he [Aurelio] said was a cousin. When the said Sienese saw him, he made the sign of the Cross . . . and said 'God give you the grace to do better than you have done in the past.'" Later this relative explained to a number of monks, including Bernardo, that Aurelio, now Marcello, "had been thrown out of two other orders." In the end, Aurelio/Marcello did not last long in Bernardo's order either: "In our monastery he did not make a profession because once he heard that we wished to throw him out, he left before we could do so."[11]

According to Bernardo, the reason for this was that he had been an "evil robber" in their house and had even had a false bottom made under his bed to hide his loot. They eventually found hidden there "a sizeable number of knives, mirrors and combs and other little things" that seemed to have been stolen.[12]

After approximately nine years, Aurelio returned to Venice and took back his original name, joining the Canons Regular (Laterensis) at the monastery of San Marco. That order sent him to their house in Padua, where he successfully made his profession as a monk. Bernardo, however, brought out the negatives even in this apparent spiritual renewal, for he reported, "After he made his profession in that order some of the friars came to ask us if the said Fra Aurelio was once one of us and they complained a great deal about him. We said to them that he was an evil person and with us he had been an evil one. After that time we did not hear anything else except that now we see him dressed as a Camaldolese [yet a third order]." Although they may not have seen much of the new Fra Aurelio, Bernardo claimed that they had in the last few years once again heard a great deal about their ex-brother, none of it positive. "I will tell you," Bernardo related, "that we know by means of confession and also outside of confession that . . . there are few men or women who do not fall into his hands as a fortune-teller. To some he says that he has a spirit in a ring; to others he says he has a fairy in the attic; but from all of them he takes money and especially from these poor women who are so credulous. According to what one hears from public rumor and reputation [*publica voce et fama*] it is said that he has his house full of prostitutes and evil men and that he lives most sumptuously there with ornate beds and pavilions."[13]

Needless to say, in this period of his life Fra Aurelio's *famiglia* was considerably larger and more prosperous than it would be in 1579. And equally evident, the testimony of Bernardo da Verona, prior of San Sebastiano, makes Fra Aurelio's relationship with Pietro Soranzo and Fantin Corner seem quite extraordinary. But the one thing that stands out in the many testimonies gathered for this case is that if Fra Aurelio was particularly good at duping poor, gullible women, as Bernardo complained, he was almost as good at convincing rich, powerful men that he could tell their future. As a result, he had ties to a number of powerful friends in high places, and through them his telling of the future may well have had an impact on the future, even on the marriage plans of Cardinal Bembo.

In fact, his reputation as a fortune-teller and his powerful friends seem to have impressed even those who were not his friends. A good example of this can be found in the generally negative and sanctimonious testimony of Francesco Giustinian, a leader in the reforming intellectual circles of the Venetian nobility associated with the Camaldolese order and nephew of the better-known Tomaso Giustinian, who in 1510 dropped out of society to join the order (changing his name to Paolo) in the hope of leading a reform movement from within the Church. From Francesco's testimony it becomes evident that the new Fra Aurelio dressed, in the habit of the Camaldolese order, was not entirely a sham. He had entered that order about a year after leaving the Canons Regular, and this time had become not only a monk but also a priest. But after a short time, Aurelio had once again begun to live on his own and follow his questionable ways. As a result, when two hermits of the Camaldolese order came to visit Francesco—it seems such hermits visited regularly because close ties had been maintained between his family and the order—he reported: "These two friars, having heard what was being said about the life that this Don Aurelio was living in the habit of their religion, wished to have him arrested by the secular authorities."[14]

Giustinian, however, was anxious to avoid "confusion and loss of honor" and devised a more devious plan to try to bring Aurelio under control. As he explained to the Holy Office, "One night I went and brought him [Fra Aurelio] to our house with the excuse that I wanted to have the pleasure of his ability to tell the future and his art of chiromancy [palm reading]." As a ruse, it was a clever one that successfully avoided any of the adverse attention that an arrest might have entailed, but curiously it appears that even with Giustinian the interest in the future was not entirely a ruse. For rather than taking Aurelio immediately into custody when he arrived, Francesco admitted, "having gathered together in our house some foreign gentlemen by chance, he [Fra Aurelio] told the future of everyone."[15] Dinner followed, and presumably only after when the guests had left with their curiosity sated, Fra Aurelio was taken into custody by the friars and carried off to the order's monastery of San Matteo on the island of Murano.

The special relationship between the Giustinian family and the order alluded to earlier was nicely demonstrated in what followed. "And because I had intervened in his arrest," Francesco continued, "I demanded that those friars promise me that they would not use any corporal punishment but only take away his habit and give him a good dressing down and send him away. After a few days in chains when it appeared that he was ready to give up the habit, change his way of life and leave . . . having been begged and advised to do so by me . . . he asked me if I would have brought to him all his things." Among those things, Francesco noted, were "many books on palm reading and many others on telling the future." Typical of Francesco's tone in his testimony, he made sure to point out that Aurelio's decision to leave the order was not for good reasons. He judged it to be motivated by "a greater concern for the shame of the world than for fear of God."[16]

If it was reputation and a fear of "shame" in the secular world that motivated Aurelio, ironically he was not long for that world. For after a few months' absence from Venice, Aurelio returned once again, dressed in the habit of the Camaldolese order. Neither "gentle admonitions" nor "threats" from Giustinian worked to get Fra Aurelio to change his way of life or give up his habit. Nor, for that matter, according to Giustinian, did the active efforts of the general of the order or of many Venetian nobles succeed. This led him to conclude that Aurelio had ties to important protectors both within the Church and without, a surmise that seems to have merit given the friar's ability to not only survive but thrive in his renegade style of life. "Moreover," Giustinian concluded with resignation after speculating vaguely about Aurelio's protectors in high places, "I have heard it said that this Sienese [Aurelio] promised the Monsignor Legate that shortly he would have a licence from Rome that would give him permission to continue the life that he lived in that habit. I know that with the passage of time, Don Aurelio has continued in this manner of living up to the present. I have heard his neighbors and others lament about the things contained in the complaint against him. In the house . . . where he lived when I visited him . . . there were to be seen women of evil fame [i.e., prostitutes] and according to the neighbors . . . he said it was not a sin to tell the future."[17]

Giustinian's testimony fleshes out to a degree the animosity of Bernardo da Verona and confirms a rather unflattering picture of Aurelio. In Venice he had passed through three orders, breaking his ties with each under questionable circumstances to take up a life that was, to put it mildly, highly questionable. Moreover he had done this while claiming to be a monk, which, needless to say, in the eyes of the clerics who testified against him and their supporters greatly increased his guilt. Still, clerical attacks on other clerics must be viewed with caution; that was especially true in the sixteenth century, when accusations of misconduct by clergy, particularly sexual, often masked or were merely a facet of general attacks motivated by confessional issues. And, in fact, Fra Aurelio's case involves some hints that there might have been confessional issues involved. Giustinian, for example, noted that one of Aurelio's important relatives was a certain Soccino in Padua. The Soccino family there was prominently associated with anti-Trinitarian views.[18]

We will see in this light also that Aurelio never said Mass and avoided confession and communion, all of which might suggest that his case was really one of a confessional nature. But as will become evident, these issues are details in a case that went in a very different direction: the evidence gathered focused on Aurelio's renegade lifestyle, his telling of the future, his keeping of mistresses and concubines, his use of love magic and healing magic, and ultimately, the large profits he seemed to make from all of this activity. And in all of this, Fra Aurelio in many ways sums up the essays that have preceded his, for as a renegade priest and monk he ties together many of the threads of those tales. In two areas, however, he appears to stand apart: as a man and as more clearly a charlatan than most of the others encountered. Still, even with those apparent differences, Aurelio's tale will qualify in ways that are revealing for understanding the world of the illicit (his world) and the ties that bound passions and people.

Neighbor's Complaints and Neighborhood

One thing that fosters a view of the case as truly concerned with Fra Aurelio as a renegade priest and brings us back to earlier themes is the heavy reliance on testimony by his neighbors, who emphasized neighborly complaints and the friar's reputation. They did not speculate about confessional issues, heresy, pacts with the Devil, or even the typical attack on clerics, sodomy. Rather, their complaints focused on what a dishonorable neighbor Fra Aurelio was and how his living in their neighborhood disrupted their lives: "We are pretty close neighbors, so close that only a small canal separates [us] and my balconies are in the middle of his," Ghielmina, wife of Antonio, explained to the Holy Office. "And certainly I do not want to look because I mind my own business [non me impazzo delli fatti d'altri] but one has to see the neighborhood from the balcony and I have seen in the three years that I have been in this house that this friar has a reputation for a most evil life and keeps dishonest people in his house. Moreover, he rents it . . . in part to infamous and dishonest people and there they maintain many bordellos because of the throng of evil people that come to hear the future told or for the pimping [that goes on] there."[19] Ghielmina's last reference to pimping, ruffianerie, as well as her mention of bordellos, may have been a generic way of referring to the questionable honor of Aurelio's house. Actually there was probably no space in the house to keep a bordello, and the Holy Office's careful questions to the women who lived there about the rent they paid seemed to convince them that Fra Aurelio was not renting at the exorbitant rates that landlords charged to profit from prostitution. Still, the bordello theme is a popular one with neighbors, probably reflecting their anger about the coming and going that so disrupted their lives. Or it just may be that this fortune-telling, renegade friar was somehow a bordello master as well.

Ghielmina had more precise complaints about the friar's sexual activities: "About two months ago this ribald friar while he was standing on his balcony made certain gestures towards certain good women [donna da ben] that is young girls [donzelle] who live above me—definitely Godly people."[20] Suggestively, Ghielmina's evaluation of the reputation of her women neighbors focuses on their sexuality, yet moved beyond it to their religiosity, demonstrating once again, as in Feltre, that there was more to a woman's honor than virginity before marriage and chastity thereafter. Still, their honor was at risk because Fra Aurelio's gestures were part of an ongoing campaign, she explained, to lead the young girls astray. And that day he had taken matters a step further. "From his balcony he threw a letter wrapped up in a hanky with a small round piece of soap tied together with a gold string. He wanted to throw it to the balcony of those girls, but by chance it fell in the canal. A woman named Francesca who lived in his house called me and said that I ought to take it out of the water. I went to the bank, [got in] my husband's small boat, picked the package out of the water and returned to my house. There [when I opened it] I found that piece of soap and a letter. While I was in my house the friar came with two armed men and as luck would have it found the door unlocked. He entered my house and tried with honeyed words to convince me to give him the hanky [presumably the hanky-wrapped package]. But I did not want to give it to him because I wanted to know what he had wanted to do with it in order to see justice done."[21]

In the rush of the action, tossing a letter from the balcony, fishing it from the canal, and Aurelio's walking into Ghielmina's home, a significant detail should not be overlooked. The two young girls who were to have received Aurelio's letter presumably were expected to read it. And Ghielmina wanted to hold on to it because she apparently planned to read it to see if there was something there that could be used in court against her neighbor. It may have been that she could not read and was planning on keeping it until someone could read it for her, but the written word was not alien to her and she apparently was prepared to take advantage of it even in court if the opportunity arrived. Again here there are indications of literacy or at least the ability to work with the written word among women, and in this case even good women.

But as is often the case, power over the written word was no match in a direct confrontation with the more straightforward force of two armed men. Ghielmina continued, "He said to me that they could tear my house apart and I replied 'if you tear my house apart and do not leave Venice, the result might be that you will leave your head among the ruins [of my house].'" This nicely turned counterthreat failed to impress Fra Aurelio or his thugs: "in response those armed men took away the package by force." She concluded her testimony by returning to the general theme shared by the complaints of most of her neighbors: "This friar is a man of evil reputation [*fama*] and worse deeds and of such great scandal that everyone complains about him. I believe that he has the support of some gentlemen to be able to stay there and do the most horrible things with pimps, whores and other evil types. The only people who frequent his house are people of evil life. Otherwise I do not know anything, but this I see everyday because of the closeness of the house [even if] certainly I do not wish to see such things and I am even forced to close the balconies."[22]

Clearly, Fra Aurelio was no more popular with his neighbors than he was with ecclesiastics. And the former were not limited to merely complaining about the disruption he was causing in their neighbor-hood. A renter who lived in the attic of Aurelio's house, after briefly complaining about his rent gouging, provided the typical picture of the friar's questionable life, adding an interesting detail at the end. "In his house . . . there gather an infinite number of people of every sort young women both married and unmarried, gentlemen, foreigners and people of every sort . . . what they do I really have not paid much attention to but it is said publicly that he tells the future . . . and does evil things. Moreover it is said throughout the neighborhood that he has corrupted some of the daughters [of the neighborhood] . . . and has made love with them. . . . This one may give credence because three times at night there have been *romanzine* against his house breaking down his balconies and throwing stones at his windows and his doors and hurling insults [such as] 'scum' and 'unfrocked friar' and other similar insults."[23]

Although an English translation cannot do justice to the force of the insults hurled, as the Italian *iniurie* suggests they were words designed to injure and were an integral part of charivari-like attacks on Fra Aurelio and his house. Although in this case *romanzine* was the Venetian dialect term used, often in the sixteenth century such disturbances were referred to as a *baia*, a "yelling." Their purpose was, as with the charivari, to tie a community together by using group violence that dishonored. Such violence highlighted group values and honor by dishonoring those who had demonstrated that they were not adhering to those values; thus yelling insults, hurling stones, or singing mocking songs dishonored and broke the ties that had bound that person to the community. Ideally the response to such treatment was for the victim to *mend* his or her ways, that is, change behavior to re-create the ties that bound one to the group. Although in this case the group or groups who carried out the *romanzine* are not identified, presumably it was largely a local affair led by the young men of the neighborhood. In other brief references to *baia* in Venice and Florence, young men appear to have organized and led these events, which could run the gamut from merely yelling outside the home of the person to be shamed to elaborate gatherings with hired musicians and, in one case, even hired painters who decorated the victim's house with paintings of the genitals reputedly involved in their misdeeds.

The Arrest of Fra Aurelio in 1549 and Bianca Sanuto

Fra Aurelio and his friends come across in these testimonies as virtually the quintessential denizens of the world of the illicit. The 1543 complaint, however, was apparently not pursued by the Holy Office and thus provides little sense of the man beyond complaints. Yet even the most evil men can have supporters, and the friar was not without his defenders, as became evident when his renegade life was again considered by the Holy Office in 1549. This also brings us back to the first marriage of this chapter, for one of his defenders was none other than Bianca Sanuto, the illegitimate daughter of Marin Sanuto.

When she came to his defense in 1549, Bianca Sanuto painted a different and much more positive picture of the friar. Bianca returns to the tale during the arrest of Fra Aurelio, at least as reported by the officers of the Holy Office who went to take him into custody before dawn on 17 October 1549. After the friar had tried to escape by jumping from a window of his house into a canal, things settled down quickly. He was bundled off to jail, and a search was begun of his papers and belongings for incriminating evidence. One thing discovered immediately was that whether or not his practices were heretical, they were profitable. Among his papers and books were found sizable sums of cash. And as that money appeared, so too did Bianca Sanuto to make a plea that not all of it be confiscated. Apparently she was living in separate quarters in Fra Aurelio's house with an old woman who had been her nurse, but had easy access to the friar's rooms, and was familiar with them and the location of at least some of his funds. In the words of the notary of the case, the searchers reported to him that "that woman of the house called madonna Bianca Sanuto . . . asked him [an official of the Holy Office, the *procurator fiscal*] to leave her some of the money saying to him 'one has to do the shopping and there are many mouths to feed as well as dogs, cats and chickens. Look, look, how is one supposed to do the shopping!' In response this lord *procurator fiscal* left her fifteen *moceneghi.'*[24]

It appears from Bianca's concerns about money and feeding the denizens of Fra Aurelio's house that she was more than a mere renter. Her own testimony before the Holy Office that same day begins to give a more detailed picture of her ties to that *famiglia* and of how her life had changed since her father had married her to Anzolo di Gratariol sixteen years earlier. First, as the Holy Office made clear from their registering of her name, "Donna Biancha Sanudo fu del quondam Messer Marin relicta del quondam Messer Anzolo Gratariol," her father was dead (*quondam*) and her husband was as well. As a widow and an illegitimate daughter of a noble family, her chances of remarriage or even finding an acceptable place in society were almost entirely determined by the size of her dowry, her own financial assets if any, and her ability to find support. Without the support of her father and his family, she could not expect a new wedding to someone of social stature with senators as guests. In fact, one may assume that if she had problems recovering her dowry, a woman like Bianca could find that the floor had literally dropped out from under her place in society and that she could be reduced to doing the shopping for a renegade priest and his dogs, cats, and chickens.

The Holy Office began by asking Bianca how long she had lived in Aurelio's house. She replied with unusual precision for an age when the remembering of exact dates was of little utility, "On the fourteenth of next March, it will be five years that I have lived in this house."[25] She explained under questioning that she rented a room above the quarters of Fra Aurelio where she lived with "her nena," her childhood wet nurse. Asked if she paid rent, Bianca replied, "I pay nine ducats, but the first year that I came here to stay I paid twelve. Then a cousin of mine recommended me to the Father [Aurelio] who has the whole house . . . and he lowered the rent out of kindness by three ducats." These are literally the first positive words about Aurelio in the records of the Holy Office, and they seem so out of place that they ring a little false. But immediately Bianca revealed what was already evident from the testimony of those who had searched the house: that she was not a mere renter; that, in fact, she provided additional services that helped to explain her lower rent. "I do for him [Aurelio] certain services and my *nena* does so as well, but many times he takes care of himself."[26] The sense of Bianca's rather vague testimony was that she and her ex-wet nurse occasionally did the shopping and cooking for Fra Aurelio.

If there was more to it than that, it appears that the Holy Office was not particularly concerned at this point and let the matter drop, turning to inquire about what kind of work Fra Aurelio did. "He does not do anything else," she replied, "except tell the future and read the hands of people who come to the house." She confirmed the wide range of people who visited, a staple of the negative testimony against the friar, but put it in the best possible light. "There come to him some of the great, some of the small [people], gentlemen, gentlewomen, captains and diverse types for this reason. And in the name of the true God who rules in heaven and over the universe in our house nothing has been done that is dishonest for the world, but it has always been as if it was a monastery."[27] Bianca's recasting of this commonplace in the testimony offers a hint that there is more to the incessant refrain about the social diversity of people that visited the friar than might at first meet the eye.

What might have seemed merely a complaint about numbers or the wide range of people bilked or corrupted by Fra Aurelio, when put in a positive light takes on a slightly different coloring that is suggestive. Bianca, after admitting that a broad cross section of people visited, felt compelled to explain that nothing went on that was dishonest in the house; rather, it was just like a monastery. The contrast is evident when we remember that the negative testimony that focused on the social diversity of people almost always followed this with an accusation of the friar of maintaining a bordello or at least arranging illicit sexual assignations. This monastery/bordello contrast suggests that the mixing of classes was seen as inappropriate (in Venice at least) and a fairly self-evident sign that something illicit was happening.[28] It was this that underlay the repeated accusation of such mixing, as if it proved some-thing significant in the earlier testimony. The monastery/bordello con-trast also evokes a commonplace about illicit sexuality, and especially prostitution and sodomy, in the Renaissance: these were areas where the classes mixed and were potentially bound to one another in antiso-cial and ultimately dangerous ways.

By this point, however, even Marin Sanuto's daughter was not likely to convince the Holy Office that the house she called "our house" was a monastery. But as it was her first testimony, and as frequently the inquisitor did not press reluctant witnesses too hard at first, he sprang what might well have seemed a very strange question. He asked, "The dogs that are in the house, who do they belong to?" She explained that they belonged to Aurelio, as he paid for their food. Then she seemed to try to return the interrogation to what was for her a more crucial issue, the probity of their house: "I know that before I came to stay here there was a woman who seemed good, however, when he [Aurelio] realized that she was bad he sent her away."[29] Ignoring insignificant dogs, their "monastic" house had once had less than monastic inhabitants, but by returning to and transforming its rental history into a morality story of sorts, she could demonstrate its honesty and his.

The inquisitor, however, was waiting to hear about Aurelio's dogs; thus, with no response to her aside on the casting out of the evil woman, Bianca returned to the dogs. "The dogs are called one Silver, another Prized, one Red Snout, the one who is the guard dog Falcon, and her son Little Rooster."[30] This attention to dogs seems to offer a view of another side of Fra Aurelio. He kept dogs, and he kept them as pets. Bianca intimated as much: only one dog, Falcon, was a guard dog; the rest, as their names indicated, had a different role. Of course, the Holy Office's concern with these pets was motivated by quite different considerations than discerning the friar's affection for animals. The paw of a dog had been found among his possessions, and they were concerned that he was using dogs or parts of them for his magic. This was, however, one line of questioning that would bear little fruit, as Aurelio was savvy enough to avoid the issue by stressing his love of dogs—he had kept the paw as a memento of a much loved dog after it died—and no one provided any information that undermined that stance. Still, keeping Silver, Red Snout, Little Rooster, and Prized, along with the guard dog Falcon, gives Aurelio a more human side.

More significantly, the Holy Office was interested in what else the friar was keeping. This became evident in the next line of questioning pursued, although it had been lurking behind the questioning all along. They asked Bianca if Fra Aurelio had kept her as his concubine. The inquisitor queried, "Do you pay for your expenses yourself?" "Yes sir," she replied "and I would be in trouble if my sister and my cousin did not help me and for instance last night I worked until the tenth hour." What she worked at she, unfortunately, did not specify, but her answer seems to make it clear that she understood exactly what was implied by his question. When she said she supported herself, she was saying that she was not being kept by Fra Aurelio—her sister, Marin Sanuto's other illegitimate daughter, and her cousin did help her out, as she explained—but both she and her examiners knew that that was not the issue. One thing at least in the testimony already heard seemed to contradict her denial: her familiarity with Fra Aurelio's finances and her request for some of his money confiscated that very morning; that suggested that her ties to the friar went beyond those of a renter to a landlord.

In the face of her denial, the inquisitor turned to that issue, asking, "Were you given [money] this morning by the *procurator fiscal* or the captain?" She admitted that she had been given fifteen *mocenigi* and that she had asked for it, but in the process gave a pretty good explanation, claiming that she had done so as someone who lived in the house and no more. Again that last question had not been asked, but she answered it anyway, as it clearly lay behind the train of the questioning. "When they took the money, I said to him [the *procurator fiscal*], 'sir here there are so many animals, dogs, and cats and fourteen or fifteen chickens and roosters, it does not seem fair that I should pay the expenses myself.' Thus he gave me ten *mocenigi* and then seeing how many animals there were he gave me five more which made a total of fifteen."[31]

In the name of fairness and taking care of the household animals, then, she had asked for some of Fra Aurelio's money. And, of course, this did make some sense, as her reduced rent was, as she had explained earlier, in part predicated upon her taking care of the shopping when Aurelio could not. Still, Bianca was much more domesticated than the others who rented from the friar; she appears to have moved about his part of the house with considerable familiarity and to have known where at least some of his money was hidden. Moreover her memory of the exact date of her arrival in the house and her careful defense of the friar suggest that the Holy Office was correct in suspecting their relationship. Their suspicion was further strengthened by the testimony of neighbors and others who concurred that Bianca Sanuto was Fra Aurelio's mistress.

In fact, one of the things that the Council of Trent and subsequent reforms attempted to do was limit the practice of clerics keeping concubines. Nobles like Marin Sanuto and their concubines were beyond the actual control of the Church (although moral pressure could be put on them), but an aggressive campaign was launched against clerics keeping concubines, even at the highest levels. It would become more and more difficult to live Cardinal Bembo's life—at least at his level of visibility—after Trent. And it was a campaign that was supported often by secular authorities as well, at least in Venice and the Veneto. Still, the problem did not disappear, and concubinage remained a problem often in the context of the relationship between a priest or friar and his housekeeper. The frequent attempts to set minimum age limits for the female servants of clerics, if followed, would have surrounded churchmen with older women (and in the process perhaps helped to place a few older women left on their own). It appears, however, that after some initial aggressive enforcement, the Church found that such rules were difficult to apply even in larger urban centers like Venice.[32]

If, as seems likely, the illegitimate daughter of Marin Sanuto had become Fra Aurelio's concubine following the death of her husband, it is unfortunate that the Holy Office was more interested in the friar's telling of the future than in that relationship. For it would be interesting to see how that young widow had come to live with the friar on the day that she remembered so exactly. It is evident that whether she was his mistress or not, she was closely linked to his household and their relationship was a rather symbiotic one. One gets a good sense of this also from the testimony of the elderly widow Anna Padoana, whom Bianca labeled her old nurse and who still lived with her. Anna described her relationship with Bianca as follows: "I do not stay with anyone, but I stay together with madonna Bianca because I was part of the household and lived with messer Marin Sanuto, her father, for twenty-four years."[33]

It may be, however, that Anna Padoana had been more than a nurse to Bianca Sanuto. She may actually have been her mother. The evidence is tenuous but suggestive. Marin Sanuto's will clearly shows that Anna was no ordinary servant. In that document Sanuto spent an unusual amount of time praising Anna's loyalty and noting that she had served him like a member of the family "day and night for which I may laud her greatly." Wills at times do sing high praises of servants, but Sanuto went beyond praise, bestowing considerable rewards as well. He created a special document, which does not survive, with the notary Girolamo Canal that recorded his debts to her and a program for repaying her. While it is difficult to surmise much about a document that no longer exists, the mere fact that Sanuto had taken the time to draw it up suggests a special tie. In addition, in his will he made a point of noting that she was to retain three rings and other jewelry he had given her; that she be given ten ducats in cash from his estate; and that "no one ask her for an accounting of anything." Finally, he left her for the rest of her life "the house in San Simeone which was our mother's," which she had the right to live in or rent as she pleased. Clearly, Anna had been no ordinary servant. That fact was further recognized in a later codicil to the will that briefly adjusted several bequests. While decreasing several bequests, Sanuto carefully stipulated that all earlier provisions for Anna, "to whom I am most obligated," be fully observed.[34] Had Sanuto honored his binding passions to Anna, his longtime mistress rather than his faithful servant?

As Bianca's mother or merely her nurse, the fact that the two women were still together in 1549 suggests strong ties. Anna, nonetheless, claimed to support herself with her own resources and not to serve as a servant of the friar. She did admit, however, "if he ordered something madonna Bianca and I, we did for him some services."[35] Rather than pursue this vague reply, the Holy Office moved on to ask why so many people came to visit the friar; a question that Anna, like Bianca, used to try to convince the Holy Office that both the friar and his household were quite holy places. "I do not know [why people come] but I have heard it said that he tells the future and that people come running to him for this reason. And as God is the guarantor of my soul, the said friar fasts every day of Lent, all the saints days, [and] all Saturdays, he says prayers [and] he goes to [hear] preachers. Certainly he lives the life of a saint and certainly he is the best soul that there is in Venice as far as I know."[36] Obviously even if the friar was not quite the best soul in Venice, he had strong supporters in Bianca Sanuto and her nurse Anna. In fact, none of the other people in the house or supporters of the friar were willing to be even a fraction as positive, and thus when neighbors like the ducal secretary, Alexandro Busonello, labeled Bianca as the friar's "kept woman,"[37] the accusation seems more than an empty one.

The Friar's Defense

There was, of course, one other person who felt that the friar was above reproach: the friar himself. When he was brought before the Holy Office in 1549, they asked first about his rather questionable track record in the various orders he had joined. His recounting of that story provides some colorful, if questionable, detail about his life and a slightly clearer sense of its timing. Asked about the context of his abandoning the monastery of San Sebastiano, he replied that he had left after only a four-month stay while he was still a novice in about 1520 and explained, "I left that order because every month I went about looking for wood with the other friars. And a Messer Giacomo Senese master of grammar and teacher of the friars . . . recognizing me [as a fellow Sienese?] took me aside to say to me 'You are young, what are you doing here in the monastery?' Thus I decided to leave and with the license of the prior— who took more than eight days, because he did not want to give me the license—I left with my secular clothes."[38] Bored with the manual labor of the monks and impressed with the reasoning of the master of grammar that life had more to offer a young man, Aurelio had left before he formally professed and became a monk. The story sounded logical and had nice details, such as the gathering of wood that gave it the ring of truth, even if it does not square too well with the testimony of Bernardo da Verona, prior of the house, who had already explained that Aurelio had been thrown out for his thievery and misdeeds.

Aurelio then left Venice for Siena, where he remained for about nine years, returning sometime in 1529–30. "Returning to Venice I went to stay in the house of messer Alvise Morosini, who knew me and my family." Could Morosini have been one of Fra Aurelio's important protectors that so many witnesses speculated about? Aurelio did not go into detail, merely stating that after staying with him for a few months, Morosini helped him to enter his next order, the Canons Regular. They sent him to a house of theirs in Padua, where he managed to last for around fifteen months. In that house he admitted making his profession but denied having taken sacred orders. Again his explanation of why he left is interesting, "Being in Padua I was very unhealthy and I was always sick. When the prior saw that he had me bled following the advice of doctors and it was decided to send me to Venice because to tell the truth that air did not suit me and I was always sick. Then in Venice I was not able to recover as I was always sick with asthma and also with spleen problems. So I asked the Prior if he would be willing to call a doctor so that he could cure me. The Prior refused saying that he did not want to have doctors underfoot all the time. When I understood that, I left without license to do so."[39]

Leaving without a license was, of course, forbidden, and things did not go well for him on the lam. "When I left the monastery of the Carità, I stayed on in the city about twenty days. And because I did not have the money to leave and because I went about through the city and the squares in my habit the friars had me arrested and they kept me locked up in a room for fifteen days until I escaped. I then went to Padua to messer Marian Soccino, who is my cousin, and had him loan me five scudi with which I returned home." Again his family ties rescued him, and as the Soccino name was an important one in reforming circles in Padua dangerously associated with anti-Trinitarian views, he revealed that he was not without contacts in such circles as well. In fact, this admission may have piqued the Holy Office's curiosity, for once he explained that after approximately a year in Siena he had joined the Camaldolese in about 1532, taking holy orders and becoming a priest as well in Puglia, they turned for a moment to confessional issues, completely ignoring the question of how he had been able to join a new order after leaving the Canons Regular under such questionable circumstances. "I stayed in this order [the Camadolese of Puglia] about two years," Fra Aurelio explained, "and I made my profession and took holy orders and moreover became a priest." The Holy Office asked immediately if he had ever said Mass. The friar answered, "Neither in the order nor outside of it did I ever celebrate Mass." Before they could pursue the issue, he explained, "This happened because in our group where I was in the monastery the plague sprang up and almost everyone died, so that there remained only four people and thus with the permission of my superiors I left and went to Siena from where I returned here . . . that would be about fourteen years ago."[40] The Holy Office returned briefly to the issue of why the friar had not said Mass and why he had avoided confession and communion as well, but in the end it seems clear that they were less concerned with such things as signs of confessional disagreement with Rome than with them as signs of his renegade life.

With the return of Aurelio to Venice in 1535 the questioning began to zero in on that renegade life, first focusing on how he had supported himself. "For two years I did not do anything because I had my own wealth to live on. Afterwards I began to practice medicine treating skin problems, wounds, and syphilis using medicinal herbs." Without having studied medicine and without any degree, much like the women healers of Latisana, Aurelio claimed to have made his way treating people with simple remedies. Given the testimony that they already had, the Holy Office, however, was not prepared to accept the friar as merely a folk healer. They asked, "Did you do anything else or follow any other art?" The friar quickly expanded the horizons of the investigation, admitting, "I also worked on the art of chiromancy [palm reading] and also a little with geomancy [divination by use of figures or lines] and I even enjoyed a bit of astrology, but I did not do these things as a profession."[41] His last qualification, that he did not practice these things as a profession, was probably an attempt to contain the damage of his admission; he did these things out of intellectual curiosity, not for personal gain. Again the story as Aurelio was telling it made him a folk healer who, given his training, also had the intellectual curiosity to be interested in some more esoteric and intellectual arts.

Rather than confronting him on this, the Holy Office moved on to a related issue, the house that he had rented after his return to Venice. It probably seemed significant not only because it was the scene where he carried out his activities, but also because the Holy Office saw it and the style of life he maintained there as beyond the reach of a simple folk healer. Thus this line of questioning circled back to his work and perhaps could undermine his defense. Fra Aurelio explained that he had lived in the house since his return to Venice fourteen years ago, aside from a short absence when he had returned to Siena. His rent had been a hefty thirty-four ducats a year, which had just recently been raised to forty ducats. The Holy Office asked with seeming innocence what he did with such a big house, living as he claimed by himself. Not making any admissions, Fra Aurelio explained, "I live only in my half, which comprises two small rooms with my stairs and my entrance."[42]

The house would become less humble under questioning, but first the friar related its rental history in a way that allowed him to present himself as an honest landlord concerned with the reputation of his house and his tenants. Once again he seems to have been appealing to the values of his listeners, especially their assumptions about household and honor. Ideally, as head of the house, he was responsible for the people who lived with him and their honor; thus, his rental history had the potential to be no mere economic tale—it could be a significant morality tale. First, he had rented part of the house to a messer Vincenzo Sirapesse, "a man of good reputation" who came on bad times and could no longer afford the rent. In contrast, his next renter was "a certain Chechino and his daughters, who were evil. When I became aware of their evil way of life, I threw them out and they came to offend me with arms." The contrast was clear: in Fra Aurelio's house, good renters were appreciated and evil ones were driven out even when they threatened the honest friar with arms. "After that I rented to madonna Antonia, a widow and a good woman who stayed three years and then not being able to pay so much rent left." Which brought the friar to his present renters and the conclusion of his morality tale: "and then there came to live madonna Bianca Sanuto, who still lives there now. She pays ten ducats for rent even though she used to pay twelve. But because she cooks some things [for me] I lowered her rent two ducats. There also is another who lives there, madonna Isabetta, kept by a German named Giacomo Vaislante and it is more than twenty years that he has kept her. But he does not ever come into the house, because I rented him the room on that condition. Instead she goes to the Fontego [dei Tedesci] when he wishes and she pays ten ducats rent. Also there is an old woman who was the nurse of the said madonna Bianca. Because she did not have any place to stay I gave her for the love of God the kitchen where she stays."[43]

Once again each rental has its moral evaluation, with the interesting exception of Bianca Sanuto. Isabetta, apparently the long-term mistress of the German, although kept by him, did not actually cohabit with him in Fra Aurelio's house; that was part of the rental agreement. Implicitly their immoralities were done elsewhere. Even Bianca's old nurse had a slightly different role that enhanced the moral reputation of the friar's house in his narration. As we have seen, Bianca testified that she kept her old nurse out of loyalty; the old nurse testified that she paid her own way with the help of relatives and her work; but Aurelio testified that he allowed her to stay in the kitchen out of a sense of charity, "for the love of God." The morality play of rental was complete; an honest and honorable life with a dose of charity had triumphed in his house, at least in the friar's account.

But the friar's tale of a just house virtually "like a monastery" was not to go unchallenged. The Holy Office asked immediately, "Did there come to your house quite a number of people?" Aurelio tried to be as noncommittal as possible as he fell back on his earlier defense of being merely a practitioner of folk medicine. "Sometimes there were quite a number," he admitted, "sometimes not, because I went about the land practicing medicine and exorcizing spirits." The Holy Office continued, inquiring. "What type of people came to your house?" The friar appeared to give in before this line of questioning with disarming ease, perhaps because he was aware that he had little possibility of denying the range of his clients. As a result he answered, sounding rather more like his irate neighbors than like his defenders: "There come diverse sorts both gentlemen and gentlewomen as well as prostitutes, Jews and various other kinds including foreigners who were men and women." Under questioning he clarified further: "there were those who came to be treated with medicine, those who came to see their future, some for one thing, some for another."[44]

The interrogation was becoming more probing, and in quick succession he admitted that he told the future for these people and that "that which I could not read in their hand, I read by making judgements [iudicii] using geomancy."[45] But the friar drew the line at admitting any kind of witchcraft: "never, never did I say any spells of any sort." Again, however, the inquisitors did not back down, asking pointedly, "have you ever used witchcraft or herbal magic . . . for these people that came to you either in order to hammer others or to cause them to fall in love or for other similar things?" "I did not do such things," he maintained, "nor have I ever done them. Actually I was asked to do them often enough but I counseled those people who wanted to try such things against doing so."[46]

With that firm denial his interrogators had the friar just where they wanted him, for in searching his home they had found a great deal of material that would cause serious problems for his testimony. One of their most common strategies was to milk such moments of confrontation with unpleasant evidenciary counterrealities to try to break the defense of those they assumed were lying. Thus they promptly showed Fra Aurelio some hair wrapped in paper that had been found in his house and that had been labeled "number one," asking him, "what did you do with this hair?" They suspected that he had used the hair for exactly the type of witchcraft he had just denied. Apparently trying to dodge the trap, Aurelio replied, "that hair was brought to me by a woman who had found it on her doorstep." Doorstep magic, as noted, was a fairly typical form of hammering magic, and Aurelio's answer makes it clear that he was as aware of that as were his interrogators.

Rather than taking his shaky explanation any further, Aurelio, probably all too aware of the other incriminating things to be found in his house, began quickly building a defense. He continued, "and I have been brought a world of similar things such as quicksilver . . . and various kinds of evil stuff by people who asked me to tell them what they were and signified. I always told them that they were evil things and that they should throw them away and thus I sent them away." This was a defense that could explain the things found in his honest and honorable house, but it clearly was not a very good one, and his interrogators were not going to let him out of their trap so easily. They raised perhaps the most obvious difficulty, asking: "Given that such things were evil as you say, why did you keep this hair?" It was not an easy question to answer and Fra Aurelio clearly had trouble with it, responding in a disjointed fashion: "a woman brought me it, as I said, and I believe that I will remember and explain also for that woman who brought it to me, having found it on her doorstep. [I still had it(?)] because many people came to my house and I took it and wrapped it in paper and I put it in that vase which was I believe about two years ago." The passage is not too clear, but it seems that Aurelio was claiming that he had hidden the hair in a vase two years earlier when many people were visiting him and then forgot it. A weak answer, it did not tackle the central issue that the Inquisition relentlessly came back to: "Does it seem good to you that you who are a cleric kept such an evil thing in your house?" Fra Aurelio was forced to concede, "this I did evilly and badly; I just didn't think."[47]

This was just the beginning. Next, he was faced with a small package labeled by the Inquisition "number two" with the letters "Alpha" and "Omega" on it in a hand that he admitted was his. Asked what it was, he replied weakly, "A woman came to me and she brought me parchment that had been written on with that white magnet [*calamita biancha*] inside. She told me that she had found it in the bag of a gentleman who was her lover. She brought it to me to ask me if I understood about white magnets. I said to her that it was a white magnet and she asked me if during the first quarter of the moon, I would put it inside [the parchment] with red and white silk, as well as cloves and incense because she had been taught that one had to wrap these things up in this way so that the person who wore it would have especially good fortune. So I wrapped it up as you see."[48]

For all his denials just a few minutes earlier, we are back with the friar in the familiar world of love magic. And, of course, his interrogators were not impressed with his explanation. They asked: "How can it seem true that that woman ordered you to wrap those things together in that way when it seems clear that she could have done it herself?" His response seemed unlikely but had the merit of admitting little. He replied that the woman had not really understood the phases of the moon; therefore he had had to do it. Again he was asked why he had kept such an evil thing in his house, but this time he tried to shift the blame to the woman who he claimed had brought the package in the first place. He related that she had come back "four or five times" for it, but there were always too many people around and eventually she had stopped coming; thus it had been left for about a year. Attempting to shift the blame, however, Aurelio was making dangerous admissions. The fact that he felt he could not return the package when other people were present implied that he knew it was evil and to be kept hidden, just as was the case with the earlier hair. Moreover the crowds that he had asserted were only occasionally heavy had now become conveniently heavy every time the woman had returned. When questioned about the letters "Alpha" and "Omega" that he had written on the package, he replied that he had done so "because it seemed to me that the name of God would have greater power and *virtù* than the other things."[49] Once more this might have sounded good, but it implied what he was trying to deny—that he was taking an active role in this love magic and using the holy to do so.

Rather than challenging the friar the Inquisition went on to the third exhibit, perhaps because it was so similar to the second. Asked to identify what was in that packet, he admitted, "In this package there is a white magnet." He continued to explain that a servant of the Zen family had brought it to him to find out if it really was a white magnet. If so, he had wanted to use it to win the good graces [*per esser ben volesto*] of his master. Here the double sense of *voler bene* (to be loved, to be well thought of) again allowed binding magic to move beyond love to cement other relations based on friendship and good will. Such magic, as we have seen, could literally provide the social ties that bound. Once more the friar explained that there had been too many people present: thus he had asked the servant to leave it and come back later, after he had had a chance to decide if it really was a white magnet. The servant, however, had not returned, and as a result, it too had been found among the friar's possessions.

Next, the Inquisition asked him about yet another packet, and finally Aurelio admitted that he had concocted this one himself for a sailor. Nicely, just in case the Holy Office was beginning to seem too modern, with all its evidence so neatly labeled and so effectively introduced, this packet was introduced as "the other number two"! Like the first number two, this one contained a magnet wrapped up with red and white silk, a clove, "and other things." Aurelio confessed that it was to be worn by sailors for good luck. Of course, as already noted, he was well known for telling the future; thus, it was perhaps quite natural or at least good business that he would also produce charms to help deal with the future, charms that brought good luck.

Significantly his charms seem to overlap; virtually the same charm that brought luck to sailors brought love to women and brought a master's good will to a servant. This overlapping may well be an illusion, as Aurelio was not a very cooperative witness and was trying to avoid incriminating himself. Still, there seems to have been a logic to this overlap. Many of the things used for love magic played upon broader forces of attraction, much like Aurelio's white magnets. Using them to attract friends as well as lovers was logical and common as well. This may have been especially true when that friendship was seen as based on the self-interest of the person using the magic. Taking this type of magic a step further to bind to oneself fortune or the good things of the future seems to fit as a more generic aspect of a similar binding. Whether there was such a logic behind Fra Aurelio's magic, his clients seemed to believe in it. He admitted making up "twelve or fourteen" such packets for sailors to carry with them, and others as well for women.[50]

It appears that his interrogators felt that finally he had begun to admit what he had previously denied: that he had practiced love magic and other forms of magic. Thus they asked him point blank: "What profession do you call this?" Though cornered, the friar did not give in, dodging with "this is not any profession." Once again he was asked if he thought these things were good, and once again he admitted they were not. This time, however, he was asked why he had done them if he knew they were evil. And once more this direct question dragged him a little deeper. "I did those things," he answered, "to make people pay me, more than for anything else. Because then some gave now four soldi, now eight, some a marcello, but not more. [And they did this] without me asking them for anything."[51] Here the friar began to allow the Holy Office to see where the wealth discovered in his house had come from. And it is clear that from the very beginning they had been interested in this aspect of his life, for the wages of sin in Fra Aurelio's case seemed to have been extensive and his high style of life—renting a house of his own, hobnobbing with nobles and others of importance, and even per-haps having the illegitimate daughter of Marin Sanuto as his mistress—had attracted attention. If social mixing was questionable, rising above one's station to do so was especially troubling. And although the for-tune-telling friar appeared to be from a noble Sienese family, he was still the fortune-telling friar and a renegade cleric who, from the perspective of licit society, belonged outside the pale. As with Andriana Savorgnan, part of what was wrong with Fra Aurelio was that he had constructed ties that allowed him to move beyond his place and to have *and* display more wealth and power than seemed right.

One very profitable area of that power was his magic based on magnets to bind love, friendship, and fortune. The Holy Office brought out several more examples of confections made with magnets, as well as a small package of magnets given to him, he claimed, by a man from Crete whose name he did not remember. Perhaps this was his supplier, but when pressed to explain why this Cretan had given him the magnets, he weakly explained that he had given them in return for the friar's making up one of his packets wrapped in a prayer to Saint Augustine written on parchment. Unfortunately, by this time Fra Aurelio had ad-mitted enough on this score that the Holy Office did not even bother to ask him the reason for this or to specify what prayer he was referring to. In the end the Holy Office faced him with confections made up of mag-

nets with red and white silk, cloves, and incense; with incense and
needles; or with all of these plus holy oil. Although it was not always
specified, it appears that some of these packets were wrapped in parchment that had written on them just a simple Alpha and Omega; others
had more elaborate prayers such as the prayer to Saint Augustine.

Behind this mix of holy and profane, however, the main common
ingredient in this form of Aurelio's magic was the white magnet. Magnets were popular in the love magic practiced by women, and they were
also quite popular in learned magic coming out of a medieval tradition
that saw the power of the magnet to attract as indicating some deeper
power of attraction. Had Fra Aurelio, then, taken his magic from the
popular traditions around him, or had he found it in the learned tradition that presumably was his as a cleric? It is suggestive that in the
beginning, when he was trying to deflect blame and picture himself as
merely executing the orders of others or as the mere recipient of others'
magic, the people who had the know-how and had brought him things
were usually women. At the same time, when he felt pressed to admit
that it was he who had actually put together the magic, he then admitted
that certain men had brought him raw materials.

Could it be that the friar, in constructing this tale, consciously or not,
felt more comfortable blaming women for an active knowledge of such
magic, because they were often his source for it, and less comfortable
building his alibi using men, because they were not? Clearly, there is no
evidence to make this more than a tentative hypothesis, but the friar did
usually portray women as instructing him and men as merely receiving
his magic, and that in itself is unusual enough outside of the world of
love magic to attract attention. Also his comment, when asked what
kind of "profession" or "art" such magic was, could be read without
being forced too much to mean slightly more. His answer had been that
it was "no profession," which may have simply been an attempt to claim
that he had not been doing such things for money, something that he
had quickly been forced to contradict. But it could also have been said to
denote a distinction between women's magic and the male world of the
profession/arts. In earlier chapters, we have seen that such assumptions
were widespread and apparently shared by both the clerics who manned
the Holy Office and the people they interrogated as witnesses and as
accused.

The fact that the Holy Office considered this type of evidence as a
separate category and moved into it by questioning Fra Aurelio about
love magic may also reflect this distinction. After they finished asking
him about the confections found in his house, they moved on to ask him
about written materials found there—even though, of course, there had
been writing involved in the earlier magic. But as the host of letters,
writings, and books that had been discovered in his house was brought
before him, we enter a world that for the Inquisition seems to have been

seen as more involved with high culture. Yet, in fact, this was not an exclusively clerical or male world either, as noted earlier. And in his explanation of that series of books and libretti, about twenty in all, women figured prominently. Moreover, what might be called "learned magic" in Fra Aurelio's practice seems frequently to intersect with the more popular practices already encountered, and tellingly, this intercutting seems to have not been limited to the friar.

One of the most learned forms of magic that Aurelio claimed to practice was geomancy. The letter labeled "number two" by the Inquisition, for example, he explained, had been written to him by a German, Guglielmo da Costanza, who had written him regularly to ask him to make predictions concerning his business dealings. According to the friar, unfortunately, Guglielmo had not heeded his advice. "If he had done things according to my advice, he would not have gone bankrupt as you can see from this same letter," he explained with evident pride.[52] As a practitioner of geomancy, the friar once again was not without his detractors. A wine dealer named Zaneto complained to the Holy Office, "I had a fourteen year old daughter, who a young man wanted to marry. To tell the truth I had not planned to marry her until she was about twenty. . . . He came to me to ask for my girl, but because I refused . . . he said he would have her one way or another. So as happens having heard about this friar who could foretell these things and what should happen, I went to this friar." Zaneto explained the situation to Aurelio and asked his advice. "The friar took a pen in his hand and on a piece of paper he began to make signs [*segni*] and push and turn [the paper] in such a way that he said to me that she should never be his wife."[53] Evidently geomancy here was supported by common sense. This father had made no attempt to hide from Fra Aurelio his aversion to his daughter's marriage, and the friar's figures confirmed those patriarchal desires. It was a good bet at several levels, and one might assume that part of the friar's fortune-telling reputation was due to the fact that such predictions usually came true. This time, however, fathers did not rule, as Zaneto ruefully admitted. "Actually everything he [Aurelio] told me was false. . . . I gave the girl to that young man as his wife and he is in my house and they live as man and wife."[54]

Marriage predictions were a large part of the friar's practice. He was involved in such matters at the highest levels, having interfered even with the marriage plans of Cardinal Bembo, but he sold his predictions to people of all social levels. And it seems clear that in making them he was providing a service that was widely seen as helpful and much used. Again the Holy Office found itself in a borderland where what they deemed illicit was seen by a large segment of the community as useful. Marriage was so important a tie that knowledge of its future was certainly worth buying. The market remained strong; thirty-two years later, in 1571, when Aurelio was once again before the Holy Office, such predictions were still highly profitable.

Numerous people in 1571 again claimed that he used his fortune-telling abilities for families at all social levels concerned about arranging good matches. When the Holy Office asked him about this, he dissimulated: "I do not remember [very well] but it is certainly true that I spoke to some people who came to ask if certain marriages would work out. I said to them that they should go and have said the Mass of the Holy Spirit and that in addition they should inquire into the life and status of that man or woman that they wanted to marry because this marriage was not something that one did more than once. And this is what I said to them and I could have said it to them thusly and in no other way."[55] This commonsense advice seems hardly the kind of fortune-telling that would have created the streams of people reported flocking to his door, nor would it have filled his coffers with the new riches confiscated at the time, but it does illuminate why his fortune-telling in this area was so important. As the friar asserted, marriage was a major decision for a family and it was a matter not to be entered into lightly. With a reputation for offering good information on the future of matches, Aurelio could charge a good price for his advice. Moreover, if as it seems, he tended to side with the potential winners, his predictions may have been especially appreciated by fathers, uncles, and others in positions of power. And, as we have seen, he was also not adverse to guiding his predictions of the future and the future itself for the right price, which made his services even more valuable to the powerful who wanted that extra advantage.

In his marital predictions Fra Aurelio fit within the more general schema of popular love magic, even if both he and his examiners tended to see his practice as of a different more learned order. Just as there was a whole series of love magic techniques to determine the force of the ties of affection or love between people—casting beans, measuring chords and chains, and so on—the friar offered a similar service. The difference was that he merely foretold the future, and at least before the Inquisition he was anxious to claim that he did only that; he did not try to bind that future magically. Be that as it may, his wide range of magic, drawing on magnets and other forms of written prayers and spells, several of which were clearly *carte di voler bene*, demonstrated otherwise. He provided, in fact, both predictions and solutions to love and marriage concerns; he both measured the ties that bound in love and bound the passions necessary to make marriage work. In this he was much like the women encountered earlier, except that he claimed to draw on a higher culture—a claim that was accentuated by the habit of the Camalodese order that he insisted on wearing, against the wishes of the clerical establishment.

While his habit and claims of higher learning may have impressed his clients, even the more learned nobility among them, it appears that the learned area of his fortune-telling magic was actually rather limited. In the early 1570s when Fra Aurelio, having returned to his earlier practices of fortune-telling against the express orders of the Holy Office, was again examined by that tribunal, much of his questioning focused on these activities. At that time he again denied that he had ever practiced love magic or predicted the future of marriages; he had apparently decided that these were issues that had been significant in his earlier problems with the Holy Office. Instead he stressed his "scientific" use of astrology and geomancy to predict the future. Once again the Holy Office put pressure on his claims by presenting him with a mass of writings, most of which he admitted were his and most of which he labeled as examples of his practice of one of those two sciences.

He did deny, however, having copied a series of pasquinades, which touched off an interesting sequence of questions that laid out his professional claims and allowed him to parry some of the Holy Office's suspicions. The pasquinades, he claimed, had been given to him by their author, a certain Dal Sabelli, who had been hanged at the Arsenale. Ignoring his relationship with the executed man and the nature of the satirical verses, the Holy Office asked if he had predicted that execution. Aurelio could not resist admitting: "My Lords, yes I did predict that. I had asked him what month he was born in and when he told me I told him that he would die at the hands of Justice."[56] After denying that spirits had helped him make such predictions, he was questioned more directly about his practice of astrology. First, he was asked if, using astrology, he could predict elections and who would be elevated to high office. With caution he replied, "These are secrets of God, who can know?" Of course, if he had said that *only* God could know such things, he would have given the answer the Holy Office deemed correct.

Nonetheless, it was not the answer they expected, as they had testimony that he had been doing just such things, as well as proof among the writings confiscated and identified by him as his. Thus they asked, "Why then have you cast figures of astrology to find out if messer Antonio Donato would be elected to a post and if a certain Cardinal would be elected Pope?" Aurelio gave a brief but careful answer: "One sees by means of the figures of astrology that the planets have certain properties in that there are four signs of the sky that are bad, that is that lean towards evil and four that are perfect and four that are mediocre that lean towards the good."[57] This position he clarified better later in his testimony when the Holy Office returned to this issue: "I did not say who would be elected nor what they would be elected to. I did say, however, that the figures demonstrated favorable or unfavorable conditions."[58]

This does not reveal much about Aurelio's practice of astrology, but it was a good answer for the Holy Office. The distinction that lay behind it was very important to the distinction between legitimate astrology and illegitimate attempts to know what could only be known by God. That the heavens contained signs of future events was a commonplace. That one could judge whether or not celestial signs were propitious or not was also widely accepted—in fact, so widespread that it is easy to overlook how closely it was aligned with the forms of thinking later labeled scientific (especially with its attempts to measure numerically and relationally the probability of change over time). The trick was to concentrate, as Aurelio claimed, on probabilities based on signs, rather than claim any knowledge of God's preordained future. Still, here we may be on to another reason why Fra Aurelio had had so many powerful friends over the years. He seems to have had enough of a reputation to be consulted not just about marriage and love, but also about offices and political power. It may have been that he was consulted on these matters for purely political ends; knowing if the stars favored one's election could be quite useful if one was considering trying to marshal votes or buy them in the well-known Venetian style of corruption known as *broglio.* But the sixteenth century had also seen grow up in Venice and elsewhere a formally illegal but very popular form of betting on the results of elections. There were handsome rewards to be won, and people who could predict the future in this area could sell their information at a good price. Fra Aurelio almost certainly did so, as the Holy Office assumed.[59]

Returning to the friar's answer, although it was a good one, the Holy Office was not sure it was an honest one. They were particularly concerned about two things. First, they wondered whether he was using illicit arts that relied on the aid of the Devil. Second, they were worried that without following any specific art, he was calling on evil spirits to help with his predictions, perhaps taking advantage of their ability as noncorporeal beings to move over vast distances quickly and report back information that would not arrive in Venice until well into the future. During his questioning on 30 June 1571, the issue of how his astrology and geomancy worked and whether they went beyond *scientia* was an underlying theme. The matter was so central that the Holy Office actually had called in an expert witness on the matter, Giacomo Zarlino, who himself was a cleric. Zarlino closely examined a number of texts written by Fra Aurelio, looking at both the content and the vocabulary, and concluded: "I believe that these writings are a form of divinatory art, a mixture of geomancy and astrology from what one can tell and conjecture from the signs and characters and the unknown names written there which are neither Hebrew nor Caldean."[60] The Holy Office was particularly concerned about those unknown names, fearing that they were appeals to evil spirits or the Devil. Aurelio, faced with this conclusion, denied that the names had a divinatory scope, insisting that they merely helped him to tell whether or not the signs were favorable. He also questioned their expert's evaluation, suggesting that they call in a true expert in geomancy and astrology, one Bartolomeo Raines.

Needless to say, this piqued the Holy Office's curiosity, and they promptly asked who this Raines was and how Fra Aurelio knew about him. Aurelio responded that Raines practiced these arts only for himself and that he had learned about him when "a merchant who worked for him . . . brought me a figure of geomancy asking me to tell him my opinion of it and I responded to him that I did not understand such things."[61] The association of Raines with merchants seems to suggest that he might have been using geomancy to gain some advantage in mercantile endeavors. If that were true, there certainly was a vast potential market for his services in Venice. Whether this was the case for Raines or not, shortly afterward Fra Aurelio admitted that he had tried to tap that market, claiming that virtually the only type of fortune-telling he had done lately had been concerned with the probability of "sickness on voyages and whether merchants would have good fortune on their expeditions."[62]

The Holy Office took Aurelio's advice and brought in Bartolomeo Raines to testify on 6 July. If he had expected support from Raines, he did not get it. Raines did admit knowing some geomancy, implying that it was a purely intellectual interest. Shown some of Aurelio's figures and writing and asked if they were geomancy, he was unsparing. "This is divinatory art," he explained and then added without being asked, "it is art badly done and a *bagatella* [worthless or lightweight]."[63] Raines, it appears, either saw Fra Aurelio as a not very knowledgeable practitioner or wanted to portray him as one. In this vein he continued to testify that he knew the friar and knew that he made his living by telling the future. He also admitted that he had asked his opinion about a figure of geomancy, but again he denigrated the friar's knowledge, claiming that the latter had been able to say no more about it than that it was "okay." Finally, when asked if the friar relied on demons for his fortune-telling, he rounded off his negative testimony by implying the worst without saying much: he admitted that he did not know if the friar had done such things, but claimed that he had indeed heard this.[64] One further expert witness who was called in confirmed that the friar's writings were a mix of astrology, geomancy, and other arcane arts, again giving the impression that the level of his knowledge and his art was not very high.[65]

Given the friar's success as a fortune-teller, this strengthened the Holy Office's fear that he was relying on spirits to gather information. This had been a concern in his first trial, when several of his confiscated books were discovered to contain spells for calling evil spirits. One is reminded of the roughly contemporary autobiographical account of the famous sculptor Benvenuto Cellini's attempt to call up spirits to tell his future with the aid of a priest. Needless to say, the friar was considerably more circumspect before the Holy Office than Cellini—who, with his colorful autobiography, managed to continue his self-display even after his death. Aurelio denied strongly any implication of working with spirits or demons, usually claiming that the incriminating texts had been given him by women to copy or evaluate.

In the 1570s, however, the Holy Office had a new suspicion about his use of spirits that centered on his servant Dorothea, the woman he was so anxious to reward with a dowry. They came to the crux of his last long interrogation in 1572 by asking him how long Dorothea had been his servant. Nine years, he replied. Then they asked a rather strange-sounding question that, given the friar's laconic response, seemed to have worried Aurelio. They inquired about Dorothea's health when she entered his service. He replied that she had been sick. The Holy Office pressed, asking what her illness was, and once again they drew the friar into their game, for he had to admit that she was possessed by a spirit. That, of course, was the focus of their suspicions.[66] "What was the name of her spirit?" they demanded. "I do not know," he parried, "because I never asked her about that." Asked if he had ever talked with the spirit, he averred, "I never talked with the spirit but I certainly [tried to] exorcize it." That led to a question about the form of exorcism he had used. Again his answer was vague. He appeared to be attempting to turn the questioning away from the subject: "[I did] the same thing done by a monk of San Domenico. But because I was sick I was not able to continue and I brought a priest Giuliano Fiorentino into the house and paid him to exorcize her."[67]

But the Holy Office was not about to allow him to shift the questioning away from his exorcism and his relationship with Dorothea's spirit. "Father, you are lying," they admonished, "because exorcists want to know the name of the spirits that they exorcize and their number, because a spirit is never alone in a body. Moreover if you had not asked his name the priest Giuliano certainly did and you ought to know it from him. So tell us his name." Fra Aurelio remained firm, claiming that the priest had carried out his exorcism in another room and had not told him any names. He added a few details about his own exorcism procedures, perhaps trying to reassure them that they had not involved learning the name of the spirit. His examiners pushed on, however, coming to the heart of their fears. "Have you ever questioned the spirit of Dorothea," they asked, "in order to know from him what was happening in Rome or other cities or places?" The friar denied this absolutely. "Never did I ask that or anything else." They then shifted to a more theoretical tack: "Do you believe it would be a sin to want to know from a spirit what a man was doing who was far away?" "It would be a sin, worse even than a sin," he retorted. Perhaps trying to trip him up, the Holy Office asked if he thought a spirit could do such things. But in the abstract area of theory the friar knew how to play it safe and he replied, "I believe that only God would know that."[68]

It appears that the Holy Office had no proof that they considered adequate to corner Fra Aurelio; thus, faced with his denials, they made one last try with a theoretical question that seems to reflect what they suspected. They inquired if he believed that a demon who was a spirit could move from west to east in a small amount of time and report what happened in distant places. The friar, perhaps sensing that the worst was past, sidestepped. "I believe that people say a great number of lies."[69] The members of the Holy Office were left with their suspicions, but the friar had avoided successfully becoming entangled in their fears. Nonetheless, those fears are quite revealing, as many even in the 1540s had believed that one of the reasons the fortune-telling friar was so successful was that he had bound to himself a spirit to aid him with predictions.

In the 1570s with Dorothea as his servant, such suspicions, perhaps fed by his reputation and even by his deeds, found an especially fertile climate in which to grow. How convenient it was to have in your house a servant who was possessed by a spirit or spirits, which as a priest you could master and use for your own ends. Unlike la Draga or other women who claimed that their special powers came from spirits that possessed them, Fra Aurelio could claim that he himself was unpossessed and thus in a position of greater power over the spirit that he manipulated. Unfortunately, the information does not exist to demonstrate that the friar did use such claims, but given his apparent readiness to profit wherever he saw a possibility to do so and his willingness to take on a servant who was possessed and to reward her as well, the suspicions of the Holy Office do not seem quite so fantastic as they might at first appear.

The High Road and the Low Road to Discovering Lost Treasure

The exclusive relationship that priests and clerics had begun to claim with the spiritual world following Trent may have had a long way to go to win general acceptance, as the investigations of love magic and the women of Latisana have suggested, but whether licit or illicit, for them such relationships usually wore a more learned veneer. Much erudite discussion had focused on the relationship between humans and spirits, and some of the best intellectuals of the Renaissance had written extensively on the issue, as the work of modern scholars like Francis Yates, Eugenio Garin, and Lynn Thorndike has amply shown. With Fra Aurelio, however, it appears that in his dealing with the spiritual as with most of the rest of his activities, he mixed the theoretically high and the formally low with a clever eclecticism. Unfortunately, that mix cannot be too closely analyzed because of his evasive testimony and the lack of details about what he was actually doing. Yet given his eclecticism, if he used spirits, one might assume that he used them as much in the manner of la Draga as in the manner of the followers of Hermes Trismegistus or other classical authorities on Renaissance magic. That hypothesis can be given some context by examining many other cases brought before the Holy Office in this period involving clerics and the conjuring of spirits. While virtually all make reference, and often extensive reference, to learned treatises and classical authorities, most of them seem inextricably intertwined with the more everyday world we have been studying as well.

Perhaps the most interesting and well-known example is the treasure hunt that came to the attention of the Holy Office in 1579 and involved as its major protagonists two Franciscan priests, Cesare Lanza and Antonio Saldagna, as well as Don Gregorio Giordano, another priest and monk who had fled his order; Francesco Oglies, a Spaniard from Valencia; the Venetian noble Giulio Francesco Morosini; and the priest Giovanni de Schioffi.[70] Morosini, a well-to-do noble, had learned from a certain Armenian about a large ancient treasure that was hidden in a cave in the hills above Verona.[71] According to Morosini the Armenian had actually been in the cave with the treasure: "In the territory of Verona in a mountain . . . there was a cave in which there was a King made of solid gold, with three mounds of gold around him. It was a great treasure. At the mouth of the cave there was a lamp or eternal flame and that treasure he [the Armenian] could not take out of the cave because of the demons."[72] Together with a certain Giulio Cesare Mutio, they had sought to rediscover the cave several times, Morosini admitted, but without luck.

Mutio, the tutor of Morosini's son, in turn gave a detailed and rather humorous account of their search. "Because it was not convenient [for Morosini to go], as an expedient he sent me with the aforementioned Armenian. And because I ate his bread and he is a Venetian Gentleman and I am a subject of theirs and my duty is to obey, I went. . . . When we reached the mountain of Suacie [we entered] a cave and instead of finding the chamber of the king and gold, we found shepherds and goat manure."[73] Muti claimed that when he returned to Venice he tried to dissuade Morosini from continuing the venture, but to no avail. Shortly thereafter the Armenian claimed to have rediscovered the treasure. This time all three went, at Morosini's expense: "So we left again and I went along more to serve him [Morosini] than with any hope of finding anything."[74] His lack of hope was amply rewarded; they found only an empty well. Later another fruitless search was made at the behest of the Armenian in the area of Soave.

Finally, they decided to try in the region of Monte Birone, where local legend had it that there was an ancient horde of gold. Muti related that when the news got out that they were there to find a buried treasure, "a great multitude of peasants came running . . . with shovels, picks and hoes, hunting for the fortune. All they found were soil and rocks and in one place a great number of bones. Returning home, and disillusioned about the whole enterprise, I avoided it."[75]

Morosini was not the first to seek this treasure. There had been at least one earlier failed search that had ended in murder.[76] But he believed that he could succeed because he had more going for him than the Armenian's faulty recollection of the treasure's location. First, there was Don Gregorio Giordano, the onetime friar and priest who had lived for many years in the monastery of San Salvatore and who had once studied with the well-known theologian and magician at Padua, Cesare Lanza. Giordano had early on won Morosini's confidence by showing him a book, *The Forty-Three Kings of Spirits*, which both men were sure would be their key to gaining the treasure. This book Giordano described to the Holy Office as follows: "there was written there on each page the name of a spirit, its powers, its characters, and the methods of conjuring it . . . and among other things there was one who said after his name 'I am the God of Treasure,' another 'I am the God of Knowledge [*Scientiarum*],' another '[I am the God] of Arms and Armies,' another 'I am the God of Victory,' another 'I am Slaughter of Armies and Men,' another 'Invisibility,' another 'Love,' another 'Hate and Discord.' . . . and it went on in that way one after another for each spirit."[77] It is noteworthy that many of the things that these spirits offered through high magic were the same things offered in the everyday world by powerful women. Moreover, although the Holy Office was very worried about the diabolic in the practices of such women, rather than relying on spirits, they often relied on Christianity in a broad sense or the powers to be found in the everyday. Thus, ironically, they might be seen as offering the same services as the high magic of their male competitors, with considerably less danger to the soul.

Be that as it may, Don Giordano's book was the key. Morosini explained to the Holy Office that the friar had claimed that once the book was consecrated, it could be used to overcome the spirits that guarded the cave where the treasure was hidden. Moreover, as rediscovering the treasure became more difficult, especially after the Armenian disappeared, it appears that they considered using the spirits in the book to help them find the treasure as well. In this process the noted theologian and magician Cesare Lanza played a crucial role.

Lanza conveniently had come to Venice to publish a book, *L'accademia del pastore*, at just the moment the treasure hunt had run into snags. As a Franciscan he had stayed at the Franciscan house at the Frari, but after a few days, perhaps persuaded by his old student Giordano, he moved in with Morosini. "Being in my house," Morosini recalled, "Don Gregorio with me present discussed with this Master Cesare his desire to consecrate this book in order to have the treasure. Both of them told me that I needed many types of spices which I should buy. . . . And I bought as well two knives with white handles and two pieces of crimson taffeta and four small incense holders. . . . Later all these things, that is, the spices, the knives, and the incense holders were put on a table where there was laid out a small cloth from my house, that is a hand towel, which was new. And they had me also get two pens and ink to write with. Several times the said Master Cesare and Don Gregorio conjured [spirits] there in my house and they went around the table burning incense and saying the [prayer] 'Veni Creator Spiritus' and certain psalms and other prayers turning towards the four corners of the world. And both Maestro Cesare and Don Gregorio said the prayers."[78]

To this point, it seems that we have entered a different and higher world where the written culture of clerics and, to a lesser extent, that of the social elite dominated. Aside from spirits/gods who could also move to love or hate, the magic involved seemed high and the goals, treasure and power over spirits, quite different. But even these practitioners of high magic were much more in the world we have been exploring than they might at first appear to be. Two of the clerics involved, Antonio Saldagna and Francesco Oglies, were especially so.[79] Saldagna was a renegade cleric from Portugal somewhat in the mold of Fra Aurelio. He had deserted the Franciscan order for a while and appears to have been ready to do so again at the first opportunity. One of the most hostile witnesses against him claimed that he was so busy and successful pursuing women that he had bragged that he and Oglies had contemplated "setting up a harem just like that of the Great Turk."[80]

Saldagna became involved in the case at Don Gregorio's behest. Just how that occurred was retold in several versions under fairly intense pressure from the Holy Office, so it is difficult to decide what details are accurate. But it is clear that Saldagna, along with Oglies, had met with Don Gregorio several times to discuss Morosini's treasure search, and that they had debated strategies for calling up spirits for it, as well as to bind the love of women and the support of their superiors.[81] And significantly binding love remained an aspect of their alliance. Even for Morosini, Saldagna admitted writing out several texts, including "one that began 'conjurations to discover treasure,' another to call spirits with, I don't remember how many spells, and other little things on the order of *secrets relating to love.*'[82] Cesare Lanza may also have attempted to play on this less threatening aspect of their magic when he sought to portray Morosini as virtually a libertine. He claimed that Morosini had little interest in high magic, being much more interested in "eating and drinking well" and being one who had a wild imagination and loved to make "fun of the world."[83]

If that description did not do justice to Morosini, it fit Saldagna well. His friend, Francesco Oglies, under close questioning never quite admitted what several other people had claimed—that Saldagna in Venice had

had affairs with several nuns and had actually made plans to carry off
two. Perhaps he stayed so loyal to his old friend because most of those
who reported such plots named him as a co-conspirator. Nonetheless, in
the end he admitted, "It is true that he, Saldagna, innumberable times
returned to similar subjects, that is wishing to carry nuns off from the
convent without naming any particular one. I always replied 'God keep
me from getting involved' . . . and often he told me about certain loves
that he had had in Neapolitan territory . . . and of those women who
had wanted to come with him, who he had left behind to re-take the
habit of a monk."[84] He had also claimed that if certain nuns saw him
without his habit, they would run off with him immediately. Oglies
reported that he had reproved the Franciscan for this and that Saldagna
had replied colorfully that even Saint Francis had always "had God in
Heaven and women on earth."[85]

Even the theologian and ex-professor of theology at Padua, Cesare
Lanza (who has been seen as the one cleric involved who had lived a life
in consonance with his calling and worked entirely in the context of
learned magic),[86] reveals a much more familiar reality. In fact, he was
heavily involved in both high and low magic, with a suggestive mix of
theory and pragmatism. It appears that to some people he had claimed
that he had become deaf earlier in his career, when trying to control
demons for his magic—a claim that echoes rumors about la Draga's
blindness and other women magicians' disabilities. But when the Holy
Office faced this priest, friar, and theology professor with that claim, he
countered that his deafness was the result of an illness that he had
contracted about nine years earlier. When pressed on the subject, he
labeled the accounts of his youthful battle with demons as "fables" and
went on to explain, "I had this problem because of an illness and this
illness was syphilis."[87] To some extent, then, Cesare had also experienced the world of the illicit.

His formal confession provides a good picture of yet another unbound passion that had led him astray—his desire for magical knowledge. He ruefully admitted that about sixteen years earlier he had been
seduced by a desire to master magic: "I went out to search for books of
this art such as: Cornelio Agrippa, *De occulta philosophia*, Mercurio Tris-
megisto, Appolonia Thianeo in the *Cantica*, Apuleio's *Asino aures*, Arte-
sio, *Delle virtù delle parole et carattere*, Orfeo in the hymns, songs and
Geneologia del Mondo, La Luna, De Imaginibus and other works."[88]
Finding that he could not make much progress in Padua, where he was
teaching theology at the time, he went to Paris to pursue his interests.
There he lost himself in his studies, and he admitted that he left behind
his Franciscan habit to "live . . . against nature," taken in by his belief
in the reality of the things that he had "only imagined."

After he returned his search for magical power continued, and he
confessed that he was capable of putting his discoveries to quite mun-

dane purposes. "I taught to some and I promised to teach to others," he admitted, "how to make a ring to be used to win in gambling and have money." He had actually made such a ring using learned magic, which he briefly described, but his goals were decidedly mercenary. "With this ring," he continued, "a friend of mine, gambling in the evening, won and in the morning he gave me two scudi. Afterwards at the request of Giulio Francesco [Morosini] and Francesco Oglies, I promised to make them each one."[89] Moving from Hermes Trismegistus to a two-scudi payoff for gambling magic or from searching for a lost horde of gold to confecting magic rings for friends might seem great leaps from the high to the low, but for all of our searchers they were part of an eclectic mix of the high and the low that made up the world of renegade priests and clerics of the late Renaissance.

How many magicians working to find the lost knowledge of the ancients were also willing to seek knowledge in the culture today labeled low needs serious rethinking and research. Even at the level of high thought that can be clearly traced from ancient texts, one must be ready to ask the difficult question: how much was that ancient wisdom empowered by similar practices encountered in the everyday world? Quite simply, here once again we are confronted with a complex discourse that resonated between the high and the low. And in their resonances, each may well have created significant harmonies for those seeking power wherever it could be found. For the priest or scholar, finding apparent echoes of the ancient in popular practice must have been a potent reinforcement of their truth; the same may well have been true for women practitioners, who found that their learned customers appreciated and seemed to understand their magic even from the context of another form of learning.

Cesare Lanza not only demonstrated this, he apparently was aware of it. Early in his testimony, he explained rather cryptically that the high magic he studied had had true power before the coming of Christ, but that after Christ's coming it was much less likely to work. He even claimed at times that his high magic was a fraud, although his actions and most of his testimony presented a different picture. But in the midst of questioning about his methods for consecrating the book of forty-three spirits, he interjected, "If you knew those who are interested in magic and those who are greedy and if you had the eyes of Argos you would not be able to see all the evil that there is in this land. *Today a lowly little woman does more than all the necromancers accomplished in the ancient world.* Moreover there is not a person who is not wearing some kind of charm with characters."[90]

Cesare's point, even if it is obviously self-serving, made sense. Apparently it hit home even for the Inquisition, for they responded immediately and rather discursively: "Even if in a city as populated as Venice there were one or even ten who arrogantly attempted similar deeds, you speak evilly of the whole of the city in which you are one evil person, but you miss the thousands of good people just as among the thousands of good friars it would be difficult to find a friar like you."[91] Certainly this is a logical response and perhaps statistically speaking a true one, but it seems also unusually defensive for the Holy Office. Yet they had good reason to be defensive. Such practices were extremely widespread, with people as diverse as peasant women in the countryside, Fra Aurelio in Venice, and even Cardinal Bembo drawn at one time or another into their web.

But Cesare may have been saying something more that the Holy Office missed or passed over, for he made a distinction between ancient practice and its implicitly learned magic and the modern practice of everyday magic done by "lowly little women." The former, he asserted, was much less powerful than the latter; modern women were more powerful than the greats of the ancient world. That certainly is a reversal of the typical Renaissance vision of the ancients! What made the difference? Earlier he had stated that with the coming of Christ the nature of the universe had changed—a good and fairly standard staple of medieval theology. Could he have been claiming that with the aid of Christ, using Christian-based magic and characters, even the humblest woman could accomplish more than an ancient wise man? If so, it was a clever and in a way an accurate appraisal of just what many of those women practitioners and their clients believed. And in the end he was correct to a degree, as humble women often did seem to succeed in their binding and healing magic, whereas he and his motley crew were unable to bind spirits at least to win their treasure. This reading may press his comments too far, especially as it was likely that they were primarily another attempt to distract the Holy Office from the issues at hand. But even at that level we see Cesare well aware of the common culture of magic that lay below his higher claims. And he was not adverse to attempting to use it, at least in his own defense. I would suggest that given his desire to know about such matters and the sacrifices that he made for magical knowledge, his awareness of that supposedly other world was not that of a disinterested observer. Certainly that was true of his compatriots in their failed search for treasure, and of many other clerics of the late Renaissance, especially those who moved in and out of the illicit world and whom we have labeled renegades.

Fra Aurelio and Power

Certainly that was true of Fra Aurelio. Across his long career he made many claims about his mastery of high culture and clearly used his habit to reinforce those claims. Yet perhaps his greatest skill was mixing the high with the low in a package that convinced, whether his client was a learned noble or a common boatman. In fact Fra Aurelio was so successful at this that even with his continuing run-ins with the Holy Office and his occasional convictions as well, from the late 1530s at least until the early 1570s, excepting his years in jail and away, he managed to remain a fairly powerful person in Venice with a large practice, important friends, and considerable wealth. The first accusations against him, it will be remembered, in 1543 were allowed to drop. Why this happened is not clear. It may be that the ecclesiastical authorities were sidetracked by other issues that seemed more important. A mere renegade friar who told the future may have seemed a small problem in those days of much more serious fears of Lutherans and Anabaptists. But in 1543 Aurelio, in his early forties (probably forty-four years old), also had powerful connections in the city. It was in just this period that he was interfering at the behest of noble friends in the marriage plans of Cardinal Bembo and attempting to secure his own papal dispensation for having left the Camaldolese without permission. Still, it may be that it was precisely his interference at the highest levels of power that led to his downfall. Given the information that remains this cannot be proven, but what can be ascertained from closely reading his case is that in 1549 Fra Aurelio found himself in a particularly exposed position vis-à-vis some important enemies he had made when he interfered in the marriage plans of the cardinal.

In his first brief reference to the marriage of Bembo's daughter in his testimony of 20 October 1549, Fra Aurelio began talking about the issue in response to a letter that had been found among his possessions written to him by the powerful Venetian noble Fantin Corner. This Fantin had been the leader of the Piscopia branch of the Corner family, one of the richest and most noted of a generally rich and noted family. In 1511 he had married Marietta Foscari, daughter of another major family, served as a senator, and held the important post of Rettore in Cyprus. The couple had four sons who reached adulthood, the most famous of whom, Franco, had a notable career in politics and as a naval officer and finished his life as a Procurator of San Marco.[92] Fantin's power had recently come to its end, however, as the friar remarked with some emotion, "he has died, God give him paradise." Given the warmth of his remarks about his deceased "friend," the Holy Office asked about the nature of their relationship. The friar replied, "I was always at his house and he was my closest friend and patron."[93] Was this hyperbole or had Corner truly been his patron, protector, and close friend as well? We already know that Aurelio had entered the lists against Cardinal Bembo's marriage plans at the behest of Corner. But there were closer ties as well, as his first rather confused attempts to explain the contents of that letter from Corner suggest.

Before admitting that the letter referred to an attempt to derail Bembo's marriage plans, Aurelio attempted to give it another reading. He claimed that it referred to an argument that had sprung up between

Corner and another noble, Gerolamo Querini, over a certain Elisabetta
Masolla: "Masolla was loved by both of them," the friar explained.
"Thus for that reason messer Fantin had written to me asking that when
messer Gerolamo came to me for a reading of his fortune I ought to tell
him as [Fantin had written] in the said letter." Putting the best face on
the matter, Aurelio explained that fortunately Gerolamo had never
come to have his fortune told, and thus he had not been put in the
position of giving him a false reading. This was especially good because
"it did not seem honest to me to sow hate between people especially
because this messer Gerolamo had lived for years and years in the house
of that Massola and he was poor and what he had he had had from
messer Fantin according to what messer Fantin had told me." He continued that the references in the letter to a "lover" referred to Massola. But
he ran into trouble when it came to explaining references to marriage in
the same letter. At that point he quickly backtracked, claiming he had
gotten things wrong—"now that I have read the whole thing, I realize
that I have made a mistake"—and he went on to reexplain Corner's
letter as asking him to interfere in Cardinal Bembo's marriage plans for
his illegitimate daughter with Pietro Soranzo.[94] In this reading, he
claimed that he had been asked by Corner to give an incorrect prog-
nostication of the future to Pietro Soranzo, the disputed potential husband.

If Fra Aurelio's memory of the meaning of Corner's letter was confused, his memory of Gerolamo Querini and his love for Elisabetta Masolla seem to have been equally so. For Elisabetta was attractive to many
men—including Fantin Corner and Cardinal Bembo, who was reputed
to have taken up with her after the death of his earlier mistress, la
Morosina, in 1535. But it is less likely that she was a love of Gerolamo
Querini, at least in the sense that the friar implied. She was his sister.
Given Renaissance mores that may not entirely rule out Fra Aurelio's
claim, but the close and long-lasting friendship between Cardinal
Bembo and Gerolamo Querini would seem to settle the issue. In fact, the
cardinal and Querini carried on a long and warm correspondence over
the years, and Querini was even named one of the executors of Bembo's
will. Perhaps behind this close relationship there stood, rather than incest and a shared mistress, a bond based on Querini's acceptance of the
cardinal's affair with his sister.[95]

Whatever the relationship was based upon, it was strong enough
that in the early 1540s the two men corresponded about Bembo's marriage plans for his illegitimate daughter, and the cardinal even sought
Querini's advice on the matter.[96] In fact it appears that the real problems
between Fantin Corner and Querini stemmed from Corner's attempt to
use Fra Aurelio to trick Querini into believing that the cardinal was not
his friend. The aim may have been to use him, as discussed earlier, to
disrupt the cardinal's marriage plans but it may have also involved the

deeper potential conflict between the cardinal and Corner over Elisabetta Masolla. What is clear is that Querini felt he had been the victim of a complex plan to break his close ties with the cardinal and that Aurelio was at the center of the plot.

Gerolamo Querini testified before the Holy Office on 13 November 1549 that about five or six years earlier there had been a conflict between the cardinal and Corner. "This messer Fantin," he explained, "seeking to invoke discord, enmity, and evil wishes between this Cardinal Bembo . . . and myself, where previously there had been such great friendship, concord and love decided among other things to try the following plan."[97] The key to the plot, as he described it, was Corner's man, Fra Aurelio. Corner was to write to a certain friend of his in Rome, asking him to get as close as possible to Flamminio Thomarozzo, who was in the service of Cardinal Bembo. Once this was accomplished, this Roman accomplice was to ask Flamminio to write to Querini as a friend of the cardinal's in Venice to help with a problem—the Roman's desire to know the fate of a certain young man who had disappeared. The solution, of course, was to have Flamminio send Gerolamo Querini a nativity of this nonexistent young man and ask him to take it to the famous fortune-telling friar of Venice, Fra Aurelio.

In this way Querini met Fra Aurelio for the first time, asking him to read the false nativity and discover the fate of the lost youth as a favor to Flamminio in Rome. It must have seemed truly impressive to Querini when, a few days later, the friar returned to him with a very detailed account of a young man who neither of them knew and whose life had been centered in distant places. In Querini's words, Fra Aurelio judged, "This nativity was of a young man who had served a great prelate at court and had secured a great number of benefices. Later he returned to his homeland where he fell in love with a young woman for whom he not only spent all his income and sold all his things but he also sold his benefices and consumed all his wealth." To this point the story had the vague truth of any love story, even if it reminds one of Boccaccio's tale of Federigo degli Alberighi, who eventually served up even his falcon to his love out of his consuming desire to win her. But in the friar's tale, love had a much less happy ending. "Then as one desperate, he went into a distant land, where not having the wherewithal to live, he began to live by robbery [and captured] he was hanged."[98] An impressive story, it became even more so when Gerolamo sent it to Flamminio in Rome; for, of course, when Flamminio gave the friar's judgment to his friend there, his friend feigned amazement at the friar's ability and confirmed his reading as totally true. Flamminio, in turn, wrote to Querini, one assumes honestly impressed, informing him that "that friar was the most important astrologer that there was in the world." Querini claimed, however, that he was not impressed, because he did not believe in such things.

Still the plot went ahead, and Querini related that shortly thereafter he had met the friar again. Alvise Michael, along with several other nobles from important families, having nothing particular to do one evening after a marriage celebration, dragged him along to visit the friar as a lark. Again Querini implied that he had been set up, as the friar made several true judgments about Michael even though both claimed never to have met. The ground then was well prepared when the friar turned to Querini and offered to read his hand. He, however, claimed to have avoided the offer by saying that he did not believe in such things. Whether this was true or merely a way of avoiding making any untoward confessions of his own temptation, Querini reported that the friar, undaunted, said "that I knew a magnificent prelate that I thought was my greatest friend and he asked me that I give him the nativity of this prelate."[99]

Reluctantly, but pressed by Alvise Michael, a few days later he brought the nativity of Cardinal Bembo to Michael, and together they went to the house of Aurelio. Corner's plot had come to fruition. Querini had seen with apparently independent and impressive proofs that Fra Aurelio was a great astrologer, and important people around him like Michael and even Flamminio in Rome had confirmed the fact. The friar gave his reading of the cardinal's nativity "immediately . . . when he saw the year of his birth." It was devastating and directly aimed at Fantin Corner's goal of breaking the friendship between Bembo and Querini. Querini reported that the friar said "that this prelate was suited to be the most evil, ribald, and infamous man that there was in the world and that I ought to watch out for him because he would make me lose my possessions as well as my life and my soul." If Querini had believed the friar, he might well have broken his ties with the cardinal and pressed his sister to do the same, leaving her presumably in the hands of Corner.

The story hardly loses anything before the convoluted twists and turns of a typical sixteenth-century comedy. Querini, however, refused to believe the friar and left, much upset by the whole matter. Later, when Flamminio visited Venice, Querini learned that he had been pressed to praise the friar. And eventually he learned from Corner's contact in Rome that the whole thing had been engineered "by Fantin so that I would give faith to that ribald friar in order to create discord between the Most Reverend Cardinal Bembo and myself . . . and I have heard said publicly that there was not an evil or ribald deed that was not done with the aid of the said friar in his house."[100]

The fortune-telling friar had worked to control the future for his patron and friend Fantin Corner, and it may well have been true that there were few evil or ribald deeds that were not committed by the two together. But one thing is clear: if Querini's tale is true, the friar, with Corner as his patron, was not afraid to take on major figures, and from the perspective of many, he had clearly made his mark and won a reputation. Corner, it seems recognized this and worked behind the scenes to protect and even advance his protege. When Aurelio was questioned about his wealth and especially his substantial deposits in the Zecca of Venice, he revealed that Corner had counseled him on investing and had helped him place the deposit.[101] He admitted as well that Corner had tried to aid his ecclesiastical career, something that is rather difficult to imagine given his questionable status at the time. "When messer Fra Gasparo went off to become chaplain to the most distinguished General of the Order . . . ," Aurelio reported, "Fantin Corner offered me his mansionary priesthood at San Zacharia."[102] Aurelio, however, turned down his friend's offer, claiming to the Holy Office that he did not feel spiritually up to the task of celebrating Mass.

What other favors Corner had done for his client Fra Aurelio one can only guess, but it may well be that the lack of action on the original complaint against him in 1543 turned on the fact that Corner was still alive then; in turn, the case brought against him in 1549 may have hinged on the fact that Corner had just died on 15 October. The investigation against Aurelio had begun a few days earlier; the first reference to it was dated the 12th. Aurelio was arrested on the 15th, the same day that Corner died, and things were off and running. It may be mere coincidence that the friar had lost his patron at just the moment that the Holy Office began to investigate him again, but it certainly did not help his chances of escaping their clutches a second time. And it may have been just by chance that one of his earliest accusers was one Nicolo Bembo, a member of one of the more important branches of Cardinal Bembo's family in Venice. Suggestively, however, this Bembo in his testimony reminded the Holy Office of the earlier investigation of the friar, even giving the names of the main people who had testified against him six years earlier and going into some detail about the damning testimony of Francesco Giustinian. Beyond that he had little to offer, merely adding that "that friar has the reputation . . . that he tells the future and lives by geomancy and that he keeps in his house his woman who was the illegitimate daughter of Marin Sanuto. Moreover from what I have heard he rents rooms . . . to evil women."[103]

Be that as it may, the investigation was underway, and while magic and fortune-telling would be the main features of the case, there seemed to be a subtext that turned on the revenge of the Bembo family and Gerolamo Querini for the friar's ''magical'' interference in their affairs. How important that other force of attraction that we label patronage was in the friar's demise we cannot know, but even here it should be noted that we are dealing with the world of binding and *voler bene*. Corner had felt strong ties to the friar and wished him well, but the Bembos and Querini clearly did not; the friar at that moment could have used some of the very love magic that others claimed he sold! And the upshot was that there was no escape from the Holy Office this time. The trial proceeded with relative alacrity, and by early December the tribunal had called in a number of clerics to review the case and make suggestions on penalties. All were in agreement that the penalty should be severe, and a number even argued that he should be stripped of his habit and turned over to the civil authorities to be burned as a "manifest heretic." Others held him only under suspicion of being a heretic and leaned toward the lesser punishment of perpetual imprisonment and the confiscation of his ill-gotten gains, which would be given over to the pious causes of the Church.[104]

On 7 December, after reviewing the case against him, the Holy Office declared Fra Aurelio a "notorious heretic" and asked him to confess and abjure his sins. This was common practice, for if heretics were willing to admit true contrition for their deeds, their culpability would be greatly mitigated. Two days later Aurelio complied, admitting virtually everything he had been accused of by the Holy Office. Of course, this "confession" must be treated with caution, because by this time the friar knew that he was to be punished and that his best chance lay in asking forgiveness in each area where the Holy Office believed him guilty. Later he would claim that he had been talked into confessing things he had not done by the inquisitor and the executive officer of the tribunal, who had promised to free him from jail "in a couple of days" if he confessed.[105] This claim may not have been entirely self-serving, as it appears that members of the tribunal at times did advise prisoners to confess in order to secure lighter sentences. To a degree this was a corruption of the procedure, but as confession and salvation of souls were the theoretical goals of the Holy Office, there was a logic in such actions. Moreover, although there was little chance that the friar would get out of jail "in a couple of days," even that claim may have been only an exaggeration of a promise that his sentence would be lighter if he confessed.

Nonetheless, even with a confession probably solicited under false pretenses, the mass of testimony and the friar's wealth both demonstrate that he had told the future, using at best questionable means; done love magic and healing magic, following both the high and the low forms available to him; lived as a renegade priest and monk; and, perhaps most damning of all, lived as a relatively powerful figure, moving among the rich and powerful of the city for years. As a result, in sentencing the friar, the Holy Office labeled him a "notorious and manifest heretic" who deserved to be perpetually imprisoned and to have his wealth confiscated and dispensed for pious causes. Instead, because of his confession and contrition, they decided to deny him perpetually the right to give the sacraments or say Mass. He was also ordered to confess his guilt in Saint Mark's Cathedral; surrender his habit; serve ten years in jail; and then be banned perpetually from the city and all its territories. Finally, his wealth was to be confiscated and distributed to pious causes. A brief accounting of the disbursement reveals that more than 2000 ducats were divided among various monasteries, convents, hospitals, and hospices.[106]

At about fifty years of age, when this sentence was pronounced, one wonders if even the fortune-telling friar would have been able to foretell what lay ahead. Certainly the clerics who sentenced him must have felt that while appearing compassionate, they had realistically eliminated for good at least one renegade cleric from Venice. But as we know already, Fra Aurelio went on.[107]

In May 1568, Aurelio, now out of jail and nearing seventy years of age, was again briefly a matter of concern for the Holy Office. They brought in a priest who had been a neighbor of his for about a year and a half. Again Aurelio was wearing a white habit, and the priest labeled him as one ''who had the reputation'' of reading hands and telling the future. He also repeated a familiar refrain that conjures memories of the 1540s: ''and I have seen coming to him many people.'' It appears that the fortune-telling friar was back in business. But perhaps Aurelio had learned something over the years, for this priest made a point of stating what a fine man he was in terms of the charity that he gave out in the neighborhood: ''And certainly in this he is a great man for the good and a great giver of charity and there is not a day that he does not give some charity.''[108]

The wages of his sins were again handsome, it appears, as at his advanced age he had once again gathered the wealth to rent a house, as well as engage in his highly visible charity. But fortunately for Fra Aurelio's renewed practice, the priest's reflections on the good side of the friar led him to remark that there was another person in the neighborhood who was really an evil man, a certain Paolo Magno. This Paolo was a lawyer and an official at the Giustizia Vecchia (an office concerned with the regulation of guilds in Venice) who ate meat on Fridays and feast days and never confessed or went to Mass; moreover, he forced his servants to follow a similar regimen and had cast aside his wife to keep a concubine. On the scent of a man who was risking not only his own soul but that of his servants and concubine, the Holy Office let the matter of Aurelio drop to pursue more important game.

In June 1571 Fra Aurelio, now about seventy-two years old, regained the Holy Office's attention apparently because of the complaints of his local parish priest, Angelo Rocha. This priest had become aware of the friar's activities and reputation as a fortune-teller and had asked him to stop, but to no avail.[109] Another priest from the same parish reiterated similar concerns, adding, ''I yelled at quite a number of women who I saw going to his house.'' He also reported that the friar ''did not have a good reputation and was reported to look at those women.''[110] In this he seems to have been implying quite a lot against a friar who was in his seventies and who claimed to have been bedridden for more than a decade. But perhaps Aurelio's recuperative powers should not be underestimated either in the realm of magic or sex.

Under questioning, the friar gave a brief account of his peregrinations after leaving jail. He had lived for a short time after his release in the house of a certain Gasparina Tessara; then he had moved into a house that he had rented for himself from the Barbarigo family; and about fifteen months earlier he had moved into his present house, which he rented from the Da Lege family for thirty-two ducats a year. When asked how he got the money to live so well, he fell back on his old defense of practicing medicine using simple herbal cures.[111] As in the 1540s, however, the Holy Office slowly forced him to admit that he had been doing more, primarily by confronting him with the testimony of others and pressing him about the details of his own reluctant admissions. On the whole, however, this time the friar was an even more recalcitrant witness, and made heavy use of his old age and physical infirmities as an explanation for not remembering anything that might incriminate him.

One area where he had particular trouble denying everything was in his movements following his release from jail. According to his original sentence of 1549, he was supposed to have left Venice after he was freed in 1559 to finish his life in banishment. But when he was released, it seems that he had been given special permission to remain in the city if he stayed in the house of Gasparina Tessara and did not return to his old practices. Upon leaving her house, however, he violated those conditions and quickly returned to being the fortune-telling friar. The picture he painted of all this is revealing and, of course, was designed to elicit sympathy. "I consulted with people [about the future]; [this] I did moved by necessity and my infinite suffering finding myself poor, paralyzed in the legs and arm for more than sixteen years, and my head full of dizziness. . . . For this reason more than six years ago now I sent to this Holy Office the most excellent Piero Moretto, my lawyer, to ask that you give me permission that I might practice this art of astrology so that I might support myself and not have to sit on some bridge and beg for charity."[112]

Sorting through the hyperbole of Aurelio's testimony, it seems likely that he was quite infirm and had spent a good part of the last few years in bed. It may also have been true, as he claimed, that his lawyer had been told that they had to wait for interpretations of decisions of the Council of Trent to know for sure if astrology and other such practices would be allowed.[113] But given the friar's style of life over those last few years, it seems problematic that he would have been begging on a bridge if denied the opportunity to practice astrology. More central and more problematic yet were the friar's claims that he had never been informed of any limits on his movements or practices when he was released from jail. At first he asserted that he had simply been told that he was being freed and could go. As the case moved on, however, he fell back more and more on his inability to remember what happened and on his appeals through his lawyer for clarification of his status that had gone unanswered.

The Holy Office, for their part, focused on the nature of his fortune-telling, as we have already seen, attempting to determine whether it was astrology, geomancy, necromancy, or perhaps something even worse—that he was using evil spirits to help him, perhaps those that possessed his servant Dorothea. But the friar remained firm in his denial and even attempted to recant the admissions he had made in his earlier trial of 1549. Given his age and those denials, the Holy Office seems to have been content to hold the friar in jail, waiting for him to confess or perhaps pass away and on to a higher judge.

Suggestively, however, in one area they did not remain passive. Once again they moved to confiscate the friar's wealth. Learning from an anonymous informant in April 1572 that the friar had been warned about his impending arrest the year before and had taken advantage of that warning to hide four chests of his ill-gotten wealth with a widow whose daughter he had cured, they sent their minions scurrying to her house.[114] They found, however, only the widow, who remembered the friar fondly. There then followed a troubled search, with the "anonymous" informant being somehow called in to help find the chests. Eventually, by tricking Aurelio's servant Dorothea and perhaps by means of some added double dealing, two chests were located and confiscated.[115] They contained a little more than 734 ducats in cash, plus some silver and other valuables. The other chests had apparently disappeared or perhaps never existed.

There were those, however, who believed that the friar had much more money. The friar himself reported that another ex-employee of his "believed that he had eight or ten thousand ducats."[116] The reason for this estimate is suggestive; it seems that the friar had once had the man buy twenty sacks for storing his money and the man had calculated his wealth, figuring 400 to 500 ducats per sack. Although the Holy Office did not choose to follow up on the implication that the friar had much more wealth than they had recovered, it seems clear that even in his early seventies and largely bedridden, for Fra Aurelio the wages of sin were still excellent. And it is not surprising, given what we have seen about his practice and the world of the illicit in general in late Renaissance Venice, that this should be the case. Wealth accumulates around power and Fra Aurelio's world was one of unusual if still largely unrecognized power.

In the end, the fate of Fra Aurelio and his wages of sin are unclear. His case transcript ends with him still in jail petitioning for release. Perhaps that was the best solution for the Holy Office: to leave the old, unrepentant, renegade, friar bedridden in jail until death dissolved the last ties that bound him to his world. If freed from jail, from their perspective there was every reason to fear that, like a spider, he would begin spinning anew his binding webs drawn from high culture and low to entrap fresh victims. If that was their decision, time had finally caught up with the fortune-telling friar. It was no longer his to manipulate. Of course, the one thing we can be sure of is that time did take its due, for it refuses to be bound—by renegade priests, by people's passions, or even by historians.

AFTERWORD

The Poetry
of the Everyday
and Binding Passions

It is not easy to end these tales. Fra Aurelio, Apollonia, la Draga, Paolina and Don Felice, Elena and Lucretia, and Andriana have been fascinating people to discover in the past, to try to know, and to try to write about. Their passions—both unbound and bound, both binding and unbinding, both to bind and to unbind—were in themselves never meant to be history of the great tradition. Yet I hope their tales have provided good history to read and good history to think, for theirs is a history that until recently we had lost—the history of the everyday; of the infinite complexity of small lives, of the decisions that individuals and groups make within the webs of values, beliefs, and ideologies; of the play of the personal within fields of power that discipline and control. In these tales I have sought to reverse the classic discipline of history itself, eschewing broad structures and great changes, great men and government, to offer a small carnival that starts with prostitutes, peasant healers, and rene-gade clerics to create narratives that, at least to a degree, reflect the infinite layerings of life at the personal and local level that also make up the past; narratives that are intentionally not prescriptive but rather signs of passing intelligences in Calvino's sense, to be read by others and reintegrated into their own passing.

That perspective makes conclusions difficult. In a way, one can only pull these tales together by bringing their carnival to an end, reversing the local and personal perspective to return to the general. Thus my conclusions are both hesitant and reluctant. My feeling is that you now know these people as well as I, and perhaps with a greater distance and a clearer eye you may know them better. But turning to what their lives and tales mean for understanding the end of the Renaissance, I would start with the obvious: they suggest to me at least that there is a great deal more to know about power and the poetics of the everyday at the local and individual level. In each of these narratives we have merely revealed the edges of what appear to have been complex and highly articulated discourses on how life was organized and lived at the end of the Renaissance. Marriage, fittingly, started and ended our tales. Andriana Savorgnan tried to thwart the order that marriage ideally imposed upon aristocratic society to marry Marco Dandolo and cross the perceptual boundaries of class and status. Passions that were to be bound in marriage for the purpose of constructing families and larger social solidarities she had bound magically for her own gain, it was claimed, threatening literally all that was held sacred. Fra Aurelio, as he lay at the end of his life in jail—a life often enriched by his claimed ability to foretell the outcome of matrimony—we still find petitioning to be allowed to use the power of his wealth to reward his loyal servant with a dowry that would allow her the ideal normal placement for a woman even at the bottom of society: marriage.

Throughout these tales, marriage comes back again and again as a crucial moment of binding, underlining the evident fact that marriage was a central institution of late Renaissance life, but opening out around it we have only begun to encounter the complex cultural constructs and fields of power that intersected with its central binding of passions. Thus with Elena Cumano, a broken promise of marriage led through honor codes for men and women on to local perspectives on reputation, with excursions into the uses and often unrecognized powers of local politics and local courts in response to changing legal requirements for marriage, and finally to the binding world and words of the local witch Lucretia Marescalio, who may well have been as much a marriage broker as a witch. Paolina di Rossi, as a courtesan, speaks to marriage from beyond, from the illicit world of extramarital relations. But the love magic that was the focus of her tale was a crucial weapon both in breaking marriages and in forming them; from beyond, we encounter perhaps unexpected dimensions of love in marriage. And in that magic we see how women had found in the world that had been assigned to them the powers necessary to bind in love, marriage, and friendship, even if we only begin to see the edges of the complex and poetic discourses that stand behind those powers. Finally, in Latisana, Apollonia and her co-healers and signers reveal once again the centrality of marriage and power over it in a rural setting, and how this power intersected with popular religion, curing, and women's networks.

If marriage was the central point of reference for the binding of passions in this book, magic was the central discourse of binding. Magic was a system (or systems) of signs that incorporated the most basic values of society, and within its multilayered and polyvalent discourse virtually all forms of power, from the religious to the institutional, were tested and vetted. Even if magic was not central to the life of the Renaissance, it would provide a unique perspective on how that life was perceived as being ordered, bound, and lived. But, in fact, it was perceived as central, as our tales have shown. Starting with Andriana Savorgnan, even if she was falsely accused, it is evident that the fear of magic and its binding powers was so widespread that noble families could construct their attack on her marriage within that discourse of fear, and authorities could hear with sympathy their reasoning. Moreover, already in the accusations leveled against her, we encounter the broad outlines of love magic as it was practiced in Venice. In the tale of Elena Cumano, her needle-pierced doll and the carefully observed actions of Lucretia take us deeper into that discourse and its power-seeking play with the symbols—physical, Christian, and verbal—that made up the cultural context of daily life.

But in Paolina di Rossi's encounter with the Holy Office we finally begin to discover the range and complexity of that magical world. Without paradox it could be both Christian and diabolical at the same time. Christian in that it drew on the way in which Christianity had deeply penetrated the culture and the perceptions of power of the age. Diabolical in that the Devil and his minions seemed to offer another range of powers, over the flesh and the darker passions of life in this world that even the Church to an extent validated. The formal logic of theology may have asserted that these two sources of power were antithetical, but the complex realities of everyday life seemed hardly to fit with such logical niceties. As Isabella Bellocchio explained to the Holy Office and as the Devil pointed out to Andrea Meri, real people took power where it could be found and left the theological niceties to theologians, who had the aesthetic luxury perhaps of creating a logical universe. That did not mean that Isabella's and Andrea's world did not have its aesthetic as well, but it was more a poetics of the everyday based upon the poetic and metaphoric resonances found in the contingent world in which they lived.

Rather than logic and metaphysics, perhaps their dominant cultural paradigm was poetic, as poetry was more suited for building a culture out of the highly complex, layered world of resonant repetition that they encountered in the everyday. That poetics was, one may assume, a significant aspect of life for people often seen as having only a limited and materialistic culture; the stereotype is of simple, confused, and ignorant people mired in the suffering of everyday life. Of suffering there was no lack, but it would be unwise to underestimate a culture of which we have still encountered only the edges, I would argue. From the edge of love magic, the poetics of the everyday can be seen in the complex vision of the intersection of Christianity and the forces of evil in daily lives; in the intricate understanding of the body, both male and female; in the deeper meanings of the physical spaces in which people moved and the

things that they used; and in the signing qualities and underlying realities of the very words used to deal with the everyday and construct
culture. And crucially, that poetics at the heart of everyday life offered
power: power over love for those who understood, and ultimately
power over the most basic building blocks of social life such as marriage
and friendship. The tales of Apollonia Madizza and Fra Aurelio confirm
this and with Aurelio reveal how this culture interesected in significant
ways with high culture. Apollonia and her fellow healers in Latisana and
Venice also reveal another way in which this poetics of the everyday
empowered women and was empowered by them—in a Christian curing that brought a rather different religion (in some ways perhaps quite
true to early Christianity) into daily life in a particularly powerful and
significant manner. Certainly both healing and love magic merely touch
the edges of a rich and complex discourse here labeled the poetics of the
everyday, but the vibrancy and poetry of what may be a mere glimpse
suggest that it is a world that merits further exploration.

It also merely begins to suggest the powers that were to be found
there. Certainly those powers seem far distant from the traditional world
of power that historians have so successfully studied for generations, but
as Fra Aurelio's much noted and often lamented close relationships with
the rich and famous of Venice and beyond suggest, the separation between even high and low power may not be as neat and clean as one
might at first assume. Although he claimed to use high magic, his practice, and that of Cesare Lanza and his fellow treasure seekers as well, was
intimately intertwined with love and healing magic. Aurelio moved between the two worlds with ease and great profit, at least until more
traditional power realities caught him in their web at midcentury. But
nicely, Aurelio was only momentarily stripped of his clout and fortune,
to reappear in the 1570s once again as a relatively rich and powerful
figure who was still dealing with prostitutes and humble washer women
as well as nobles. More significantly perhaps, most of the powerful
women of these tales also operated across a wide spectrum of late Renaissance society. Healers did not deal solely with the poor and those
who did not have access to regular medical practitioners. Benetta in
Venice cured "lady Gaspara," as well as her husband and brother; Apollonia Madizza had been called to the homes of Venetian nobles from
Latisana, apparently to cure. In turn, the power of love magic penetrated
the sanctity of the marriage bed of the Dandolo family, interfered with
the noble Faceno clan's plans in Feltre, upset the noble life of Gian
Battista Giustinian, and may have thwarted the marriage plans of Cardinal Bembo for his daughter. But much more important, I would assert, it
opened up a rich realm of power in the everyday world for people often
perceived as essentially powerless, especially women. Foucault suggested that we need to search out the "micro-powers" that he saw as
permeating every aspect of social life in infinitely complex ways. These

tales, I hope, have shown how much such research can reveal even if one does not follow rigorously Foucault's broader methodological injunctions. In the end, Cesare Lanza epitomized how completely such a change of perspective can open new vistas on power when he lamented: "Today a lowly little woman does more than all the necromancers accomplished in the ancient world." At the time he made this statement, it went against all the accepted visions of power, especially the assumed superiority of the ancient world and high culture. For an important theology professor at Padua, one of the leading universities of the day, it was an astounding admission to make and an astounding thing to think. Today, after encountering the women of these tales, his statement merely underlines their evident significance and power. They hardly needed his grudging respect, but that they got it says worlds about their power.

Yet crucially, in the longer run their world and that of Fra Aurelio and Cesare Lanza was coming to an end: magic, marriage, and power were sliding into different realities with different meanings and different forms. That is a tale that we cannot tell here, but with the advantage of hindsight it seems clear that the world was losing its poetry, its multiplicity of meanings, signs, and powers for better and worse. The old ties that bound individuals, families, and communities were dissolving slowly into modern metaphors, rituals, and ideologies—perceived more as word play and pyrotechnic display than reality. The poetics of the everyday, in its polyvalent beauty and in its dangerous ability to disguise flowers of evil, also slowly withered, to bloom more and more rarely in cultures labeled popular.

Teased from this massive dying off or this harvest tide (depending upon one's perspective) and well underway was a new world that we have called, with perhaps unwarranted pride, modern. We have lost the world of Andriana, Elena, and Lucretia, Paolina and Don Felice, Apollonia and la Draga, and Fra Aurelio. It has been left behind not just because of the quantification of the world picture, or the triumph of capital, or the development of the modern state, or even the cultural hegemony of modern science and technology. Our lives, our bodies, and, most important, our passions have become bound in other ways. And even if we still speak about love, marriage, friendship, and community, without making a value judgment, to put it tritely but precisely—the magic is gone.

Yet as I sit here thinking about the meaning of such a change, gazing out over my computer at the spring breezes playing over the golden mustard colors of wild flowers and shiny green olive leaves of the Tuscan Hills of I Tatti, the landscape does seem alive with the promise of spring and life—perhaps much as it once seemed alive to another band of storytellers in these same hills, Boccaccio's. And feeling the world alive for an instant, it is evident that from moment to moment we are still capable, for better or worse, of feeling the need to bind our passions and those of the cosmos, and we are still capable of being bound by them. In the end, something of the poetry of the everyday may be more than a cultural construct. My suspicion is that if we could return to la Draga and her peers and listen as the Holy Office never could, they might offer an explanation for that mystery as well and provide the ending for these tales that they deserve.

NOTES

Introduction

1. Natalie Zemon Davis, "The Reasons of Misrule," in *Society and Culture in Early Modern France* (Stanford, Calif.: Stanford University Press, 1975), p. 103.

2. His nickname was Rossetto, which means in Venetian dialect a little noisy bird called in Italian today a *scricciolo;* on this see Giuseppe Boerio, *Dizionario del dialetto veneziano* (Venice: Tipografia di Giovanni Cecchini, 1856), p. 556.

3. Archivio di Stato of Venice (A.S.V.), Sant'Ufficio, Busta 30, Giacomo Zorzi and Zaccharia Lombardini, testimony of Zaccharia, 5 March 1571, f. 5v.

4. Geronimo Bragadin, was the son of a certain Rocco, who was a minor official. Rocco filed the formal complaint; on this see ibid., testimony of Rocco Bragadin, 5 March 1571, f. 3v–4r.

5. Those powers, however, were to be curtailed for a moment in the 1580s, when the size of the council was increased to make it in theory more representative (and in fact less secretive and efficient), and it was forced to divest itself of much of its economic and some of its criminal authority. Reformed, it remained nonetheless a very powerful body, probably the single most important council of government.

6. The literature on the Venetian Holy Office is large and growing rapidly. For an excellent discussion of its organization and operation see Brian Pullan, *The Jews of Europe and the Inquisition of Venice, 1550–1670* (Totowa, N.J.: Barnes and Noble, 1983), pp. 3–142. Paul Grendler has also published several important works that draw heavily on documents from the Holy Office and provide a careful analysis of it as an institution, especially his *The Roman Inquisition and the Venetian Press, 1540–1605* (Princeton, N.J.: Princeton University Press, 1977) and his "The Tre Savii Sopra Eresia 1547–1605: A Prosopographical Study" in *Studi Veneziani,* n.s., 3 (1979), pp. 283–340. Perhaps the institution has been most thoroughly studied, as one might expect, from the perspective of how it dealt with heresy; for this John J. Martin's book *Venice's Hidden Enemies: Italian Heretics in a Renaissance City* (Berkeley: University of California Press, in press) will provide a significant new overview and a thorough review of previous scholarship. Finally, for an important·overview of its creation, its relationship with the Roman Inquisition, and its early activities in Venice and its territories, see Andrea Del Col, "Organizzazione, composizione e giurisdizione dei tribunali dell'Inquisitione romana nella Republlica di Venezia (1500–1550)," in *Critica Storica/Bollettino Arte, Scienze, Economia (A.S.E.),* vol. 25, n. 2 (1988), pp. 244–94. Magic and witchcraft in Venice have also recently been studied from a more traditional and institutional perspective, with a significantly different vision of

popular culture from mine, in Ruth Martin's *Witchcraft and the Inquisition in Venice 1550–1650* (Oxford: Basil Blackwell, 1989).

7. For the most recent overview of this situation that incorporates the pioneering work of John Tedeschi and William Monter in the area and provides a suggestive overview of the Inquisition in Italy, see Giovanni Romeo, *Inquisitori, esorcisti e streghe nell'Italia della controriforma* (Florence: Sansoni, 1990). An introduction to the work of Tedeschi and Monter can be found in their joint article "Toward a Statistical Profile of the Italian Inquisitions, Sixteenth to Eighteenth Centuries," in *The Inquisition in Early Modern Europe: Studies on Sources and Methods,* ed. Gustav Henninsen and John Tedeschi with Charles Amiel (Dekalb, Ill.: Northern Illinois University Press, 1986), pp. 130–57. See also, for Monter, his *Witchcraft in France and Switzerland; The Borderlands During the Reformation* (Ithaca, N.Y.: Cornell University Press, 1976) and "Women and the Italian Inquisitions," in *Women in the Middle Ages and the Italian Renaissance and Historical Perspectives,* ed. Mary Beth Rose (Syracuse, N.Y.: Syracuse University Press, 1985), pp. 73–87. For Tedeschi see "Preliminary Observations on Writing a History of the Roman Inquisition," in *Continuity and Discontinuity in Church History,* ed. F. Forrester Church and Timothy George (Leiden: E. J. Brill, 1979), pp. 232–49. On the often noted restraint of the Venetian Holy Office in its treatment of those accused of witchcraft, Marisa Milani provides a brief statistical background in "L'ossessione secolare di suor Mansueta. Un esorcismo a Venezia nel 1574," in *Quaderni Veneti* 7 (1988), pp. 129–31. Although these figures should be used with caution, it provides a good general overview.

8. On this see Martin, *Venice's Hidden Enemies.*

9. A.S.V., Sant'Ufficio, Busta 30, Giacomo Zorzi and Zaccharia Lombardini, querela, 1 March 1571, f. 1r.

10. Ibid., testimony of the priest Andrea Berengo, 5 March 1571, f. 4v.

11. Ibid., testimony of Zaccharia Lombardini, 5 March 1571, f. 7r. Zaccharia was also forced to admit that their costumes might have made them look like priests, but he insisted that that had not been their intention.

12. Edward Muir, *Civic Ritual in Renaissance Venice* (Princeton, N.J.: Princeton University Press, 1981), p. 177; see there also the excellent general discussion of carnival in Venice, pp. 156–81.

13. Most scholars hold that it comes from *carnem levare,* "take away the meat, flesh"; on this see Muir, *Civic Ritual,* pp. 177–78. A popular etymology also held that it came from *caro vale,* "goodby flesh"; for this see *The Oxford Dictionary of the Christian Church,* ed. F. L. Cross (London: Oxford University Press, 1957), p. 238.

14. Romeo's book *Inquisitori, esorcisti e streghe,* cited above, argues this point well. His analysis, however, is stronger on how this position won out in the administration of the Inquisition than on the cultural factors involved.

15. Lately, the very existence of witches in early modern Europe has been questioned. Those who have argued this have pointed out that the classic picture of the witch was one largely based on the fears of the Church about devil worship and then pressed on the populace of late medieval Europe. There is some truth to this contention; in many instances, the persecution of witches and witch crazes appear to have been simply that—persecution and moments of madness. But things were not so simple. And I fear consigning the witch to an existence solely in the fantasy of misguided (or perversely misogynistic) eccle-

siastics and their uneducated or gullible followers plays on, if anything, even more unfounded stereotypes than the traditional stereotype of the witch. Moreover, it seems evident to me that among those labeled witches, many believed in witches and witchcraft as labels that fit others and often as labels that fit themselves. Thus I decided to follow the usage of the documentation, and I believe the period, while at the same time trying to reveal a more complex, nuanced witch and world of witchcraft. Still, examples of such projections did occur, and at present I am working on a book tentatively titled *Lucca in the Year of the Witch*, which will look at one of the relatively rare moments of such persecution of witches in late-sixteenth-century Italy. In Lucca in 1589 secular authorities pressed women to admit that they had gone to the Sabbat, had sexual intercourse with the Devil, flown on brooms, and sucked the blood of babies in a show trial that reveals a great deal about the social fabric and the ties that bound society together. It reveals much less about witchcraft, which in this case seemed to be a broad, rather empty conceptual frame of fear with certain points of reference like the Sabbat as given, but with large areas free to be filled in with the anxieties and discontents of late-sixteenth-century society.

16. These works were originally published in Italian as *I Benandanti, Stregoneria e culti agrari tra Cinquecento e Seicento* (Turin: Einaudi, 1966) and *Il formaggio e i vermi, Il cosmo di un mugnaio del'500* (Turin: Einaudi, 1976). Both have been translated into English by John and Anne Tedeschi as, respectively, *The Night Battles, Witchcraft and Agrarian Cults in the Sixteenth and Seventeenth Centuries* (Baltimore: Johns Hopkins University Press, 1983) and *The Cheese and the Worms, The Cosmos of a Sixteenth-Century Miller* (Baltimore: Johns Hopkins University Press, 1980).

17. The significance of *Quaderni Storici's* leadership in this area led to the publication of a volume of articles translated from that journal edited by Edward Muir and myself, *Microhistory and the Lost Peoples of Europe, Selections from Quaderni Storici* (Baltimore: Johns Hopkins University Press, 1991). Muir's introductory essay to that volume provides an important overview of the approach, and our discussions of the issues involved have had a strong influence on this book. The first volume of that series, *Sex and Gender in Historical Perspective: Selections from Quaderni Storici* (Baltimore: Johns Hopkins University Press, 1990), also was very important for the telling of these tales.

Chapter 1

1. Pietro Aretino, *Sei giornate*, ed. Giovanni Aquilecchia (Bari: La Terza, 1980), p. 139. There is a long tradition of literature on Renaissance prostitution. For Venice, perhaps most important is the nineteenth-century collection of documents published anonymously by Giovanni Battista de Lorenzi, *Leggi e memorie venete sulla prostituzione* (Venice, 1870–72). The recent volume *Il gioco dell'amore. Le cortigiane di Venezia dal Trecento al Settecento* (Milan: Berenice, 1990) provides a general overview of the literature, especially the articles of Giorgio Padoan, "Il mondo delle cortigiane nella letteratura rinascimentale," pp. 63–71, and Giovanni Scarabello, "Le 'signore' della repubblica," pp. 11–35. Nineteenth-century scholars wrote extensively on the topic. Perhaps the most prolific in Venice were Arturo Graf and Giuseppe Tassini; for Graf's work see *Attraverso il Cinquecento* (Turin: Chiantore, 1888); for Tassini, see *Cenni storici e*

leggi circa il libertinaggio in venezia dal secolo decimoquarto alla caduta della repubblica (Venice: Fontana, 1886), published anonymously. More recent works include Rita Casagrande di Villaviera, *Le cortigiane veneziane del Cinquecento* (Milan: Longanese, 1968); Antonio Barzaghi, *Donne o cortigiane? La prostituzione a Venezia. Documenti di costumi dal XVI al XVIII secolo* (Verona: Bertani, 1980); Kathy Santore, "Julia Lombardo, 'Somtuosa Meretrize': A Portrait by Property," *Renaissance Quarterly* 41 (1988), pp. 44–83; and my own *The Boundaries of Eros: Sex Crime and Sexuality in Renaissance Venice* (New York: Oxford University Press, 1985). Perhaps the best general overview remains Paul Larivaille, *La vie quotidienne des courtesanes en Italie au temps de la renaissance* (Paris: Hachette, 1975).

2. A more complete treatment of this theme can be found in my "Re-Reading the Renaissance: Civic Morality and the World of Marriage, Love and Sex," in *Sexuality and Gender in Early Modern Europe: Institutions, Texts, Images*, ed. James Turner (Cambridge: Cambridge University Press, in press).

3. On the Renaissance perception of convents, see Ruggiero, *Boundaries*, pp. 70–86. There were approximately ten convents in Venice that were well known in the Renaissance for their lax discipline. Probably best known among them was San Angelo di Contorta, where in the fifteenth century no fewer than fifty-two nuns, including several abbesses, were involved in affairs significant enough to become public knowledge.

4. Aretino, *Sei giornate*, p. 50.

5. Ibid., p. 90.

6. A.S.V., Sant'Ufficio, Busta 47, Andriana Savorgnan, testimony of Laura Savorgnan, 24 October 1581, f. 116r. This case is bound in the middle of the case of Margarita di Rossi and thus is rather difficult to find. The cover is labeled "Margarita di Rossi," but after 39 folios the foliation begins again and the case against Andriana continues for 157 folios. After this section, Margarita's dossier picks up again for a few unfoliated pages, only to be followed by the insertion of yet another case against Diana Passarina, followed by one against Margarita Squarcie. The unpublished and at times unreliable set of genealogies in the Archivio di Stato of Venice attributed to Marco Barbaro lists a Marco Dandolo born in 1558, brother of Francesco and son of Gerolamo, which matches the genealogical information given in the transcript for Marco; see Barbaro, vol. 3, pt. 11, p. 196. This is also confirmed in the index to the *Libro d'oro, Nascite* (a list of noble births kept by the Avogaria di Comun), where his date of birth is given as 21 October 1558 and his mother is listed as Cecilia Michael q. Francesco.

7. Ibid., ff. 116r–v. It appears that Laura claimed that she had at least attempted to get a license from the patriarch for the wedding, sending her parish priest to ask for it. Also, at Dandolo's behest, she had had a mass said in the name of the Holy Spirit for the matrimony.

8. Ibid., f. 116v.

9. For a discussion of the impact of the Council of Trent in general on marriage, see Jean-Louis Flandrin, *Families in Former Times, Kinship, Household and Sexuality in Early Modern France*, trans. R. W. Southern (Cambridge: Cambridge University Press, 1979), pp. 130–38. Christiane Klapish-Zuber, "Zacharie ou le père évincé: Les rituels nuptiaux toscans entre Giotto et le Concile de Trente," *Annales Economies, Sociétés, Civilisations (E.S.C.)* 34, no. 6 (1979), pp. 1216–43; translated as "Zacharias, or the Ousted Father: Nuptial

Rites in Tuscany between Giotto and the Council of Trent," in *Women, Family and Ritual in Renaissance Italy*, trans. Lydia G. Cochrane (Chicago: University of Chicago Press, 1985), pp. 178–212, also reviews much of the relevant Italian literature on the topic. A brief review of the Venetian legal view of marriage can be found in Marco Ferro, *Dizionario del diritto comune e veneto . . .* , vol. 7, "Matrimonio" (Venice: Modesto Fenzo, 1780), pp. 145–63; for a more detailed and slightly different perspective on what this meant, see Chapter 2. On the significance of marriage for the Venetian nobility in the period and some interesting anecdotal and statistical background, see Alexander F. Cowan, *The Urban Patriciate: Lübeck and Venice, 1580–1700* (Cologne: Böhlau Verlag, 1986), especially pp. 126–73.

10. A.S.V., Sant'Ufficio, Busta 47, Andriana Savorgnan, testimony of Laura Savorgnan, 16 October 1581, f. 75v.

11. Ibid., testimony of Catarina, wife of Josep Furlani, 11 September 1581, f. 3v.

12. Ibid., testimony of Aloisio Soranzo, 31 October 1581, f. 11r. Andriana was described as "una donna mecanica, infame, et publica meretrice." For another case of a marriage in the early seventeenth century between one of the richest patricians of the city, Giovanni Battista Corner, and a courtesan, Zanetta Boni, which also created quite a scandal, see Cowan, *Patriciate*, pp. 70–71.

13. Ibid., testimony of Domenico Buccolo, 25 October 1581, f. 9r. Late in the investigation, Fillipo was called in to testify about his relationship with Andriana and confirmed that she had been "my woman for about twenty months." Testimony of Fillipo, 10 March 1582, ff. 154v–56r.

14. This will be discussed in more detail in Chapter 2.

15. A.S.V., Sant'Ufficio, Busta 47, Andriana Savorgnan, testimony of Catarina wife of Josep Furlani, 11 September 1581, f. 4v.

16. Ibid., testimony of Giovanni Pietro Moschino, 1 November 1581, f. 14r. Evidently Andriana's supporters painted a different picture. A servant of hers, when asked if Andriana had used magic to win Dandolo, denied it firmly: "My Lords no! On my soul this Dandolo was sick and he made a pledge to marry her if he recovered. And thus he took her for his wife." Testimony of Paolina, daughter of Jacobini Grandessi, 16 October 1581, f. 72r.

17. Elisabetta Margerita, wife of Bernardo Sansoni, provided one interesting account of how Andriana and she threw beans together. Ibid., testimony of same, 7 October 1581, f. 57v.

18. Ibid., testimony of Franceschina, wife of Vincenzo Savoner, 27 October 1581, f. 125v.

19. Ibid., Notarile Testamenti, Marcantonio Cavanis, Busta 195.712, 27 January 1583.

20. Ibid., Sant'Ufficio, Busta 47, Andriana Savorgnan, testimony of same, 16 October 1581, f. 76v.

21. Archivio di Stato of Florence (A.S.F.), Filze Medici, Filza 753, letter dated 24 November 1581, no folios.

22. A.S.F., Onestà, Practica Secreti, Busta, 201, f. 37r.

23. Niccolò Machiavelli, *Tutte le opere*, ed. Mario Martelli (Florence: Sansoni, 1971), p. 1112.

24. Matteo Bandello, *Le quattro parti de le Novelle del Bandello*, ed. Gustavo

Balsamo-Crivelli (Turin: Unione Tipografico-Editrice Torinese, 1924), pt. III, novelle XLII.

25. Ibid. The theme was an ancient one found in Diogenes Laertius and Seneca. The Renaissance context of such pretensions is reinforced by the extensive literature that complained about them. In the *Ragionamento di Zoppino*, for example, Giulia Ferrarese, herself a Roman courtesan, seeing the mother of Tullia d'Aragona, remarked, "Now that woman claims that her daughter is the daughter of the Cardinal of Aragon. I certainly believe that the ass (mule) of the Cardinal crapped in her house [giving birth to Tullia] and thusly many courtesans ennoble themselves." Cited in Giorgio Padoan, "Il mondo delle cortigiane" in *Il gioco dell'amore*, p. 65.

26. *La Bulesca*, edited by Bianca Maria da Rif in *La letteratura ''alla Bulesca''; Testi rinascimentali veneti* (Padua: Antenore, 1984), pp. 48–84; for Marcolina's evaluation of the advantages of practicing outside the bordello, see pp. 58–59; for Zuana's soliloquy, see pp. 69–70; for da Riff's discussing of the dating and ambience of the play, see pp. 9–28 of her introduction. Although the play has little in the way of plot, action, or humor by modern standards, for a young aristocratic audience it must have been an interesting presentation of what set them apart and above those below them on the social scale. With a laugh, they could enjoy seeing why Bio and Bulle would never be real threats, not even for the attentions of Marcolina, who rejoiced in having escaped their violent earthiness and graduated to more refined clients.

27. A.S.V., Sant'Ufficio, Busta 47, Andriana Savorgnan, testimony of Zaccharia, a servant of Andriana, 3 November 1581, f. 14v. For her earlier sentencing to jail by the Magistrato alle Pompe, see Lorenzi, *Leggi*, p. 13.

28. For this, see Larivaille, *La vie quotidienne des courtesanes*, and the colorful, brief account of Lynn Lawner, *Lives of Courtesans, Portraits of the Renaissance* (New York: Rizzoli, 1987), pp. 4–5.

29. Bandello, *Novelle*, pt. III, novelle XXXI.

30. Ibid.

31. Ibid. It is interesting to note that such behavior in Venice continued to attract attention and comment in the seventeenth century. At midcentury Francesco Pannocchieschi wrote, "And as far as sexual freedom is concerned in Venice it is very great. What is really amazing, however, is to consider how four or six people together and peacefully keep a woman in whose house they drink and play and they find themselves together virtually every day. Thus they build their friendship where normally one would expect jealousy and animosity." Quoted in Scarabello, "Le 'signore' della repubblica," in *Il gioco dell'amore*, pp. 25–26.

32. A.S.F., Otto Suppliche, Register 2241, n. 412, 17 March 1563. For the Otto see John K. Brackett, *Criminal Justice and Crime in Late Renaissance Florence 1537–1609* (Cambridge: Cambridge University Press, 1992).

33. Ibid. In the end, the Otto did provide him some small redress, ordering Giulia to render the services paid for: "to go and sleep with him and give him the use of her body" or repay to him the four *scudi* plus whatever additional fine the Otto would deem just. This Giulia was very likely the Giulia Napolitana referred to in several poems by Lasca. See, for example, Anton Francesco Grazzini, called Il Lasca, *Le rime burlesche edite e inedite*, ed. Carlo Veronese (Florence: Sansone,

1882), poems 18, 19, and 20. I would like to thank Meg Gallucci for tracking down these references.

34. And, as noted earlier, literature also provided many cautionary tales based on complaints about the airs that courtesans had taken on and their overweening pride. Bandello's tale of the young Milanese noble's suicide, discussed above, certainly draws on the theme, even if avarice is stressed more than pride. One of the most troubling examples of this literature, not surprisingly, was written in Venice in the sixteenth century: the poem *La Zaffetta*, sometimes referred to as *Il trentuno della Zaffetta*, attributed to the Venetian noble Lorenzo Venier. In violent, misogynistic language the poem details the gang rape of the Venetian courtesan Angela del Moro, called La Zaffetta, offering the attack as a justified joke played on an overly proud prostitute. While arranged and participated in by nobles, it should be noted that a major aspect of her demeaning involved being victimized by common men. Even in the cruelest misogynistic fantasy or deeds (critics debate whether the rape occurred or not), social hierarchy played a crucial role.

35. A.S.V., Sant'Ufficio, Busta 47, Andriana Savorgnan, testimony of Catarina, wife of Josep Furlani, 11 September 1581, f. 3v.

36. Ibid., testimony of Catarina, wife of Josep, 11 September 1581, f. 4r.

37. Ibid., testimony of Laura Savorgnan, 16 October 1581, ff. 76r–v.

38. Ibid., 16 October 1581, f. 76v.

39. Ibid., Busta 65, Jacomina di Seravallo (Locatelli), testimony of same, 1 September 1590.

40. Ibid., testimony of Marco son of Pietro di Bassano, 10 February 1590. Marin Sanuto, earlier in the century, provided a description of another casino set up for carnival by some nobles on Murano. "On that evening [in 1524] some of our gentlemen organized a party at the home of ser Lunardo Giustinian son of the deceased ser Bernardo knight and Procurator with approximately 15 sumptuous whores, who danced and ate there with virtuosity and great pleasure." Marino Sanuto, *I diarii di Marino Sanuto*, 58 vols., ed. Rinaldo Fulin et al. (Venice: Deputazione R. Veneta di Storia Patria, 1897–1903), vol. 35, col. 375.

41. Ibid., testimony of Giacomina, 4 January 1590.

42. Ibid., Busta 66, Cassandra Lizzari, testimony of same, 26 May 1590.

43. Ibid.

44. Ibid.

45. For Veronica and her literary production, see Margaret F. Rosenthal, *The Honest Courtesan: Veronica Franco, Citizen and Writer in Sixteenth-Century Venice* (Chicago: University of Chicago Press, 1992).

46. A.S.V., Sant'Ufficio, Busta 46, Veronica Franco, deposition of Rodolfo Vannitelli, undated (the case is dated on the back as beginning 3 October 1580); much of this case was published by Marisa Milani in "L''Incanto' di Veronica Franco," *Giornale storico della letteratura italiana* 162 (1985), pp. 250–63.

47. Ibid. and Milani, *Giornale storico*, p. 259.

48. Ibid.

49. Ibid., testimony of Veronica Franco, 8 October 1580; and Milani, *Giornale storico*, p. 261.

50. Ibid., Signori di Notte al Civil, Capitolare I, f. 113r; published in *Leggi e memorie*, p. 92.

51. In fact, in the early sixteenth century, things had gotten so bad that Dionisio Malipiero tried to sell his family's monopoly rights over the Castelletto brothel but could not find a buyer. His son Priam, in 1537, complained that in good times there were only ten or fifteen prostitutes working for him, and often only three or four. He may have been exaggerating about his problems, as he was using these figures to petition to have his taxes, already reduced because of declining revenues from forty to ten ducats, reduced further. For Malipiero's complaint see Scarabello, "Le 'signore,'" pp. 14–15.

52. Such legislation, however, was passed and repassed in the sixteenth century, suggesting that it too was regularly ignored. For example, in 1571, referring to legislation of 1539 by the Council of Ten, the Provveditori alla Sanità forbade prostitutes to attend church on holy days or to sit there next to noble-women or cittadini. It also limited the hours when they could go to confession. On this, see *Leggi e memorie*, p. 119.

53. On the first, see my *Violence in Early Renaissance Venice* (New Brunswick, N.J.: Rutgers University Press, 1980), pp. 125–37; for the second, see *Boundaries*, pp. 21–24, 46–49, and especially 70–88.

54. On this, see *El vanto de la cortigiana ferrarese qual narra la bellezza sua. . . . Seguita l'epigramma con el Purgatorio delle Cortigiane* (Venice, 1532); this purgatory was the Incurabile. On the Incurabile see Brian Pullan, *Rich and Poor in Renaissance Venice, The Social Institutions of a Catholic State* (Oxford: Basil Blackwell, 1971), pp. 233–38 ff.; see also the brief account of Nelli Elena Vanzan Marchini, "L'altra faccia dell'amore ovvero i rischi dell'esercizio del piacere," in *Il gioco dell'amore*, pp. 47–56.

55. On this see Pullan, *Rich and Poor*, pp. 377–79.

56. A.S.V., Sant'Ufficio, Busta 47, Andriana Savorgnan, testimony of Laura Savorgnan, 16 October 1581, f. 76r.

57. See Chapter 5 and, for an earlier period, see Ruggiero, *Boundaries*, pp. 70–88 and 146–48.

58. That sermon (or at least a reputed transcription of it) is preserved in the Biblioteca Correr, manuscript Cicogna 2082. Pompeo Molmenti, in his *La storia di Venezia nella vita privata*, 3 vols. (Trieste: Lint, 1973), vol. II, p. 450, n. 8, gives a brief account and reports the date of these events as 1551.

59. Quoted in Pullan, *Rich and Poor*, p. 382. For the earlier period, see Ruggiero, *Boundaries*, pp. 41–42. Note that the Italian term for bawds, *ruffiane*, has a feminine plural ending, implying that this rhetoric was particularly concerned with women recruiting women.

60. Pullan, *Rich and Poor*, pp. 388–91.

61. Ibid., p. 391. For a similar institution in Bologna, see the important article of Lucia Ferrante reprinted and translated as "Honor Regained: Women in the Casa del Soccorso di San Paolo in Sixteenth-Century Bologna," in *Sex and Gender*, pp. 46–72.

62. On the number of women in these institutions, see Pullan, *Rich and Poor*, p. 378 for the Convertite and p. 391 for the Zitelle; for Bologna's Casa del Soccorso, see Ferrante, "Honor Regained," p. 48; and for Florence, see Sherrill Cohen, *The Evolution of Women's Asylums since 1500: From Refuge for Ex-Prostitutes to Shelters for Battered Women* (New York: Oxford University Press, 1992).

63. A.S.V., Sant'Ufficio, Busta 47, Andriana Savorgnan, testimony of An-

tonio q. Bartolomeo di Pistori, 24 October 1581, f. 6v. He reported that Andriana had been in Padua since Easter and had been helped there by one of the brothers of her ex-lover Lorenzo Celsi. Lorenzo was the son of the noted Admiral Giacomo Celsi.

64. Ibid., testimony of Marco Dandolo, 22 October 1581, ff. 101r–102v.

65. Ibid., undated and unsigned letter, folded and inserted before f. 40r; folded inside this letter is a second letter from the Patriarch of Venice, dated 16 November 1581, ordering Andriana to come before the Holy Office or be declared a heretic. In the unsigned letter, the author refers to himself as the husband of Andriana and states explicitly that she cannot come to Venice because that would be too dangerous.

66. Barbaro, vol. 3, pt. 11, p. 196. According to Barbaro, he died in 1616 at about fifty-seven years of age.

Chapter 2

1. A.S.V., Sant'Ufficio, Busta 61, Elena Cumano, testimony of Andrea da Canal, 12 May 1588. This testimony was originally taken in Feltre for the bishop of that city. For this, see Archivio della Curia Vescovile (A.C.V.) di Feltre, Busta 60, ff. 321–336r (12 May–19 May 1588). It was then briefly passed to the Podestà of that city, a Venetian official; finally, the case was taken over by the Holy Office of Venice in July. The figure was referred to as a *tosato*, which is defined by Boerio as a small child; see Giuseppe Boerio, *Dizionario del dialetto veneziano*, p. 760, col. 1. An abbreviated form of this chapter was originally published in Italian as "'Più che la vita caro': Onore, matrimonio, e reputazione femminile nel tardo Rinascimento," in *Quaderni Storici*, 66 (1987), pp. 753–75. Recently, the main Venetian texts of the case have been published as *Un caso di stregoneria nella Feltre del '500*, ed. Marisa Milani (Belluno: Tipolitografia Trabella, 1990) (Comunità Montana Feltrina Centro per la Documentazione della Cultura Popolare, Quaderno n. 7). I would like to thank Gigi Corazzol and Daniela Perco of the Communità Montagna Feltrina for securing me a copy.

2. A.S.V., Sant'Ufficio, Busta 61, Elena Cumano, undated denunciation by Gian Battista Faceno. It appears that this denunciation was sent to the Sant'Ufficio of Venice and that they dated it 24 May 1588, probably the date when they began to look into the matter.

3. Ibid., Collegio, Relazioni di Rettore ed altre cariche, Busta 41, letter of 24 May 1589 by Vincenzo Capello. On the whole, Capello's letter was rather general and tended to repeat the cliches of earlier Podestà. The report that followed by Francesco Sagredo, the next Podestà, was much more detailed and analytical. He noted that the city was divided into four districts "in which there are 8715 inhabitants of every age, class and sex, divided into nobles of their council, *cittadini*, and *popolani*." He also discussed in some detail the dissensions he found in the city between the nobility and the *cittadini*, dissensions that may have played a role in this case. Sagredo's letter is found in this same Busta immediately after Capello's dated 14 November 1591.

4. Although the investigation was begun by the bishop of Feltre in May 1588 and continued by the Podestà, it was taken up actively by the Sant'Ufficio of Venice in Venice in July and then dragged on until September, when the case was dropped with an admonition to Elena and a letter to the Podestà of Feltre

informing him that the case was closed from the perspective of the Holy Office. For an excellent overview of the procedural issues involved, see Andrea Del Col, "Organizazzione, composizione e giurisdizione," pp. 276–94. Also, in May of that year, a countercase concerning infractions of local marital law was brought before the Podestà of Feltre that was eventually reviewed by the Avogadori di Comun of Venice. This aspect of the case will be discussed below.

5. A.S.V., Sant'Ufficio, Busta 61, undated denunciation by Gian Battista Faceno.

6. For a discussion of some of these problems in Venice, see Ruggiero, *Boundaries of Eros*, pp. 26–39; for the broader context, see Beatrice Gottlieb, "The Meaning of Clandestine Marriage," in *Family and Sexuality in French History*, ed. Robert Wheaton and Tamara K. Hareven (Philadelphia: University of Pennsylvania Press, 1980), pp. 49–83; see also the excellent article by Gaetano Cozzi, "Padri, figli e matrimoni clandestini (metà sec. XVI—metà sec. XVIII)," in *La cultura* 15 (1976), pp. 169–212. An additional bibliogɩ ‚phy may be found in note 9, Chapter 1.

7. On the role of honor and the disciplining of women, see the important articles by Sandra Cavallo and Simona Cerutti, "Female Honor and the Social Control of Reproduction in Piedmont between 1600 and 1800," in *Sex and Gender*, pp. 73–109; Luisa Ciammitti, "Quanto costa essere normali. La dote nel Conservatorio femminile di Santa Maria del Boraccano (1630–1680)," *Quaderni Storici* 53 (1983), pp. 469–97; and Lucia Ferrante, "Honor Regained," in *Sex and Gender*, pp. 46–72. For a discussion of honor in the context of the prosecution of sex crimes, see Ruggiero, *Boundaries*.

8. Cavallo and Cerruti, "Female Honor," pp. 88–89.

9. A.S.V., Avogaria di Comun, Misc. Penale, Busta 444:16, testimony of Elena Cumano, in Feltre, 24 May 1588, f. 1v. This case, brought before the Podestà of Feltre, was transcribed and reviewed by the Avogadori di Comun in Venice. On the complexities of this review process and the interrelationship between local justice and central justice in the Venetian terraferma, see Claudio Povolo, "Aspetti dell'amministrazione della giustizia penale nell'Repubblica di Venezia. Secoli XVI–XVII," in *Società e giustizia nella Repubblica Veneta (sec. XV–XVIII)*, ed. Gaetano Cozzi (Rome: Jouvence, 1981), pp. 155–257, and Enrico Basaglia, "Il controllo della criminalità nella Repubblica di Venezia. Il secolo XVI: Un momento di passagio," in *Atti del Convegno "Venezia e la Terraferma attraverso le relazioni dei Rettori"* (Milan: A. Giuffrè, 1981), pp. 65–78.

10. A.S.V., Avogaria di Comun, Misc. Penale, Busta 444:16, testimony of Elena Cumano, 24 May 1588, ff. 1v–2r.

11. Ibid., f. 2v.

12. Ibid., Sant'Ufficio, Busta 30, Elena called la Draga, testimony of same, 17 August 1571, ff. 5r–v. It is also interesting to note that this woman healer used the term *fior*, or flower, to refer to menstruation; often it was referred to in a much less positive manner. On this, see Ottavia Niccoli, " 'Menstruum quasi monstruum': Monstrous Births and Menstrual Taboo in the Sixteenth Century," in *Sex and Gender*, pp. 1–25.

13. Kristin Ruggiero reports similar remedies in a similar context of curing late periods in both rural Argentina and Italy in the nineteenth and early twentieth centuries. Frequent references to cures for late periods in American and

English women's magazines at the same time probably had a similar market in mind.

14. A.S.V., Avogaria di Comun, Misc. Penale, Busta 444:16, testimony of Elena Cumano, in Feltre, 24 May 1588, f. 2v.

15. Ibid., ff. 3r–v. The specific date of the meeting in bed comes from a complaint brought by her father before the bishop of Feltre, where he provided the date; on this, see Archivio della Curia Vescovile di Feltre, Busta 64. For examples of similar situations in fifteenth-century Venice, see Ruggiero, *Boundaries*, pp. 27–28, 36. Such forced marriages were a common theme in literature as well. Beyond the well-known tale of the nightingale in Boccaccio, Bandello used the theme in tale 58 of the third part of his *Novelle,* where the noble Tigrino Turco was caught in bed with the young and very independent widow of Lanciloto Constabile by her brother-in-law, who forced the couple to marry immediately. In this tale, interestingly, it was the widow who was the aggressive character sexually, and it was her brother-in-law who was hard pressed to defend the honor of his family. In fact, at the death of Tigrino, the problem reemerged until she joined the convent and, at least, in Bandello's telling, everyone lived happily ever after.

16. A.S.V., Avogaria di Comun, Misc. Penale, Busta 444:16, testimony of Elena Cumano, in Feltre, 24 May 1588, f. 3v; frequently scribes included references to the formal structure of the examination in Latin, in distinction to the vernacular of the testimonies in this period.

17. Ibid., ff. 3v–4r. Again Elena's testimony seems self-serving in claiming that Gian Battista specifically admitted that the marriage was unforced. According to both Venetian and canon law, forced marriages were not valid; see Ferro, *Dizionario del diritto,* vol. 7, "Matrimonio," pp. 145–48.

18. Actually, it had just begun. For the bishop's ruling, see Archivio della Curia Vescovile di Feltre, Busta 60, 7 January 1588, ff. 64r–65v. Elena provides a brief account of the Faceno family's attempt to pressure witnesses in her first deposition before the Podestà of Feltre, which was later forwarded to the Avogadori in Venice: A.S.V., Avogaria di Comun, Misc. Penale, Busta 444:16, testimony of Elena Cumano, in Feltre, 24 May 1588, ff. 4r–v.

19. A.S.V., Avogaria di Comun, Misc. Penale, Busta 444:16, text provided by Zuan Cumano, in Feltre, 26 May 1588, ff. 18r–19v, where Zuan quoted a *parte* passed by the Council of Ten on 27 August 1577. Although he slightly misquoted its terms, they were particularly relevant to the case and our discussion and suggest that he was far from alone in his travails. "It is understood that in this our city of Venice there has been introduced [the practice] by various evil men who under the pretext of marriage take women with only the pledge of those present . . . without observing the solemnities required by the Church. Then after they have violated and enjoyed them . . . they leave them gaining dissolution of the marriage made contrary to the rules of the Holy Council of Trent. Thus it is necessary to provide for the glory of God and the preservation of the honor of such women who are easily led astray in this manner." The Ten ruled, therefore, that men who committed such deeds should be condemned as seemed just, "having the option to condemn them to galley service or ban them or fine them according to the quality of the person as well as the impression of their guilt." For the original ruling passed by the Ten, see Consiglio dei Dieci,

Comune, filze 129, no folio, 27 August 1577. In Feltre, as one might expect, Elena was not the only victim of such activities. An indication of this is provided by a public announcement ordered by the bishop there two years later warning that cohabitation or sexual intercourse should not begin after a promise of marriage, but should await marriage itself. Archivio della Curia Vescovile di Feltre, Busta 64, 1 June 1590, f. 554r.

20. A.S.V., Avogaria di Comun, *Misc. Penale*, Busta 444:16, written complaint of Zuan Cumano, in Feltre, 25 May 1588, f. 8r.

21. Ibid., ff. 8r–v. On this see Archivio della Curia Vescovile di Feltre, Busta 60, 7 January 1588, ff. 64r–65v.

22. On the delicate calculus that joking promises of marriage created, see Cavallo and Cerutti, "Female Honor," in *Sex and Gender*, pp. 78–82. On the significance of the *beffa*, see *Formes et significations de la "Beffa" dans la littérature Italienne de la Renaissance*, ed. André Rochon (Paris: Université de la Sorbone Nouvelle, 1972), *Centre de Recherche sur la Renaissance Italienne*, I. I would like to thank Allen Grieco for the reference to this latter work.

23. A.S.V., Sant'Ufficio, Busta 61, Elena Cumano, testimony of same, in Venice, 30 July 1588. The earlier testimony she was referring to in Feltre occurred on 19 May 1588. The apparently close ties between the Podestà and the noble Faceno family may have been reinforced by the political reality that the Podestà was formally advised on criminal matters by a committee of local nobles. For this see ibid., Collegio, Relazioni di Rettori ed altri cariche, Busta 41, letter of Francesco Sagredo, 1591. This committee was elected by the local noble Major Council.

24. Francesco Sagredo, the next Podestà of Feltre, labeled him as potentially dangerous in his report to the Collegio (ibid.); at much the same time, he reported in a letter to the Ten that he feared that Galeazzo was a ringleader in a murder plot against several leading nobles. For this, see Consiglio dei Dieci, Capi, Lettere dei Rettori, Busta 159, Feltre, letter from Sagredo, 22 April 1591. It should be noted that Zuan was also seen as a leader in his community and had served Venetian interests well in the early 1580s as a lawyer in the complex border disputes in the area between Venice and the Duchy of Austria. Thus it may have been that he hoped to play upon a mix of fear and obligation to make the authorities see that Gian Battista's "joke" was no laughing matter. On his role in the border disputes, see *I libri commemoriali della Republica di Venezia, Regesti*, ed. Roberto Predelli (Venice: Deputazione Veneta di Storia Patria, 1907), vol. VII, pp. 32–33.

25. A.S.V., Collegio, Relazioni di Rettori ed altri cariche, Busta 41, letter of Francesco Sagredo, 1591. Interestingly, much like the late medieval antimagnate legislation of north Italy, Sagredo attempted to pacify the situation by forbidding the carrying of arms, limiting both public and private gatherings, and working assiduously to discipline the public conduct of the nobility.

26. Bandello, *Novelle*, pt. 2, novella 31; vol. 3, p. 37.

27. A.S.V., Avogaria di Comun, *Misc. Penale*, Busta 444:16, written complaint of Zuan Cumano, in Feltre, 25 May 1588, ff. 8r–v.

28. See Ruggiero, *Boundaries*, pp. 21–31, 43–44, 46–49.

29. A.S.V., Avogaria di Comun, *Misc. penale*, Busta 444:16, written complaint of Zuan Cumano, in Feltre, 25 May 1588, f. 6v.

30. Ibid., testimony of Elena Cumano, in Feltre, 24 May 1588, f. 2r. For a

similar vision of the exchange of honor involved in a marriage promise, see Cavallo and Cerutti, "Female Honor," in *Sex and Gender*, pp. 75–80.

31. A.S.V., Sant'Ufficio, Busta 61, Elena Cumano, testimony of same, in Venice, 30 July 1588 (italics mine).

32. Ibid.

33. Ibid.

34. On the Christian element in this, see Chapter 4.

35. A.S.V., Sant'Ufficio, Busta 61, Elena Cumano, testimony of same, in Venice, 30 July 1588. Elena calle Lucia "mia nena," which would be translated as "my wet nurse," but Lucia had worked for the Cumano family for only six years. For this, see in the same busta the testimony of Zuan Giacomo, Lucia's husband, taken in Feltre, 21 May 1588.

36. Ibid., testimony of Pietro Grevo, in Feltre, 12 May 1588.

37. Ibid., testimony of Elena Cumano, in Venice, 30 July 1588.

38. For a more detailed discussion of hammers, see Chapter 3.

39. A.S.V., Sant'Ufficio, Busta 61, Elena Cumano, testimony of same, in Venice, 30 July 1588.

40. It should be noted that while this was the case in Venice and the Veneto, other researchers have reported more extensive activity by men. See, for example, Luisa Accati's study of nearby Friuli in the seventeenth century, "The Spirit of Fornication: Virtue of the Soul and Virtue of the Body in Friuli, 1600–1800," in *Sex and Gender*, pp. 117–18.

41. A.S.V., Sant'Ufficio, Busta 61, Elena Cumano, testimony of Bartolomeo Bressano, in Feltre, 22 May 1588.

42. On this, see Ottavia Niccoli, "*'Menstruum quasi monstruum,'*" in *Sex and Gender*, pp. 1–25, and her book *Prophecy and People in Renaissance Italy*, trans. Lydia G. Cochrane (Princeton, N.J.: Princeton University Press, 1990), originally published as *Profeti e popolo nell'Italia del rinascimento* (Bari: Laterza, 1987).

43. The cowl, or placenta, was often seen as a protection against enemies and wounds and, as Carlo Ginzburg has demonstrated for Friuli in his *Night Battles*, it was also central to the self-identification of the night-battling Benandanti. In fact, Bartolomeo noted that the cowl was reputed to be worth at least twenty-five ducats, but Giorgio had decided to keep it rather than sell it. A.S.V., Sant'Ufficio, Busta 61, Elena Cumano, testimony of Bartolomeo Bressano, in Feltre, 22 May 1588.

44. Ibid. It is interesting to note that men in this case primarily name other men to support their testimony.

45. Ibid., testimony of Giacoma Patugalla, in Feltre, 26 May 1588. The literature on witches destroying young children is extensive and well known. The topic will be discussed further in Chapter 5. *Male* in Italian had the double sense of evil and sickness. Both senses seem to apply in this type of description, and thus it is used frequently to refer to the condition of bewitched people.

46. As witches were often seen as being able to know what was done in secret, and as Lucretia was accused of that as well, that "somehow" may be more important than it seems in the brief account of Giacoma's testimony. On this score Zambetta Galletto related: "I was astonished that this donna Lucretia came one morning to complain to me that I, Bragato, and Bortolomeo Bonamigo had spoken evilly about her. I knew that we had spoken together with messer Nicolo

Cavallero [and no one else] and later we agreed that no one had spoken about it with her." Bragato the same day labeled her knowledge of that conversation as "witchcraft." Ibid., testimonies of Zambetta Galletto and Battista Bragato, in Feltre, 25 May 1588.

47. Ibid., testimony of Giacoma dal Cumo, in Feltre, second testimony on 25 May 1588.

48. Ibid., testimony of Orsola, wife of Vettor Buziga, in Feltre, 25 May 1588; that same day Bastiano Horon recalled the incident, and the next day Pasqualo Franceschino also remembered it.

49. Ibid., Busta 64, Helena Pedra, testimony of Faustina, widow of Giovanni Dominici Nordio, 22 June 1589.

50. Ibid. Another good example of explicit reference to vendetta is the case of Laura Casabria. She was accused of a wide range of witchcraft, including the killing of a neighborhood child, and was reported by her neighbors in Murano to have also claimed that she had been licensed by her confessor to pursue her vendettas! As unlikely as that may sound, some women did claim to have the license of their confessors to use certain forms of magic; this will be discussed in Chapter 4. For Laura's case, see Busta 65, Laura Casabria, 1 July 1589.

51. Ibid., Busta 61, Elena Cumano, testimony of Zuan Victor, in Feltre, 15 May 1588.

52. On this in Venice see Ruggiero, *Boundaries of Eros*, pp. 71, 85. It was also a theme that appeared regularly in the novella literature of the period.

53. On this see the next two chapters.

54. A.S.V., Sant'Ufficio, Busta 61, Elena Cumano, testimony of Zuan Victor, in Feltre, 15 May 1588.

55. Ibid.

56. This was reported by Antonio Argento, who had heard it from her husband. Ibid., testimony of same, in Feltre, 16 May 1588.

57. Ibid., testimony of Andrea da Canal, in Feltre, 13 May 1588.

58. Although Lucretia was carefully examined in Feltre and was the focus of the investigation there, it appears that the Holy Office in Venice was not interested enough in her to bring a case against her. Elena Cumano was the focus of their inquiries. Their official reasoning for taking up the case is contained in their letter of 5 July 1588 to the bishop of Feltre, which argued that in ecclesiastical matters they were the correct, regular investigating body for the Veneto in such matters, and that it was important to not let cases of such importance to the Church be handled by secular courts like that of the Podestà of Feltre. Ibid.

59. Ibid., testimony of Piero Trento, in Feltre, 13 May 1588.

60. Ibid., testimony of Antonio Argento, in Feltre, 16 May 1588. He reported that she said that "she [usually] told her own sins to the confessors as it was not right to tell the sins of others."

61. Ibid.

62. Ibid., testimony of Andrea da Canal, in Feltre, 13 May 1588. Interestingly, however, Lucretia did not avoid asking him for some payment for her advice. Informed as he was leaving that she was a poor woman, he understood her drift and went home immediately and got her some bread.

63. Ibid., testimony of Andrea da Canal, in Feltre, 12 May 1588.

64. Ibid.

65. Ibid., testimony of Andrea da Canal, in Feltre, 13 May 1588. He did

admit, however, that Zuan Vettor had warned him recently that she was a witch.

66. Ibid. The lighting of holy candles was a prominent part of the Mass said the Saturday before Easter. Normally there were three special candles used by the priest to light the others. It appears that Andrea had used these candles for his magic. I would like to thank Monica Chojnacki for alerting me to the significance of these special candles.

67. Ibid.

68. Ibid., testimony of Antonio Argento, in Feltre, 16 May 1588.

69. And, of course, on this I may be simply the last and most gullible victim of Lucretia's *fama*, presuming a form of her guilt 400 years later. Still, if Andrea had been the culprit, as Lucretia maintained, it would have been unwise for him to attempt to incriminate a woman whose magical powers he clearly respected and who also knew enough about his private problems to create potentially serious problems for him with his superiors.

70. A.S.V., Sant'Ufficio, Busta 61, Elena Cumano, testimony of Paula daughter of Lucretia, in Feltre, 25 May 1588.

71. Ibid., testimony of Giacomo Cambrucio, in Feltre, 25 May 1588. Later that same day his neighbor Lucia, wife of Simeon Brustolini, provided a slightly different account in her testimony, but with the same implied witchcraft and outcome, the death of Giacomo's daughter.

72. Ibid., Avogaria di Comun, *Misc. Penale*, Busta 444:16, 15 December 1588, f. 33v. Although this decision was not made until December, it also required that Gian Battista take over and raise the child who had in the meantime been born to Elena, a daughter called with rather sad irony Victoria. It appears, however, that Gian Battista did not live long enough to take on these responsibilities, perhaps dying in the wars of Flanders. In 1592 the bishop of Feltre, at Elena's petition ordered the Faceno family to desist from hiding his will and turn over a copy of it to the priest, Pietro Trento. On this see Archivio della Curia Vescovile di Feltre, Busta 70, ff. 639r–v.

Chapter 3

1. A.S.V., Sant'Ufficio, Busta 66, Andrea Meri, testimony of Giuseppi q. Paolo, 28 April 1590. This case is briefly alluded to in the suggestive article of Giovanni Scarabello, "Paure, superstizioni, infamie," in *Storia della cultura veneta. Il Seicento*, ed. Girolamo Arnaldi and Manlio Pastore Stocchi (Vicenza: Neri Pozza, 1984), vol. 4, pt. 2, p. 370.

2. The *necessario* was an early euphemism for a toilet; see Boerio, *Dizionario del dialetto veneziano*, p. 438, col. 3.

3. Again this is an area of rapid scholarly developments. Perhaps most important for stimulating Italian scholarship has been the work of Carlo Ginzburg, especially his *The Night Battles* and *The Cheese and the Worms*. For a quick overview of the issues involved, see Peter Burke, *The Historical Anthropology of Early Modern Italy* (Cambridge: Cambridge University Press, 1987) and *Popular Culture in Early Modern Europe* (London: Temple Smith, 1978).

4. A.S.V., Sant'Ufficio, Busta 66, Andrea Meri, testimony of same, 12 May 1590.

5. Ibid.

6. Ibid., Sentence, 7 August 1590.

7. Ibid., Busta 63, Paolina di Rossi and Don Felice di Bibona, testimony of Paolina, 26 April 1588. This case at present is the seventh fasiculo of Busta 63, approximately 120 pages long, without folio numbers. It runs along pretty much in chronological order except for some administrative business involving Paolina's penalty from September 1588 (after the case was over) inserted toward the front.

8. Ibid.; on the casting of beans, see the discussion below.

9. Ibid.

10. Ibid.

11. Ibid.

12. Ibid., testimony of Argenta wife of Giovanni Magni, 7 May 1588. In fact, Argenta's husband had left her.

13. The case actually was brought to the attention of the Holy Office by an undated denunciation written for the mother of Gian Battista, Laura Giustinian, by Geronimo Cantinella. This is bound in at the front of the case and was probably written in early April 1588. Ibid.

14. Ibid., testimony of Paolina, 26 April 1588. "Lying through one's throat" was a popular accusation in criminal testimony in both Florence and Venice in the sixteenth century.

15. Ibid. Menstrual blood was an important part of the corpus of magic associated with the body. For an earlier case involving menstrual blood, see Ruggiero, *Boundaries*, pp. 33–35. On similar practices in the Middle Ages, see Cleto Corranin and Pierluigi Zampini, *Documenti etnografici e folkloristici nei sinodi diocesani italiani* (Bologna: Forni, 1970), p. 13. For the learned vision of the relationship between menstrual blood and conception, see Ian Maclean, *The Renaissance Notion of Woman, A Study in the Fortunes of Scholasticism and Medical Science in European Intellectual Life* (Cambridge: Cambridge University Press, 1980), pp. 35–37; and for a suggestive discussion of its role in the economy of body fluids, see Thomas Laqueur, *Making Sex, Body and Gender from the Greeks to Freud* (Cambridge, Mass.: Harvard University Press, 1990), pp. 35–36.

16. Ibid.

17. The primary use of beans was in a relational context to determine the emotional relationship of one person to another. This will be discussed in more detail below.

18. A.S.V., Sant'Uffizio, Busta 63, Paolina di Rossi and Don Felice di Bibona, testimony of Don Felice, 26 April 1588.

19. Ibid.

20. Ibid. Although he did not give the words of the secret in his testimony, both he and his examiners were well aware of the words referred to. In several other cases the secret written on the host or sage was used; its wording was explicitly noted in Sant'Ufficio, Busta 31, Fra Aurelio di Siena, Sentence of 19 December 1589, and again (to be said when casting beans) in Busta 69, Paolina Bianchini, testimony of Julia Fabreta, 22 February 1593. The secret was also used for other forms of magic. A brief but interesting reference was made in a case of 1587 to the lover of a certain Lucia, who wore an amulet that contained the cowl (discussed in Chapter 2) and the words of the secret that supposedly protected him from evil. For this, see Busta 59, Lucia, testimony of Margarita wife of Niccolo, f. 1v, no date, probably October 1587.

21. Ibid., Busta 63, Paolina di Rossi and Don Felice di Bibona, testimony of Don Felice, 26 April 1588.

22. Ibid. Troubling as it may seem, ingesting parts of the lover or beloved literally (as in the case of Paolina's menstrual blood) or symbolically were an important part of love magic. For a suggestive discussion of medieval visions of the power of the host, including a brief reference to its use for love magic, see Carolyn Walker Bynum, *Holy Feast and Holy Fast, The Religious Significance of Food to Medieval Women* (Berkeley: University of California Press, 1987), pp. 54–65, and Peter Browe, "Die Eucharistie als Zaubermittel im Mittelalter," in *Archiv für Kulturgeschichte* 20 (1930), pp. 134–54.

23. Ibid., Busta 66, Cassandra Lizzari, testimony of same, 3 April 1590.

24. This healing type of magic will be discussed in more detail in Chapter 4. For the general concern about the illicit use of holy oil in the Veneto, see Corrain and Zampini, *Documenti etnografici,* pp. 74–75.

25. See below, note 30. The association of holy oil or at least blessed oil and love magic can be found even in the early Church. Peter Brown reports the case of an Eastern hermit who was consulted by a wife whose husband had been bound by magical means to a concubine. He took pity on the woman, and, according to a relatively contemporary account, "he quenched the power of the magic by prayer, and blessing by divine invocation a flask of oil she had brought, told her to anoint herself with it. Following these instructions, the woman transferred to herself her husband's love, and induced him to prefer the lawful bed." Quoted in Peter Brown, *The Body in Society: Men, Women, and Sexual Renunciation in Early Christian Society* (New York: Columbia University Press, 1988), pp. 327–28.

26. Ibid., Busta 63, Giulia, daughter of Gismondo, deposition of Paolo Amici, 20 October 1588.

27. Ibid.

28. Ibid., Busta 61, Angela Salo, complaint of Antonio Gaietta, 21 March 1588. Angela and Antonio's relationship, although never defined in the brief investigation, may have been predicated on the fact that they were originally from the same place, Salo. Holy oil's use was so ubiquitous that it was even reported as being used to dress a salad in order to bind love. In 1581 a certain Bertola, probably a prostitute and the sister of the concubine of a priest, was reported to have "dressed a lettuce salad with [holy] oil in order to give it to a gentleman lover of hers to eat." The oil had been given to her sister by her priest lover. For this, see Busta 49, Pre Andrea de Perin, testimony of magister Bernardo, 6 November 1581, f. 2v.

29. Ibid., Busta 65, Giacomina di Seravallo (Locatelli), testimony of Diamante wife of Bernardo Ortolano, 4 January 1591. Giacomina, incidentally, was a prostitute who could read and write and who demonstrated eminent good taste. Asked about her reading habits, she responded, "I certainly do have books to read, history and other things because I enjoy reading history." Ibid., testimony of Giacomina, 1 September 1590.

30. Ibid., Busta 63, Isabella Bellocchio, testimony of same, 27 June 1589, f. 155r.

31. It may be as well that Isabella was also playing on the distinction between honoring and worshipping here. In a society where honor was so

important, it was necessary to honor many powers, but that did not imply that one rejected other powers by honoring one particular one. Ibid. It is possible in Isabella's case to see how this magic was passed from one courtesan to another. Three years earlier, a servant of the courtesan Emilia Catena had testified that her mistress had been taught this very magic by Isabella Bellocchio. At the same time, she was learning a wide range of other love magic from an old woman noted for her magical medicines and throwing of beans named Anastasia; for this, see Busta 58, Emilia Catena, testimony of Magdalena, wife of Giovanni, 26 March 1586.

32. Perhaps the technologically advanced or the powerful few in certain situations can force their environment to adapt to tighter cultural symmetries; this may ultimately be closely related to the "civilizing process" of Norbert Elias. But the rest are forced to build cultures with more flexibility and more ambiguity in order to survive.

33. A.S.V., Sant'Ufficio, Busta 64, Girolama di Venezia, *carta di voler bene,* 21 March 1589.

34. Ibid. It was reported that this *carta* was to be used only on certain days: Easter, Christmas, and the feast day of Saint John the Baptist before the sun rose. In addition, it was supposed to work before sunrise on all Fridays. Many *carte* were not so time specific, but often, especially for magic that drew on the holy, certain holy times were more significant than normal time.

35. It should be noted that literature of the period often referred to lovers being hammered. The Venetian comedy *La Bulesca,* for example, opens with a reference to the female lead, Marcolina, and her maid using "el martello" as their weapon against the aggressive prepotency of the male leads, Bule and Bio. *La Bulesca* has recently been edited by Bianca Maria Da Riff in her *La letteratura "Alla Bullesca";* see p. 49 and passim for this apparently gendered reference to a hammer. For a husband who was typically "wrecked" (*guasto*) by such magic, see the case of Giovanna di Cesari, A.S.V., Sant'Ufficio, Busta 59, 23 October 1587. In the case of Giovanna Falconetta, a widow accused of wrecking children, she refers in turn to how she was "wrecked" by the famous la Draga, and makes a tantalizingly vague reference to knowing that the same la Draga had wrecked the patriarch of Venice so badly that he had died. Busta 37, Giovanna Falconetta, testimony of same, 21 October 1574. A dramatic recounting of the effects of such magic is also provided by Elena Zamberti, who was hammered by Isabella Bellocchio because she was her rival in love. This will be discussed in more detail below.

36. Ibid., Busta 66, Cassandra Lizzari, testimony of same, 26 May 1590.

37. Ibid., Busta 41, Fra Aurelio di Siena, *carta di voler bene,* undated. Aurelio was an exemplary renegade cleric, whose life is the focus of Chapter 5.

38. Ibid.

39. Busta 63, Paolina di Rossi and Don Felice di Bibona, testimony of Don Felice, 26 April 1588.

40. Ibid.

41. Ibid.

42. Ibid., Busta 63, Isabella Bellocchio, testimony of same, 23 June 1589.

43. Italo Calvino, *Le Cosmicomiche* (Turin: Einaudi, 1965), p. 50.

44. Numerous explanations of how beans worked were given to the Holy Office. In the case involving Andriana Savorgnan discussed in Chapter 1, for

example, a certain Betta reported that when beans were thrown she read them as follows: "When the beans that marked the man and the woman come together, it signifies that those people talk, because they fell together. When they fall parallel to each other, they signify that they lay down together, that is that they go to bed together. But when one bean falls with its head against the head of the other, it means that they argue." Betta also claimed that she said a prayer to Santa Elena before casting beans. Ibid., Busta 47, Andriana Savorgnan, testimony of Betta Marangoneta, 27 October 1581, f. 10r. In almost all the reports, the details of the procedure varied slightly. Many, for example, used the other materials thrown with the beans to determine certain things. Thus the relationship of the beans to a piece of bread marked who was eating with whom (Busta 59, Lucia, testimony of Margarita wife of Nicolo, f. 1r, no date, probably October 1587); the relationship of the beans to a piece of coal denoted who was sharing a hearth. But behind the variety, the underlying continuity was the relational nature of space, which as a true metaphor could mirror human relations.

45. Ibid., Busta 53, Giulia, daughter of Lodovico di Verona, testimony of same, 24 August 1584. Giulia admitted that she had once bought a new pan and some swaddling in the name of the Great Devil (*Gran Diavolo*). After binding a lizard with the swaddling, she boiled it, apparently alive, in oil, saying, "I do not bind this lizard, rather I bind the heart of him [the man sought] in the name of the Great Devil who rules and governs." Giulia also was quite eclectic in her magic, confessing that she relied on the holy as well. As one might imagine, such magical associations of hearth, cooking of things, and women had a long tradition. In her highly suggestive discussion of the relationship between women and food in the Middle Ages, Carolyn Walker Bynum notes that men were suspicious of women's control of the preparation of food, and ecclesiastical authorities like Burchard of Worms listed a range of magic associated with the manipulation of food, "for example, increasing or decreasing sexual ardor of a husband by adding to his food such things as menstrual blood, semen, or dough kneaded with a woman's buttocks." Walker, *Holy Feast*, p. 190.

46. A.S.V., Sant'Ufficio, Busta 63, Isabella Bellocchio, testimony of same, 23 June 1589.

47. Ibid.

48. On this see Martin, *Witchcraft*, pp. 104–5.

49. Ibid., Busta 59, Elisabetta Giantis, testimony of Isabella Seghetti, 26 June 1587.

50. Giulia, the daughter of Lodovico di Verona, made such a division explicitly in one of the incantations that she confessed to the Holy Office in 1584. She offered to split the blood of her intended lover two-fifths for herself and three-fifths for the eclectic mix of damned and divine spirits that she called on to help her. For this, see ibid., Busta 53, Giulia, daughter of Lodovico di Verona, testimony of same, 24 August 1584. In 1586 Emilia Catena was accused of using very similar magic and dividing her lover's blood in exactly the same proportions with the Devil; see Busta 58, Emilia Catena, testimony of Magdalena, wife of Giovanni, 26 March 1586.

51. Ibid., Busta 63, Isabella Bellocchio, testimony of Elena Zamberti, 4 May 1589. On signing in the form of a cross, see Chapter 4.

52. Ibid. Elena's suffering finds a humorous parallel in the suffering for love

that the character Menato felt at the beginning of the comedy by Ruzzante titled *La Moscheta*. There, while lamenting the mad passion that he feels for Betìa, wife of his friend, he momentarily decides that he must have been bewitched. "I believe she has put me under a spell or bewitched me," he complains in a soliloquy. "She has bewitched me as I stand here, because I feel always on this left side a pain, a fire, a burning, a ripping apart so bad that it seems to me that I have some workers with two hammers working away: bim bam! bim bam! And when one diminishes the other increases. . . . I am almost dead. . . . Why not, yes, I will die, collapse which will feel good to me since I am so afire. Yes, yes, yes, for it swirls through my stomach and I feel how strongly it makes my heart beat, and my lungs, and all the rest." Ruzzante [Angelo Beolco], *Teatro*, ed. and trans. into Italian by Ludovico Zorzi (Turin: Einaudi, 1967), pp. 591–93.

53. A.S.V., Sant'Ufficio, Busta 63, Isabella Bellocchio, testimony of Elena Zamberti, 4 May 1589.

54. Ibid.

55. Ibid., Busta 66, Elisabetta Greca, testimony of Lutieta widow of Giovanni Mane, 12 July 1590.

56. Ibid., testimony of Clareta wife of Ambrosio, 12 July 1590.

57. Ibid., Busta 65, Rosa and Caterina, testimony of Lucretia, wife of a carpenter, 24 September 1589.

58. The inadequacy of the modern terms "public" and "private" is manifest here. Certain rooms of the private house were quite public, with people (at least certain people, family, neighbors, and friends) and animals wandering in and out with relative freedom and others peering in through windows or chinks in the fabric of the house. Other areas were more clearly private, but even the privacy of a bedroom was relative when several people slept in the same bed. Wealth, status, and increasingly demanding gender and honor concerns had begun to separate off a form of domestic private space, but it was still a long way from the modern concept of the private, populated as it was at the upper social levels at least by servants and a normally fairly extended family.

59. A.S.V., Sant'Ufficio, Busta 63, Isabella Bellocchio, testimony of Elena Zamberti, 4 May 1589. It will be remembered that the Columns of Justice were where ritual executions were carried out; thus the earth there was believed to be soaked with the blood of criminals. A year earlier, Regina Vassalin was accused of using earth from a new grave for similar door magic in order to hammer a rival for her ex-lover, who was trying to avoid honoring a promise of marriage to her. Suggestively, he, much like Gian Battista Faceno in Feltre, had used the new rules of Trent to block the marriage; for this, see Busta 61, Regina Vassalin, testimony of Polisena, wife of Giovanni Miola, 10 December 1588.

60. Ibid., Busta 77, Bellina Loredana et al., Denunciation of Alvise Ongaretto, 15 December 1615. Loredana was another interesting and powerful woman. About seventy years old when this case was brought to trial, she apparently had started her career as a prostitute, then moved on to selling love magic and a number of cures, including a special oil that she had had licenced by the Sanità, a magistracy responsible for public health. In this way she had made enough money, it appears, to keep a substantial house where she rented rooms to prostitutes, and had lived virtually all her life as an independent woman on her own. Martin's account of Loredana stresses the gambling aspect of her magic and provides a briefer version of her simulated execution; see *Witchcraft*, pp.

112–13. Given the detail of cutting off the right hand, it is likely that this Bellina was reenacting the traditional execution for a thief or murderer. For a discussion of ritual executions in Renaissance Venice, see: Ruggiero, *Violence,* pp. 1–2, 47–49, 180–81.

61. What follows in many ways qualifies Thomas Laqueur's one-sex model for premodern society advanced in *Making Sex.* There he argued that behind the apparent diversity of premodern European visions of the body, sex, and gender, society perceived essentially only one sex, with the female sexual organs being merely a reversed and imperfect form of the male organs. His argument is based, however, primarily on medical and philosophical texts. Nonetheless, he seems to needlessly compress the diversity of premodern thought to make his hypothesis work; on this, see the excellent review essay of Katherine Park and Robert A. Nye, "Destiny Is Anatomy," in *The New Republic* (18 February 1991), pp. 53–57. His argument might be better served by shelving the radical-sounding claim of only one sex and positing a tradition (as opposed to *the* tradition) that emphasized one body, with various shades of sex hierarchically arranged and gendered into male and female. This would still be an exciting vision that would promote some useful rethinking, and it would fit better with the material that he has presented.

62. In many societies, of course, breasts were also closely associated with fertility and reproduction. Representations of multibreasted ancient fertility figures immediately come to mind. And for the Renaissance, one could read the myriad representations of Mary nursing the Christ child in a similar light. Magic, however, seems to suggest that that may be an incorrect parallel. The general practice of using a wet nurse to breast-feed infants also suggests a less automatic connection between the breasts and fertility and fecundity, as the wet nurse's breasts were not so much a sign of fecundity (she was not the mother) as a sign of someone else's wealth and status. Breast-feeding a child, moralistic appeals aside, may not have been seen as a central aspect of maternity; in fact, it may have been seen as a menial task below the honor of important women. That, in turn, suggests that the fascination with Mary feeding Christ was more attuned to the Virgin's self-sacrifice and Christ's humanity and frailty as a child.

63. A.S.V., Sant'Ufficio, Busta 59, Splandiana Mariani, testimony of Lucretia Cillia, undated, probably July 1587. Interestingly in this case, another neighbor reported that when someone else drank this wine by mistake, he became an unintended victim of the magic.

64. Ibid., testimony of Splandiana, undated, probably July 1587. Most accounts of this magic leave out the Devil, which may have been a wise strategy since they were being given as testimony to the Holy Office. The Holy Office usually pressed people to admit that the White Angel was the Devil, but most resisted. In Splandiana's testimony, while she is willing to admit that the Devil was involved, the Devil and the White Angel do not seem to be equated; rather, the Devil is called in the name of the White Angel.

65. Ibid., Busta 63, Franceschina, testimony of Marieta, daughter of Antonio, 28 April 1588.

66. On this case see Ruggiero, *Boundaries,* pp. 33–36.

67. A.S.V., Sant'Ufficio, Busta 57, Diana and her mother Faustina, unsigned denunciation, 10 July 1586.

68. Ibid., Busta 59, Elisabetta Giantis, testimony of same, 26 June 1587.

69. Ibid.

70. Ibid.

71. Ibid.

72. Ibid., Busta 63, Paolina di Rossi and Felice di Bibona, testimony of Sebastian Meliori, 23 June 1588. For his trial also involving love magic, see Busta 65, Sebastian Meliori, 9 September 1589.

73. Ibid., Busta 63, Paolina di Rossi and Felice di Bibona, sentence of Paolina di Rossi, 30 June 1588; sentence of Felice di Bibona, 23 August 1588. There was, however, a chance that as his confinement was to be in a monastery, Don Felice may have ended up in a more relaxed house and enjoyed a rather lax confinement. Although following the Council of Trent, the drive to reform monastic orders accelerated, research strongly suggests that there were still a goodly number of not particularly strict monastic houses in Italy in the late sixteenth century.

74. This line of investigation was suggested to the Holy Office by Tomaso Trevisano, Paolina's lawyer, in a letter dated 31 May 1588. Among other potential witnesses he named Salvatore. For Salvatore's testimony see ibid., testimony of Salvatore Samater, no date, probably 4 June 1588. A case from 1589 refers to him as Sebastiano and as Paolina's lover, Busta 65, Paola Padova, testimony of Magdalena, 18 July 1589.

75. Ibid.

76. Ibid.

77. Ibid., testimony of Angela, wife of Domenico Toscano, 4 June 1588. Here again it should be noted that this testimony may have been suborned as calling Angela to testify had been suggested by Paolina's lawyer.

78. Ibid.

79. Ibid., testimony of Argenta, wife of Giovanni Magni, 7 May 1588.

Chapter 4

1. *Oxford Annotated Bible*, p. 1471.

2. Ibid., pp. 1255–56.

3. The very cases that Ginzburg used for his discussion of the Benandanti suggest the continued domination of rural Christianity by nonclerics, especially women, in the late sixteenth century. And this domination was by no means entirely broken even two centuries later. Edward Muir, who has been working on a study of violence and vendetta in Friuli and who kindly read and commented on this chapter, suggests that these tendencies may have been stronger in the region because it had been an ecclesiastical principality for such a long time that the established Church had become particularly subject to the corruption of aristocratic patronage. Moreover mendicants never really flourished in the region, perhaps for similar reasons. As a result, popular Christianity may have been freer to flourish in Friuli than elsewhere in rural Europe.

4. Ginzburg, *Night Battles*, p. 75.

5. Ibid.

6. A.S.V., Sant'Ufficio, Busta 68, Latisana, testimony of Pietro di Venezia, 14 May 1591, f. 1r. The folio numbers in this file are a modern addition in pencil. As it presently stands, the file breaks up fairly naturally into a first section, which is a copy of testimony collected in Latisana, followed by major testimony heard

by the Holy Office in Venice and lesser investigations carried out at their behest in Latisana. The text was also published by Marisa Milani in *Antiche pratiche di medicina popolare nei processi del S. Uffizio* (*Venezia, 1572–1591*) (Padua: Centrostampa Palazzo Maldura, 1986) (*Corso di Letteratura delle Tradizione Popolari* (*a.a. 1985–86*), pp. 106–229. As her edition is difficult to find, I will cite the archival references as well. Her edition is useful, as it gathers together several other cases dealing with healing practices from the period and has helpful notes. My own reading, however, is based on the archival texts. For an important discussion of clerics and healing magic, see Mary R. O'Neil, *"Sacerdote ovvero strione,* Ecclesiastical and Superstitious Remedies in Sixteenth Century Italy," in *Understanding Popular Culture, Europe from the Middle Ages to the Nineteenth Century,* ed. Steven L. Kaplan (Berlin: Mouton, 1984), pp. 53–83.

7. Ibid.; Milani, *Antiche pratiche,* p. 106.

8. Pietro Bembo, *Gli Asolani,* trans. Rudolf Gottfried (Freeport, N.Y.: Books for Libraries Press, 1971), pp. 111–12; for the Italian original, see *Bembo, Opere in volgare,* ed. Mario Marti (Florence: Sansoni, 1961), pp. 96–97.

9. A.S.V., Collegio, Relazioni, Busta 54, report of Piero Zen, Francesco Falier, and Filipo da Molin, 5 April 1591, ff. 36v–37r.

10. Ibid., Collegio, Relazioni Ambasciatori, rettori ed altre cariche, Busta 41. This is a later copy of the *relazione* with some material added from a survey of 1557. It also appears to be filed out of place at present after the *relazione* of Alvise Foscarini of 1637.

11. Ibid., Notarile Testamenti, Marsilio, Busta 1214.1039. Zaccharia was dead by 9 December 1563, when a number of witnesses certified that this was his will in his own hand. He did require, however, that this land in Latisana be returned to the male line of his brothers at the death of Elena.

12. According to the index of the *libro d'oro, nascite,* Zaccharia was born in 1557 and would have been thirty-two at the time of these problems. For these complaints, see Consiglio dei Dieci, Criminale, Filze 26, 23 August 1589, no folios. Nicolo was already living with his father in Latisana in August 1581, when they reported to the Capi of the Council of Ten in Venice at the latter's request about activities of outsiders from Church territories operating in the area, which creates some doubts about his marriage being the reason for his living there. On this, see Consiglio dei Dieci, Capi, *Lettere dei Rettori,* Busta 188, letter n. 20, 25 August 1581; see also the letter of 20 August, n. 29, which suggests that these outsiders were a problem because of a shortage of grain in the area. The locals were apparently selling their grain to them rather than to the Venetian Rettore and Capitano.

13. On this, see John Bossy, "The Counter-Reformation and the People of Catholic Europe," *Past and Present* 47 (1970), pp. 51–71; and his more synthetic overview, *Christianity in the West 1400–1700* (Oxford: Oxford University Press, 1985). The thoughtful essays of Peter Burke in *The Historical Anthropology of Early Modern Italy* are also suggestive.

14. A.S.V., Sant'Ufficio, Busta 68, Latisana, testimony of Pietro di Venezia, 14 May 1591, f. 1r; Milani, *Antiche pratiche,* p. 106.

15. Ibid., testimony of Apollonia, 6 June 1592, f. 64v; Milani, *Antiche pratiche,* p. 163.

16. Ibid., f. 65r; Milani, *Antiche pratiche,* p. 163.

17. Ibid.

18. Ibid., testimony of Sensa, wife of Tonigucci, 28 April 1591, f. 26v; Milani, *Antiche pratiche*, p. 112.

19. Ibid., testimony of Paolo de Casteon, 28 April 1591, f. 27r; Milani, *Antiche pratiche*, p. 113. Paolo explained that Apollonia was "mia cognata"—my relative—and went on to explain the precise connection: "the deceased Jaco, husband of the said Apollonia, was the brother of my wife Maria."

20. "Last Friday . . . when he [Gasparo] came to ask and invite me as I said, there was with him Jacomo, the brother of Domenico Committo from Latisanotta [a small neighborhood on the northern edge of Latisana]. This Domenico is a relative of Gasparo having married a sister of his. With them there was also Valentino Bracetto who lives in Piscarola." This Valentino was also a relative, Antonio clarified; "he is married to a cousin of ours." Ibid., testimony of Antonio Madizza, 28 April 1591, ff. 27v–28r; Milani, *Antiche pratiche*, pp. 114–15.

21. A.S.V., Sant'Ufficio, Busta 68, Latisana, testimony of Antonio Madizza, 20 May 1591, f. 28v; Milani, *Antiche pratiche*, p. 116. Concerning Antonio's reading of the transcript of his earlier testimony, ecclesiastical courts did at times allow such rereading, but usually only after they had tried to trap witnesses in self-contradictions. Given the evident suspicions about his role in the escape, accepting his request may have been a bit of special treatment reflecting his and his family's standing in the community.

22. Ibid.

23. Ibid., testimony of Apollonia, 6 June 1591, f. 64v; Milani, *Antiche pratiche*, pp. 162–63.

24. Ibid., testimony of Apollonia, 18 June 1591, ff. 70r–v; Milani, *Antiche pratiche*, pp. 168–69. On this, see also the interesting discussion of the early modern sense of conscience in David Warren Sabean, *Power in the Blood, Popular Culture and Village Discourse in Early Modern Germany* (Cambridge: Cambridge University Press, 1984), especially pp. 45–46.

25. One reason that Camilla was well known as a healer was that she was the niece of the even more famous healer, la Draga, who will be discussed in more detail below. A.S.V., Sant'Ufficio, Busta 67, case of Camilla Orsetta (labeled incorrectly on the wrapper "Orsola Garzolo"), complaint of Fioralisa, wife of Giovanni, 5 December 1590, f. 1v.

26. Ibid.; italics mine.

27. Ibid., testimony of Leona di Belluno, f. 5v, 10 January 1591.

28. Ibid., Busta 68, Latisana, testimony of Apollonia, 18 June 1591, f. 70v; Milani, *Antiche pratiche*, p. 169.

29. Ibid.

30. Ibid.

31. Ibid., f. 71r; Milani, *Antiche pratiche*, p. 169.

32. Ibid., f. 71v; Milani, *Antiche pratiche*, p. 170.

33. Ibid., f. 72r; Milani, *Antiche pratiche*, p. 170.

34. Ibid.

35. Ibid., f. 72v; Milani, *Antiche practiche*, p. 171.

36. Ibid., f. 72r; Milani, *Antiche practiche*, p. 171.

37. Ibid., f. 73r, Milani, *Antiche practiche*, p. 171.

38. To some extent, once the disruptions of this status quo settled out into a new status quo for rural Catholicism, a similar symbiotic relationship appears to

have been established. On this, see Luisa Accati, "The Spirit of Fornication" in *Sex and Gender*, pp. 128–29.

39. A.S.V, Busta 68, Latisana, testimony of Apollonia, 10 June 1591, ff. 65v–66r; Milani, *Antiche pratiche*, p. 164.

40. The first investigation of her activities occurred in 1571, recorded in Sant'Ufficio Busta 30; the second in 1582, recorded in Busta 49. Curiously, la Draga may have had a son who was a priest, Benedetto Naracio. He denied this when questioned about it by the Holy Office, but an ex-lover provides some interesting details. She claimed that while they were living together for about six months shortly before he was banned for ten years for heresy, she had seen magical books that belonged to his mother, la Draga, and that when they were about to break up, she had been hammered by her. Taking pity on her because of her suffering, Benedetto had returned to la Draga, asked her to lift the hammer, and threatened. "If she dies I will accuse you of having made the patriarch die (about 1564) down at the Arsenal." Supposedly, la Draga gave him a cure to undo the magic and she recovered. Ibid., Busta 37, Giovanna Falconetta, testimony of same, 21 October 1574, no folios. Her account is corroborated to an extent in that the Sant'Ufficio did investigate a Benetto Naracio in 1558 for using love magic and banned him for ten years. No patriarch died, however, in 1564. Interestingly, Naracio was reported to have been willing to give out love magic only to help in reconciling married couples with marital problems. On this, see Sant'Ufficio, Busta 14, Pre Benetto Naracio.

41. Ibid., Busta 30, Elena called la Draga, testimony of same, 11 August 1571, f. 2v; also see Milani, *Antiche pratiche*, p. 27.

42. Ibid., f. 2v–3r; Milani, *Antiche pratiche*, p. 27. *Spasemo* was used here and elsewhere in these cases in the sense of being overwhelmed by an evil force; the sudden fear of Fiordilisa's child, noted above, suggested to his mother a similar evil force coming over him.

43. See *Catholic Encyclopedia*, "Extreme Unction."

44. James, V, 14, 15; *Oxford Annotated Bible*, p. 1471.

45. See, for example, Peter Brown, *The Cult of the Saints: Its Rise and Function in Latin Christianity* (Chicago: University of Chicago Press, 1981), pp. 77–78; Vivian Nutton, "Murders and Miracles: Lay Attitudes to Medicine in Classical Antiquity," in *Patients and Practitioners: Lay Perceptions of Medicine in Pre-industrial Society*, ed. Roy Porter (Cambridge: Cambridge University Press, 1985), pp. 45–53. The case of Orseta Padova, heard by the Holy Office in 1590, provides an interesting confirmation that holy oil was still seen as central in rites for the dead. Accused of using holy oil for magical purposes, she denied the accusation and stressed that she had never even had holy oil in the house except for when there were dead there. "I do not know anything about herbal remedies or witchcraft. Moreover I have never had holy oil in my house except when I saw it given to the dead." A.S.V., Sant'Ufficio, Busta 66, Orsetta Padova, testimony of same, 24 May 1590.

46. A.S.V., Sant'Ufficio, Busta 68, Latisana, testimony of Antonia, widow of Giovanni Maria Bologna, 20 May 1591, f. 19v; Milani, *Antiche pratiche*, pp. 146–47.

47. Ibid., testimony of Apollonia, 11 June 1951, f. 66r; Milani, *Antiche pratiche*, p. 164.

48. Ibid., ff. 66v–67r; Milani, *Antiche pratiche*, p. 165.

49. Ibid.

50. "Mouthful" [*boccolina*] probably has here the sense of "cute little thing"; the double meaning nonetheless was unfortunately suggestive. Ibid., testimony of Antonia, widow of Giovanni Maria Bologna, 20 May 1591, f. 20r; Milani, *Antiche Pratiche*, p. 147.

51. Ibid., Busta 30, Elena called la Draga, testimony of same, 11 August 1571, f. 3r; also see Milani, *Antiche pratiche*, pp. 27–28. Milani's transcription omits "in the form of a cross" from the Virgin's instructions on how Lazarus should place the olive leaves on his forehead.

52. Ibid., f. 3v; Milani, *Antiche pratiche*, p. 28.

53. Ibid. We might speculate that this was merely a clever coopting form of defense on her part, but la Draga had so many problems with her multiple personalities that that seems unlikely. Also, the enthusiasm with which she tells in detail her curing technique suggests that rather than defending herself, she was interested in relating her knowledge, at least in this part of her testimony. At this point the transcript has a second folio numbered 3; thus the folio numbers cited from folio 3 on are actually one off.

54. Ibid.; Milani, *Antiche pratiche*, pp. 28–29.

55. This is not to suggest that resignation was the only option or the only form of behavior chosen, but lower-class life in the city and the life of peasants in the countryside probably entailed far more acceptance and resignation than resistance in even the most rebellious.

56. A.S.V., Sant'Ufficio, Busta 68, Latisana, testimony of Maria Madizza, 14 October 1591, f. 110v; Milani, *Antiche pratiche*, pp. 204–5. Although it is not a self-evident reading, the structure of the tale seems to play on the difference between positive male hospitality and negative female lack of same. The significance of the bow and the arrow is less self-evident and it may well be that the story was not clearly remembered. But with a less literal translation the tale might be read to suggest that as the bow goes with the arrow so should a man and a woman go together (even with the evil deed of the latter) and the child in their midst will be well. The proverbial nature of the bow and the arrow going together in peasant culture is humorously played upon in Ruzzante's play *La Betia*. There in a take-off on Pietro Bembo and the conceits of love poetry several peasants in colorful dialect discuss in a pseudo-Bembian manner their sufferings for love. Bazzarello, however, sees the whole discussion as absurd and is constantly trying to call his comrades back to reality. When he hears that a pudgy little winged child/god (Cupid) is responsible for their suffering, shooting lovers in the "guts" with a bow and arrow that he always carries (just like Bazzarello and his friends when they go hunting), he is suitably unimpressed. After a few obscenities about the type of men who would let such a god shoot them in the ass, Bazzarello offers manfully to take him on and rip off his wings. Ruzzante, *Teatro*, pp. 172–76.

57. A.S.V., Sant'Ufficio, Busta 68, Latisana, testimony of Maria Madizza, 14 October 1591, f. 110v; Milani, *Antiche pratiche*, p. 204.

58. Ibid., testimony of Margarita, wife of Nicolo del Gobbo, 13 August 1591; Milani, *Antiche pratiche*, p. 180.

59. Ibid.

60. Ibid., testimony of Aloysia, wife of Daniele Pasut, 20 May 1591, ff. 11r–v; Milani, pp. 130–31.

61. Ibid., Busta 30, Elena called la Draga, testimony of same, 14 August 1571, f. 4v; Milani, *Antiche pratiche*, p. 32.

62. Ibid., 17 August 1571, f. 5v; Milani, *Antiche pratiche*, pp. 33–34.

63. Ibid., ff. 5v–6r; Milani, *Antiche pratiche*, p. 34. That is, obviously no problems. The play on inside/outside—the safety of Mary's womb for Christ and the danger of the street—is particularly compelling here. Also, the emphasis on the feminine and its protective, mothering qualities appears once more well suited to this Christianity dominated by women. Even Christ is protected by Mary's body. I would like to thank Lucia Bertolini for help with the reading of these players.

64. Ibid., f. 6v; Milani, *Antiche pratiche*, p. 35.

65. Ibid.

66. Although she and her husband were labeled lady and lord, they appear to have been merely important people. He may have been from Bergamo and seems to have been a merchant selling velvet. Still, they were substantial people, and once again we get a sense of how widely healers moved even in Venice. Ibid., Busta 68, Benedetta, wife of Batista Samiter [also called a widow], testimony of Gaspara, wife of Christoforo, 12 January 1591; Milani, *Antiche Pratiche*, pp. 76–77. There has been considerable debate about whether women healers treated men or even dealt with more than illnesses related to reproduction. Evidently they dealt with a much broader range of problems in Venice and the Veneto, and men went willingly to them for treatment. For a recent overview of the debate, see Monica Green, "Women's Medical Care in Medieval Europe," in *Signs: Journal of Women in Culture and Society* 14 (1989), pp. 434–73.

67. Ibid.; Milani, *Antiche pratiche*, p. 77.

68. Ibid., testimony of Benedetta, wife of Batista Samiter, 15 January 1591; Milani, *Antiche pratiche*, p. 79.

69. Ibid.

70. Ibid.; Milani, *Antiche pratiche*, p. 80.

71. Ibid., disposition of case, undated, probably 7 February 1591; Milani, *Antiche pratiche*, p. 85.

72. Ibid., Busta 68, Latisana, testimony of Nicolo Romaneto, 21 May 1591, ff. 23v–24r; Milani, *Antiche pratiche*, pp. 152–53.

73. On this, see the section on *carte di voler bene* in Chapter 3.

74. A.S.V., Sant'Ufficio, Busta 68, Latisana, testimony of Nicolo Romaneto, 21 May 1591, f. 24r; Milani, *Antiche pratiche*, p. 153.

75. Ibid., testimony of Apollonia, 11 June 1591, f. 67v; Milani, *Antiche pratiche*, p. 166.

76. Ibid. One reading is suggested by the association of urination and ejaculation that is encountered in Italian folklore and elsewhere. Edward Muir suggests that if the ring is associated with the vagina, urinating through a ring would be metaphorically parallel to ejaculating within the vagina. This magic would then be very similar to the metaphoric type of magic so typical of the period.

77. This has been a presupposition of much of Ginzburg's earlier work now made clear by his *Storia notturna: Una decifrazione del sabba* (Turin: Einaudi, 1989), translated as *Ecstasies, Deciphering the Witches' Sabbath*, trans. Raymond Rosenthal (New York: Pantheon, 1991).

78. That is, if Freud had not written about a much different time, place, and

human personality. Magic was not adverse to using things and beings that in a way stretched beyond life, as we have seen, but that evidently entailed a different vision of death than Freud's. Taking a tack perhaps more attuned to Renaissance sensibilities, the association of certain kinds of suffering with love—not being able to sleep or rest, and so on—that were used as a *martello* to force someone to love might be seen as reversals of the situation that led the lover originally to seek magical aid. The lover who was unloved was actually the one who could not eat or rest. Love magic reversed this situation. The one who did not love felt the pains associated with love until he or she gave in and loved.

79. This does not preclude achieving a certain level of knowledge about such things. The more hypotheses overlap and reinforce one another, the more they become revealing, useful, and true.

80. A.S.V., Sant'Ufficio, Latisana, testimony of Apollonia, 11 June 1591, ff. 67v–68r; Milani, *Antiche pratiche,* p. 166.

81. Ibid., f. 68r; Milani, *Antiche pratiche,* p. 166.

82. Ibid., f. 68v; Milani, *Antiche pratiche,* p. 167.

83. Ibid., f. 67r; Milani, *Antiche pratiche,* pp. 165–66.

84. Ibid., testimony of Maria Madizza, 14 October 1591, f. 111v; Milani, p. 206.

85. Ibid., testimony of Mario Roma, no date, probably 21 May 1591, ff. 22v–23r; Milani, *Antiche pratiche,* p. 151. Even if the story sounds unlikely, it was confirmed in a general way by Apollonia in her testimony of 11 June 1591, f. 168r.

86. Ibid., Sentence of Apollonia, 22 June 1591, f. 77r; Milani, *Antiche pratiche,* pp. 175–76.

87. There was another case involving a group of women in Latisana heard by the Holy Office in 1618; see ibid., Busta 72, Penzona, Maria, Tabacco, Luigia, Tazzorra, and Orsola di Latisana. This case involved both accusations of witchcraft and of being Benandanti. Ginzburg discusses it from the latter perspective in *Night Battles,* pp. 99–106. On the same region in the seventeenth and eighteenth centuries, see Accati, "The Spirit of Fornication," in *Sex and Gender,* pp. 110–40. For the modern period, see the anecdotal but interesting collection of oral testimony by the students of Marisa Milani, *Streghe, morti ed esseri fantastici nel veneto oggi* (Padua: Editoriale Programma, 1990).

Chapter 5

1. "Fo in questo zorno fate et compite le noze de Bianca mia fiola natural in Anzolo di Grataroli fo di messier Alexandro dotor fisico, et fu fato belle et honorate noze, perche a farle fo assai senatori et altri mei parenti." Sanuto, *Diarii,* vol. 58, col. 495; the date is recorded in col. 541.

2. Quoted in Robert Finlay, *Politics in Renaissance Venice* (New Brunswick, N.J.: Rutgers University Press, 1980), p. 257. This translation is slightly different from Finlay's. Actually, Sanuto had married Cecilia Priuli in 1505 shortly before he turned forty, but that marriage seems to have been a traditional one of family alliance rather than a result of passion. Cecilia already had a grown daughter from an earlier marriage, and their union produced no children.

3. Given the values of the age, however, Sanuto should have given up his taste for young males well before he married in his late thirties. At the time of

Malatesta's letter, Sanuto was in his sixties, and although Malatesta was referring to an earlier time, it seems likely that Sanuto was being accused of pursuing
his homoerotic interests well beyond the age when such behavior could be seen
as a youthful indiscretion. On the Venetian laws concerning sodomy, see Patricia
Labalme, "Sodomy and Venetian Justice in the Renaissance," *The Legal History
Review* 52 (1984), pp. 217–54; for age distinctions and attitudes toward homoerotic relationships, see Ruggiero, *Boundaries*, pp. 109–45, 159–61; and Michael
J. Roche's *Homosexuality in Late Medieval Florence: Male Sociability and the Policing of Illicit Sex*, to be published by Oxford University Press.

4. I say "seems" because it appears that the printed version of Sanuto's
diaries were slightly edited to eliminate some material deemed unseemly. Bianca
was not the only daughter that Sanuto refers to in his diaries. Earlier he had
recorded the marriage of another natural daughter, Candiana, to Zuan Morelo.
Apparently this marriage was less impressive socially, as Sanuto reports only a
"good dinner" at home to celebrate the wedding; then the bride had been
quickly sent off to the house of her husband. *Diarii*, vol. 53, col. 268. No senators
seemed to have graced this affair; Morelo's parentage is not noted; and the
relatives, if any, went unreported. Still, Sanuto had at least two illegitimate
daughters, and one, Bianca, he seems to have been able to marry quite well.

5. For a brief discussion of this form of adoption, see Ruggiero, *Boundaries*,
pp. 150–52.

6. Vittorio Cian, "Fra i penetrali del patriziato veneziano cinquecentesco:
Pietro Bembo e Pietro Gradenigo," *Atti veneto di scienze, lettere ed arti* 106 (1947–
48), pp. 80–81.

7. Ibid., p. 84 from *Lettere* IV, I, 95–96, Venezia, 1729.

8. A.S.V., Sant'Ufficio, Busta 31, Fra Aurelio, testimony of same, 20 October 1549. The material now in Busta 31 was once divided in different buste. It
consists of three fasciulli: the first was titled "1543 contra Fratrem Aurelium
Senem" (not foliated); the second was labeled "contra Fratrem Aurelium Stichiano Senesem 1572" (foliated, but inaccurately); and the third began with a
letter by Fra Aurelio that opens "La lunga mia fede" (without wrapper or folios).
The plan probably was more complex than this letter suggested. Unfortunately
the letter no longer exists, but it and the plan it referred to will be considered in
more detail below.

9. Gradenigo, in a letter to the cardinal, complained that although according to rumor he had received a dowry of 16,000 ducats, it had been much less.
Nonetheless it was widely assumed that the cardinal, following this expense,
went to live in Gubbio, where he held one of his many benefices, to live more
cheaply there away from the papal court and replenish his coffers. Cian, "Pietro
Bembo," p. 91.

10. A.S.V., Sant'Ufficio, Busta 31, Fra Aurelio, testimony of Bernardo da
Verona, undated, probably November 1543.

11. Ibid.; "profession" was the moment when one vowed to live in accordance with the rule of a monastic order and according to the general monastic
requirements of obedience, poverty, and chastity. The time frame of the friar's
monastic career will be discussed in more detail below.

12. Ibid.

13. Ibid.

14. Ibid., testimony of Francesco Giustinian, 5 October 1543.

15. Ibid.

16. Ibid.

17. Ibid.

18. Who this Soccino was he did not specify. The most famous member of the family was Lelio Soccino, the reformer, who in 1547 briefly deserted Padua to live in Switzerland. Giustinian's account referred to 1534–35, when Lelio, born in 1525, would have been only ten; thus it could hardly have been him. His father, Bartolomeo, better known as a jurist at Bologna, may have been living in Padua at the time. As will be discussed later, Aurelio refers to a Marian Soccino in Padua loaning him 5 scudi at about this time; this was almost certainly another member of the family.

19. Ibid., testimony of Ghielmina, wife of Antonii, 9 November 1543. *"Non me impazzo delli fatti d'altri"* was a very common way of saying "I mind my own business." Neighbors often used the phrase before demonstrating that, in fact, they did not mind their own business when it came to Fra Aurelio.

20. Ibid. Interestingly, *donzelle* is used here in the sense of being young and pure, for these young women are referred to as godly as well.

21. *"Per via de iustitia"*; ibid.

22. Ibid.

23. Ibid., testimony of Vicenzo Scitapesse, 13 November 1543.

24. Ibid., report of the arrest of Fra Aurelio, 17 October 1549.

25. Ibid., testimony of Bianca Sanuto, 17 October 1549.

26. Ibid.

27. Ibid.

28. Sodomy legislation shares a similar concern even in the fifteenth century, focusing regularly on indiscriminate mixing of age groups and classes. See Ruggiero, *Boundaries*, pp. 121–25, 139–40, and Labalme, "Sodomy and Venetian Justice," pp. 217–54.

29. A.S.V., Sant'Ufficio, Busta 31, Fra Aurelio, testimony of Bianca Sanuto, 17 October 1549.

30. Ibid.

31. Ibid.

32. For an example of the complexity of this issue and the life of a cleric and his concubine in the Veneto, see A.S.V., Sant'Ufficio, Busta 35, Abbot Alessandro Ruis, 1573.

33. Ibid., Busta 31, Aurelio di Siena, testimony of Anna Padoana, 17 October 1549.

34. Sanuto's will and its codicil are published in Guglielmo Berchet's introduction to Sanuto's Diaries, *Diarii,* vol. I, pp. 101–9. The original, in Sanuto's infamous hand, is in A.S.V., Notarile Testamenti, Girolamo Canal, Busta 191.546I; a badly damaged legal copy may be found in the same notary's only surviving protocol book, Protocollo, Busta 192.

35. Ibid., Busta 31, Aurelio di Siena, testimony of Anna Padoana, 17 October 1549.

36. Ibid.

37. Ibid., testimony of Alexandro Busonello, 19 October 1549.

38. Ibid., testimony of Fra Aurelio, 20 October 1549. Fra Aurelio remembered leaving the monastery of San Sebastiano twenty-six years earlier, but as he

told his story, referring every now and then to the time that had passed, it requires approximately twenty-nine years to make his account work. Figuring that he was probably more accurate in remembering smaller spans of time, such as how long he stayed in a certain order or city rather than in estimating long periods, I have dated his narrative based on the twenty-nine year scheme of things. That means that the years add up, but it also means that they may be as much as three years off.

39. Ibid.

40. Ibid.

41. Ibid. On the practice of magical medicine by clerics in the period, see Mary R. O'Neil, *"Sacerdote ovvero strione,"* in *Understanding Popular Culture,* pp. 53–83.

42. A.S.V., Busta 31, Aurelio di Siena, testimony of Fra Aurelio, 20 October 1549.

43. Ibid.

44. Ibid.

45. Ibid. Although *iudicii* translates well as "judgments on the future," in Fra Aurelio's case at least it seems to have had a technical meaning that described a certain way of telling the future based on a more intellectual and learned approach than reading of palms or other common practices. It also seems to have implied a less secure way. With *iudicii* the future was formulated more in terms of probabilities than certainties.

46. Ibid.

47. Ibid.

48. Ibid. Although most scholars who have discussed *calamita bianca* discuss it as a white form of natural magnet, later usage suggests that it might have been a white powder that because of its adhering characteristics was associated with magnetism. I would like to thank Patricia Fara for this information. Whether *calamita bianca* was in fact a form of a natural magnet (*calamita*) or merely perceived as such, it was the ability to attract that was crucial for magic.

49. Ibid.

50. Ibid.

51. Ibid.

52. Ibid.

53. Ibid., testimony of ser Zaneto vende malvasia, 21 October 1549. Zaneto's desire to not marry his daughter until she was twenty might seem strange, but as a wine dealer and someone clearly well below the nobility, he may well have seen his daughter as an asset in his business.

54. Ibid. To add insult to injury, when he offered the friar six soldi for his prediction, the latter responded, according to Zaneto, "These are so few and he asked me for twelve soldi." Zaneto paid and, needless to say, was not particularly pleased at having done so.

55. Ibid., Fra Aurelio, testimony of same, 13 October 1571, f. 19v. This later case is now contained, along with the earlier one, in Busta 31 in a second fascicolo. Although it is foliated, numbers are both repeated and omitted, making the folio numbers only a rough reference.

56. Ibid., 30 June 1571, f. 12r.

57. Ibid., f. 12v.

58. Ibid., f. 13r. He also clarified that most of these writings were actually left over from the 1540s and his first trial.

59. Martin notes that in the seventeenth century the Holy Office began to prosecute more aggressively those who sold such information; on this see her *Witchcraft*, pp. 110–11.

60. A.S.V., Sant'Uffico, Busta 31, Fra Aurelio, testimony of Joseph Zarlinus, 30 June 1571, f. 13r.

61. Ibid., testimony of Fra Aurelio, 30 June 1571, f. 14r. This reference is so brief that it is difficult to tell if the friar was trying to imply that Raines, practicing these arts only for himself, was somehow more disinterested and thus could be relied upon as more honest. If so, in a way he would have been speaking against himself, for his own practice was evidently not so disinterested. On this point it is suggestive that in 1549, when Fra Aurelio first testified before the Holy Office, he had attempted to portray his chiromancy, geomancy, and astrology as not being a profession.

62. Ibid., Fra Aurelio, 13 October 1571, f. 19v.

63. Ibid., testimony of Bartolomeo Raines, 6 July 1571, f. 14v.

64. Ibid., ff. 14v–15r.

65. Ibid., testimony of Annibal Rimondo da Verona, 7 July 1571, ff. 15–16r. It should be noted that although the experts may have been unimpressed with Aurelio's learning in the area, apparently a number of substantial people had been. In 1549, for example, Aurelio was examined about letters showing that nobles like Giorgio Foscari had come to him to secure copies of manuscripts on the subject; for this, see testimony of Fra Aurelio, 23 October 1549.

66. Ibid., testimony of Fra Aurelio, 26 April 1572, f. 36r.

67. Ibid., ff. 36r–v.

68. Ibid.

69. Ibid., f. 37r.

70. Ibid., Busta 44, Cesare Lanza et al., 1579. This case was published by P. C. Ioly Zorattini, *Processi del S. Uffizio di Venezia contro ebrei e giudaizzanti*, vol. 6 (Florence: L. S. Olschki, 1985), pp. 133–62; as Ioly Zorattini's transcriptions are very close to mine, I include references to his edition, which is more easily consulted than the archival originals (it should be noted, however, that his folio references do not seem to match the folio numbers in the case). This case is also discussed in Pullan, *Jews*, pp. 128–29, because it involved questions about Jewish practices in the Portuguese community of Venice and has been described in more detail in Martin, *Witchcraft*, pp. 89–96, as an important example of learned magic. In addition, see Aldo Stella, *Chiesa e Stato nelle relazioni dei Nunzi pontifici a Venezia* (Città del Vaticano: Biblioteca Apostolica Vaticana, 1964), p. 288. Giovanni Romeo also mentions it briefly as an example of learned magic in *Inquisitori*, pp. 152–53. The case, however, is a very complex one and might well warrant a separate study for its rich insights into early magic/science or theology/science.

71. Ibid., Busta 44, Cesare Lanza et al., testimony of Giulio Francesco Morosini, 6 October 1579, ff. 162r–167v; Ioly Zorattini, *Processi*, pp. 231–35. Actually, in this his second testimony, he first reported that Gregorio Giordano had told him about the treasure (f. 162r); only later did he claim that an Armenian told him about it (f. 167r).

72. Ibid., ff. 162r–v; Ioly Zorattini, *Processi*, pp. 231–32.

73. Ibid., testimony of Giulio Cesare Muti, no date but probably December 1579, f. 244r; Ioly Zorattini, *Processi*, p. 292.

74. Ibid.; Ioly Zorattini, *Processi*, p. 292.

75. Ibid.; f. 244r–v; Ioly Zorattini, *Processi*, p. 293. Muti's rather deprecating account, for all its humor, must be taken with a grain of salt. His tale of the search served to distance himself as much as possible from the case and any penalties that might be imposed. As he reconstructed his actions, he was just a loyal Venetian subject following reluctantly the strange orders of his noble patron. This may not reveal much about his actual involvement, but it says a great deal about the givens of social relationships in Venice.

76. Ibid., testimony of Fra Cesare Lanza, 28 November 1579, f. 229v; Ioly Zorattini, *Processi*, p. 282. He reported that while teaching grammar in the area several years earlier, he had heard that a local lord had been looking for someone to help him find the treasure. He had contacted even Lanza, but he had told the noble that it was a project unlikely to succeed. Another friar appeared, however, who claimed to be an expert in these matters. The search produced nothing, and according to Lanza, when the lord began to believe he had been tricked, he had the friar killed.

77. Ibid., confession of Don Gregorio Giordano, not foliated, 23 February 1580; Ioly Zorattini, *Processi*, pp. 353–54. Although he had left his order without license and thus was officially excommunicated, he admitted that he had continued to act as a priest, saying Mass and performing the sacraments.

78. Ibid., testimony of Giulio Francesco Morosini, 6 October 1579, ff. 162v–163r; Ioly Zorattini, *Processi*, p. 232. Cesare Lanza was, according to Giovanni Romeo, a "noted professor of theology" and the teacher of Fra Valerio Polidoro, who wrote influential treatises on exorcism; on this see Romeo, *Inquisitori*, p. 153.

79. In fact they were so heavily involved in the illicit that Martin holds that Cesare Lanza had little hope of their spells working with such dishonest clerics involved. She also sees Lanza as having been brought in because of his higher moral standards. These, she argues, were seen as necessary to make the magic work; see *Witchcraft*, pp. 91ff. As we shall see, however, Lanza had his faults; he certainly was no Sir Gawain among the other clerics of Morosini's round table.

80. A.S.V., Sant'Ufficio, Busta 44, Cesare Lanza et al., testimony of Felix de Castello, 22 September 1579, f. 106r; Ioly Zorattini, *Processi*, p. 194.

81. This group met at Morosini's house, and Don Gregorio provides a brief account of one of their meetings: "One morning we, that is Morosini, the said friar [Cesare Lanza], Oglies, and I, ate at the house of the said Morosini. After we ate there arrived Saldagna. And Francesco Oglies showed to the friar [Lanza] a book in which there were many things and particularly the *Clavicole of Solomon*. This book had been copied by Saldagna. The priest [Lanza] after he had looked at it said that it was not a good thing and that he would make a good book of psalms, prayers and conjurations to bind these spirits." Ibid., testimony of Don Gregorio Giordano, 23 September 1579, f. 111r; Ioly Zorattini, *Processi*, p. 198. Ioly Zorattini labels this testimony as being that of Cesare Lanza, but the context makes it clear that it is actually that of Gregorio Giordano.

82. Ibid., testimony of Antonio Saldagna, 25 September 1570, f. 113v; Ioly Zorattini, *Processi*, p. 200.

83. Ibid., testimony of Cesare Lanza, 22 September 1579, f. 109v; Ioly

Zorattini, *Processi,* p. 196. On libertines and libertinage, see Giorgio Spini, *Ricerca dei libertini: La teoria dell'impostura delle religioni nel Seicento Italiano* (Florence: La Nuova Editrice, 1983).

84. Ibid., testimony of Francesco Oglies, 25 September 1579, ff. 124r–v; Ioly Zorattini, *Processi,* p. 206.

85. Ibid., f. 124v; Ioly Zorattini, *Processi,* p. 206. In fact, Saldagna's involvement with "women on earth" had led him into a complex affair with a Venetian lady the intricacies of which would challenge the credibility of even the most avid reader of harlequin romances. Saldagna claimed that he and Oglies had been drawn into a plot involving incest, the use of spirits for binding love, murder, and a plan to corrupt even the investigation of this case by the Holy Office instigated by the powerful Fiamma clan, a family with important ecclesiatical connections in Venice and beyond.

86. Martin, *Witchcraft,* pp. 91ff.

87. A.S.V., Sant'Ufficio, Busta 44, Cesare Lanza et al., testimony of Cesare Lanza, 22 September 1579, f. 109v; Ioly Zorattini, *Processi,* p. 197. Nine years earlier, he was already a friar and a priest; thus this was not merely a part of his youthful days as a scholar at the university.

88. Ibid., unfoliated and undated confession of Fra Cesare Lanza; Ioly Zorattini, *Processi,* p. 332.

89. Ibid; Ioly Zorattini, *Processi,* p. 332. The making of the ring he described as follows: "take a turquoise on Wednesday [lit. the day of Mercury] observing the conjunction [that is] that the said planet is in a good house and an uplifting one. Then one binds it [to the ring] so that it is finished that day, incising underneath the stone where it must touch the finger an Aleph and a Lambeth and below the Aleph three points so that they say El. That done I say three psalms over the ring giving it a benediction and burning incense over it."

90. Ibid., testimony of Fra Cesare Lanza, 29 September 1579, f. 137v; Ioly Zorattini, *Processi,* p. 215, where Magia in the first line is read as "Magnifici."

91. Ibid., f. 138r; Ioly Zorattini, *Processi,* p. 216.

92. The procurators of San Marco were the highest elected officials of Venice after the doge and normally were drawn from the most experienced, successful, and rich leaders of the city. That Fantin's son achieved this post was a significant sign of the family's continued power across the sixteenth century. Another son, Giovanni, revealed the family's strong ties to the mainland as well. He married Chiara, daughter of Alvise Corner, a major Paduan noble, noted for his works on agriculture and rural life and his close connection with Ruzzante. Alvise Corner was not a Venetian noble, but his wealth, connections, and reputation made his daughter an attractive match. On Franco, see *Dizionario biografico Italiano,* vol. 29, pp. 195–97; on Alvise, see ibid., pp. 142–46, and Emilio Menegazzo, "Alvise Cornaro: Un veneziano del Cinquecento nella terraferma padovana," in *Cultura,* vol. 3, pt. II, pp. 513–38. Fantin had his own literary interests. Marin Sanuto reported that in 1513 he was a protagonist in a play reading of a comedy based on Plautus held in the Cha Morosini that attracted approximately 300 people. Sanuto, *Diarii,* vol. XV, p. 535.

93. A.S.V., Sant'Ufficio, Busta 31, Fra Aurelio di Siena, testimony of same, 20 October 1549.

94. Ibid.

95. Elisabetta's will of 1 May 1537 confirms that Querini was her brother

and suggests that their relationship was a close one, as she named him one of her executors. Interestingly, she also labeled her husband, Lorenzo Masolla, a noble, even though he was not a Venetian one. In fact, his lack of a Venetian noble pedigree may have been a reason why she was available to be the mistress of powerful and noble men like Pietro Bembo and Corner. For her will, see A.S.V., Notarile Testamenti, Girolamo Canal, Busta 190.224. For Querini as executor of the cardinal's will, see Cian, "Pietro Bembo," pp. 85–91.

96. Cian, "Pietro Bembo," pp. 85–91. For example, in a letter of 4 December 1542 to Querini, Bembo revealed his interest in Mario Savorgnan, who he described as "the most handsome young man that there is among our nobility, learned in Latin and Greek, handsome like a flower" and asked both Querini's opinion on such a match and his help in pursuing it. Mario was the nephew of another mistress of Bembo, Maria Savorgnan. Their love letters were published as *Maria Savorgnan—Pietro Bembo, Carteggio d'amore (1500–1501)*, ed. Carlo Dionisotti (Florence: Felice le Monnier, 1950). I would like to thank Edward Muir for reminding me of this fact.

97. A.S.V., Sant'Ufficio, Busta 31, Fra Aurelio, testimony of Gerolamo Quirini, 13 November 1549.

98. Ibid.

99. Ibid.

100. Ibid.

101. Ibid., testimony of Fra Aurelio, 20 October 1549. The Zecca was the mint of Venice, but it had also become a place where money could be deposited at interest.

102. Ibid., testimony of Fra Aurelio, 23 October 1549. A *mansionaria* was a beneficed priesthood.

103. This terminology usually implied that the women were prostitutes. He also talked about the earlier papal legate's desire to bring Aurelio back under the discipline of his order and Giustinian's failed attempt to so. Ibid., testimony of Nicolo Bembo q. Gian Battista, 26 October 1549.

104. Ibid.; these opinions were formally called for by the Holy Office on December and came in on 5 December.

105. Ibid.; the original confession is in the first unfoliated fascicolo, dated 10 December 1549; his denial is in the foliated second fasicolo, ff. 15v–16r, 9 August 1571.

106. Ibid.; the sentence is dated 19 December 1549.

107. Actually, in 1553 the friar appears again in the records of the Holy Office when there was a jail break from the *Preson Forte,* where he was being held. One of the guards, Vicenzo di Tomaso, gave a vivid account of the event. "About the twenty-second hour [that would have been about seven or eight in the evening in July] when the captain [of the prisons] and the guards entered the prison to search it as was the custom . . . the prisoners locked them in and then jumped upon the captain and began beating and wounding him. And I . . . began to scream 'robbers, assassins, you are killing the captain.' For this the prisoners dumped a bucket full of ashes and mortar in my eyes." Ibid., Busta 11, Fra Aurelio di Siena, testimony of Vicenzo di Tomaso, 26 August 1553, f. 38r. Once the alarm had been given, however, the Signori di Notte arrived and restored order. Vicenzo thought he remembered seeing Aurelio flushed out from hiding behind a staircase and captured. But later he saw that the friar was not in his cell,

and the search for him began. As was normal Venetian practice, a clause in his sentence required that if the friar escaped from jail, whoever recaptured him would receive a fifty-ducat reward from the friar's own wealth, if possible. Thus we know that he was recaptured four or five days later near San Marco by a police patrol that claimed the reward. Ibid., 10 October 1553, ff. 14r–v. The payment of this fine itself created a bit of litigation. The Council of Ten blocked the use of some of his already confiscated wealth, because the interest earned on that wealth was committed to other causes (ff. 16–17v). A final settlement was reached when some additional wealth of the friar turned up stored in a chest, and the patrollers agreed to divide thirty-five ducats between them (ff. 19–20r).

108. Ibid., Busta 31, Fra Aurelio, testimony of Giuseppe Gidono, 6 May 1568, ff. 1r–2v.

109. Ibid., testimony of Angelo Rocha, 21 June 1571, ff. 5r–v.

110. Ibid., testimony of Giovanni Negro, 23 June 1571, f. 6r.

111. Ibid., testimony of Fra Aurelio, 28 June 1571, ff. 8–11r.

112. Ibid., testimony of Fra Aurelio, 13 October 1571, ff. 20r–v. Just before this passage, the friar is quoted as saying that he practiced ''*Negromancia*'' and thought there was nothing illicit in doing so. This apparently was a scribal error. The Holy Office had tried to get him to admit this several times, and he had always steadfastly refused. The context makes it clear that he was referring to astrology, as the passage is a defense of his use of astrology, which he saw as licit. Confirming this is the fact that the Holy Office did not return to *negromancia* after this apparent admission.

113. Ibid., f. 20v.

114. This anonymous denunciation was made by Geronimo Orsi, who had once worked for the friar. He asked as his reward one-half of the wealth confiscated. Ibid., 17 April 1572, f. 24r.

115. The Holy Office's suspicions of double dealing focused on their own minions, especially a certain Biaggio, who managed to open the chests in private and keep them in his own house for a night. This whole affair created yet another batch of testimony in April 1572, but in the end it appears that they felt they could not prove that Biaggio or anyone else had robbed the chests, in part because Fra Aurelio confirmed that the contents were pretty much what he had earlier put in them. Ibid., ff. 24–39r. There is actually more material in this section than the folio numbers indicate because several pages are not foliated.

116. Ibid., testimony of Fra Aurelio, 26 April 1571, f. 39r.

BIBLIOGRAPHY

Archival Sources

Archivio della Curia Vescovile di Feltre

Archivio di Stato, Florence (A.S.F.)

Filze Medici

Onestà
    Practica Secreti
    Suppliche

Archivio di Stato, Venice (A.S.V.)

Archivio Notarile
    Chancelleria Inferiore, Notai
    Chancelleria Inferiore, Miscellanea Notai Diversi
    Testamenti

Avogaria di Comun
    Balla d'Oro
    Contratti di Nozze
    Lettere di Rettore . . . agli Avogadori
    Libro d'Oro, Nascite
    Miscellanea Civile
    Miscellanea Penale
    Raspe, Reg. 3673/33–3691/51

Collegio
    Relazioni Ambasciatori
    Relazioni dei Rettori

Consiglio dei Dieci
    Capi, Lettere dei Rettori
    Comune
    Deliberazioni Miste
    Parti Criminale
    Parti Secreti

Esecutori conto la Bestemmia
    Processi

Quarantia Criminal

Provveditore sopra Monasteri

Sant'Ufficio
    Buste 9–70

Senato
  Misti
  Secreta
  Terra

Published Works

Accati, Luisa. "The Spirit of Fornication: Virtue of the Soul and Virtue of the Body in Friuli, 1600–1800." In *Sex and Gender in Historical Perspective: Selections from Quaderni Storici*, ed. Edward Muir and Guido Ruggiero. Baltimore: Johns Hopkins University Press, 1990, pp. 110–40.

Aretino, Pietro. *Sei giornate*, ed. Giovanni Aquilecchia. Bari: La Terza, 1980.

Bakhtin, Mikhail. *Rabelais and His World*. Translated by Hélène Iswolsky. Bloomington: Indiana University Press, 1984.

Bandello, Matteo. *Le quattro patri de le Novelle del Bandello*, ed. Gustavo Balsamo-Crivelli. Turin: Unione Tipografico-Editrice Torinese, 1924.

Barzaghi, Antonio. *Donne o cortigiane? La prostituzione a Venezia. Documenti di costumi dal XVI al XVIII secolo*. Verona: Bertani, 1980.

Basaglia, Enrico. "Il controllo della criminalità nella Repubblica di Venezia. Il secolo XVI: Un momento di passaggio." In *Atti del Convegno "Venezia e la Terraferma attraverso le relazioni dei Rettori."* Milan: A. Giuffrè, 1981, pp. 65–78.

Bembo, Pietro. *Gli Asolani*. Translated by Rudolf Gottfried. Freeport, N.Y.: Books for Libraries Press, 1971.

Bembo, Pietro. *Bembo. Opere in volgare*, ed. Mario Marti. Florence: Sansoni, 1961.

Boerio, Giuseppe. *Dizionario del dialetto veneziano*. Venice: Tipografia di Giovanni Cecchini, 1856.

Bossy, John. *Christianity in the West 1400–1700*. Oxford: Oxford University Press, 1985.

Bossy, John. "The Counter-Reformation and the People of Catholic Europe." *Past and Present* 47 (1970): 51–71.

Brackett, John K. *Criminal Justice and Crime in Late Renaissance Florence 1537–1609*. Cambridge: Cambridge University Press, 1992.

Browe, Peter. "Die Eucharistie als Zaubermittel im Mittelalter." *Archiv für Kulturgeschichte* 20 (1930): 134–54.

Brown, Peter. *The Body in Society: Men, Women, and Sexual Renunciation in Early Christian Society*. New York: Columbia University Press, 1988.

Brown, Peter. *The Cult of the Saints: Its Rise and Function in Latin Christianity*. Chicago: University of Chicago Press, 1981.

Brucker, Gene. *Giovanni and Lusanna, Love and Marriage in Renaissance Florence*. Berkeley: University of California Press, 1986.

Burke, Peter. *The Historical Anthropology of Early Modern Italy*. Cambridge: Cambridge University Press, 1987.

Burke, Peter. *Popular Culture in Early Modern Europe*. London: Temple Smith, 1978.

Bynum, Carolyn Walker. *Holy Feast and Holy Fast. The Religious Significance of Food to Medieval Women*. Berkeley: University of California Press, 1987.

Calvi, Giulia. *Storie di un anno di peste: Comportamenti sociali e immaginario nella Firenze barocca.* Milan: Bompiani, 1984.

Calvino, Italo. *Le Cosmicomiche.* Turin: Einaudi, 1965.

Camporesi, Piero. *Il pane salvaggio.* Bologna: Il Mulino, 1980. Translated by David Gentilcore as *Bread of Dreams.* Chicago: University of Chicago Press, 1989.

Camporesi, Piero. *Il sugo della vita: Simbolismo e magia del sangue.* Milan: Edizione di Comunità, 1982.

Camporesi, Piero. *La carne impassibile.* Milan: Il saggiatore, 1983. Translated by Tania Murray as *The Incorruptible Flesh: Bodily Mutilation and Mortification in Religion and Folklore.* Cambridge: Cambridge University Press, 1988.

Carroll, Linda. *Angelo Beolco (Il Ruzante).* Boston: Twayne, 1990.

Carroll, Linda. "Carnival Rites as Vehicles of Protest in Renaissance Venice." *Sixteenth Century Journal* 16 (1985): 487–502.

Carroll, Linda. "Who's on Top?: Gender as Societal Power Configuration in Italian Renaissance Painting and Drama." *Sixteenth Century Journal* 20 (1989): 531–58.

Castan, Nicole. *Les criminels de Languedoc, les exigences d'ordre et les voies du resentiment dans une société pré-révolutionnaire.* Toulouse: Association des publications de l'Université de Toulous-Le Mirail, 1980.

Castan, Nicole, and Yves Castan. *Vivre ensemble. Ordre et désordre en Languedoc (XVIIe–XVIIIe siècle).* Paris: Gallimard-Julliard, 1981.

Castan, Yves. *Honneteté et relations sociales en Languedoc, 1715–1718.* Paris: Plon, 1974.

Cavallo, Sandra, and Simona Cerutti. "Female Honor and the Social Control of Reproduction in Piedmont between 1600 and 1800." In *Sex and Gender in Historical Perspective: Selections from Quaderni Storici,* ed. Edward Muir and Guido Ruggiero. Baltimore: Johns Hopkins University Press, 1990, pp. 73–109.

Certeau, Michel de. *The Practice of Everyday Life.* Translated by Steven F. Randall. Berkeley: University of California Press, 1984.

Ciammitti, Luisa. "Quanto costa essere normali. La dote nel Conservatorio femminile di Santa Maria del Boraccano (1630–1680)." *Quaderni Storici* 53 (1983): 469–97.

Cian, Vittorio. "Fra i penetrali del patriziato veneziano cinquecentesco: Pietro Bembo e Pietro Gradenigo." *Atti veneto di scienze, lettere ed arti* 106 (1947–48): 76–97.

Cohen, Sherrill. *The Evolution of Women's Asylums since 1500: From Refuge for Ex-Prostitutes to Shelters for Battered Women.* New York: Oxford University Press, 1992.

Corrain, Cleto, and Pierluigi Zampini. *Documenti etnografici e folkloristici nei sinodi diocesani italiani.* Bologna: Forni, 1970.

Cowan, Alexander F. *The Urban Patriciate: Lübeck and Venice, 1580–1700.* Cologne: Böhlau Verlag, 1986.

Cozzi, Gaetano. "Padri, figli e matrimoni clandestini (metà sec. XVI—metà sec. XVIII)." *La cultura* 15 (1976): 169–212.

Cozzi, Gaetano, ed. *Stato, società e giustizia nella Repubblica Veneta (sec. 15–18)*. Rome: Jouvance, 1980.

da Rif, Bianca Maria, ed. *La Bulesca*. In *La letteratura "alla Bulesca"; Testi rinascimentali veneti*. Padua: Antenore, 1984.

Darnton, Robert. *The Great Cat Massacre and Other Episodes in French Cultural History*. New York: Vintage Books, 1985.

Darnton, Robert. "The Symbolic Element in History." *Journal of Modern History* 58 (1986): 218–34.

Davis, Natalie Zemon. *Fiction in the Archives, Pardon Tales and Their Tellers in Sixteenth-Century France*. Stanford, Calif.: Stanford University Press, 1987.

Davis, Natalie Zemon. *The Return of Martin Guerre*. Cambridge, Mass.: Harvard University Press, 1983.

Davis, Natalie Zemon. "The Sacred and the Body Social in Sixteenth-Century Lyon." *Past and Present* 90 (1980): 40–70.

Davis, Natalie Zemon. *Society and Culture in Early Modern France*. Stanford, Calif.: Stanford University Press, 1975.

de Lorenzi, Giovanni Battista, ed. *Leggi e memorie venete sulla prostituzione*. Venice: published privately by the Count of Orford, 1870–72.

Del Col, Andrea. "Organizzazione, composizione e giurisdizione dei tribunali dell'Inquisizione romana nella Repubblica di Venezia (1500–1550)." *Critica Storica/Bollettino Arte, Scienze, Economia*, 25, n. 2 (1988): 244–94.

Delumeau, Jean. *Le Catholicisme entre Luther et Voltaire*. Paris: Presses Universitaires de France, 1971.

Delumeau, Jean. *Le péché et la peur. La culpabilisation en Occident (XIIIe–XVIIIe siècle)*. Paris: Fayard, 1983.

Delumeau, Jean. *La peur en occident (XIVe–XVIIIe siècle). Une cité assiégée*. Paris: Fayard, 1983.

Demos, John P. *Entertaining Satan: Witchcraft and the Culture of Early New England*. New York: Oxford University Press, 1982.

Di Villaviera, Rita Casagrande. *Le cortigiane veneziane del Cinquecento*. Milan: Longanese, 1968.

Dionisotti, Carlo, ed. *Maria Savorgnan—Pietro Bembo. Carteggio d'amore (1500–1501)*. Florence: Felice le Monnier, 1950.

Farr, James R. "Crimine nel vicinato: Ingiurie, matrimonio e onore nella Digione del XVI e XVII secolo." *Quaderni Storici* 66 (1987): 839–54.

Farr, James R. *Hands of Honor: Artisans and Their World in Dijon, 1550–1650*. Ithaca, N.Y.: Cornell University Press, 1988.

Farr, James R. "Popular Religious Solidarity in Sixteenth-Century Dijon." *French Historical Studies* 14 (1985): 192–214.

Ferrante, Lucia. "Honor Regained: Women in the Casa del Soccorso di San Paolo in Sixteenth-Century Bologna." In *Sex and Gender in Historical Perspective: Selections from Quaderni Storici*, ed. Edward Muir and Guido Ruggiero. Baltimore: Johns Hopkins University Press, 1990, pp. 46–72.

Ferro, Marco. *Dizionario del diritto comune e veneto . . .* Venice: Modesto Fenzo, 1780.

Finlay, Robert. *Politics in Renaissance Venice*. New Brunswick, N.J.: Rutgers University Press, 1980.

Flandrin, Jean-Louis. *Families in Former Times: Kinship, Household and Sexuality in Early Modern France.* Translated by Richard W. Southern. Cambridge: Cambridge University Perss, 1979.

Ginzburg, Carlo. *I Benandanti, Stregoneria e culti agrari tra Cinquecento e Seicento.* Turin: Einaudi, 1966. Translated by John and Anne Tedeschi as *The Night Battles, Witchcraft and Agrarian Cults in the Sixteenth and Seventeenth Centuries.* Baltimore: Johns Hopkins University Press, 1983.

Ginzburg, Carlo. *Il formaggio e i vermi, Il cosmo di un mugnaio del'500.* Turin: Einaudi, 1976. Translated by John and Anne Tedeschi as *The Cheese and the Worms, The Cosmos of a Sixteenth-Century Miller.* Baltimore: Johns Hopkins University Press, 1980.

Ginzburg, Carlo. *Miti, emblemi, spie: Morfologia e storia.* Turin: Einaudi, 1986. Translated by John and Anne Tedeschi as *Clues, Myths and the Historical Method.* Baltimore: Johns Hopkins University Press, 1989.

Ginzburg, Carlo. *Storia notturna: Una decifrazione del sabba.* Turin: Einaudi, 1989. Translated by Raymond Rosenthal as *Ecstasies, Deciphering the Witches' Sabbath.* New York: Pantheon, 1991.

Il gioco dell'amore. Le cortigiane di Venezia dal Trecento al Settecento. Milan: Berenice, 1990.

Gottlieb, Beatrice. "The Meaning of Clandestine Marriage." In *Family and Sexuality in French History,* ed. Robert Wheaton and Tamara K. Hareven. Philadelphia: University of Pennsylvania Press, 1980, pp. 49–83.

Graf, Arturo. *Attraverso il Cinquecento.* Turin: Chiantore, 1888.

Grazzini, Anton Francesco (Il Lasca). *Le rime burlesche edite e inedite,* ed. Carlo Veronese. Florence: Sansone, 1882.

Green, Monica. "Women's Medical Care in Medieval Europe." *Signs: Journal of Women in Culture and Society* 14 (1989): 434–73.

Grendler, Paul. *Critics of the Italian World 1530–1560: Anton Doni, Nicolò Franco and Ortensio Lando.* Madison: University of Wisconsin Press, 1969.

Grendler, Paul. *The Roman Inquisition and the Venetian Press, 1540–1605.* Princeton, N.J.: Princeton University Press, 1977.

Grendler, Paul. "The *Tre Savii Sopra Eresia* 1547–1605: A Prosopographical Study." *Studi Veneziani* n.s., 3 (1979): 283–340.

Hunt, Lynn, ed. *The New Cultural History.* Berkeley: University of California Press, 1989.

Ioly Zorattini, P. C. *Processi del S. Uffizio di Venezia contro ebrei e giudaizzanti,* Vol. 6, Florence, L.S. Olschki, 1985, pp. 133–362.

King, Margaret L. *Venetian Humanism in an Age of Patrician Dominance.* Princeton, N.J.: Princeton University Press, 1986.

Klapisch-Zuber, Christiane. "Zacharie ou le père évincé: Les rituels nuptiaux toscans entre Giotto et le Concile de Trente," *Annales Economies, Sociétés, Civilisations* 34, no. 6 (1979): 1216–43. Translated as "Zacharias, or the Ousted Father: Nuptial Rites in Tuscany between Giotto and the Council of Trent." In *Women, Family and Ritual in Renaissance Italy.* Translated by Lydia G. Cochrane. Chicago: University of Chicago Press, 1985, pp. 178–212.

Labalme, Patricia. "Sodomy and Venetian Justice in the Renaissance." *The Legal History Review* 52 (1984): 217–54.

Laqueur, Thomas. *Making Sex, Body and Gender from the Greeks to Freud.* Cambridge, Mass.: Harvard University Press, 1990.

Larivaille, Paul. *La vie quotidienne des courtesanes en Italie au temps de la renaissance.* Paris: Hachette, 1975.

Lawner, Lynn. *Lives of Courtesans, Portraits of the Renaissance.* New York: Rizzoli, 1987.

Levi, Giovanni. *L'eredità immateriale: Carriera di un esorcista nel Piemonte del Seicento.* Turin: Einaudi, 1985. Translated by Lydia Cochrane as *Inheriting Power: The Story of an Exorcist.* Chicago: University of Chicago Press, 1988.

Lowry, Martin. "The Reform of the Council of Ten, 1582–83: An Unsettled Problem?" *Studi Veneziani* 13 (1971): 275–310.

Macfarlane, Alan. *Witchcraft in Tudor and Stuart England. A Regional and Comparative Study.* London: Routledge, 1970.

Maclean, Ian. *The Renaissance Notion of Woman, A Study in the Fortunes of Scholasticism and Medical Science in European Intellectual Life.* Cambridge: Cambridge University Press, 1980.

Marchini, Nelli Elena Vanzan. "L'altra faccia dell'amore ovvero i rischi dell'esercizio del piacere." In *Il gioco dell'amore. Le cortigiane di Venezia dal Trecento al Settecento.* Milan: Berenice, 1990, pp. 47–56.

Martin, John J. "A Journeymen's Feast of Fools." *The Journal of Medieval and Renaissance Studies* 17 (1987): 149–74.

Martin, John J. *Venice's Hidden Enemies: Italian Heretics in a Renaissance City.* Berkeley: University of California Press, in press.

Martin, Ruth. *Witchcraft and the Inquisition in Venice 1550–1650.* Oxford: Basil Blackwell, 1989.

Milani, Marisa. *Antiche pratiche di medicina popolare nei processi del S. Uffizio (Venezia, 1572–1591).* Padua: Centrostampa Palazzo Maldura, 1986. *Corso di Letteratura delle Tradizione Popolari (a.a. 1985–86).*

Milani, Marisa. "L'"Incanto' di Veronica Franco" *Giornale storico della letteratura italiana* 162 (1985): 250–63.

Milani, Marisa. "L'ossessione secolare di suor Mansueta. Un esorcismo a Venezia nel 1574." *Quaderni Veneti* 7 (1988): 129–31.

Milani, Marisa. *Streghe, morti ed esseri fantasici nel veneto oggi.* Padua: Editoriale Programma, 1990.

Milani, Marisa, ed. *Un caso di stregoneria nella Feltre del '500.* Belluno: Tipolitografia Trabella, 1990. (Comunità Montana Feltrina Centro per la Documentazione della Cultura Popolare), n. 7.

Molmenti, Pompeo. *La storia di Venezia nella vita privata,* 3 vols. Trieste: Lint, 1973.

Monter, William. "Women and the Italian Inquisitions." In *Women in the Middle Ages and the Italian Renaissance and Historical Perspetives,* ed. Mary Beth Rose. Syracuse, N.Y.: Syracuse University Press, 1985, pp. 73–87.

Monter, William, and Tedeschi, John. "Toward a Statistical Profile of the Italian Inquisitions, Sixteenth to Eighteenth Centuries." In *The Inquisition in Early Modern Europe: Studies on Sources and Methods,* ed. Gustav Henninsen and John Tedeschi with Charles Amiel. Dekalb, Ill.: Northern Illinois University Press, 1986, pp. 130–57.

Muchembled, Robert. *Culture populaire et culture des èlites dans la France Moderne (XVe–XVIIIe siècle). Essai.* Paris: Flammarion, 1978. Translated by

Lydia Cochrane as *Popular Culture and Elite Culture in France 1400–1750.* Baton Rouge: Louisiana State University Press, 1985.

Muchembled, Robert. *L'invention del l'homme moderne: Sensibilités, moeurs et comportementes collectif sous l'Ancient Régime.* Paris: Fayard, 1988.

Muir, Edward. *Civic Ritual in Renaissance Venice.* Princeton, N.J.: Princeton University Press, 1981.

Muir, Edward. *Mad Blood Stirring: Vendetta and Factions in Friuli during the Renaissance.* Baltimore: Johns Hopkins University Press, in press.

Muir, Edward. "The Virgin on the Street Corner: The Place of the Sacred in Italian Cities." In *Religion and Culture in the Renaissance and Reformation,* ed. Steven Ozment. Kirksville, Mo.: Sixteenth Century Studies Journal Publications, 1989, pp. 25–40.

Muir, Edward, and Guido Ruggiero, eds. *Microhistory and the Lost Peoples of Europe, Selections from Quaderni Storici.* Translatled by Eren Branch. Baltimore: Johns Hopkins University Press, 1991.

Muir, Edward, and Guido Ruggiero, eds. *Sex and Gender in Historical Perspective: Selections from Quaderni Storici.* Translated by Margaret A. Gallucci with Mary M. Gallucci and Carole C. Gallucci. Baltimore: Johns Hopkins University Press, 1990.

Niccoli, Ottavia. "'*Menstruum quasi monstruum*': Monstrous Births and Menstrual Taboo in the Sixteenth Century." In *Sex and Gender in Historical Perspective: Selections from Quaderni Storici.* ed. Edward Muir and Guido Ruggiero. Baltimore: Johns Hopkins University Press, 1990, pp. 1–25.

Niccoli, Ottavia. *Profeti e popolo nell'Italia del rinascimento.* Bari: Laterza, 1987. Translated by Lydia G. Cochrane as *Prophecy and People in Renaissance Italy.* Princeton, N.J.: Princeton University Press, 1990.

Nutton, Vivian. "Murders and Miracles: Lay Attitudes to Medicine in Classical Antiquity." In *Patients and Practitioners: Lay Perceptions of Medicine in Preindustrial Society,* ed. Roy Porter. Cambridge: Cambridge University Press, 1985.

O'Neil, Mary R. "*Sacerdote ovvero strione,* Ecclesiastical and Superstitious Remedies in Sixteenth Century Italy." In *Understanding Popular Culture, Europe from the Middle Ages to the Nineteenth Century,* ed. Steven L. Kaplan. Berlin: Mouton, 1984, pp. 53–83.

Padoan, Giorgio. "Il mondo delle cortigiane nella letteratura rinascimentale," In *Il gioco dell'amore. Le cortigiane di Venezia dal Trecento al Settecento.* Milan: Berenice, 1990, pp. 63–71.

Park, Katherine, and Robert A. Nye. "Destiny Is Anatomy." *The New Republic* 3970 (1991): 53–57.

Pavan, Elisabeth. "Police des moeurs, société et politique à Venise à la fin du Moyen Age." *Revue Historique* 246 (1980): 244–66.

Povolo, Claudio. "Aspetti dell'amministrazione della giustizia penale nell'Repubblica di Venezia. Secoli XVI–XVII." In *Società e giustizia nella Repubblica Veneta (sec. XV–XVIII),* ed. Gaetano Cozzi. Rome: Jouvence, 1981, pp. 155–257.

Predelli, Roberto, ed. *I libri commemoriali della Repubblica di Venezia, Regesti,* vol. VII. Venice: Deputazione Veneta di Storia Patria, 1907.

Priori, Lorenzo. *Practica criminale secondo le leggi della serenissima Repubblica di Venezia.* Venice: G. Girardi, 1738.

Pullan, Brian. *The Jews of Europe and the Inquisition of Venice, 1550–1670.* Totowa, N.J.: Barnes and Noble, 1983.

Pullan, Brian. *Rich and Poor in Renaissance Venice, The Social Institutions of a Catholic State.* Oxford: Basil Blackwell, 1971.

Raggio, Osvaldo. *Faide e parentele: Lo stato geneovese visto dalla Fontanabuona.* Turin: Einaudi, 1990.

Roche, Michael J. *Homosexuality in Late Medieval Florence: Male Sociability and the Policing of Illicit Sex.* New York: Oxford University Press, in press.

Rochon, André, ed. *Formes et significations de la ''Beffa'' dans la littérature Italienne de la Renaissance.* Paris: Université de la Sorbonne Nouvelle, 1972.

Romeo, Giovanni. *Inquisitori, esorcisti e streghe nell'Italia della controriforma.* Florence: Sansoni, 1990.

Rosenthal, Margaret F. *The Honest Courtesan: Veronica Franco, Citizen and Writer in Sixteenth-Century Venice.* Chicago: University of Chicago Press, 1992.

Ruggiero, Guido. *The Boundaries of Eros: Sex Crime and Sexuality in Renaissance Venice.* New York: Oxford University Press, 1985.

Ruggiero, Guido. "'Più che la vita caro': Onore, matrimonio, e reputazione femminile nel tardo Rinascimento." *Quaderni Storici* 66 (1987): 753–75.

Ruggiero, Guido. "Re-Reading the Renaissance: Civic Morality and the World of Marriage, Love and Sex." In *Sexuality and Gender in Early Modern Europe: Institutions, Texts, Images,* ed. James Turner. Cambridge: Cambridge University Press, in press.

Ruggiero, Guido. *Violence in Early Renaissance Venice.* New Brunswick, N.J.: Rutgers University Press, 1980.

Ruzzante (Angelo Beolco). *Teatro,* ed. and translated into Italian by Ludovico Zorzi. Turin: Einaudi, 1967.

Sabean, David Warren. *Power in the Blood, Popular Culture and Village Discourse in Early Modern Germany.* Cambridge: Cambridge University Press, 1984.

Santore, Kathy. "Julia Lombardo, 'Somtuosa Meretrize': A Portrait by Property," *Renaissance Quarterly* 41 (1988): 44–83.

Sanuto, Marino. *I diarii di Marino Sanuto,* 58 vols., ed. Rinaldo Fulin et al. Venice: Deputazione R. Veneta di Storia Patria, 1897–1903.

Scarabello, Giovanni. "Devianza sessuali ed interventi di giustizia a Venezia nella prima metà del XVI secolo." In *Tiziano e Venezia, Convegno Internazionale di Studi.* Venice: Neri Pozza Editore, 1976, pp. 75–84.

Scarabello, Giovanni. "Paure, superstizioni, infamie." In *Storia della cultura veneta. Il Seicento,* vol. 4, pt. 2 ed. Girolamo Arnaldi and Manlio Pastore Stocchi. Vicenza: Neri Pozza, 1984.

Scarabello, Giovanni. "Le 'signore' della repubblica." In *Il gioco dell'amore. Le cortigiane di Venezia dal Trecento al Settecento.* Milan: Berenice, 1990, pp. 11–35.

Spini, Giorgio. *Ricerca dei libertini: La teoria dell'impostura delle religioni nel Seicento Italiano.* Florence: La Nuova Editrice, 1983.

Stella, Aldo. *Chiesa e Stato nelle relazioni dei Nunzi pontifici a Venezia.* Città del Vaticano: Biblioteca Apostolica Vaticana, 1964.

Tassini, Giuseppe. *Cenni storici e leggi circa il libertinaggio in Venezia dal secolo decimoquarto alla caduta della repubblica.* Venice: Fontana, 1886; published anonymously.

Tedeschi, John. "Preliminary Observations on Writing a History of the Roman Inquisition." In *Continuity and Discontinuity in Church History*, ed. F. Forrester Church and Timothy George. Leiden: E. J. Brill, 1979, pp. 232–49.

Thomas, Keith. *Religion and the Decline of Magic*. New York: Scribners, 1971.

Tiziano e Venezia, Convegno Internazionale di Studi. Venice: Neri Pozza Editore, 1976.

Yates, Francis A. *Giordano Bruno and the Hermetic Tradition*. Chicago: University of Chicago Press, 1964.

INDEX